CONSPIRACY... BETRAYAL... BUSINESS AS USUAL

Controversial and provocative, *Bushwhacked* is a journey into the secret world of whistle-blowers and corporate-government conspirators. A compilation of Uri Dowbenko's ground-breaking articles from the Alternative Media, *Bushwhacked* includes Investigations, Interviews and Secret Histories you won't find anywhere else.

Written in Dowbenko's trademark style, this book of political and cultural commentary includes true stories of conspiracy, cover up and betrayal — the ingredients of exciting spy novels and action movies. The difference, however, is that these stories are all real —

- *Bushwhacked: HUD Fraud, Spooks and the Slumlords of Harvard* is the true story of investment banker Catherine Austin Fitts and how she was ambushed by a cabal of corporate-government criminals
- *The Man Who Knows Too Much* describes the amazing life of undercover agent Al Martin and his adventures in the world of the US Secret Government
- *Prophet of Cyber-Grunge* reveals the creative mind of acclaimed science fiction author William Gibson
- *Spiritual Wickedness in High Places* is the last known interview with the late author Malachi Martin on the End of Religion (As We Know It)
- *True Stories from the 4th Dimension* dives into the extraordinary world of remote viewer David Morehouse, author of "Psychic Warrior"
- *Mind Control for the New World Order* draws back the curtain on the bizarre life stories of mind control survivors, programmed sex slaves and assassins

Challenging traditional concepts of history, *Bushwhacked* delivers the real stories of True Conspiracy and Cover-up, which turn out to be just Business As Usual. This book contains radical reporting from the frontlines of investigative writing. It's a no-holds-barred account of secret worlds, hidden patterns and lost knowledge.

If you're interested in the haunting unexplained mysteries of life, you'll love *Bushwhacked*.

URI DOWBENKO

BUSHWHACKED
INSIDE STORIES OF TRUE CONSPIRACY

Bushwhacked
Inside Stories of True Conspiracy

By Uri Dowbenko

Copyright © 2003 by Uri Dowbenko

For additional information, please contact:
Conspiracy Digest, LLC
Post Office Box 43, Pray, Montana 59065
Email: virtualagency@yahoo.com

Conspiracy Digest: Real News that Connects the Dots
Website — http://www.conspiracydigest .com

ISBN: 0-9710042-1-8
Library of Congress Number: 20022102051

Book and cover design by
Uri Dowbenko

Cover painting by
John Beukemann

Conspiracy Digest, LLC
Printed and bound in the
United States of America

To order additional copies,
Call Toll Free 1-866-317-1390

Contents

Introduction

Today less people than ever believe the truthfulness of news reported by the networks and mega-media outlets. In fact, recent Pew Research Center surveys show that a majority of the public (56%) now believes news stories are often inaccurate. Likewise cynicism regarding government corruption has also reached epidemic proportions.

Alternative media publications and websites that don't hew to a typically "left" or "right" agenda are quietly gaining a strong constituency in America. The First Amendment obviously helps. But now there's a wide spectrum of publications and websites that provide news and information, which seem to fall through the cracks of corporate programming, i.e. mainstream news.

This historically homegrown tradition of self-publishing without interference is the energy behind today's American *samizdat*. That's Russian, by the way, for pre-glasnost self-published politically incorrect writing. These are the stories, which disappear in the Orwellian Memory Hole that lies between the magazines and the tabloids.

And so it happened that the so-called Information Age became crowded with half-baked psychological operations (PsyOps) foisted on the general population by the Government-Media Cartel.

In fact, this virtual miasma of programming, indoctrination, and brainwashing, commonly known as "news" (and even "education") is delivered incessantly through the normal propaganda organs like TV, movies, magazines and newspapers. In order to control the masses, to mold opinion and to produce order, the Power Elite (also known as the Illuminati or the Cryptocracy) continues to propagate their various frauds, conspiracies and cover-ups.

Is this too brash an assessment? I think not — for the consensus realities of everyday life are reinforced to engender obeisance to the cult of consumerism, merchandising and other cults, which act in concert to produce blind obedience to the prevailing dogmas of Civilization, in other words, the Civil Lie in Action.

The problem with so-called mainstream media is that there is no context. They may get the facts right, but without a contextual background, there really is no value in so-called "news," or any so-called "information" for that matter.

Behind the officially sanctioned lies and half-truths of the Government-Media Cartel is the hidden world of Alternative Media. It is the domain of small circulation magazines, newspapers and newsletters, typically a labor of love, which gives dissident views of politics and world events a proper airing, so that the Truth itself can be discerned within the context of the lies, which continue their deadly work in the manipulation of Terra.

The Alternative Media, therefore, is the *raison d'etre* of the First Amendment. As long as Freedom of the Press remains a freedom in America, the tireless advocates of Truth will continue to do their work. After that, it will undoubtedly go underground as information guerrillas worked during the repressions of the Soviet Union.

It should be noted that as recently as the 1600s, *avant garde* writer Francis Bacon had to incorporate ciphers and cryptograms into his works — "The Shakespearean Plays" and the "King James Bible" — to leave behind a chronicle of the hidden mysteries and his own true history. It has been said that "The truth will set you free," but as the old joke goes, "First, it'll really piss you off."

Bushwhacked is a compilation of many innovative and provocative articles, originally published in alternative media publications like *Nexus Magazine*, *Media Bypass*, *Magical Blend*, *Paranoia Magazine*, *Steamshovel Press*, *Whistleblower Gazette*, *Nationalist Times*, as well as alternative media websites like *Al Martin Raw* (www.almartinraw.com), *Conspiracy Digest* (www.conspiracydigest.com) *Steam-shovel Press* (www.steamshovelpress.com) and *Conspiracy Planet* (www.conspiracyplanet.com).

My strength, I've been told, is the ability to integrate fragments of information into a coherent whole — connecting the proverbial dots, so to speak, so that an understandable framework can emerge.

One of the joys of writing is that it remains the ultimate educational experience. As life is a continuing education program, writing is therefore the most interesting and valuable occupation ever. For it is by writing that we learn and teach others.

Bushwhacked is not only a collection of the true stories of many brave men and women, who have endured the ultimate betrayal and "punishment" as scapegoats, but also the exposure of the infamy of so-called "public servants." As Al Martin, author of *The Conspirators: Secrets of an Iran Contra Insider* would say, this is simply "How the World Works."

I hope you enjoy these Investigations, Interviews and Secret Histories, and that they may help you avoid the problems and pitfalls encountered by the heroes and heroines of this book, those who were bushwhacked by the forces of darkness, yet survived to tell their stories.

And so it goes. As long as people are fed up with tabloid trash, news-magazine bias and government spin, Alternative Media is bound to keep growing.

This ancient motto seems to be most appropriate now — The Truth Against the World.

— Uri Dowbenko

URI DOWBENKO

BUSHWHACKED
INSIDE STORIES OF TRUE CONSPIRACY

Chapter 1

Bushwhacked: HUD Fraud, Spooks and the Slumlords of Harvard

C ATHERINE AUSTIN FITTS IS STILL TRYING to figure out what happened. Her company, Hamilton Securities, Inc., was the lead financial advisor to the US Department of Housing and Urban Development (HUD).

Hamilton was hired to manage the sales of $10 billion worth of mortgages on houses, apartment buildings and nursing homes.

By all accounts, Hamilton's new program was a resounding success.

In fact, the HUD loan sales program team was even given a Hammer Award for Excellence in Re-engineering Government by Vice President Al Gore's Reinventing Government Initiative. By cutting red tape and improving the resale value of HUD owned mortgages, Hamilton Securities was a case study of a public-private partnership that saved US taxpayers lots of money.

Until…

The firm was ambushed by a series of lawsuits, audits and unsubstantiated rumors, which destroyed the business.

Catherine Austin Fitts — Maverick Banker

In the arcane but stodgy world of investment banking, Catherine Austin Fitts is a revolutionary.

1

Before founding her own firm, Fitts, a Wharton School of Business graduate, was the first woman to be promoted to managing director of Dillon, Read and Co, Inc., the prototypical elitist men's club Wall Street investment bank.

To her credit, Fitts was instrumental in building a new market for Dillon Read. She began underwriting previously unrated municipal bonds, in essence, financing large government projects which other Wall Street firms said couldn't be done.

These novel bond sales helped revive New York City's crumbling subway system, and they provided funding for the City University of New York and other major projects.

The market in unrated and low-rated muni bonds took off, earning Fitts the title of "Wonder Woman of Muni Bonds," in a glowing *Business Week* article (February 23, 1987).

In 1989, she was asked to become the Federal Housing Administrator under HUD Secretary Jack Kemp. Fitts moved to Washington to undertake the monumental task of reforming the scandal-ridden, fraud-plagued agency.

After her stint in government, she was invited to be a Governor of the Federal Reserve Board. She declined.

Instead she founded Hamilton Securities Group, an employee-owned investment banking firm, which created an innovative system for saving taxpayers billions of dollars in the sale of government-guaranteed mortgage-loan sales from HUD.

By promoting open disclosure in the HUD financial transactions, Fitts undoubtedly, and unknowingly, must have stepped on a lot of toes.

The Crony Capitalists (The Old Boys' Network — or The Octopus) must have seen Hamilton's program of financial transparency as a major threat to their system of bid rigging and insider trading.

HUD Cost Savings Lead to Hamilton's Demise

In this extremely complex case, newly disclosed evidence indicates that powerful forces conspired to destroy the financial equity of employee-owned Hamilton Securities, as well as the personal life savings of the firm's president, Catherine Austin Fitts.

Why? Because Hamilton Securities had opened up the market for defaulted HUD mortgages. In simple terms, the established network of insiders would be susceptible to — horrors! — open competition, not to mention an entire universe of new bidders.

In fact, Hamilton's plan for optimization of sales of defaulted mortgages resulted in a savings of over $2.2 billion for US taxpayers.

The numbers are staggering. Every year HUD issues about $70 billion of mortgage insurance which guarantees the mortgages used to finance homes, apartment buildings, nursing homes, assisted living facilities and hospitals.

HUD then pays out about $6 billion on claims for defaulted mortgages, which the agency has to then manage at great cost to taxpayers.

Prior to Hamilton's involvement, HUD was recovering about 35 cents on the dollar of mortgage insurance payments made on defaulted mortgages.

When Hamilton instituted their new program, HUD's recovery rate soared to about 70 to 90 cents on the dollar. How? Hamilton introduced a proprietary optimization bidding software and an on-line database of information, accessible to all investors, so that the defaulted portfolio could be bid upon in an open auction.

In October 1997, the Chairman of one Congressional oversight committee referred to the Hamilton-based loan sales at HUD as generating "eye-popping" yields.

In fact from 1994-97, HUD saved about $2.2 billion in HUD's $12 billion mortgage portfolio. These savings then allowed HUD to issue far more new mortgage insurance at a lower cost.

When Hamilton's successful loan sales-auction program was suspended due to the investigation, the old levels of government "inefficiency" were resumed. Call it "Business As Usual." Or more aptly, "Fraud As Usual."

That means HUD is now losing about $4 billion per year on its $6 billion of defaulted mortgages — instead of just $2 billion.

That's the equivalent of 20,000 taxpayers working their whole lives to pay for this boondoggle for just one year.

Anatomy of a Corporate Murder

Targeted by criminal elements within the Department of Justice (DoJ), Housing and Urban Development (HUD), as well as a Old Boys' cartel of private investment companies, Hamilton Securities has undergone an onslaught of unimaginable harassment and intimidation.

There had been a SWAT-like attack on Hamilton's office in Washington, 19 audits, countless subpoenas as well as ongoing litigation against HUD to force them to pay monies owed on their contract. It's been over four years of a long financially and emotionally draining "investigation." To-date, there has been no evidence of any wrongdoing — just rumors, innuendo, and plenty of character assassination.

First, in June 1996, a sealed *qui tam* lawsuit, a phony whistle-blower suit, as well as a Bivens action was filed by John Ervin of Ervin & Associates, Inc., a

HUD subcontractor, notorious for filing nuisance lawsuits and "bid protests" — 37 of them in the recent past. In the Bivens suit, he sued HUD itself, as well as several former HUD officials personally.

In fact, Ervin's lawsuits have cost a fortune in legal fees and overhead, estimated — from 1995 to-date — to be as high as $40 to $50 million.

An insider claims that during that time Ervin had up to 17 in-house personnel working fulltime on mountains of paperwork regarding this and other cases.

So who's bankrolling Ervin? Nobody has offered any explanations, but for a small-time HUD sub-contractor like Ervin, this has turned out to be a serious investment — or payoff.

Under the False Claims Act, a private party like Ervin, who files suit on behalf of the government, can receive 15-30% of any recovery, if the government's claim is successful. That percentage of 15-30% would have covered asset seizures of up to $4.7 billion of loan sales won by Goldman Sachs and its partners.

Is somebody just playing the odds? In this version of government "greenmail" (state-sponsored extortion), any asset seizures could be part of this 15 to 30% "bounty."

The Spooky Life of Stanley Sporkin

Then it just so happened that the judge presiding over the Hamilton case was the former CIA Counsel — Federal Judge Stanley Sporkin (recently retired).

According to Rodney Stich, author of *Defrauding America*, "Sporkin was involved with the 1980 October Surprise scheme and his judicial appointment was probably his reward by the Reagan-Bush administration for helping carry it out, and to block any judicial exposure or prosecution action."

(The October Surprise was the Reagan-Bush black-ops/covert action to delay the release of the hostages in Iran, which resulted in the electoral victory of Reagan as US President.)

Appointed to the bench by Ronald Reagan in 1985, Sporkin's spooky roots go back to the days when he was a director of the SEC's Division of Enforcement, while the infamous Bill Casey was practicing his Wall Street shakedown techniques as Chairman of the Securities and Exchange Commission (SEC).

Sporkin's other claim to fame was to encourage Casey to go after the infamous scamster Robert Vesco. The question remains — was Vesco considered "competition," or was he just another "freelancer," who needed to be put in his place?

Casey, like George Bush Sr., neglected or "forgot" to put his assets in a blind trust. Both Casey and Bush, of course, became directors of the CIA. Casey's shares, however, (controlling stock in Capitol Cities Communications) were eventually used to take over ABC in a $3.5 billion merger deal.

In the words of *Casey* author Joseph Persico, Casey as "the director of the Central Intelligence Agency was soon to be a substantial shareholder in one of the country's major forums of free expression, with wondrous opportunity for managing the news."

Also according to Persico, Casey further employed Sporkin's specious reasoning by claiming that killing "suspected terrorists" was not murder.

Reagan's infamous Executive Order 12333, which privatized dirty tricks by the US National Security State, was ostensibly the reason.

"Striking at terrorists planning to strike at you was not assassination," wrote Persico referring to Sporkin's logic, "it was 'preemptive self-defense.'"

Then Sporkin became the general counsel for the CIA (1981-86) and his mastery of coverup skills increased dramatically. For instance, in keeping the Oliver North Cocaine Trafficking Operation under wraps, it was Sporkin who invented another ingenious method of lying by omission.

Persico writes that "North's insistence that the oversight committees be cut out troubled the CIA people. But the adroit Sporkin found a loophole. The President was required to inform the oversight committees of a covert action presumably in advance of the action, except when the urgency of the situation required that notification be delayed." Result? Everybody was notified 48 hours after the operation.

According to Persico, Sporkin also perfected the techniques of writing retroactive "findings" for Congress, so that CIA criminality could always be disguised or covered up — after the fact.

Stich concludes that "to protect the incoming Reagan-Bush teams and many of the federal officials and others who took part in October Surprise, the Reagan-Bush team placed people, including those implicated in the activities, in control of key federal agencies and the federal courts. Some, like attorneys Stanley Sporkin, Lawrence Silberman, and Lowell Jensen were appointed to the federal bench, defusing any litigation arising from the October Surprise or its many tentacles... Organized crime never had it so good."

Ironic Postscript Dept.: In Feb. 2000, retired spooky judge Stanley Sporkin (Yale Law School, 1957) joined the global powerhouse law firm Weil, Gotshal & Manges LLP. The company, which boasts 750 attorneys in 12 offices worldwide, is considered one of the leading law firms in the country on bankruptcy.

The Secret Life of "Slimy Affirm"

According to documents obtained by author Rodney Stich, Stanley Sporkin was heavily involved in the Hawaii-based "investment firm" Bishop, Baldwin, Rewald, Dillingham and Wong (BBRDW), a CIA proprietary company funded by the Agency in 1979, using many of the same personnel as were used in the notorious Nugan Hand Bank. It was a CIA money laundry front with Ronald Rewald, as the titular head of the company, who later became the CIA's Fall Guy of Choice when the operation was exposed.

Stich found an envelope labeled "Attorney-Client information," which revealed secret activities, including CIA drug trafficking and the funding of secret CIA overseas bank accounts for US government officials.

According to Stich, "notes in the envelope listed high level people with secret CIA-funded accounts. The names on the left side of the notes were aliases Rewald used to identify people on the right for which there were secret bank accounts opened and funded by the CIA through BBRDW."

The hidden bank accounts were contained in Rewald's "green book, which listed all foreign accounts and the cover names used to hold funds for special people." The funds were proceeds from illicit arms deals, drug trafficking transactions and other illegal activities.

Irwin M. Peach	George Bush
Mr. Bramble	George Bush
Commander Quinstar	General Hunter Harris
Mr. Apan	Robert W. Jinks
Mr. Grey	Robert Allen
Farrah Fawn	Jackie Vos
General Shake	Arnold Braswell
Mr. Branch	Richard Armitage
Mr. Denile	William Casey
Slimy Affirm	Stanley Sporkin

The names of these characters should be familiar. George Bush, of course, is the former US President and CIA director. Arnold Braswell was Commander in Chief of US Pacific Air Force, (CINCPACAF). Richard Armitage was US Assistant Secretary of Defense and reportedly heavily involved in drug trafficking during the Vietnam era. William Casey was the late CIA director.

Stich also confirms that Ross Perot knew of these secret bank accounts and that Rewald himself answered Perot's questions about the illicit operations. Rewald acknowledges that these people "were sent monthly statements," that "the funds came from Agency funding mechanisms," and that these "bank accounts were always full. It was not unusual for us to have hundreds of millions of dollars in various banks in Hong Kong and Shanghai banks, in Cayman Islands, Netherlands Antilles banks and Swiss bank accounts."

"Slimy Affirm" seems like a fitting handle for Stanley Sporkin, the SEC lawyer who became a Political Liability Control Specialist in his role as Federal Judge. Being on the pad is more than just a perk; it's evidently a way of life for Stanley Sporkin.

The Hamilton Bushwhack

In the Hamilton Securities case, Sporkin's claim to fame is that he managed to illegally keep a *qui tam* lawsuit sealed for almost 4 years. That could be a "judicial" record.

In August 1996, an investigation against Hamilton was initiated by HUD Inspector General Susan Gaffney, serving two subpoenas on the company — and incidentally failing to tell Hamilton about the existence of the *qui tam* as required by law. The subpoenas demanded hundreds of thousands of documents, mostly HUD documents that HUD already had, or that had been supplied to them as part of the ongoing work — a clear case of burying Hamilton in paperwork as more ongoing harassment.

At the same time, a HUD audit team from Denver had completed a favorable audit of Hamilton's program. When Fitts asked HUD IG Gaffney whether she intended to "bury the Denver audit," Gaffney huffed back, "How dare you suggest that I would do any such thing? That would be unethical."

In fact, she did exactly that. HUD Inspector General Susan Gaffney never allowed the publication of the Denver Audit team's report which exonerated all of Hamilton's methodology and results.

Then, at the same time, a smear campaign against Hamilton was being waged through a *US News and World Report* hatchet-job article about HUD Secretary Henry Cisneros and the loan sales program.

Clearly the fix was in.

According to Fitts, the lead reporter had told her that he had been assured "at the highest levels" of the HUD Inspector General's office that Hamilton Securities and Fitts were the subject of a criminal investigation and were guilty of criminal violations.

There was no evidence, however, either offered by HUD or published by the magazine, and these false allegation also died with the passage of time. As did Fitts's company.

In a bizarre double-bind mentality, HUD and DoJ — in a separate court and with a different judge — had taken the position that the Ervin lawsuit was without merit — even while Hamilton's legal costs climbed into the millions of dollars.

The Dirty Fingerprints of Lee Radek

In December 1997, Hamilton wrote a letter to the President's Council on Integrity & Efficiency (PCIE), a committee in the Office of Management and Budget (OMB), to investigate HUD IG Susan Gaffney's conduct.

Hamilton's four-page highly detailed letter to Neil J. Gallagher, Acting Assistant Director of the FBI's Criminal Investigative Division and Chairperson of PCIE, was blunt.

"The HUD IG has crossed the line in its investigation of Hamilton, which was begun in response to complaints from Ervin & Associates, a disgruntled HUD contractor," wrote Fitts. "The IG's wide-ranging and unfocused 'fishing expedition' against Hamilton has failed to produce findings of wrongdoing and threatens the survival of the firm. The repeated leaking to the press of propri-etary and confidential information that only the HUD IG could know and the intervention of other Federal Agencies [IRS, FDIC] into Hamilton's affairs con-stitute a campaign of smear, slander and intimidation that should be investigat-ed and stopped."

Fitts wrote about many incidents of intimidation and harassment, which "demonstrate or suggest that the HUD IG is deliberately leaking information to the press about its investigation of Hamilton. These leaks represent serious and persistent breaches of confidentiality, unethical and unlawful behavior and vio-lations of Hamilton's constitutional rights."

PCIE declined to investigate. In her next letter to Gallagher in February 1998, Fitts wrote that "since the filing of our complaint, the Hamilton Securities Group Inc. and all of its subsidiaries have been rendered insolvent... In the face of eighteen months of Inspector General 'lynch mobbing' we have exhausted our reserves and have no means to continue an investigation that has no end..."

After another refusal by PCIE to investigate, Hamilton filed a Freedom of Information Action (FOIA) for the files.

The files revealed a heavily redacted letter signed by the Lead Coverup-Meister himself — Lee Radek, head of the Department of Justice's ironically named "Office of Public Integrity."

In a letter dated April 3, 1998 addressed to Thomas J. Piccard, Chairman of the Integrity Committee of the PCIE, Radek wrote "C. Austin Fitts, President of the Hamilton Securities Group, Inc. sent the IC a copy of a civil complaint filed by Hamilton Securities against HUD Secretary Andrew Cuomo, Assistant Secretary Nicolas Retsinas and Inspector General Susan Gaffney. The complaint alleged that HUD's OIG investigation of Hamilton and improper media leaks by the OIG about the investigation was causing Hamilton to go out of business... After reviewing the letter and the attachments, the Public Integrity Section con-

cludes that the allegations in the complaint do not provide sufficient information to warrant a criminal investigation."

The rest of the page — seven inches of what used to be text — is blacked out.

For the record, US Department of Justice apparatchik Lee Radek has held a
virtual stranglehold on DoJ "investigations," consistently covering up the criminal activities of the Clinton Administration. As a linchpin in the corrupt DoJ,
he has had many opportunities to coverup crimes and block inquiries — and he
has taken full advantage of his position as a Federal-Mob "enforcer."

It's an ironic twist of fate, then, that Neil Gallagher — the FBI staff member
of PCIE, whose job it was to investigate allegations against Susan Gaffney — and
Lee Radek appeared together in May 2000 before a Congressional hearing — as
antagonists.

Gallagher affirmed in public testimony that Radek was indeed under pressure
from US Attorney General Janet Reno to stall any investigation into the
Clinton-Gore campaign fundraising scandals.

Unsealing the Lawsuit

Finally in May 2000, US District Judge Louis F. Oberdorfer unsealed the *qui
tam* lawsuit against Hamilton — and Surprise! — the Department of Justice
decided not to pursue the groundless claims.

The suit was filed in June 1996, and DoJ's decision not to intervene in this
case came after a 1,400 day so-called "investigation" — or 1,340 days longer than
the 60 days mandated by the Federal False Claims Act.

Hamilton Securities maintained that the allegations in the complaint were
not true, and there was no evidence to support the false allegations.

In fact, HUD security procedures and overlapping levels of review associated
with the open bidding process made the alleged bid rigging and insider trading
impossible. This was corroborated by HUD's own audits.

The sources for the alleged bid rigging in Ervin's complaint, kept under court
seal for almost four years, included Jeff Parker of the Cargill Group, Terry R.
Dewitt of J-Hawk (First City Financial Corporation of Waco, Texas, and a
Cargill investment and joint venture partner), and Michael Nathans of Penn
Capital Corporation.

The Waco-Cargill Connection

In retrospect, Hamilton must have been a major threat to the nation-wide
money laundering and financial fraud network, which uses government-guaranteed mortgages and other programs to scam US taxpayers. The formerly secret

sources of the false allegations against Hamilton have some interesting connections.

SEC documents state that First City Financial Corporation (FCFC) of Waco, Texas started business in 1986 "purchasing distressed assets from FDIC and RTC."

Another subsidiary, First City Commercial Corp. was used to "acquire portfolios of distressed loans" — another hallmark of the standard money laundry operation.

According to the Houston Business Journal (Sept. 24, 1999), "First City Bancorporation, once one of Houston's largest bank holding companies, was acquired out of bankruptcy in 1995 by J-Hawk Corp of Waco and renamed First City Financial Corp."

"FCFC began its relationship with Cargill Financial Services Corp. in 1991," according to the company's SEC filings. "Since that time, the Company and Cargill Financial have formed a series of Acquisition Partnerships through which they have jointly acquired over $3.2 billion in Face Value of distressed assets. By the end of 1994, the Company had grown to nine offices with over 180 professionals and had acquired portfolios with assets in virtually every state."

But then — and now comes the sad part —- the mortgage banking subsidiary of First City Financial Corporation, Harbor Financial Group Inc., filed for bankruptcy (Oct., 1999), just as the notorious Denver-based money laundry, M&L Business Machines, had done years before.

The corporate shell game of mergers, acquisitions and liquidation is obviously in full play in this scenario.

The other false accuser listed — Cargill Financial Services Corp., — on the other hand, is a subsidiary of Cargill, the Minneapolis-based global agribusiness cartel and the world's largest privately-held company.

Cargill is a mega-corporate international merchant of agricultural, industrial and financial commodities, and it operates in 59 countries, has 82,000 employees, and about $50 billion in annual sales.

The financial subsidiary, Access Financial Holdings Corp., was formed to "manage the housing finance business" and "provide residential real estate mortgages," an unregulated arena in which money laundering is often the real business.

And here's the punchline in this revolving-door joke called the Criminal Big Government-Big Business Syndicate.

The lead law firm listed on First City Financial's 1998 registration statement is Weil Gotshal — former spooky judge Stanley Sporkin's new employer.

Whistle-Blower Stew Webb's Perspective

Federal whistle-blower Stewart Webb thinks he knows why Catherine Austin Fitts and her company, Hamilton Securities, were bushwhacked. In fact, he believes that her operation was a direct threat to the "Denver Boys" — the Bush Crime Family's money laundering operation based in Denver.

Why was she targeted? "Because she had set up a company which was showing the government how to save money through competitive loan sales programs," explains Webb. "It was a threat to [Leonard] Millman in Denver. Because they were in control of the mortgage program."

Webb is referring to the many HUD low-income housing-based frauds and scandals in Denver. He claims that one of their proxies was John Ervin himself. "He had his own office in Denver," says Webb. "One of the biggest supplies of money to these boys is the money they're stealing from HUD. They are still robbing HUD like nobody's business.

"That's a massive covert revenue stream for them," continues Webb. "As of last year, they became the largest apartment owner in the United States. AIMCO. That's Millman and Company in Denver."

Apartment Investment and Management Co. (AIMCO) is one of the largest real estate investment trusts, or REITs, in the US with headquarters in Denver, Colorado and 36 regional offices. AIMCO operates about 1,834 properties, including about 385,000 apartment units nationwide in every state except Vermont.

AIMCO is the successor to the Considine Co., founded in 1975, by Terry Considine. It was then re-organized as a real estate investment trust and became a public company through an initial stock offering in July 1994.

In an article called "HUD, AIMCO Clash Over Housing" (*Denver Business Journal*, May 8, 1998), AIMCO was excoriated by affordable-housing advocates for taking 90,000 low-income (so-called "affordable housing") apartments — bought from HUD at below market rates — and converting them into higher end properties, thereby displacing poor renters.

According to the article, "the revamping also involves upgrading bare-bones properties built with federal funds two decades ago which will allow AIMCO to boost rents."

AIMCO has also gobbled up Washington DC-based apartment manager NHP, Inc., Ambassador Apartments, a Chicago-based REIT, and the apartment portion of Insignia Financial Group.

Since AIMCO is the nation's largest owner of affordable housing and the sole provider of such homes in many markets, the implications are ominous.

More homeless people on the streets are a sure bet.

The Harvard-Bush Connection

Historically the Chinese Opium Trade and the African Slave Trade have provided the financial foundation for the Boston "Bluebloods." It should therefore come as no surprise that the Harvard Endowment Fund and the Harvard Management Corporation are involved in what can be liberally characterized as a shady deal at best — or criminal enterprise at worst.

In 1989, the Harvard Endowment Fund, became the 50% owner of HUD subsidy (Section 8) and non-subsidy apartment buildings through its purchase of NHP, an apartment management firm, headed by Roderick Heller III.

Since their plan was to do an Initial Public Offering (IPO) or a merger for NHP, they tried to run up the value by aggressive acquisition of more apartments, preferably with HUD issued mortgage insurance which could be defaulted on — with little or no consequence.

Unfortunately for Harvard, HUD had initiated its new open-disclosure and performance-based auction under the direction of Hamilton Securities. When the private market firms battled it out, Harvard was outbid by GE, Goldman Sachs and Black Rock and its sour grapes apparently turned to vengeance.

In 1996, according to Fitts, Rod Heller told her that the government had a "moral obligation" to him and his investors (Harvard Endowment) to renew or roll over the subsidies with them to maintain their profits.

In other words, an open auction-free marketplace was not acceptable to the Harvard Boys, since they were operating their business of HUD-backed corporate welfare-subsidies under what Heller claimed was "an understood handshake."

The HUD portfolio of distressed properties had traditionally been managed to derive profits for private business — like Harvard Endowment Fund — and not US taxpayers. Since Harvard was used to rigging profits through politics — and not fair business practices — it started losing income because there were less management fees and the value of its stock started going down.

In 1991, Harvard and Heller asked Fitts to do an investment bank with them. At the last minute, Harvard Management Company honcho Michael R. Eisenson told her he wanted 20% of her new company's stock, and the deal was shattered.

On the first large HUD loan sale, Eisenson complained to Fitts, "I don't like this" — referring to Hamilton's use of optimization software to auction HUD mortgages — "because the only way we can win is by paying more than our competitors. We prefer a bid process where we can win by 'gaming it' because we are 'smarter.'"

For those unfamiliar with Soviet (or Harvard Mob) nomenclature, "smarter" is code language for "we can rig it." And "gaming it" means manipulating the players to get control of them, rather than using the competitive process of free market capitalism.

Eisenson was obviously quite at home with the proverbial fix. In fact, he demanded it and was miffed when Hamilton Securities would upset his rigged deal.

And who is Mike Eisenson? He was the lead investor who eventually sold Harvard's share of NHP to the Denver-based AIMCO. Eisenson's other claim to fame is that he was on the board of directors of the infamous stock swindle Harken Energy rigged as an insider stock deal on behalf of George W. Bush — not coincidentally a Harvard grad himself.

The Harken Scam story began in 1986, when a small company called Spectrum 7, with George W. Bush as Chairman and CEO, was acquired by Harken Energy Corp.

After Bush joined Harken, the largest stock position and seat on its board was acquired by Harvard Management Co.

The oil and gas, real estate and private equity portion of Harvard Endowment also acquired Warren Buffet's position in NHP, one of the largest owners of HUD Section 8 subsidized properties in 1989.

Then the Hamilton Securities-initiated HUD loan sales were slowed down and cancelled, and, of course, Harvard's capital gains were ensured through an IPO of NHP and through a later sale to AIMCO.

The Harken Board gave the Junior Bush $600,000 worth of company stock, plus a seat on the board, plus a consultancy worth $120,000 a year — despite suffering losses of more than $12 million dollars against revenues of $1 billion in 1989.

In 1987 when creditors were threatening to foreclose, the Junior Bush himself made a trip to Arkansas to meet criminal-banking kingpin Jackson Stephens, whose Stephens Inc. arranged financing for the faltering Harken Energy from a subsidiary of the Union Bank of Switzerland (UBS).

Stephens Inc, of course, had ties to the notorious CIA money laundry bank, the Bank of Credit and Commerce International (BCCI), where drug trafficking and arms-smuggling profits mingled freely with looted S&L and fraud-scam proceeds.

Then in 1990 Bahrain awarded an exclusive drilling rights contract to Harken and the Bass brothers added more equity to the deal. Six months later George Bush Jr. sold off 212,140 shares grossing him $848,560.

When Saddam Hussein invaded Kuwait, the Harken stock dropped suddenly. The SEC was not notified, and no action for insider trading was taken against the Junior Bush. Why? SEC chairman Richard Breeden was a faithful Bush loyalist.

Today Eisenson, formerly one of the lead investors in NHP and Harken and one of the primary portfolio managers of Harvard Management, runs a private equity portfolio called Charlesbank Capital Partners LLC in Boston, which manages $1.4 billion in real estate investments for the Harvard Endowment.

One of the partners of a company doing business with NHP, Scott Nordheimer actually admitted to Fitts in June 1996 – "We tried to get you fired through the White House and that didn't work. So now the Big Boys got together, and you're going to jail."

Shortly thereafter the *qui tam* lawsuit with the bogus whistle-blower charges was filed against Hamilton.

In this complicated story, there's another part of the puzzle, which needs exposure. The Hamilton Bushwhack involved Cargill personnel falsely accusing the following companies of financial improprieties: Hamilton Securities, as well as investment bankers Goldman Sachs and Black Rock Financial, a subsidiary of PNC.

Goldman Sachs has been touted as one of the largest contributors to the Democratic National Committee and the Clinton-Gore Presidential Campaign.

Was the Hamilton Bushwhack just another outward sign of a covert power struggle? Because of its implications, it had the potential to lead to Clinton's impeachment on fundraising violations, much more significant and criminal activity than the Monica Lewinsky Sexcapades used as a cover story in the Ken Starr so-called investigation.

More Spooky Harvard Connections

The key to the mystery of the Hamilton Bushwhack may ultimately be found in the relationship between 1) government guaranteed/insured mortgages, 2) asset seizure/forfeitures, and 3) the private companies whose profits derive from an inside track with both government programs.

More lucrative than mere corporate subsidies, there are entire segments of mega-business, which depend on these government insider deals.

For example, besides Harvard, the other primary investor in apartment management company NHP was Capricorn Investments and Herbert S. "Pug" Winokur, Jr.

Winokur, former Executive Vice President and Director of Penn Central Corp, CEO of Capricorn Holdings Inc. and managing partner of three Capricorn Investors Limited Partnerships, is one of those insiders who may have benefited from the outrageous assault on Hamilton's open bid auction for defaulted HUD mortgages.

Not incidentally, from 1988 to 1997, because of his large investments, Winokur was also the Chairman and CEO of DynCorp, a US government contractor whose customers include Department of Defense, NASA, Department of State, EPA, Center for Disease Control, National Institute of Health, the US Postal Service and other US Government agencies.

Most importantly, according to SEC registration documents (S-1), DynCorp is the prime servicer on the Department of Justice Asset Forfeiture Fund, having procured a five-year contract with the Department of Justice worth $217 million from 1993 to 1998. This 1000 person contract required staffing at over 300 locations in the US and involved support of DoJ's drug-related asset seizure program. According to SEC documents, DynCorp's personnel supports "U.S. Attorney Offices that are responsible for administering the federal asset forfeiture laws."

In other words, DynCorp could have profited first from a successful seizure of HUD loan sales. Then, DynCorp could have profited from HUD "Operation Safe Home" seizures, which target low-income tenants, mortgage holders and apartment owners. And, since the company has the expertise and personnel, DynCorp could also have targeted these communities with private surveillance teams and non-lethal weapons to effect asset seizures using the phony War on Drugs as a rationale.

By all accounts, there is at least a major conflict of interest in Winokur's investments in HUD low-income housing and his role in Department of Justice seizures.

Imagine — if you're Pug Winokur, you can make money on defaulted HUD mortgages, guaranteed by US taxpayers, as well as by kicking out low-income housing tenants because of drug-related "asset seizures." The criminal-corporate-government scams don't get any better.

In the case of Hamilton's open-bid auction process on defaulted HUD mortgages, the potential $4.7 billion seizure of HUD loan sales would have been a major plum for DynCorp as the prime servicer of the DoJ Asset Forfeiture Fund.

By the way, Winokur also had the "foresight" not to board the ill-fated flight to war-torn Yugoslavia, which took Secretary of Commerce Ron Brown's life.

There are other spooky connections. According to *Newsweek* (Feb. 15, 1999), Reston, Virginia based DynCorp is a $1.3 billion firm, which also trains police in Haiti and works on coca eradication in Colombia, where three of its American pilots have died since 1997.

Reliable sources allege this shadowy outfit may be a CIA-military proprietary, in other words, a privatized entity useful for "plausible deniability." At any rate, it also provides "Yankee Mercenaries" for the Colombian campaign against drug trafficking. Employing about 30 US Vietnam War veterans, DynCorp has a $600 million contract to run and maintain the planes and helicopters used in "anti-drug" efforts in Peru, Bolivia and Colombia, according to the World Press Review (Nov. 1, 1998).

Postscript: Who says (corporate) crime doesn't pay? According to the Harvard University Gazette, in June 2000, Herbert S. "Pug" Winokur Jr. was named to join the seven-member Harvard Corporation, the University's executive governing board.

Doing Business with the Feds

Imagine having to wait more than 4 years to get paid on an invoice.

For more than $2 million.

From the US Government.

That, in short, is what happened to Hamilton Securities.

Doing business with the US Federal Government should come with a warning label: Warning — Saving money for the taxpayers can be hazardous to your health.

"HUD is withholding about $2 million of funds owed to Hamilton for services performed for HUD," says Hamilton's President Catherine Austin Fitts. "We also understand that this with-holding is at the request of the Justice Department and the HUD Investigator General.

"As the lead investment banker on $10 billion of loan sales, we have been able to preserve the integrity of these transactions. We intend to take whatever steps necessary to recover our shareholders' and employees value as we have done for the US taxpayers. The unsealing of the *qui tam* lawsuit should free HUD to meet its outstanding contractual obligations to Hamilton as quickly as possible."

Toward a Positive Future

And what is Catherine Austin Fitts doing now?

Besides trying to recover her life, she's moving ahead with her new company called Solari Inc., and her vision, the Solari Investment Model, community-based programs for local equity building and investment.

"Solari is an investment advisory service, which plans to reengineer investment and financial structures at a local level, so that new technology can be integrated into communities to increase jobs and ownership," says Fitts.

"Over the last ten years, we have prototyped a substantial number of transactions, venture capital and portfolio strategy to determine the ideal way to refinance communities in the stock market," she continues. "Our intention is to create a fund which can finance local development — and maintain local control — through an investment model geared for breakthrough transformations with individual, organizational and community change."

Her far-reaching vision is an inspiration. "By creating one or two Solari Stock Corporations (one for real estate and one for venture capital) through a community offering, and swapping non-voting stock for outstanding debt," says Fitts, "the community can lower short term debt service and realign interests between numerous constituents who can be positioned in a win-win financial model."

The problem is quite simple. The old model — the Soviet-inspired centralized command & control system which rules Washington, its agencies and the beltway bandits feeding at the trough of corporate subsidies — must give way to the new paradigm of the neighborhood investment model. It's a foregone conclusion: the corrupt system of corporate socialism which guarantees profits to insiders will be swept into the ashcan of history, just as the Soviet Union's brand of communism has been discredited forever. It's just a matter of time.

In the end — by building an alignment between spirituality and the material world — Catherine Austin Fitts believes that "everyone can prosper through actions which integrate our spiritual principles in the material world in which we live and work."

(For more information on the Solari Model of Investment and community-based profitability, read http://www.solari.com)

Chapter 2

DoJ Lies: Unsealed Court Docs Reveal How Hamilton Was Bushwhacked

RECENTLY UNSEALED COURT documents in the Hamilton Securities case show that attorneys from the Department of Justice and HUD (Department of Housing and Urban Development) lied repeatedly in court before US District Judge Stanley Sporkin.

In an outrageous example of judiciary malfeasance, Judge Sporkin himself coached the government attorneys on how they should proceed with their investigation and litigation strategy.

Prior to the lawsuit, Hamilton Securities, an innovative software company and its president Catherine Austin Fitts successfully completed an auction sale of defaulted HUD properties, which saved the government an estimated $2.2 billion in lost revenue. Then the company became a target.

In June 1996, Hamilton was served with a *qui tam* lawsuit as well as a phony whistleblower suit filed by a disgruntled HUD subcontractor, John Ervin of Ervin & Associates.

In fact, transcripts of the sealed hearings show that DoJ and HUD attorneys were clearly the strategic force behind Ervin's phony suit against Hamilton, running interference for Ervin in closed sessions with Judge Sporkin.

DoJ attorneys Barbara Van Gelder and Anthony Alexis, as well as HUD attorney Judith Hetherton then managed to keep stalling the *qui tam* lawsuit against Hamilton for an astonishing four years. This was apparently a clear-cut effort to bleed Hamilton's financial resources. The time proscribed by law, by the way, for "investigations" of this type, is 60 days.

The coordination against Hamilton seems to have originated in the US Attorney's office in the District of Columbia, as well as the Lee Radek fiefdom of the Department of Justice, misnamed "Office of Public Integrity."

Former CIA operative Lee Radek is a master of conspiracy cover-up and his office has a well-known reputation for derailing investigation and coordinating reprisals against government whistleblowers.

Hetherton was a former member of the District of Columbia's US Attorney's office, while Van Gelder worked for Eric Holder, the DC US Attorney who became the Assistant Attorney General under Janet Reno.

Van Gelder also reported to Frank Hunger, Al Gore's brother in law, head of the Civil Division of the Department of Justice.

In essence, the *qui tam* lawsuit, filed by a bounty hunter (Ervin) on behalf of the government, alleged that the government had been harmed by bid rigging between Goldman Sachs, Black Rock, HUD and Hamilton Securities.

Court documents present a convincing case that the *qui tam* lawsuit against Hamilton was itself concocted by the DC US Attorney's team — even though they knew it was completely without merit.

During the same time frame (four years), Judge Sporkin illegally kept the court documents sealed to further obfuscate DoJ's criminality.

In fact, the unsealed court transcripts reveal an astonishing disregard for evidence and normal court protocol by government attorneys as well as the judge.

It's clear that Judge Sporkin was guiding DoJ and Ervin attorneys in their "search" for non-existent evidence against Hamilton.

Sporkin, a former CIA and SEC counsel under Bill Casey, repeatedly helped government attorneys by verbally nudging them toward some semblance of professional behavior.

Sporkin, by the way, took over the case from Judge Charles R. Richey who mysteriously — and unexpectedly — died after the first several hearings.

In the March 29, 1999 transcript, for example, Judge Sporkin asked US Attorney Anthony Alexis. "Where are we on this thing here? Where's the government going? Do they know yet?"

Alexis replies. "No." Sporkin, evidently frustrated by the US Attorney's inability to present a credible case against Hamilton, asks him, "You don't know where you want to go?"

Alexis answers, "I kind of know which direction I want to go in terms of who I want to speak to, but there's well, obviously the documents which Ms. Hetherton can speak to which is before the special master."

The case, by the way, was first heard on June 20, 1996, so the preceding conversation took place three years after the supposed "investigation," which yielded no evidence of wrongdoing by Hamilton.

Each time attorneys for DoJ and HUD appeared in closed session with the judge, they would, time and again, present no evidence, no affidavits, and no documents — just a plea to postpone the case.

Judge Sporkin, time and again, acceded to their baseless request and postponed the case.

The chronology of illegal and bizarre behavior by Sporkin and government attorneys follows:

• July 1, 1996 – Judge Richey extends the case for 60 days based on Barbara Van Gelder's unsubstantiated allegations that fraud was involved. Judge Richey tells Van Gelder he won't give them another extension. Then Judge Richey suddenly gets sick and dies.

• Aug 19, 1996 – The new judge, Stanley Sporkin, extends the case another 90 days.

• December 19, 1996 – Sporkin gives government attorneys another 90-day extension. He comments on the fact that John Ervin, the disgruntled government contractor/bounty hunter would get 15% to 30% of the settlement.

"Gee, I had one of these *qui tams* where the government recovered close to 30 million. And the Realtor I guess got — what do they get, a third?" the judge asks. "Thirty percent," answers Wayne Travell, a Tucker Flyer attorney representing failed bounty hunter John Ervin.

• May 20, 1997 – US Attorney Barbara van Gelder lies once again regarding her lack of evidence in the case. She implies that if she's given more time, she'll definitely come up with something concrete.

When Sporkin asks her about consolidating the two cases, Van Gelder flirts with the judge and tells him, "Oh, it's always a pleasure to appear before you." The judge says, "You know how to butter me up, don't you? You and I go back many years…"

But Sporkin doesn't recuse himself.

Van Gelder then tells the judge, "The reason why we can't — I believe that we can't have one case consolidated is that one judge would have total knowledge of the case and the problem is in the other case we are the defendant, and so with the United States being the plaintiff and the United States being the defendant…"

In other words the government is in the bizarre situation of being the Plaintiff AND the Defendant, since Ervin has also sued the government, specifically HUD and Helen Dunlap. Sporkin is puzzled too. He asks her how the government can be both plaintiff and defendant in the case.

After Ervin and his counsel are referred to as "bounty hunters," Sporkin gives government attorneys another 90 days — illegally. Again Van Gelder lies and tells the judge she needs an additional six months.

Sporkin replies, "...these are interesting cases. I've had one of these where the Realtor I think, he recaptured abut 30 million and I think 25 percent is tops."

Van Gelder says, "Twenty five is the top, right?" Sporkin says, "And you figure 25 percent of 30 million is 7.5 million bucks."

The message between the lines is that Sporkin is wondering out loud what the patsy John Ervin is actually doing to "earn" the $7.5 million.

• Sept 10, 1997 – Sporkin recommends that Van Gelder use SEC investigators to figure out if the HUD loan sales can be construed as "securities." Van Gelder says that she wants to use SEC only in an advisory capacity. In essence, Sporkin the judge is advising Van Gelder the DoJ Attorney on litigation and investigation strategy. Improper? Sure. Has Sporkin and van Gelder been censured, fined or prosecuted? Not yet.

• October 1997 – HUD Director Andrew Cuomo abruptly cancels the Hamilton Securities contract, despite the fact that Hamilton successfully auctioned off $10 billion worth of defaulted mortgages, saving the government an estimated $2.2 billion. HUD still owes Hamilton $2.5 million for contracted services.

• March 9, 1998 – FBI loots the Hamilton Securities office in Washington, DC. A sworn affidavit by a building custodian shows DoJ's intent to plant false evidence in the basement hoard of Hamilton documents in order to frame Hamilton — and in turn, Goldman Sachs.

DoJ Attorney Tony Alexis appears and asks for another 120-day extension in the case.

• July 10, 1998 – Tony Alexis lies again and claims Hamilton isn't giving them documents they have asked for. The Judge stalls the case again.

• Nov 19, 1998 – Dan Hawke, Ervin's attorney, asks for another 90 days.

• Jan 29, 1999 – Tony Alexis, assistant US Attorney Civil Division, asks for the case to be sealed for 90 days

• June 2, 1999 – DoJ attorneys continue to mislead the court.

Judge Sporkin begins to show his frustration at the ineptness of government attorneys. You can imagine how he feels after more than three years of no results. He says, "Let me tell you what you've got to do here. What you've really got to do, because this thing is dragging on, get a team together of some very knowledgeable people. You might have to bring them in from the outside. There's a big pool of people over there at Securities and Exchange Commission you could use. And I don't know whether you're permitted to go outside of the SEC to bring in some people that are knowledgeable in Wall Street and how these things work and get into that end of it. And I don't know whether HUD has that — the Inspector General has those skills. I don't know. I really, I think it's dragging on. And the longer you wait, the harder it's going to be to reconstruct things because what you're going to have to do is reconstruct your market."

Translation: I'm really, really frustrated with the incompetence of all you government attorneys. Why can't you just do the job?

Sporkin then continues leading them, trying to motivate them to bring him something — anything with any perceived value. "I think you've really got to get a team together that's knowledgeable in this area of the law and can, you know, can go into it and see if these allegations are true or not. I don't know how you're going to do it, but you've got to get — I don't know — is the Inspector General carrying this on or do you have anybody from Justice working on this?"

The transcripts show that the Hamilton bush whack was a setup, a story of dirty politics within the DoJ and HUD. The transcripts also implicate DoJ Attorneys, the HUD Inspector General Susan Gaffney and HUD Director Andrew Cuomo in collusion, if not conspiracy, against Hamilton Securities.

Andrew Cuomo, the mob-connected son of former Governor Mario Cuomo, is currently running for Governor of New York. While he was HUD Director, HUD Inspector General Susan Gaffney revealed in March 2000 that $59 billion of HUD monies had been "lost" and the accounting could not be reconciled. Computer "error" was initially blamed for the shortfall, but this ludicrous and laughable cover story did not stand.

Furthermore it becomes clear that —

1. DoJ designed the construct and rationale for Ervin to file the lawsuit against Hamilton on behalf of the government.

2. DoJ taught Ervin how to get the ultimate kickback as a "bounty hunter." Incidentally Ervin was actually paid several million dollars when he agreed to withdraw his lawsuit against HUD and HUD officials, a backdoor payoff.

3. Judge Stanley Sporkin's egregious behavior and improper conduct is evidence of criminal conspiracy. Well-trained in dirty tricks and spooky "tradecraft," Sporkin, according to whistleblower Rodney Stich, was initially "appointed to the federal bench to defuse any litigation arising from the October Surprise or its many tentacles."

So was Hamilton Securities just another domino in trying to knock down Goldman Sachs?

Or was Hamilton and its innovative software a serious threat to the insiders who had rigged the sales of defaulted loans to hide the rampant well-documented fraud in HUD itself?

Were they so afraid that Hamilton' open auction system would cut them out and destroy their covert revenue streams and money laundering capability through HUD?

Other more serious questions also remain.

Why did HUD Director Andrew Cuomo and Al Gore' brother-in-law Frank Hunger, head of the Civil Division of DoJ, try to frame Goldman Sachs during the Clinton impeachment, despite the fact that Goldman Sachs was a major contributor to the Democrat Party?

Was this the aftermath of a failed palace coup by Al Gore, Frank Hunger and Hillary Clinton against Bill Clinton himself?

Timing, after all, is everything.

Hamilton Securities and Catherine Austin Fitts continue to struggle under the burden of a meritless lawsuit by the Department of Justice.

Hamilton has still not been paid on its invoice for $2.5 million — unquestionably and undeniably owed by HUD.

Gored and bushwhacked, software pioneer Catherine Austin Fitts has paid dearly for her company's innovations. Nevertheless she's ready to begin her new project, a book called *The Solari Spirit: How to Create Local Prosperity in a Global Economy*. (http://www.solari.com) — as soon as this outrageous case is settled...

Chapter 3

The Curious Case of the Spooky Professor

FORMER CIA INSPECTOR General Frederick P. Hitz, responsible for covering up the CIA's involvement in distributing crack cocaine to American inner cities, has been rewarded with a prestigious teaching position — the Goldman Sachs Chair at Princeton University.

Officially Hitz's title is John L. Weinberg/Goldman Sachs and Company Visiting Professor and Director of the Project on International Intelligence (CIS) at the Woodrow Wilson School of Princeton University

Here's the background on the crimes, the cover-ups and the reward for CIA's cover-up meister. On March 16, 1998, Hitz appeared before the House Intelligence Committee to report on his investigation of the CIA, the Contras and crack cocaine. He testified that in 1982 a secret agreement had been made between the CIA and the Department of Justice. This "Memorandum of Understanding" allowed the CIA to use "agents, assets, and non-staff employees" involved in drug trafficking and to refrain from reporting these illegal activities.

In essence, then CIA Director William Casey and Attorney General William French Smith had made their own twisted version of a "Don't Ask, Don't Tell" policy. This effectively gave the CIA cover to maintain their "plausible deniability" during the Iran-Contra narcotics trafficking, which brought billions of dollars in covert revenue for the Agency.

In other words, CIA officials could lie straight-faced to Congress and the American people about government-sanctioned narcotics trafficking.

When asked by Congressman Norman Dicks of Washington, "Did any of these allegations involve trafficking in the United States?" Hitz answered, "Yes." Hitz also acknowledged that the CIA knew that "dozens of individuals and a number of companies connected in some fashion to the Contra program" were involved in drug trafficking.

Later on October 8, 1998, CIA Inspector General Hitz issued *The Report of Investigation: Allegations of Connections Between CIA and the Contras in Cocaine Trafficking to the United States* (96-0143-IG).

Now that Hitz has a position at Princeton University, it's only fair to ask — was the Goldman Sachs Chair his reward for the CIA version of "omerta" or silence?

After all the timing of the release of the Report and the Goldman Sachs Connection is curious to say the least.

Clinton's Secretary of Treasury Robert Rubin was the former Co-Chairman of Goldman Sachs, one of the most powerful investment banking firms in the world. Goldman Sachs was also reportedly one of the biggest contributors to Clinton's political campaign.

The question arises — did Hitz bury the Report, which helped save Clinton from impeachment?

After all Henry Hyde's committee was ready to move forward with impeachment proceedings when Hitz's Report was posted on the CIA website. Republicans then would have been held responsible for US Government sanctioned narcotics trafficking during the Iran Contra era.

Was Hitz's maneuver an impeachment negotiating tactic?

And was the Goldman Sachs professorship a not-so-subtle payoff for "services rendered"?

Republicans continued with the impeachment process, of course, but there would be no impeachment.

Now the CIA's former cover-up meister Frederick Hitz even has his own website (http://www.wws.princeton.edu/faculty/hitz.html).

From his "official" biography, you would learn that "Hitz, a member of Princeton's Class of 1961, is the former inspector general of the CIA, appointed by the President in 1990. His experience includes serving as a congressional relations officer, deputy assistant secretary of defense for legislative affairs, a senior staff member of the Energy Policy and Planning Staff in the Executive Office of the President, and director of congressional affairs at the Department of Energy. He is the recipient of the Secretary of Defense Medal for Outstanding Public Service and the Department of Defense's Distinguished Civilian Service Medal. He served as Legislative Counsel to the Director of Central Intelligence from

1978 to 1981, and was managing partner of the law firm of Schwabe, Williamson, and Wyatt in Washington, D.C. from 1982 through 1990. JD Harvard Law School."

What the biography leaves out is that it was Hitz's CIA Inspector General's Report which "exonerated" the CIA from responsibility in distributing cocaine to black urban neighborhoods as part of illegal Iran-Contra operations.

According to a recent article on the Princeton University website (http://www.princeton.edu:80/pr/pwb/00/0110/p/espionage.shtml), the spooky Hitz will now be "teaching" Princeton undergrads a freshman seminar called "The Myth and Reality of Espionage: The Spy Novel."

"It helps that their teacher, in addition to being a lifelong fan of spy novels had a career with the CIA as a case officer running agents in West Africa, as deputy chief of the European Division and most recently as Inspector General," the article gushes.

"In his course Hitz strives not only to show how fiction and reality can mirror each other but also to raise moral questions about espionage. In addition to comparing the fantasy worlds of spy novels with the way it really happens, we're looking at the morality of espionage and how we justify this activity in the US democracy,' he says. 'The class finds out that fiction approaches reality in many ways.'"

Especially if you're going to write a CIA Inspector General's report.

In a section called "Fact vs. Fantasy," you would learn that "Hitz has put together a varied reading list which includes fiction (Tom Clancy's *The Hunt for Red October*, Ian Fleming's *Dr. No*, Graham Greene's *The Human Factor* and Rudyard Kipling's *Kim*, among others) and nonfictional accounts of espionage, such as books about the case of double agent Aldrich Ames and a CIA report on the Bay of Pigs crisis."

Maybe "Professor" Hitz needs some help with his syllabus. He certainly should have included these classic books about CIA Drug Trafficking History:

• *Defrauding America* by Rodney Stich, which documents ongoing CIA and DEA narcotics trafficking

• *White Lies: The CIA, Drugs and the Press* by Alexander Cockburn and Jeffrey St. Clair on the long twisted history of CIA narcotics trafficking and media coverups.

• *The Politics of Heroin: CIA Complicity in the Global Drug Trade* by Alfred W. McCoy, which documents CIA sanctioned drug dealing since the Vietnam War.

• *Dark Alliance: The CIA, The Contras and the Crack Cocaine Explosion* by Gary Webb, on the facts of CIA drug traffickers, which Hitz's Inspector General report suppressed

- *The Big White Lie: The CIA and the Cocaine/Crack Epidemic* by Michael Levine, a veteran DEA undercover agent for 25 years who stumbled into CIA protected narcotics trafficking in South America.
- *Drugging America* by Rodney Stich, a former federal investigator who documents decades of CIA drug trafficking and the phony War on Drugs
- *Powderburns: Cocaine, Contras and the Drug War* by DEA agent Celerino Castillo III and Dave Harmon who write about US Government collaboration with drug smugglers.

The Princeton article goes on to say that "in helping his students to examine the legality and the ethics of espionage, Hitz draws on his training as an attorney."

That should certainly help. Specious reasoning to rationalize criminal conspiracy by government employees would come in handy, since Hitz himself is a Harvard Law School graduate.

In the class, "A good number of students hone in on the moral issues," he observes. "They recognize a need to protect the national security of the U.S., but they also perceive that effort may break laws in the countries where the information is gathered" — not to mention bringing in CIA cocaine from sea to shining sea on US soil itself.

"Would Hitz recommend the CIA as an employer to current students, as it was recommended to him when he studied early European history at Princeton in the late 1950s and early '60s?

"If students are interested in foreign languages, foreign cultures or geopolitical issues," he says, "they might well explore the CIA as a career."

It remains doubtful that Hitz would inform his students that CIA recruits are required to lie, cheat and steal (and even deal drugs) for "patriotic" purposes to provide for so-called "national security."

After all, it's a tough job — but somebody's got to recruit the next generation of professional government-sanctioned narcotics traffickers.

Chapter 4

Undue Diligence: Drug Czar Walters and the Iran-Contra Connection

J OHN P. WALTERS, APPOINTED "Drug Czar" by President George Bush Jr., is
uniquely qualified for his new job. He was actually involved in the Iran-
Contra Drug Trafficking Cover-up.

In a recent interview, whistle-blower Al Martin, who testified before the congressional Kerry Commission and the Alexander Committee about Iran-Contra,
stated that "when Assistant Secretary of State Elliott Abrams went to Panama to
have a meeting with [former Panamanian ruler] Noriega, he took along Deputy
Assistant Secretary of State, Michael Kozak, and John Walters, who at that time
had been appointed special advisor to the State Department's Office of Inter-
American Affairs."

Martin says, "They went down to smooth things over with Noriega, who was
complaining that he wasn't getting a big enough piece of the pie for allowing
Panama to be used as a trans-shipping point for drugs and weapons. We were
complaining that he wasn't keeping up his end of the bargain, making facilities
secure for the storage of drugs and weapons. His G-2 was pilfering a lot of
materiel. Meanwhile Noriega was complaining that he wasn't getting a big
enough slice of the pie.

"This came soon after Oliver North had ripped Noriega off for $5 million dol-
lars in that boat deal with Donald Aronow [See Chapter 18 of *The Conspirators*
by Al Martin]. He was still upset about Ollie taking his money. So the three of

them went down to have a discussion. They met at the Intercontinental Hotel in Panama on December 10 to smooth things out.

"Noriega was promised a bigger cut of the pie, when he said he wasn't making enough money," Martin continues. "He claimed there were a lot of people on his end within G-2 that had to be paid. Abrams tried to tell him that everybody was not getting the cut they had. The price of cocaine was falling so rapidly because we were importing so much of the stuff. Consequently the whole pie had become smaller than before. And that's what John Walters was all about. Now he's appointed 'drug czar,' which is not only ironic, it's absolutely laughable.

"When he went down to meet with Noriega, John Walters was the 'special advisor.' His father Vernon Walters got him the position. His father is very, very loyal to the Bush Cabal and had been for years. You don't see Vern much anymore. Vernon Walters was one of the original post-war Military-Industrial Complexers."

John Walters denies that Vern is his father. The late US Army Lieutenant General Vernon A. Walters was the deputy director of the CIA from 1972 to 1976 during the Nixon administration.

When the Watergate scandal erupted, Walters was very adept at covering the CIA's liabilities. After all, Agency fingerprints were all over the Watergate burglary, and the prime players — the Cubans, Hunt and McCord — were all CIA agents or assets. Later, according to Silent Coup author Len Colodny, his old friend General Alexander Haig was instrumental in getting Walters the job of translator for the secret Paris talks between Henry Kissinger and the North Vietnamese. Walters was also the acting Director of Central Intelligence in 1973 (between James Schlesinger's and William Colby's directorship). Later Vernon Walters was appointed Ambassador-at-Large by President Reagan.

In his book The Conspirators: Secrets of an Iran Contra Insider, Al Martin describes the real reason why the price of cocaine kept falling in the mid 1980s. In a chapter called "Classified Illegal Operations Cordoba and Screw Worm," he describes how Oliver North planned to distribute "more cocaine into the United States than ever imagined before. 'Operation Screw Worm' was the last and the largest. It envisioned a tremendous expansion of 'authorized' narcotics trafficking."

Martin writes, "North had set up the time in May 1986 of the first biweekly policy and planning session of the FDN and this absolutely astounded me. Fred Ikley was there. Donald Gregg himself was there. The usual cast of characters, Manuel Diaz, Nestor Sanchez.

"North envisioned an increase of 50,000 kilograms a month which absolutely astounded me," Martin continues.

"Jeb Bush [the current governor of Florida], I think, correctly voiced concerns that had already come into play that the Agency [CIA] was dealing in so much cocaine that its street value was becoming depressed. This had already happened. In 1985, cocaine was commanding $30,000 per kilogram. By 1986, it had dropped to $15,000 per kilogram and was continuing to drop.

"But North felt it was important to raise the revenues, so there was going to be a tremendous increase in importation," writes Martin. (p. 65, *The Conspirators* by Al Martin; National Liberty Press LLC; Order Line: 866-317-1390; Website: Al Martin Raw http://www.almartinraw.com)

The appointment of John P. Walters as Head of the White House Office of National Drug Control Policy makes him the perfect "Drug Czar." His previous job was Deputy Director for Supply Reduction, the No.2 position under William Bennett in George Bush Sr.'s administration.

According to the Washington Post, "Walters stresses the importance of criminal penalties for drug users and openly opposes the use of marijuana for medical purposes."

What makes Walters uniquely qualified, however, is his intimate knowledge of how to cover up US Government drug trafficking. And, of course, he has vowed to continue the pretense of the Phony War on Drugs.

And here's the context. According to the Department of Justice, there is $500 billion to $1 trillion of money laundering a year in the United States. Financing the federal deficit and keeping the stock market buoyed actually depends on the daily reinvestment of laundered monies. A large percentage of that depends on the cash flow from the high-margin profits of narcotics trafficking, government contract fraud, the burgeoning for-profit prison industry and its concomitant slave labor market — all key components of the Phony War on Drugs."

With his "hands-on experience" in Iran-Contra drug trafficking, the appointment of John Walters as George Bush's new "drug czar" is a fitting crown for a man who knows what it takes to keep the flow of drugs moving into the country — and the necessary cash flow moving through Wall Street.

By the way, the AP story is ironically headlined – "Bush's choice for drug czar vows to help addicts." (May 11, 2001)

Who knows? Maybe John Walters will make the price of cocaine drop again.

BUSHWHACKED

Chapter 5

On the Take: IRS Chief Rossotti Gets Kickbacks

T HE MULTI-MILLIONAIRE IRS Commissioner Charles Rossotti acts as if the usual rules don't apply to him. And actually he's right. They don't. In a glaring conflict of interest, Charles Rossotti, Commissioner of the US Internal Revenue Service and former Chairman of American Management Systems Inc. (AMS), has retained between $16 million and $80 million of AMS stock.

It's the ultimate insider's deal. In essence, Rossotti gets a kickback every time AMS, a computer data-processing company based in Fairfax, Virginia, gets a new government contract.

Rossotti's ownership of AMS stock was revealed in financial disclosure forms filed in May 2000.

In 1998, the New York Times reported that Rossotti was the largest individual shareholder in AMS, a company that had revenues of $1.28 billion in 2000.

Unlike Vice President Dick Cheney who sold his Halliburton Corp. stock and Treasury Secretary Paul O'Neill who sold $100 million worth of his Alcoa Corp. stock, Rossotti refuses to divest.

In fact, Rossotti flaunts his conflict of interest and ethically challenged behavior.

Appointed by President Clinton in 1997, Rossotti's brazen ethics-be-damned position is buttressed by the fact that later he received an executive waiver of conflict of interest rules from the Clinton Administration.

According to *Insight Magazine* ("IRS Boss Snagged Clinton Waiver" by John Berlau, April 30, 2001), Rossotti got a waiver from Stuart Eizenstat, Clinton's deputy Treasury Secretary. This last minute waiver allows Rossotti to participate in decisions regarding AMS contracts with the IRS. In essence, Rossotti can continue to ensure that AMS interests — and his own — continue to be served by new as well as ongoing government contracts.

Incidentally AMS is supposed to be paid more than $17 million by the IRS this year for "add-ons" to existing contracts for internal software systems — the so-called Custodial Accounting Project (CAP).

IRS continues to give AMS these add-on contracts without taking new bids from any AMS competitors.

This egregious corporate-government fraud by IRS Commissioner Charles Rossotti is unprecedented in recent history.

AMS: *Corporate Insiders at the Government Trough*

Founded by Charles Rossotti in 1970, AMS has leveraged its insider contacts and government contracts into a $1.28 billion global business with clients that include more than 43 state governments and federal agencies.

From 1965 to 1969, Rossotti himself was one of the so-called "Whiz Kids" of Defense Department Secretary (and unindicted war criminal) Robert McNamara, whose legacy remains the failed policy to prosecute the bogus Vietnam War.

Rossotti worked in the Office of Systems Analysis within the Office of the Secretary of Defense. The Office's claim to fame was inventing the use of "body counts" (dead "enemy" soldiers) as a gauge of "success" during the infamous war. McNamara received an MBA from Harvard Business School in 1939, and Rossotti got his MBA from Harvard in 1964.

Headquartered in Fairfax, Virginia, AMS has approximately 8,750 employees in 512 offices worldwide. According to the AMS website, its clients include the Environmental Protection Agency (EPA), General Services Administration (GSA), the Army Reserve, State Department, Treasury Department and the Department of Defense.

In its 1997 Annual Report, AMS claims that the "U.S. Department of Defense (DoD) has contracted with AMS for the Standard Procurement System to automate and streamline the DoD-wide procurement system."

The automation has evidently been so "successful" that four years later whistle-blower Al Martin, a former Naval Intelligence officer, reports that Defense Department fraud is at an all time high. (See "Fraud for Lunch at Redstone Arsenal," http://www.almartinraw.com/column11.html).

In his report on government fraud, Al Martin writes that "at the party, there was an active lieutenant general, an active three star general no less, who was talking about moving his fraud money to Corsica. This is the type of scam that's been done for years. He's just doing it a little more professionally. It's called the Old Double-Inventory-Whammo-Scam, and it's often done against the Department of Defense. The general is doing it with his clique of ten confederates. Some are in DoD Procurement. Some are in DoD Inventory Control. Some are in DoD Payment and Disbursement. And some are in DoD Audit. You have to have someone in each of these offices to make the scam work.

"He was bragging about it," Martin continues. "'We just committed this scam last week. It cost $40,000 and it netted $2.5 million.' He said his end was $250,000 and it just got wired to his offshore account. He's going to bury the money by buying a piece of beachfront property in Corsica because he doesn't have anything else to do with it.

"The scam is relatively simple," Martin writes. "They are reselling back to the Department of Defense actual Department of Defense inventory items that the Department of Defense already owns, but doesn't realize it owns. They go through the massive Department of Defense inventory list. They look for some esoteric but generic part. It doesn't have to be big. Just something that can be easily misplaced or mislaid.

"What this guy does on the inside is he simply deletes from the computer. That's all he does. He deletes it. He doesn't leave a paper trail pretending it was sold to some other company. It's just erased. It's just deleted."

By the way, at Donald Rumsfeld's confirmation hearing, Senator Robert Byrd (D-WV) said, "I seriously question an increase in the Pentagon budget in the face of the Department's recent Inspector General's report. How can we seriously consider a $50 billion increase in the Defense Department budget when DoD's own auditors say the Department cannot account for $2.3 trillion transactions in one year alone?"

Rossotti's IRS Shakedowns: Political Enemies Audited

The long-standing tradition of failing upward has finally landed Rossotti in the office of Commissioner of the Internal Revenue Service.

According to his website bio, (http://www.ustreas.gov/press/officers/rossotti.htm) Charles Rossotti "assumed his duties as Commissioner on November 13, 1997, pledging to turn the IRS into an organization that will consistently provide first-class service to the American public."

This stance belies the ugly reality of the IRS and its ongoing shakedowns of perceived political enemies. Its well-known tactics of fear and intimidation have been increasing steadily, marking the IRS as a reasonable facsimile of Soviet thuggery and/or banana republic corruption.

Since Rossotti assumed office, many political enemies of the administration have suffered IRS audits. These audits can only be construed as politically motivated *de facto* harassment.

A partial list of those targeted by Rossotti and his allegedly "kinder gentler" IRS include:

- Joseph Farah and The Western Journalism Center
- Juanita Broaddrick, who publicly accused Clinton of raping her while he was Arkansas attorney general
- National Center for Public Policy, a group critical of Clinton's environmental policies
- Citizens Against Government Waste.
- Catherine Austin Fitts, former FHA Commissioner under Jack Kemp and President of Hamilton Securities, a company which ironically saved HUD $2.2 billion through its innovative loan sales/auction

Rossotti Hires AMS Pals for High-Paying IRS Jobs

The IRS Restructuring and Reform Act of 1998 mandated that the IRS Commissioner hire non-IRS personnel for top positions in the tax-collection agency.

In an obvious *quid pro quo*, IRS Commissioner Rossotti then managed to hire two state tax honchos who had a prior history with AMS.

John LaFaver, Secretary of Revenue for the State of Kansas, was appointed IRS deputy commissioner for modernization, while Val Oveson, formerly chairman of the Utah State Tax Commission, was appointed national taxpayer advocate.

Even though both officials have since left IRS, both LaFaver and Oveson headed state agencies, which hired AMS to oversee the modernization of their respective states' tax collection computer systems.

In another instance of the revolving door syndrome between corporate and government networks, LaFaver's successor as Kansas Secretary of Revenue, Karla Pierce, went to work for Computer Sciences Corp, the lead contractor in IRS "modernization" project. Pierce, likewise, had been project manager when AMS's Kansas contract began.

Rossotti's AMS Sued for Breach of Contract

The corporate history of AMS is rife with lawsuits.

According to its Proxy Statement (2000), AMS has been sued at least several times by its own clients for sub-standard performance, shoddy work and breach of contract.

For example, in 1993, the State of Mississippi had contracted with AMS to improve and integrate its tax collection software. By April 1999, "not a single tax-collection software program was operational," read the lawsuit, filed on April 22, 1999 against AMS.

On August 23, 2000, a jury found AMS guilty of breach of contract and ordered to pay the State of Mississippi $474.5 million in actual and punitive damages.

Eventually the case was settled for $185 million, of which about $102 million was paid by its insurers.

In 1999, AMS Technical Systems (an AMS subsidiary) was sued by Bezeq, the Israeli telecommunications company. Bezeq alleged that AMS was in breach of contract and sought damages for $39 million. The case was later settled out of court.

In 1995, AMS's Form 10-K reported that Andersen had also sued AMS for copyright infringement and appropriation of trade secrets

Rossotti's AMS and the "Missing" $59 Billion at HUD

One of the most outrageous breaches of public trust (or in-your-face fraud) has been the Department of Housing and Urban Development's (HUD) "loss" of $59 billion in Fiscal Year (FY) 1999 and $17 billion in FY 1998.

According to the Government Accounting Office (GAO), the company responsible for the HUD software system called HUDCAPS was Rossotti's company, AMS, as well as a company called Advance Technology Systems (ATS).

Despite the poor performance, HUD continued to pay on its contract to AMS, even though the system didn't work and $59 billion was "missing."

The HUD Audit Debacle was then blamed on the agency's financial reporting systems, i.e. accounting software. In fact in her statement to Congress, HUD Inspector General Susan Gaffney reported that she could not validate an audit of the books. In other words, there has been no audit of HUD financial statements for 1999. And $59 billion is still "missing."

In May 2000, Gaffney herself told lawmakers that "the material weakness is that HUD does not have a single financial ledger system in place... the financial systems flowing in were incompatible and the system rejected the transactions. The rejected transactions weren't corrected in the new ledger system."

Gaffney's conclusion was that "HUD does not have a reliable and accurate statement of its financial condition."

In other words, then HUD Commissioner Andrew Cuomo (who plans to run for Governor of New York, while "losing" $59 billion during his tenure at HUD) used AMS to install an accounting system, which has never worked.

The HUDCAPS system has supposedly been going online since 1997. According to Gaffney, HUDCAPS does not work and that a new so-called "add-on" system is being implemented.

It's well known among insiders that "computer glitches" are often used as an excuse to hide fraud within government agencies.

The Office of Management and Budget (OMB), which has the power to rein in this fraud by cutting the HUD budget, has heretofore refused to take responsibility.

And, so far, AMS has avoided a PR debacle — primarily because mainstream media has studiously avoided mentioning its role in HUD's "missing" $59 billion scandal.

AMS, however, continues to be paid on its $250 million HUD contract — despite its non-performance and its breach of contract in providing HUD with a useable accounting system.

Rossotti must be smiling. But you'd be smiling too. If you weren't held accountable. If you had between "$16 million and $80 million" worth of AMS stock that was going up while you slept.

As IRS Commissioner, Charles Rossotti has reached the pinnacle of corporate-government fraud.

After all, who's going to trifle with the guy?

Chapter 6

Power Scam: The Bush-Enron Connection

The phony US energy crisis has deep ties to the Bush Family.

One of the prime beneficiaries of the "crisis" is Enron Corporation and its Chairman Ken Lay, a major corporate and personal contributor to George Bush Jr.'s presidential campaign.

Even though California Gov. Gray Davis has reached into California residents' deep pockets to bail out the utility companies through emergency legislation, Washington Gov. Gary Locke has balked.

According to KCPQ-TV's Chris Daniels' "A Disturbing New Twist in Western Power Troubles," "Governor Locke says, 'It's unjustified, it's obscene, and clearly hurting all consumers.'"

Like other western governors, Locke has had to pay for electricity at any price. In November of 1999, for example, electricity was purchased for $29 a megawatt hour. A year later, the price increased to $160 an hour, according to sources at Tacoma Power. In the spring of 2001, it was at $525.

Locke expressed his indignation saying, "I'm very disappointed in President Bush that the new administration will not be intervening." Locke should know better. Why should Bush intervene?

One of Bush's largest campaign contributors is Enron Corporation, a Texas-based company which is part of the defacto global energy oligopoly-cartel. Although diversifying into other business, Enron has been best known as the largest buyer and seller of natural gas in the United States. Its 1999 revenues of $40 billion had made it the 18th largest company in the United States.

Enron is also invested in energy projects around the world, including the UK, Argentina, Bolivia, Brazil, the Philippines, Indonesia, China, India and Mozambique.

One of the global energy cartel's most visible players, Enron saw its corporate profits rise 34 percent in the fourth quarter of 2000.

Enron shareholders should ask — did dividends come from price gouging US citizens?

How George Bush Jr. Got Layed

Federal Election Commission records show that Enron Chairman Kenneth Lay donated more than $350,000 directly to Bush campaigns since 1997. Lay also gave another $100,000 to Republican candidates and fundraising committees. In addition, Enron Corporation, including employees, also donated $1.5 million in soft money to Bush and Republican committees. More recently, Lay and his wife donated $10,000 to the "Florida Recount Fund," and another $100,000 to the "Presidential Inaugural Fund."

As one of his fundraising "Pioneers," Lay helped raise more than $100,000 for Bush's campaign for president. In consideration of these numbers, is it too much to ask for a phony contrived power "crisis" as a payback? Naah, not at all...

According to newswire reports, as a new energy advisor for President Bush, Ken Lay says that precap prices for wholesale electricity in the West "is not even a short-term solution."

Not coincidentally, Enron is the largest power marketer in the United States. A cap would limit the prices it and other wholesalers could charge to utilities. Wholesale power prices were deregulated under the landmark 1996 law but retail rates were not.

Lay said the federal government should limit itself to an "advisory" role, letting California leaders resolve a "pretty much self-inflicted problem."

California's rolling blackouts have come as the two large utilities, PG&E Corp. and Southern California Edison, have struggled under huge debts through buying electricity at higher wholesale prices than they can recoup under the retail rates they are allowed to charge.

In the short term, Lay said, the state government will have to "buy the power to fill the short positions of the utilities." And to ensure Enron's unconscionable profit, he should have added.

Enron's Pug Winokur, Shadow Government Insider

On the Enron corporate website, one of the Board of Directors, Herbert S. "Pug" Winokur, Jr., is described as Chairman and CEO of Capricorn Holdings,

Inc., and Former Senior Executive Vice President, Penn Central Corporation. As the Insiders' Insider, "Pug" Winokur has been such a permanent fixture in the Washington Old Boy Network that he's even mentioned in a 1978 book by Daniel Guttman called "The Shadow Government."

Historically Winokur's Capricorn Holdings was used as an investment vehicle in NHP, an apartment management firm headed by Roderick Heller III. In turn, NHP's assets included oft-purloined and defaulted HUD Section 8 subsidy housing, a notorious and well-known vehicle for fraud and money laundering. Winokur was also on the Board of Directors of Harvard Endowment Fund, which purchased 50 percent of NHP, making the prestigious Harvard a prototypical, but very low-profile, slum landlord.

It should also be noted that George Bush Jr. attended Harvard Business School. Later, after Bush joined Harken Energy Corp and became a director, the largest stock position and seat on the board was acquired by Harvard Management Co.

Ironically, from 1988 to 1997, Winokur was also the Chairman and CEO of DynCorp, one of the government's largest contractors in data acquisition and management.

Since DynCorp had a contract from the Department of Justice, Winokur would have profited from the DoJ Asset Seizure Program, as well as HUD's Operation Safe Home seizures which targeted low-income tenants and mortgage holders in the inner cities.

In addition, DynCorp is one of the lead contractors for the new phony War on Drugs in South America called "Plan Colombia," another tax-payer supported scam to bring monies into DynCorp's coffers.

Now there's a guy who understands that the only way to do a deal is to get it rigged from the very beginning.

Enron's Son of a Spook

Enron dealmaker Frank Wisner, Jr. muscled the company into lucrative overseas contracts, most notably in India and the Philipines.

Enron's deal to manage a power plant in the Philippines was due largely to Wisner's efforts. Based in Subic Bay, a former US military outpost, the power planet was taken over by Enron in 1993, two months after the last US troops left the base.

Wisner is also credited with helping Enron win a $2.8 billion deal in India, building a power plant near Bombay. Now the project is under heavy fire for being over-priced, and the deal continues to simmer with allegations of bribery. (News flash: the Dabhol Plant project has gone belly-up.)

Wisner Jr. must have learned his tradecraft from his father Frank Wisner Sr., one of the CIA's prime operatives.

Wisner Sr., who worked at CIA from 1947 until just before his "suicide" in

1965, was involved in 1) the 1954 CIA coup in Guatemala, toppling the government of Jacobo Arbenz for United Fruit Company, 2) the 1953 overthrow of Iranian Prime Minister Mohammed Mossadeq, and 3) the secret operations against Indonesian President Sukarno. Unlike his spooky father, Frank Wisner Jr., however, was a former Pentagon official before his job at Enron.

Enron's Ken Lay and the Bush Boys

Enron Founder and Chairman Kenneth Lay also worked in the Pentagon for the Nixon administration during the Vietnam War. Lay is a close friend of George Bush, Sr. In fact, his Houston home in River Oaks is near the Tanglewood residence of the former President and CIA Director. Although there have been no published reports of Bush Sr. doing favors for Lay, three of the Bush Boys have used their father's name to get contracts for Enron.

According to an article by Seymour Hersh in the New Yorker, Neil and Marvin Bush tried to influence government officials for an Enron bid to rebuild Shuaiba North power plant in Kuwait.

Ironically this power plant was destroyed in George Bush's Persian Gulf War. Enron abandoned the bid a year ago.

In 1988, then Texas governor George Bush Jr., reportedly telephoned Rodolfo Terragno, Argentina's Public Works Minister, to ask him to award Enron a contract to build a pipeline from Chile to Argentina.

"He assumed that the fact he was the son of the president would exert influence. I felt pressured. It was not proper for him to make that kind of call," Terragno told The Nation.

Finally, when Carlos Menem, another Bush Sr. crony, became president of Argentina, Enron won the bid. Neil Bush, director of the failed Denver-based Silverado Savings and Loan, created a subsidiary of his oil company to conduct business in Argentina in 1987.

Argentina finally got so fed up with the Bush Boys, they formally had a parliamentary investigation regarding their so-called "business dealings.

Enron Rigs Washington in the Clinton Years

Even though it has strong ties to the Republican Party, Enron also did remarkably well during the Clinton years. Most importantly, they got a ban lifted on Export-Import Bank financing of projects in China. This allowed Enron to move forward on overseas projects guaranteed by US taxpayers. In other words, if Enron "fails," you pay. You're on the hook, not Ken Lay or Enron.

Enron also got new rules instituted at the Ex-Im Bank that allowed the bank to finance projects on the basis of projected cash flow. This insider track helped Enron make multi-billion dollar deals overseas with US taxpayers guaranteeing

their performance.
- March 1993, Enron made a deal to develop new European markets for Russian gas.
- November 1993, Enron made a $1 billion deal with Turkey to develop two power plants. Ex-Im Bank provided $285 million in financing. The Overseas Private Investment Council(OPIC)covered insurance costs.
- August 1994, Enron made a deal to build a power plant in India. ExIm provides major financing and OPIC provides an additional $100 million.
- November 1994, Enron made a deal to build a $130 million power plant in China. Ex-Im Bank again provided the financing.

Moral of the story? When you're a monopoly capitalist, it doesn't matter who's in office. Republicans. Democrats. They all bribe the same. Those offshore Enron slush funds work great during any administration.

Lawsuit Against Enron Alleges Conspiracy

Unfazed by the bogus contrived energy crisis, the San Francisco City Attorney is filing a lawsuit against Enron and eleven other companies. The filing says that Enron "conspired to restrict supplies and drive up prices" costing consumers additional charges "on the order of 1 billion dollars."

Washington's Governor Locke says President Bush needs to take counter-measures or the economy will suffer on a national level.

"If the federal government doesn't act, you're going to see a lot of jobs go away, a lot of business close down..." says Locke. "We need help from the federal government immediately to help stabilize the situation."

Is this Enron's first visible and public Bush payoff? It just might be the best "energy crisis" money can buy.

(Author's note: This article was written and published in the spring of 2001 before the dramatic crash and burn of the mega-corporate money laundry known as Enron.)

BUSHWHACKED

Chapter 7

Dirty Tricks, Inc.: The DynCorp-Government Connection

O RGANIZED WHITE-COLLAR CRIME is the absolute essence of mega-corporate-government business. As Jim Hougan wrote in his landmark book, Spooks: *The Haunting of America – The Private Use of Secret Agents,* "With their cultural and career investments in upholding the stereotype of the Mafia as the vehicle of organized crime, the public and the press have generally failed to grasp the felonious nature of the outfit's WASP counterparts on the Big Board. Whereas some petty hoodlums put out contracts on individuals, the multinationals have begun to place contracts on entire countries (for example, ITT versus Chile). With that difference, their operational styles are similar: offshore laundries used to wash bribes paid in clandestine support of a sales effort designed to create and satisfy the potentially lethal addictions of their would be customers. Whether the product is heroin or Starfighter jets, the result is often the same: profits that corrupt and impoverish… In short it appears that some multinationals had evolved into genuinely criminal enterprises." (p. 441)

Likewise, outsourcing State Terrorism is the fastest growing segment of the US Government market. In fact, white-collar criminal activities, like Federal IT, or Information Technology, which involves "privatizing" the financial database management of government agencies, accounts for some of the most lucrative contracts available anywhere on earth.

The practice of privatizing (using private companies for government work) has been long exploited by the CIA and the Pentagon, who like to use proxies, like contractors or mercenaries, to fight their covert wars.

The benefits for federal agencies include "plausible deniability" with respect

45

to assassination and drug trafficking, as well as the ability to bypass the Military Code of Honor and the accords of the Geneva Convention, which hold "official" combatants to a different standard.

In other words, by privatizing "dirty tricks," a federal agency cannot be held liable to the standards one would expect of, well, the US Government.

Acting as one of the US Government's primary privatized Dirty Tricks Divisions, DynCorp has become one of the leading prime federal contractors, reaping a global harvest of shame and disgrace.

The Murky Origins of DynCorp

And where did DynCorp come from?

In the apocryphal story, DynCorp began as an Air Force contractor in 1954. Since then, however it has garnered a reputation as a shadowy company with a spooky pedigree, rumored to be a CIA "cutout," or front company, for the Agency's dirty tricks.

Using high-level government insider connections, DynCorp provides a range of "services" one would expect to facilitate fraud and money laundry activities, acting like a virtual conduit between the corporate (private) and government (public) worlds.

According to DynCorp, the US Government is its biggest client, accounting for more than 95% of its revenues.

After it gobbled up GTE Information Services LLC in 1999, DynCorp has become one of the nation's largest Federal contractors for IT, or Information Technology, services. Along with Lockheed Martin, SAIC, AMS, and others, DynCorp contracts with federal government agencies to "manage" federal databases.

Dyncorp's clients include the Drug Enforcement Agency, the Department of Defense, Department of State, Department of Justice, Internal Revenue Service, Securities and Exchange Commission, FBI, CIA, and HUD — all government agencies notorious for rampant, unchecked and egregious fraud.

For example, the Pentagon cannot account for a mind-boggling $2.3 trillion. In fact, at Secretary of Defense Donald Rumsfeld's confirmation hearing in January 2001, Sen. Robert Byrd wondered aloud, "How can we seriously consider a $50 billion dollar increase in the Defense Department's budget when the DoD's own auditors cannot account for $2.3 trillion in transactions?"

After September 11, of course, fresh fraud at DoD will become virtually limitless because of the new "War on Terrorism," a black hole of a boondoggle that may surpass even the "Cold War" in Pentagon corruption, waste and malfeasance.

Meanwhile, HUD cannot account for $59 billion, according to the testimony of former HUD Inspector General Susan Gaffney. (See "Why Is $59 Billion Missing from HUD?" by Kelly O'Meara, Insight Magazine)

Coincidentally, that was the year that "HUD Taps DynCorp for Services," according to a Washington Post headline from August 2, 1999, describing a new $51 million contract to provide desktop services to the Office of Inspector General at Housing and Urban Development.

Even more sinister is the fact that DynCorp manages email and information systems for many federal investigation agencies like FBI, DOJ and SEC. What does that mean? Whenever criminal behavior is detected, DynCorp controls the information, giving it defacto power to subvert the process of law and cover-up corporate-government criminal activities.

And guess who's DynCorp's auditor of record?

It's none other than Arthur Andersen, the best Corporate Cooking-the-Books-and-Shredding-Documents firm money can buy. If this Big Eight Firm did it for Enron, you can bet they're doing it for most of their other clients.

Corporate Insiders at the Government Trough

So who's minding the store at DynCorp?

The sordid cast of characters includes Herbert S. (Pug) Winokur, member of the Council on Foreign Relations, as well as a director of DynCorp since 1988, according to a May 9, 2001 Proxy Statement.

By the way, the Council on Foreign Relations, which has been liberally described as a think tank, is actually "a clearinghouse for the really choice frauds," according to whistleblower Al Martin, author of *The Conspirators: Secrets of an Iran Contra Insider.*

In fact, Winokur was the also Chairman of the Board of DynCorp from 1988 to 1997.

So here is the connection between criminal corporate and government networks.

Winokur is also on the Board of Directors of the notorious Enron — the notorious slush fund/ money laundry disguised as a corporation. It should be noted that Enron has declared bankruptcy after paying corporate insiders hundreds of millions of dollars for their "services."

As the chair of Enron's Finance Committee, Winokur approved the creation of more than 3000 offshore limited partnerships and subsidiaries, used by the corporation to hide losses from derivative trading, other bogus transactions and money laundering.

Winokur is also a director of Harvard Management Company and a member of Harvard Corporation.

Harvard, of course, has all the trademarks of a highly successful money laundry, but is cleverly disguised as a prestigious "educational institution." Its endowment fund rose remarkably from $5 billion to $19 billion in just 6 years.

(Imagine if you could get that kind of return.)

Winokur also has the ability and the means to coordinate money flows in and out of offshore slush funds with little or no public supervision — as Chairman and CEO of Capricorn Holdings, Inc., a "private investment company" and Managing General Partner of three Capricorn Investors Limited Partnerships "concentrating on investments in restructure situations." That's code for "bottom feeding" on so-called "distressed" properties.

As far as DynCorp is concerned, though, there's Winokur's pal, Dudley Mecum, DynCorp Director since 1988, who just happens to also be the managing director of Winokur's Capricorn Holdings Inc., as well as CitiGroup, the New York banking conglomerate, convicted of serial money laundering and other criminal offenses.

The DynCorp Board itself is filled with so many shadowy characters that the company could be rightly considered a retirement/ slush fund for former spooks and military honchos.

They include General P.C. Carns, a retired General US Air Force who served as Vice Chief of Staff and as Director of the Joint Chiefs of Staff. According the DynCorp Proxy statement, Carns is also a member of the Defense Science Board and the Board of Advisors, National Security Agency.

Then there's General Russell E. Dougherty, Director since 1989, whose term as director expired in 2001. He was an attorney with the law firm of McGuire, Woods, as well as a retired General US Air Force, who served as Commander in Chief, Strategic Air Command and Chief of Staff, Allied Command, Europe.

Who needs a pension when you have the coffers of the government open to you?

Dirty Business, Dirty Clients

One of the DynCorp's biggest clients is the US Department of Justice. The ironically named JCON (Justice Consolidated Office Network) also awarded DynCorp a $500 million contract to design, implement and manage and integrated hardware and software program as early as 1996.

Reliable inside sources claim that a new improved PROMIS software with increase real-time tracking capabilities has also been used by DynCorp in recent times. By all accounts, it comes in very handy when you're trying to coordinate government interagency fraud.

JCON after all is available to Executive Attorneys (USA), Executive Office for US Marshals, Executive Office for Immigration Justice Management Division, Office of the Solicitor General and the six litigating divisions including Civil, Civil Rights, Environmental, Tax Criminal, and Anti Trust Divisions of the US Department of Justice.

Between its DoJ contracts (PROMIS) and HUD contracts, it's not unlikely that DynCorp may have had the ability to falsify evidence of HUD system e-mail and offshore accounts. After all, DynCorp is also in charge of so-called asset seizure (forfeiture) programs for HUD and Treasury.

DynCorp's sweet contract deal with JCON is the ultimate insider scam. The fed-speak for it is "a single-vendor indefinite delivery, indefinite quantity contract."

Another major client of DynCorp is the FBI. DynCorp will do a $51 million upgrade of the FBI network for the information technology and transport network components of its Trilogy program, a $300 million, three-year initiative to update the FBI backbone network. By the way, the notorious Andersen will be doing the audit. Imagine how many documents will be shred in that deal...

DynCorp's RICO Problems

According to *Washington Technology Magazine* (April 2, 2001), DynCorp's revenue for 2000 was more than $1.8 billion, up from $1.4 billion in 1999. Its contract backlog at the time was $6 billion, and about half of DynCorp's revenue comes from the Department of Defense.

With little or no public scrutiny, DynCorp has acted like a white-collar organized crime outfit. Besides being a federal contractor with insider deals for rigging computer systems to facilitate government fraud and malfeasance, whistleblowers working in Bosnia have revealed that DynCorp supervisors are engaging in sex slavery and prostitution of local 12-year old girls. [See "DynCorp's Disgrace" By Kelly O'Meara, *Insight Magazine* (http://insightmag.com/main.cfm?include= detail&storyid=163052)

In Johnson v. DynCorp Inc., et al, DynCorp employee Ben Johnston alleges that his former employer breached his three-year contract, firing him without cause in June 2000 because of Johnson's whistleblower activities. The lawsuit alleges that DynCorp engaged in racketeering activities in violation of the RICO, the Racketeer Influenced and Corrupt Organizations Act, and that Johnson was fired because he refuse to commit an illegal act.

The suit alleges that DynCorp engaged in peonage and slavery, sexually exploiting children, dealing in obscene material and procuring fraudulent identification documents for the underage victims. When Johnston told his DynCorp supervisor that co-workers were buying women from the mafia, he was told to mind his own business.

Johnston is not the only DynCorp employee to blow the whistle on Dirty Works, Inc., otherwise known as DynCorp. A UN International Police Force monitor called Kathryn Bolkovac has also filed a lawsuit in Great Britain against DynCorp for wrongful termination.

Bolkovac discovered that DynCorp, whose $15 million contract to train police officers in Bosnia, had officers who were also participating in sex- trafficking.

And you'd think that government fraud would be enough?

DynCorp Drug Trafficking and Cover-Up?

"The Resister," a US military J358 whistleblower publication, has claimed that DynCorp was also contracted by the CIA to "observe" activities against the Kosovo Liberation Army (KLA) on the part of the Serbs.

For the record, the KLA was a drug-financed army of gangsters, murderous thugs and terrorists, trained by the CIA, and used to undermine attempts at peace between Kosovars, Albanians and Serbs.

DynCorp's contracted employees are typically ex-military, probably "sheep dipped" (moved into a new cover) into DynCorp, standard operating procedure for black ops and other covert activities by US military and intelligence organizations.

Most recently, DynCorp's use of military veterans and retired spooks to do the dirty work for the phony War on Drugs in Colombia, known as "Plan Colombia," is no exception.

In June 2001, DynCorp's unsavory presence in the War on Drugs in Colombia was exposed when an American missionary plane was shot down in Peru, leaving a mother and her baby daughter dead.

DynCorp Technical Services had been paid hundreds of millions of dollars by the CIA, Customs Service, Defense Department and State Department for "missions" like these, everywhere from Bosnia, Rwanda, Haiti, Colombia and Peru.

According to an AP story ("Peru incident shines spotlight on shadowy practice," by Lisa Hoffman, April 24, 2001), "DynCorp has supplied dozens of mechanics, trainers, maintenance and administrative workers, logistics experts, rescuers and pilots" for a price tag of $600 million.

The UK Guardian describes DynCorp's role in the five-year $200 million contract as providing "crop dusting pilots for eradication of coca plantations [could they be CIA competitors?] and helicopter pilots to ferry Colombian troops and DynCorp's own security personnel."

Another DynCorp Aerospace Technology subcontractor in the so-called War on Drugs (Plan Colombia) called EAST (Eagle Aviation Service and Technology, Inc. has an equally notorious past.

EAST "helped Oliver North run guns to Nicaraguan rebels in what would be known as the Iran Contra affair," wrote AP reporter Ken Guggenheim on June 5, 2001.

Founded in the 1980s by Richard Gadd, EAST helped North secretly supply weapons and ammunition to the Nicaraguans.

General Richard Secord hired Gadd in 1985 to oversee weapons deliveries, and it's a good bet that drugs would have been flown north on the return trip in Oliver North's infamous "Guns-For-Drugs" operation.

Bid Rigging De Rigueur

Here's another example of insider government contract shenanigans.

According to a General Accounting Office report of Feb. 28, 2001, "the Department of State awarded two contracts to DynCorp Aerospace technology for aviation services to support the Bureau's counter narcotics aviation program." One five-year contract for $99 million was awarded by State in 1991. Then in 1996, State awarded DynCorp another sole-source contract for another $170 million without competitive bidding.

Rigged deals can't get much sweeter, can they?

At the time, DynCorp's Jim McCoy got new contracts from the State, Treasury, and Commerce Departments, as well as the CIA and NASA. It became common knowledge that DynCorp acted as a front-company on behalf of the CIA, hiring mercenaries and "assets" in order to distance itself from the manipulation of US foreign policy from behind the scenes.

According to an article in *The Nation* ("DynCorp's Drug Problem," by Jason Vest), DynCorp employees have also been implicated in narcotics trafficking. It must be remembered that US involvement in Colombia is ultimately a gambit to control the lucrative drug trade, as well as the oil fields, explored by Bush Family connected Harken Energy.

DynCorp Charged with Terrorism

Most recently DynCorp has been charged with terrorism.

According to NarcoNews.com reporter Al Giordano (http://www.narconews.com), a class-action lawsuit has been filed in Washington, DC, on behalf of 10,000 farmers in Ecuador and the AFL-CIO-related International Labor Rights Fund. Why? DynCorp has US Government contracts to spray toxic herbicides over 14 percent of Colombia, supposedly to eliminate coca in the phony War on Drugs.

Giordano writes, "Although DynCorp's taxpayer-sponsored bio-warfare has not made a dent in the cocaine trade, it has caused more than 1,100 documented cases of illness among citizens, destroyed untold acres of food crops, displaced tens of thousands of peasant farmers, and harmed the fragile Amazon ecosystem, all in the name of the 'war on drugs.'"

"DynCorp may be about to get its comeuppance in federal court," continues Giordano, "where Justice Richard W. Roberts is presiding over a lawsuit brought by labor, environmental and indigenous groups against the aerial herbicide program. The text of the legal complaint is available online for all to read: http://www.usfumigation.org/compliant.htm

In addition, NarcoNews.com writes that DynCorp's top corporate director, Paul Lombardi, attempted to intimidate the International Labor Rights Fund, one of the plaintiffs in the lawsuit.

According to documents obtained by NarcoNews.com , on October 25, 2001, "Lombardi wrote to each of the board members of the AFL-CIO allied Rights Fund in an unsuccessful attempt to scare them off the lawsuit. In that letter,

Lombardi accused the group, without offering evidence, of fronting for illicit 'drug cartels.' Lombardi also attempted, bombastically, to portray the Rights Fund as an enemy in the war on terrorism. He wrote: 'Considering the major international issues with which we are all dealing as a consequence of the events of September 11th, none of us need to be sidetracked with frivolous litigation the aim of which is to fulfill a political agenda.' And DynCorp's Lombardi attempted to cause the Rights Fund to drop the lawsuit, saying, 'Clearly it is not in our mutual best interests to continue politically charged litigation.' Bishop Jesse DeWitt, president of the International Human Rights Fund, responded in a November 5, 2001 letter to DynCorp's Lombardi, suggesting that it is DynCorp that engages in terrorist actions."

In this letter, Bishop DeWitt called DynCorp's actions in South America "terrorism." He wrote "we found your reference to September 11 particularly apt, but for a very different reason. Based on what appear to be uncontested facts, a group of at least 10,000 Ecuadoran subsistence farmers have been poisoned from aerial assault by your company."

"Imagine that scene for a moment. You are an Ecuadoran farmer, and suddenly, without notice or warning, a large helicopter approaches, and the frightening noise of the chopper blades invades the quiet," he continues. "The helicopter comes closer and sprays a toxic poison on you, your children, your livestock and your food crops. You see your children get sick, your crops die. Mr. Lombardi, we at the International Labor Rights Fund, and most civilized people, consider such an attack on innocent people terrorism. Your effort to hide behind September 11 is shameful and breathtakingly cynical."

"Bishop DeWitt put Lombardi on notice that he and other DynCorp officials may be added as defendants in the lawsuit, now having been officially informed of the harm done by their fumigation program: 'If there is any further spraying done that causes similar harm, we will amend the legal complaint and name you and other DynCorp decision-makers as defendants in your personal capacities, and will charge you with knowingly conducting aerial attacks on innocent people. Again, based on well-established principles of international law, that would be terrorism.'"

Lombardi has shown that Homegrown Terrorism (or White-Collar Terrorism) is alive and well at DynCorp.

Translating the "Drug War" into Dollars: How Much Pop Per Dead Colombian?

So how much does DynCorp really make on the notorious War on Drugs Scam? According to Catherine Austin Fitts, former FHA Commissioner in the Bush I Administration and former CEO of Hamilton Securities, an investment banking/ software company, the creation of Stock Value, also referred to as Capital Gains, is called "Pop" in Wall Street jargon.

She explains the money dynamics of DynCorp's business model with regard to its War on Drugs activities.

"If DynCorp has a $60 million per year contract supporting knowledge management for asset seizures in the United States," she says. "The current proxy shows that they value their stock, which they buy and sell internally, at approximately 30 times earnings."

"So, if a contract has a 5-10% profit, then per $100 million of contracts, DynCorp makes about $5-$10 million, which translates into $150 million to $300 million of stock value."

"That means that for a $200 million contract, with average earnings of 5-10% ($10 million to $20 million), DynCorp is generating $300 million to $600 million of stock value. Pug Winokur of Capricorn Holdings appears to have about 5% ownership, which means that his stock value increases $15-$30 million from the War in Colombia."

"If the DynCorp team kills 100 people, as an example, then that means they make $1.5 - $3 million per death. That way the Pop per Dead Colombian can be estimated, or, how much capital gains can be made from killing one Colombian. Since DynCorp was also in the Gulf and in Kosovo, we should be able to calculate the relative value of killing people in various cultures and nationalities. Under these assumptions, Pug Winokur then makes $75,000 to $250,000 of Pop per Dead Colombian."

"Since the stock of prison companies trades on a per bed basis, my guess is that defense stocks are going to evolve towards a per person expenditure and other similar performance rules-of-thumb for profit-making opportunities."

"One of my expectations is that the numbers for the Colombian war will yield a very high per death cost," Fitts continues. "That means lots of shareholders' profits, but probably very few American Jobs Created per Dead Colombian. That's because the big money is not made on labor intensive contracts, but on switching ownership of land, natural resources and other resources, including control of the drug markets and their reinvestment in our stock market and university endowments like Harvard, as opposed to local Colombian investments. This insider trading cabal is where the real money goes."

"That's why DynCorp's role as a knowledge manager (managing federal agency databases) is so important," she concludes. "It's worth far more money than the straight-up government contract. The profit will not show up for insider trading on DynCorp's portfolio, but in other capital gains that flow to the players of the Chase and Council on Foreign Relations syndicates and their private and institutional portfolios."

Outsourcing State Terrorism

This analysis of Catherine Austin Fitts, currently CEO of Solari, Inc. (http://www.solari.com) is probably the best model available for calculating the cost-benefit numbers in this egregious corporate-government scam.

The implications are ominous. By subcontracting (outsourcing) State Terrorism to so-called "private" entities like DynCorp, the US Government abdicates any moral/ ethical high ground in future confrontations. The proverbial "Iron Fist in the Velvet Glove" of the US Military in a Global Imperial Rampage is all that's left.

It was Executive Order 12333 that precipitated the shift during the Reagan-Bush Regime — a policy change in which so-called "national security" and "intelligence" functions were "privatized."

Likewise the DOJ-CIA Memorandum of Understanding allowed the outsourcing of illicit drug trafficking and weapons sales to private firms and individuals.

According to *Washington Technology Magazine*, this is the future. "The global market for outsourcing of government services is growing faster than outsourcing in any commercial segment, and is likely to more than double over the next five years, according to a new study by Accenture Ltd.," writes Patience Wait in her article "Government outsourcing grows fastest of all sectors" (March 4, 2002) http://www.washingtontechnology.com/news/16_23/cover/17920-1.html.

In this outsourcing market, DynCorp has an estimated 5% market share, while Lockheed Martin leads the proverbial pack with 30%.

However there's a bigger question. When a handful of federal contracting firms with lucrative insider deals control federal accounting and computer systems, does US Government sovereignty even exist anymore?

In other words, if the US Government and its agencies do not control their proprietary accounting, payment, and information systems, it becomes questionable whether we even have a sovereign government at all.

The outsourcing of these systems, then, in essence has become a silent coup d'etat by Corporate-Government Insiders.

According to *Washington Technology Magazine* (March 4, 2002), top outsourcing vendors to the US Government in fiscal 2000 are Lockheed Martin Corp (30% market share), CSC (13%), EDS (7%), DynCorp (5%), TRW (5%), Raytheon (4%) SAIC 4%) Northrop Grumman (3%) and Unisys (2%).

This is America's Corporate/Public Enemy #1 — the parasitic constituents of the so-called Military-Industrial-Pharmaceutical Complex.

Now that the parasites have literally overwhelmed the host (the US Government), the question remains — how long will companies like DynCorp continue to give America the finger?

Another question, however, is even more important — how long will America put up with this Enemy Within?

Chapter 8

Catch & Release Justice:
The Story of the Freemen Trial

I T WAS MY FIRST DAY AT THE Freemen Trial in Billings, Montana and I was trying to be as non-provocative as possible. I even took my Swiss army knife off my keychain before going into the US Courthouse.

Why? Because I was prepared for a Close Encounter with Friendly Fascists. You see I was thinking ahead. When I come face to face with the feds, I thought, I'm going to be completely harmless. After all, I had read the new Antiterrorism and Effective Death Penalty Act of 1996, just signed into law by Clinton. I knew that anybody could be designated a terrorist. Who knows? Maybe carrying a keychain with a Swiss army knife might be too politically incorrect. You just can't be too careful.

You see, according to this new legislation, if you're charged with violating the law and so-called "classified" information is involved, they hold a Star Chamber-like hearing which keeps out your evidence. Then if they say you're a terrorist, you can't deny it —it's the law.

Here's what it says in Sec. 219 (8): "If a designation under this subsection has become effective under paragraph 1B, a defendant in a criminal action shall not be permitted to raise any question concerning the validity of the issuance of such designation as a defense or an objection at any trial or hearing."

Got that? Read it again, then stop and think about what it means.

(Fax a request to 202-228-2815 and ask for Public Law 104-132.)

"America today exists in a twilight zone, not a democracy or a Republic, but not yet a police state," writes author Gurudas in his book, *Treason — The New World Order*, (Cassandra Press, Box 150868, San Rafael, CA 94915, 800-255-2665). "America has become an elitist corporate oligarchy."

Welcome to the post-modern National Security States of America.

Live and In Person at the "Freemen" Trial

The so-called Montana "Freemen" trial could have been performance art or maybe a scene out of Kafka. Men were carried out of the courtroom for swearing at the judge and the attorneys. Someone else yelled at the judge that he was under arrest. It was like the Marx Brothers in *A Day at the Courthouse*. The Freemen claimed they were beyond the prosecutors' jurisdiction. They acted like 60s radicals — Civil Disobedience For the Hell Of It. The spectacle of justice as political theater. Maybe Freemen wasn't such a good handle. How about the Montana 8 — like the Chicago 7 or the Seattle 5?

After all, the Nineties are just the Sixties upside down. But, here's a bummer — you can't get it on Court TV and you can't get it on C-SPAN. You have to go there in person. Reading Associated Propaganda, I mean Press, stories is just not the same.

The Feds, in fact, have descended on Billings. Cheap blue suits everywhere you look. Don't kid yourself. It's a political show trial. Less than a step removed from Stalin's kangaroo courts.

In "show trials," key issues are not addressed. They're excluded by the judge who filters out so-called "sensitive" information as "irrelevant." When the judge is the gatekeeper, information inimical to the prosecution is ruthlessly repressed. Recent trials including the Oklahoma City Bombing trial have proven this point conclusively.

As a political show trial, the Montana Freemen case was to be a public condemnation of anti-fed ideology. Though it had the pretense of law, the issues of the case were strictly political. The judge refused to discuss "jurisdiction" let alone establish it. Trials typically are not based on law, but on judicial policy. Like the Soviet refuseniks, who dared to challenge the former totalitarian regime, the so-called Freemen must have known they would end up in the federal gulag.

Billings is a squalid grease-spot of a town in eastern Montana. Earlier in the century, it was supposed to be a place where mobsters would lay low when things got too hot in Chicago. Today it's a haggard looking burg. Pedestrians look like they're waiting for their next dose of crystal meth. It's a sleazy town with undercurrents of crime and corruption. The feds fit right in.

Coming into town, you see billboards for "K-BULL Non Stop Country" and "Ostrich Farm Investors Welcome" then at least four used car lots for mobile homes. It's an overcast winter sky and a bleak forecast for freedom in America.

Inside the courthouse, you sit on hard wooden benches like church pews. Justice evidently requires patience and a hard rear end. His Honor (I just love titles of nobility, don't you?) US District Judge John C. Coughenour from Seattle is presiding. The chief prosecuting attorney is Assistant US Attorney Jim Seykora, overbearing and arrogant as if he had all the power and resources of the federal government behind him. Don't kid yourself — he does.

Five of the defendants were not in the courthouse. Only two of the defendants remain — Edwin F. Clark, 47, and Elwin Ward, 57. From the timely and speedy trial department: they've been in prison for more than 600 days refusing to recognize the jurisdiction of the court.

The subtext? The prosecutors tried to paint anyone with a gun as "militant agitators" or "anti-government extremists" (phrases commonly used in AP stories) even though the defense attorneys showed that all the weapons in question were "legal" by all current standards.

Wrong Place, Wrong Time, Wrong "Friends"

"For Elwin Ward, this case is about his family," said attorney David A. Duke in his opening statement. He showed the jury photos of Ward's wife and children as well as a map of the United States, which marked Ward's journey to retrieve his kidnapped children held by a disgruntled ex-husband of his wife.

And how did they get involved with Leroy Schweitzer, the kingpin Freeman? "They were seeking a legal way to get Steve Magnum [the ex] out of their lives," said Duke. "They took the class [referring to the school on common law practices] and the proof packet, proof and evidence from Schweitzer that things were working. They were not motivated by money, but resolving their custody problem."

"…They showed up in Justus Township in the 17th month of the 18 month investigation by the government, on March 25, 1996, starting the 81 day stand-off," Duke continued. "The US Government promised the Wards that he wouldn't be arrested and charged." So much for promises. And why were the Montana 8 brought to trial?

You've probably heard of Catch 22. How about Rule 35? Federal prosecutors' win-at-all-cost tactics have a name — Rule 35. Call it coercion. Call it intimidation. Call it legal threats. It all works.

"When a person agrees to plead guilty to the charges, you can throw in what's called Rule 35," Duke explained later. "The judge can give the defendant a break on the sentence, if he cooperates or gives substantial assistance to the government. It's from the Federal Rules of Criminal Procedure."

According to Duke, it's often used by the Feds to coerce small fish to testify against the big fish. "In the federal system there's no parole, as opposed to the state system, when you can get out early if you appear before a parole board. Whatever sentence you get, that's the sentence you have to serve. The only relief available to you is what's called Rule 35."

"It's very common," continues Duke. "Anybody who doesn't want to go to trial and plead guilty instead has the option to enter into a Rule 35 with the government."

Liberally speaking, federal sentences are draconian. After all imprisonment is a growth industry in America. More people are imprisoned in America than in any other country in the world, according to Amnesty International. Then there are the mandatory sentencing guidelines, which prohibit a judge from using his or her own discretion. It's the formula for a *de facto* Police State.

In the case of the Freemen, the usual intimidation tactics of the Feds hadn't succeeded. According to attorneys, the Feds had fully expected these "secondary participants" to testify against the so-called "kingpins." They miscalculated badly, and the prosecutors' lack of evidence of criminal intent was obvious.

These were not the "big fish" the Feds desperately wanted.

Here's the Uncensored Testimony

Defendant Edwin Clark was the first — and only — witness on behalf of his own defense. He was universally credited with resolving the so-called standoff so it didn't end up like Ruby Ridge or Waco, incidents decried by civil libertarians in which the FBI killed first and asked questions later.

A lifelong resident of Montana and a Vietnam veteran, Clark looks like actor Wilford Brimley, the guy who does the Quaker Oats commercials. According to his testimony, he'd been married for 25 years to Jan Clark with two children, Dawn, 21, and Casey, 23. His occupation, he said, was rancher-farmer with a welding shop and fabrication business on the side. "I love to design farm equipment," he said. "My grand-dads on both sides of my family homesteaded in the area [Garfield County, Montana] in 1913."

When attorney Steve Hudspeth asked him about his farm, Clark replied, "I don't own nothing now. It's all been taken from me." Why? He failed to make a land payment and the property reverted to his uncle under a contract-for-deed deal he had made.

"It was a very long complicated dragged-out affair," he said. "We'd been fighting this foreclosure for 18 years. We said it was an unlawful foreclosure."

So how do you get recourse when corrupt government practices have a stranglehold on your life? People look for alternatives to a legal system dominated by lawyers and federal agencies. Hence the popularity of classes in common law and other exotic tactics of courtroom battle.

Fighting against intimidation and corruption, his father was charged with 48 counts of fraud by the government which were later dropped, according to Clark. There were more broken promises later.

"The government said 'we'll give you a new security agreement.' Then the FmHA (Farmers Home Administration) filed for foreclosure. I was aggravated," Clark testified.

And what about the FmHA? According to Brian Kelly, author of *Adventures in Porkland: How Washington Wastes Your Money and Why They Won't Stop*, the Farmers Home Administration "is widely believed to be one of the worst managed government giveaways ever. Whatever you think of the philosophical arguments of saving farms or not saving farms, the way the government goes about it is a disaster for everyone concerned."

As James Bovard wrote in *The Farm Fiasco*, "The FmHA is a welfare agency that routinely destroys its clients lives,"… In repeated studies the General Accounting Office had found FmHA an incomprehensible mess." It makes you think of Willie Nelson and Farm Aid and what's the point of it.

Clark continued, "I didn't know Rodney Skurdal [one of the Freeman defendants] or any of them. I didn't trust legal counsel. I couldn't afford it, so I was forced to learn as much as I could."

Frustrated by his inability to make headway in these complex legal entanglements, Clark said, "when my father was brought in on 48 criminal counts and when the government backdated the agreement, they threw it out of court. My dad took me to see Schweitzer.

"I got a very big monkey on my back," Clark continued. "We were completely dried up on operating credit. I had to have money for fuel and operating expenses. Then they said we filed for bankruptcy which was not true." All of Clark's vendors and suppliers cut off his credit, which was used to run the farm.

When his lawyer asked him why he continued the operation, Clark replied, "That's the $64 question. My wife asked me 33,000 times.

"I don't know," he said with a sad finality.

Clark, a rancher caught up in a land dispute maelstrom, testified that he had 1500 acres in the CRP program which yielded $33 per acre, or a total of $48,000 per year. Then large debts of $100,000 would come in. "We had several years of 100% hailouts," he said — bad weather which totally destroyed the crops. "We sold all our sheep because of predators. I planted all of it to alfalfa, a strictly haying operation."

First, it was years of bad luck farming, then a medical emergency struck. Clark says he needed a pituitary tumor operation for Casey. When they arrived at the hospital in Rochester, Minnesota, "the hospital wanted $25,000 up front in cash." So he drove 1,100 miles back home to his bank.

Attorney Hudspeth asked Clark, "Why did you allow these people [the Freemen] you hardly knew to come?"

"They moved to Richard Clark's [a relative]. I didn't allow anybody," Clark replied. "Yes, it concerned me. We all had our problems and I knew it would bring it all to a head. I was a member of the ad hoc committee of Justus Township. We elected commissioners, constables and clerks."

And what was the reason for creating Justus Township? asked the attorney. Clark replied, "We're not anti-government. We're pro-government. We just want government to follow the law, to follow the Constitution."

Was it your intent to learn anything illegal from Schweitzer? asked the attorney. "Oh, absolutely not," replied Clark.

Criminal intent was sorely lacking in the prosecution's case. Their usual intimidation tactics hadn't worked either. And frustration at government corruption was running high.

"Our county government totally shut us out — commissioners, clerks and recorder," said Clark. "They were so much against us. We had no redress."

The latest statistics, according to a recent poll by the Pew Research Center, claim that only 39% of Americans trust the government to do the right thing at least most of the time.

That's considered an "improvement" because four years ago, it was only 21%.

The survey suggests that this distrust is driven by two principal factors: discontent with the honesty of public officials and dissatisfaction with the way the government does its job.

Concerning his involvement with Leroy Schweitzer's "system," attorney Hudspeth asked Clark, "You wouldn't consider yourself gullible, would you?"

Clark replied, "I'm starting to find out I am."

FBI Propaganda

With uncharacteristic candor, the AP (March 24, 1998) wrote that "one of the FBI's top con men described Monday how he lured the leaders of the Montana Freemen into a sting operation that toppled their multimillion dollar hot check operation."

The FBI's top con man? It's like a job description, right?

You know I've always admired the FBI, ever since I found out that J. Edgar Hoover liked to wear black cocktail dresses to intimate Washington parties.

According to Anthony Summers, author of *The Secret Life of J. Edgar Hoover*, "Hoover's preference for pedophilia was well known in the capital's power elite circles. But the cover story of the tough guy Hoover was kept sacrosanct."

After all it's not such a stretch to have a closet gay/transvestite as the top cop in the National Security States of America. Maybe Wilhelm Reich was right. He believed that repressed sexuality is a prerequisite for police-state mentality and behavior.

Then, when Hoover was finally knocked off, he was eulogized by "Tricky Dick" Nixon who, after hearing the news of his demise, reportedly said, "He's dead. That old cocksucker."

But where did the FBI come from? According to *Treason — The New World Order*, there was no federal police force until the twentieth century since it wasn't allowed by the Constitution. "The FBI was established in July 1908 as a branch of the Justice Department. Between 1917 and 1921 its agents compiled files on 200,000 people and organizations... Harassment of political protesters and minority groups has long existed and been well-documented..."

Throughout the 1960s and 1970s, a secret domestic program aimed at American citizens called COINTELPRO was established by the FBI "to expose, disrupt, misdirect, discredit or otherwise neutralize American citizens who were political dissidents."

You can think of the FBI as a Kinder Gentler Home-Grown Gestapo. If you have any doubts, just remember the travesty of justice against hapless security guard Richard Jewell. He was publicly accused of being the Olympics bomber, then finally released after his crucifixion by the media and non-stop harassment by the FBI. (And that even before the Los Alamos Wen Ho Lee debacle.)

"The FBI created violence in the ghettos and destroyed civil rights groups discrediting them with forged documents," the author continues in *Treason*, an excellent history of the burgeoning police state in America. "There were hundreds of illegal break-ins, theft of membership lists, encouragement of gang warfare and infiltration of groups with agent provocateurs.

"At a 1971 conference on the FBI held at Princeton University, Thomas I. Emerson said: 'The inescapable message of much of the material we have covered is that the FBI jeopardizes the whole system of freedom of expression which is the cornerstone of an open society...' The Bureau's concept of its function, as dedicated guardian of national security, to collect general political intelligence, to engage in preventive surveillance, to carry on warfare against potentially disruptive or dissenting groups is wholly inconsistent with a system that stipulates that the government may not discourage political dissent to achieve social change as long as the conduct does not involve the use of force, violence or similar illegal action.'

"'...The government is so obsessed with its law and order function, so ridden with bureaucratic loyalties, so vulnerable to its own investigators that it cannot be trusted to curb its police force.'"

The rampant and epidemic corruption of the US Department of Justice and so-called national security agencies (CIA, NSA, DEA, etc.) has been extensively documented in Rodney Stich's encyclopedia of government-sponsored crimes and coverups, *Defrauding America* (Diablo Western Press, Box 5, Alamo, CA 94507; 800-247-7389; $28, http://www.defraudingamerica.com)

In the Freeman case, media bias is also worth noting. Unproven allegations against the defendants were called a "hot check operation" according to the AP slant. Elsewhere AP stories, supposedly the paragon of "objective journalism," refer to "worthless comptroller warrants," "phony checks," and "freemen's bogus warrants."

No explanation is necessary for the unwashed masses of how financially sophisticated outfits like banks and the IRS would accept so-called "worthless" financial instruments as the real thing.

The AP version of reality and news is simply "Associated Propaganda." AP is a virtual mouthpiece for government-sponsored, condoned and manufactured "news."

In his book *Propaganda: The Formation of Men's Attitudes*, author Jacques Ellul explains that "only through concentration in a few hands of a large number of media can one attain a true orchestration, a continuity and an application of scientific methods of influencing individuals. A state or private monopoly is equally effective... This concentration itself keeps accelerating thus making the situation increasingly favorable to propaganda."

When you look at the few mega-corporations, which control information in the United States as an *ipso facto* monopoly of the so-called news and media outlets, this point becomes completely transparent and obvious.

The question is — was the Freemen's operation just a bogus check scam? Or is there a basis to the Freemen's "perfected liens," which became "credit" and later collateralized as "cash?" Even now some claim that offshore banks hold billions of dollars worth of financial instruments based on the Freemen's paper.

Bad Cop. No Donut.

When the judge called a recess for lunch, I went outside to take a picture of the courthouse. There are no photos allowed inside, no video cameras, no tape recorders. So I took the picture, got back in my car and drove off. On a one way street, I stopped the car at the curb to find an address in my book. A police car comes up behind me and blocks me in. The cop asks me for my license and I hand it over.

Then I asked him, "So what did I do? Make a wrong turn?" He shakes his head no and smiles and tries to change the subject.

I looked closer at his badge and I realized it wasn't the Billings Police.

It wasn't the Montana State Police.

It wasn't the Montana Highway Patrol.

It wasn't the FBI or the US Marshals.

It was — surprise! — Federal Protective Services. There on his badge, it said "GSA."

Wha'? The GSA police are stopping me on the streets of Billings?

When I got back, I tried to figure out what's going on. I called Bill Bearden in Washington. He's the media spokesperson for the GSA and the Federal Protective Service. Bill defended his friendly fascists in Billings saying, "Federal Protective Service is part of the Federal Building Service of GSA. They are the Federal police force."

"What's their domain?" I asked, surprised that they would have the run of downtown Billings. "If you have a federal building, if it's a GSA controlled building," said Bearden, "we provide the security for that building and that's the Federal Protective Service."

So why did they stop me? I asked. "If you were near a federal building and they thought you were suspicious, if they didn't know you were a reporter, they just saw you taking pictures of a federal building, it would send a flag to them to be security conscious enough to at least check out who you were," Bearden huffed. "Because if they didn't do things like that, you could have the recurrence of the Oklahoma City Bombing. It sounds like they were simply doing their job."

I continued, "To you, it's doing their job. To me, its harassment and intimidation. I was stopped for no reason. Then I left — for good. I figured I had better leave while I still had the chance."

"It doesn't seem to be anything improper about what they did," Bill said. "If you were doing nothing wrong and you're a law abiding citizen, I don't understand why you would care if someone just checked you out."

"So they're stopping me for my own good? Where does the Federal Protective Service domain begin and end? They boxed me in and then a brand new taxpayer-paid for $50,000 white Suburban pulled up," I told him.

Bearden was having trouble following. "Something doesn't sound right to me," he said. "It doesn't sound like it's normal, that it's their domain."

"That's right, Bill," I said. "It didn't sound 'normal' to me either."

"You know what the spin on this story is?" I asked him. "It's kinder gentler nazis in Billings Montana."

"Ha-ha-ha," Bill laughs.

"You laugh there in Washington D.C.," I said, "but this is absolutely outrageous."

"If you look suspicious on the street, a law enforcement person has the right to question you," said Bill.

Suspicious? "While I was standing on the sidewalk, I told them I was intimidated. I asked the cop, 'how would you feel if you were me?' He said, 'I wouldn't be too happy, sir.' 'If I were black,' I told him, 'I'd probably get beat up first, then you'd ask me questions later.'"

Bill says, "Let me read you a sentence here — the Federal Protective Service provides physical security, law enforcement and other services in federal buildings, US courthouses and GSA controlled-leased space."

"So what the hell are they doing — stopping me on the Billings sidewalk?" I asked.

"They have the right to stop you."

"By what law?"

"You don't have to have a law. They have arrest authority. They thought you were suspicious. They have a right to ask you who you were."

I said, "We have a creeping police state, and you're a spokesman for it, Bill."

"Have a nice day," he said, and I hung up.

The Spectacle of Justice

On March 31, 1998, Edwin F. Clark was found not guilty of all charges.

The AP headline — "Freeman Trial: Five guilty, one released."

Like its fishing analogue, catch & release justice is alive and well in Montana.

And the Associated Propaganda subtext? We've been telling you they're guilty. One just got away. That's all.

When Big Media is a mouthpiece for Big Government, You're in Fascist Country, Pardner.

Chapter 9

Near-Death Experiences 101

"YOU KNOW THE DIFFERENCE between God and a doctor?" asks Dannion Brinkley. "God never thinks he's a doctor." For a man who reportedly "died" three times, he looks — and speaks — remarkably well, his punchlines delivered with the ease of a professional.

Brinkley, best-selling author of *Saved by the Light* and *At Peace in the Light*, spoke in Montana at a conference called the "Gathering of the Mystics" as part of his cross-country speaking tour.

His high-energy, take-no-prisoners style would have been right at home in the night life of Las Vegas. In fact the show had the rhythms of a world-class stand-up comedy routine.

What's he like? Imagine Richard Pryor — before crack ate his brain.

Taking the tragi-comic details of his "near-death experiences," Mr. Brinkley transforms them into powerful entertainment as well as deep spiritual insights about what happens after and during death.

Mr. Brinkley makes light of his being struck by lightning while talking on the phone in September 1975. He was clinically dead for 28 minutes.

People say to him, "Dannion, you're so special."

And he answers, "How special could I be? God called me on the telephone."

In an astonishing synchronicity, he claims he was again struck by lightning in September 1978 — again while talking on the phone. In 1983, he collapsed and had to have emergency open-heart surgery. And in 1987, he had brain surgery.

Despite this astounding run of serious health crises, Mr. Brinkley's deprecating deadpan style and his southern accent serve him well.

Since he's been a hospice volunteer for the past 22 years, people ask him, "Why do you do so much hospice work?"

He answers, "You just tell them [in heaven] I'm doing a good job."

"I come from the deep south. Everybody goes to hell," he confides. "You know how stupid that is? I didn't go to hell — and if I didn't go to hell, not one of you turkeys is going to go either."

In an almost nostalgic retelling of his near-death experience, Mr. Brinkley describes his journey to the afterlife. "You go to crystal cities," he says. "You dwell with the violet flame. In each of my near death experiences, I have seen it and dwelled in it."

Regarding life on earth, Mr. Brinkley presents an iconoclastic view. "Life is like summer camp. God sent us here to get out of her hair," he insists.

Then he says, "I'm going to tell you what you've been taught to be afraid of — what happens at death. First comes a panoramic life review.

"You will see everything you ever did," he says. "You will watch yourself from a second person point of view. I saw everyone I had ever hurt. I was such a jerk. It broke me of the habit.

"You see and feel the pain you caused," he claims. "That's bad enough."

Hospice work, he believes, is one of the most important things that people can do for one another. His organization is called Compassion in Action, with chapters around the country.

(Note from the Cosmic Irony Dept.: Brinkley's website opens up with two inch high letters that screams "CIA." It's all the more jarring when you remember that he is a self-admitted former CIA assassin. Referring obliquely to his own sordid history in his book, he was supposedly a trained government killer working in the notorious Phoenix Project in Vietnam, which used mind-controlled agents to slaughter thousands of Vietnamese. Is this website the Agency's not-so-subtle way of saying he's still working for them? After all, CIA insiders jokingly refer to themselves "Criminals In Action.")

When Brinkley visits the VA hospitals, however, he says he tells people, "God couldn't come today, and that's why he called me."

In a more metaphysical vein, he explains, "We are multi-dimensional spiritual beings. In your breath, you pull at least eight levels of consciousness from at least eight different levels. That's the purpose of life — that spirituality can dwell on these rocks [Planet Earth]."

Brinkley's positive and life-affirming message goes out to everyone. "The day you took your first breath, you became a hero," he continues. "This [life] is only a nanosecond in how long you are. Because this [life] is an illusion."

His candor is refreshing. One of the greatest problems that people have, he claims, is their lack of self-forgiveness. "Pick something everyday, and forgive yourself," says Brinkley.

And for those who think his attitude toward religion is sacrilegious, Brinkley challenges them on any further repercussions, "What are they going to do?" he asks rhetorically. "Kill me?"

BUSHWHACKED

Chapter 10

Gorby and the Illuminati Wannabes

WHERE DO DICTATORS GO after they've been give the boot? Many former dictators end up on the French Riviera. Mikhail Gorbachev, the former chairman of the Soviet Communist Party, however, is no ordinary ex-dictator. He ended up on a former US Army base in San Francisco called the Presidio. He got the best place he could find, a cute two-story former officer's residence overlooking the Golden Gate Bridge with a great view of the San Francisco Bay. Gorby doesn't actually live there, but it is the home of the Gorbachev Foundation USA.

And what does the Gorbachev Foundation USA actually do? Most recently it sponsored the State of the World Forum, held in the posh Fairmont Hotel in San Francisco.

According to the Gorbachev Foundation, the purpose of the Forum is to "articulate a clearer vision of new international priorities" and "to bring together in working dialogue some of the most thoughtful individuals in the world...senior statespeople, current political leaders, business executives, scientists, artists, intellectuals, spiritual leaders and youth."

Hey, I'm in at least four of those categories, but I didn't get a single invitation. Am I surprised? No, not at all.

You see, the Power Elite likes to pick and choose its own front men, straw men and women to give the appearance of grassroots participation. You wouldn't want the appearance of top-down global economic and social planning in the old monopoly capitalist or communist mold. No, the kinder gentler New World

Order wants the semblance of so-called roundtable discussions by panels of brand-name celebrities.

The State of the World Forum, after all, was attended by people, hand-picked by Gorby, who consider themselves visionaries and with great foresight paid $5000 to prove it. In other words, it was a closed-to-the-public event.

But if you can even imagine Gorby as a visionary, you'd fit right in. Then you could mingle with retired bureaucrats like former Secretary of State George Schultz (Chairman of the Gorbachev Foundation Advisory Board), former National Security Advisor Zbigniew Brzezinski and former US majority leader George Mitchell.

Or you could share celebrity chef prepared dinners with New Age author Deepak Chopra or scientists like Nobel Prize winner Arno Penzias, science standup guy Carl Sagan, primatologist Jane Goodall, media mogul Ted Turner and his former actress wife Jane Fonda, actress Shirley MacLaine or a host of other people who like to consider themselves as part of what the Gorbachev Foundation calls "a global brain trust." Then you could "analyze the current state of the world and articulate the fundamental priorities and values necessary to constructively shape the early 21st century."

Since I consider myself at least a visionary (not to mention artist, scientist and business leader), I called up Gorby's PR contingent and asked about press credentials. Oh no, she said, we're sorry, but all the press passes have been taken. So, in the spirit of visionary investigative journalism, I decided to go incognito. I thought I'd just crash the party.

Would I run into Ted Turner? I could ask him if he was really serious when he said "Christianity was a religion for losers" and that "if you want to fish, put down a million dollars and buy your own damn stream."

(Or did he say those things on a day when he forgot to take his Lithium?) You see I've always been curious about rich socialist manic depressive, I mean bi-polar disordered, types.

But I didn't run into Citizen Turner. The first roundtable forum I attended was called "Social Values and Economic Renewal." There was Jeremy Rifkin, author of *Beyond Beef* and *The End of Work*, talking about Surprise! The World According to Jeremy Rifkin.

Rifkin actually said that "the industrial age brought the elimination of slave labor, and that the information age brought about the end of wage labor." Huh?

Earth to Rifkin, come in, dude, you're fading fast.

I wanted to invite him to McDonald's to ask the wage slaves working there what they thought about his theories — but he was rushing off to the airport. Those busy visionaries gotta run. Pick up that Gorby Foundation check and get out of town.

So I stood in the hallways of the majestic Fairmont Hotel seeing what else I could stumble into. Soon enough, an entire procession of State of the World people were walking down the hall. I joined in and found myself in the outdoor garden on the rooftop. I noticed that this odd parade was being videotaped, and since I was incognito, I stepped out of line and watched from the sidelines. All the people moved in slow motion. It was like a trance-walk, slow deliberate steps, in a circle around the garden. I watched for a while, and then asked a media-type guy what was going on. There was Shirley MacLaine and Dennis Weaver and a monk in saffron robes going around and around.

"What's that?" I asked. "Are they practicing The Zombie March of the New World Order?"

The guy gives me a dirty look and says, "No, that's a meditation." I got the impression he meant to say, who let you in, pal?

"Oh," I said and kept quiet after that.

Then I tried to get into the roundtable discussion called "Towards an Earth Charter in the 21st Century," which featured Gorby himself. He was going to discuss such important issues like — "Should there be a Bill of Rights for the earth similar to the UN Declaration of Human Rights?"

How do you like that? Gorby, the former Commie dictator, is now an advocate for "rights" — not "human" rights, but "earthly" rights. It's like the guy's an advocate for all of us. Imagine an ex-dictator is going to fight for Gaia's rights. It's pretty awesome.

The Gorbachev Foundation writes that "the framework of a new Earth Charter would provide a moral and legal basis to evolve a new relationship between people and their planet. The question is how such a charter is to be implemented and with what kind of sanctions for global violations. Would this require a global ombudsman or a global court which can give final verdicts on violations of the Earth Charter and the time frame within which such a Charter should be evolved and gradually introduced."

You gotta love the "sanctions" part. And even a "global court" appointed by Gorby's pals, no doubt. Imagine a UN global court that's going to fight for eco-rights.

Now, I don't know about you, but the idea of Mikhail Gorbachev pontificating on the environment is the ultimate in "Cosmic Irony." It's an irony that transcends the ordinary, everyday, mundane kind of irony. It's like Hitler appointing an all Nazi committee to look into the "allegations" of genocide against the Jews, the Gypsies, and other "useless eaters." It takes a certain ballsiness and a certain denial of reality, if you know what I mean.

Today Gorby's the head of an environmentalist group called Green Cross International, but while he was dictator supremo of the Soviet Union, there was more environmental pollution Back in the USSR, than any other time in recent history, anywhere in the world.

Let me refresh your memory. According to the *Weekly Telegraph (UK)* (30 November-6 December 1994), "Moscow has confirmed that it spent 30 years of disposing of atomic waste by pumping directly into the Earth. Worse still the pumping is still going on. Already it is suspected to have leaked into rivers leading into the Caspian Sea and the Arctic Ocean and has been blamed for the rise in cancer deaths in several locations where the waste has started returning to the surface."

"The dumped atomic material is reported to measure up to 3 billion curies of radiation. This compares to about 50 million curies released in the Chernobyl accident and 50 curies released at Three Mile Island in Pennsylvania. Even a small amount of this waste could totally sterilize vast areas of the northern oceans, destroying and contaminating the food chain for the entire northern hemisphere and rendering vast areas uninhabitable for centuries."

Does Gorby want to clean it up? Sure why not. As long as you're paying the tab.

Does Gorby and Company want to strand trial for High Crimes against Gaia, the Planet Earth in question?

It's doubtful, but the Illuminati wannabes in attendance obviously agreed with him, because I neither saw nor heard anyone expressing outrage that the man responsible for such monumental environmental havoc had the nerve to talk about an "Earth Charter" with a straight face.

But you gotta hand it to him. The guy is a wizard of Hegelian Dialectic. This is how it works, so the Illuminati/Power Elite control the outcome.

By the way, this is called "Crisis Management" in the West. First, you set up the thesis (or create the problem), i.e. environmental disaster. Then you set up the anti-thesis (or create a phony solution), i.e. environmental regulations. The synthesis is a UN Global Court which can "give final verdicts on violations of the Earth Charter."

And what do we get? A greater centralization of global economic and political power under the guise of UN "arbitrariness" and "equanimity."

What a deal.

After a while, I went off to make a phone call. I had the phone booth on the hotel open, my legs sticking out into the hallway. I'm looking straight ahead and out of nowhere, he appears. It's Gorby himself, and he's flanked by two ear-jacked security guys with shades.

Somehow our eyes meet and he gives me a small nod of recognition, with his Mark of the Beast birthmark on his forehead just like in the pictures. Momentarily I thought, "Gee you'd think the guy could afford a laser tattoo removal process or something." But he was gone, moving on to his Gorbachevian destiny in the Grand Ballroom.

You'd also be interested to find out about the "Global Security Programme" of the Gorbachev Foundation. When you get past the Recommendations for Nuclear Weapons Disarmament, Neutralizing Nuclear Weapons, Making START Reductions Irreversible, and Moving to the Final State of Nuclear Arms Control, you get to where Gorby's Boys are really doing some creative thinking.

It's called "Controlling Conventional War Weapons." You see, according to the Gorbachevian think-tankers, "we live in a world awash with an unnecessarily high level of armaments."

That's code for "Americans need to be disarmed."

And what do they, the Jim Garrisons and other Illuminati lackeys, propose? "A programme of step-by-step restraints on procurement; namely production, sale and transfer of military technology. To start this process of global restraint in arms procurement, the scope of the existing UN arms registry should be expanded to cover... information on production and national holdings of weapons... The coverage of conventional arms in the registry should be expanded to the small arms that play so large a role in local and regional conflicts. Later reporting on all items in the registry should become mandatory and implementation should be verified by an international authority..."

"The costs of maintaining an expanded UN registry and its verification should be raised from the proceeds of a UN excise tax on arms procurement, whose level might be increased to meet expenditures for these purposes and also used to finance peace-keeping."

What does it mean? Well, first, you register your guns with the appropriate United Nations agency. Then you pay a tax on it. Then the UN Peacekeepers, who are stationed in your neighborhood, will be paid by the revenue from your gun taxes.

Sounds simple, doesn't it? It is. There's no messy Bill of Rights or Constitutional arguments here.

By this time you're probably wondering who helped pay for the State of the World Forum?

Archer Daniels Midland, whose advertising tagline is "Supermarket to the World." gave the largest single amount: $250,000. This food monopoly corporate giant, one of the global oligopoly, is under investigation by the US Justice Department for price-fixing. The company is known by insiders as the "CIA Supermarket."

According to Forbes Magazine, ADM's in-house philosophy is "The customer is our enemy. The competition is our friend." Huh?

But all is not well in Illuminati Kingpin Dwayne Andreas's global fiefdom. ADM's clients aren't as stupid as ADM thought they were. According to the Wall Street Journal, ADM is currently facing over 70 lawsuits, "at least 21 suits by users of its high-fructose corn syrup, a sweetener used in soft drinks; 11 suits by users of its lysine, a nutritional supplement given to hogs and poultry; and four suits by customers of its citric acid, a widely used flavoring agent in beverages."

Yep. The chickens are coming home to roost, as they say. According to the Wall Street Journal, "the lawsuits, which generally accuse ADM of artificially raising product prices through anticompetitive behavior, seek treble damages and class-action status."

You see ADM loved working with the USSR dictator because they understood that it was the best way to get things done. No messy laws. Just a bunch of payoffs to the right politburo guys and that's it.

Smaller contributors to this Gorbachevian love-fest included $100,000 from the Red Rose Collection (a new age kitsch mail order company), $50,000 each from UPS, HarperCollins Publishers and seven others, $25,000 each from Carnegie Corporation of New York, Capital International Inc., David Packard, Prodigy, United Airlines, The Well and two others and a measly $10,000 each from British Airways, The Economist, Johnson & Johnson, Montgomery's Securities, SunAmerica Inc. and Occidental Petroleum (the old Armand Hammer company).

The grand finale of the State of the World Forum was a conversation between Mikhail Gorbachev, Margaret Thatcher and George Bush on the role of the United Nations. Carried live on CNN, it was held in the Masonic Auditorium on Nob Hill, but I watched it from the comfort of my easy chair. I had done enough incognito work for one weekend.

And what happened in this Battle of the Cold Warriors? Gorby was on the defensive against his former so-called foes Bush and Thatcher, and he even laid off his non-stop message of environmental alarmism and pushed his other line.

"The United Nations alone is able to deal with conflicts," said Gorbachev. "You can't persuade me the United Nations is not necessary. This is the time for the United Nations." He went on and on that the UN should be given more power rather than use the United States as a "Global Policeman."

But Gorby knows darn well he can have it both ways.

As soon as US servicemen fight under UN colors in Macedonia, or Chechnya, or wherever, you'll know he's more than just a former dictator or Illuminati Wanna-Be.

Gorby's the Real Thing.

Chapter 11

Globalist Chic

I F YOU THINK IT'S HARD WORKING full time, running a business, or raising a family, try running the world. The headaches are tremendous. The "useless eaters" keep multiplying and using up your resources — your food, your oil, your minerals. The "useful idiots" (the global gofers and asset managers of your planet) can hardly ever do anything right. Plus you have to make sure they're not skimming too much. It's a tough job — running the world — but somebody's got to do it.

Once upon a time there was a Cold War. The Bad Communists were engaged in a nuclear standoff with the Good Capitalists. Then all of a sudden, as if by Magic, the Evil Empire crumbled. The Cold War was over, and the Bad Communist, Mikhail S. Gorbachev, became a Former Communist. So, in a truly Hegelian dream sequence, the Capitalists and Communists became united, establishing a New World Order. And everybody lived happily ever....

This is the Fairy Tale Version of Recent History.

And what really happened to Gorbachev — now affectionately called "Gorby" by the media? When his Olympian sponsors bankrolled him with over $3 million, the Gorbachev Foundation found a new home in the Presidio, a former Army base in San Francisco. Gorby's paymasters were the Carnegie Endowment for International Peace, the Ford Foundation, the Rockefeller Brothers Fund, and the Pew and Mellon Funds.

They even established a foundation for him — while he was still a Soviet dictator. The Berlin Wall hadn't come down. The Iron Curtain wasn't lifted, but

Gorby was the bossman of the Tamalpais Foundation, incorporated in California by his "capitalist" pals. Gorby, you see, got the proverbial deal he couldn't refuse. Leave the country and come to America as the head of your very own capitalist-funded foundation.

Initially Jim Garrison was the frontman, but soon the Gorbachev Foundation had become a high profile vehicle for spreading the gospel of the "New Global Civilization." Meanwhile Gorby, the former Communist dictator with the blood-red splotch on his forehead, got a political (but not a cosmetic) makeover and became a roving evangelist for the New World Order.

He has served his Illuminati Masters well. For the second year in a row, an annual meeting called "The State of the World Forum," held in the luxurious Fairmont Hotel high atop San Francisco's Nob Hill, has emerged as a prime mover to deliver the message of *globalism uber alles.*

And who attended this confabulation? It was a world-class namedroppers' dream. Besides former USSR frontman Mikhail Gorbachev, there were geopolit-ical celebrities galore — former Israeli Prime Minister Shimon Peres, feminists Betty Friedan and Bella Abzug, primatologist Jane Goodall, former Haitian President Jean Bertrand Aristide, former California Senator Alan Cranston, best-selling author John Naisbitt, and a supporting cast of hundreds. There was even entertainment provided by musicians John Denver and Graham Nash.

Power elite types, like bureaucrats, ideologues, and policymakers got to mix it up with just plain folks. Actually they were more of the "limousine liberal" per-suasion — at least 375 of them who paid $5,000 per person to attend. It was a prime networking opportunity for globalist types to make sure the right message was getting out.

And what was the message? The same old Globalist line. Nuclear arms con-trol ("elimination of nuclear weapons"). Gun control ("a Global Code that would ban transfer of arms"). Chemical control (elimination of production and use of "toxic chemicals"). The operative word here is "control." The Globalist Control Freaks get a warm fuzzy feeling knowing everything's in control.

Not unlike a "secular religion," Globalism has a set of tenets, which are as strict as any sect you'll find anywhere. Their primary belief is that the usefulness of the nation-state is at an end, that One World Government must be estab-lished, but that this effort at least for now must be couched in cryptic language for the unwashed masses. Globalist spokesman and New World Order Godfather, Zbigniew Brzezinski, a former Columbia University professor and President Carter's former National Security advisor spoke at the State of the World Forum in 1995, saying, "We cannot leap into world government in one quick step... [It] requires a process of gradually expanding the range of democratic cooperation."

In plain language, that means that ordinary people must be indoctrinated a lot more before they'll "buy" into the program. Cooperation toward a one-world government and economy is, in fact, one of the reasons for the Forum. Despite the carefully crafted perception of consensus building, the programs are strictly from top-down dictatorial management. The Forum, a four-day, four-night gabfest, is another way of making sure the *hoi polloi* get their marching orders straight.

Inside the Fairmont Hotel's Grand Ballroom, they've finished their dinner of Grilled Aromatic Herb Marinated Tenderloin of Beef on Garlic Artichoke Focaccina washed down with a Wente Bros. Estate Selection Pinot Noir 1994. Coffee is being served with dessert, Ghirardelli Chocolate Paté with Orange Sauce and Almond Cookie, as preparations are made for the keynote speaker. The people are looking forward to four days listening to significant speakers speak on significant topics like "The Price of Peace," "The Definition of Wealth," and "Challenges to Democracy in Times of Turbulence."

When the applause dies down, the man with the red birthmark across his forehead steps up to the podium and begins the keynote address. It's Mikhail S. Gorbachev, one of the world's foremost evangelists for the New World Order.

Gorby himself gave the keynote address the first night, addressing what he called the issues of "21st Century Globalization." He talked about the "death of many peoples from epidemics and wars" and said not surprisingly that the "alternative is a managed process."

"Managed," by the way is another code word — as in crisis management, asset management, and risk management. The Global Ruling Class hates those pesky unplanned or unforeseen situations.

The audience was mesmerized by Gorby's intoxicating words. In his role as unstoppable U.N. booster, Gorby said there should be a new role for the United Nations. He used statistics like a pro, claiming that "73% of people polled said that the U.N., not the US should take the role of global policeman," and that "84% spoke in favor of the UN right to institute pollution taxes on toxic waste."

I'm quite sure you voted in that poll, right?

And the next step if Gorby gets his way? You can expect green-helmeted U.N. Environmental Police patrolling your neighborhood. You see, by then, according to Gorby, there will be an Earth Charter as well as an Ecological Tribunal to take care of all of your environmental crimes.

The audience was mesmerized by the former soviet leader's intoxicating words. Here was Gorby, having received less than 1% of the vote in the Russian election, and now he's in the USA telling the people how it's going to be.

Then Gorby started praising Hazel Henderson. Was this his pet ideologue?

Billed as an economist, a futurist and a human ecologist, Hazel Henderson is the author of *Paradigms in Progress: Life Beyond Economics*.

And what exactly is "life beyond economics?"

Yep, you guessed it. She's got a chapter called "Toward a New World Order."

"In the space of a few short years, the reality of global interdependence has restructured global geopolitics irrevocably," she writes. "Leaders shorn of national sovereignty are now forced to seek partners, deal with a still dangerously anarchic world system via ad hoc alliances and act pragmatically — even when at odds with their existing world views."

(Is this a subtle reference to Globalist arm-twisting?)

"The United States went from the Soviet-bashing escalating military budgets and UN baiting of the Reagan years to the 1990 UN courting and alliance-building so as to prosecute Iraq," writes Ms. Henderson. And lest we forget, she restates the obvious, that "during the Persian Gulf War, President George Bush referred repeatedly to a New World Order for the 1990s as a rationale for US policies and military action."

She's got that right, invoking King George Bush I as a Globalist precedent for Caesar-like rule over the plebes of America. The "commoners" didn't raise too much of a fuss, though, did they? Remember any anti-Gulf War demonstrations? Not on my TV.

"Mr. Bush's New World Order was widely construed as a New Pax Americana in global geopolitical terms since the United States had military superiority even if its economy was weakened," she writes.

And, yes, comparing America today with the last days of the Roman Empire and its Pax Romana, which by the way granted full citizenship to people conquered by the Roman legions, not unlike the exalted status of illegal aliens today.

"New definitions of a new world order must include security from environmental pollution, poverty, hunger and diseases..." writes Henderson, picking up her international socialist drumbeat.

"Security," by the way, is another Globalist codeword for covert control of your life. Watch for that word.

"Now is the time for debate on the ways of shifting the world's priorities and redirecting the current $1 trillion a year spent on weapons toward investments in the areas of health, education and environmental restoration."

And you know what? Ms. Henderson's right again. It's not such a big step from today's national-corporate socialism in America to international socialism on a global scale. You want to guess who's going to pay for it — this redistribution of wealth on a planetary level? I guarantee you — it won't be Hazel Henderson and her futurist comrades.

The next day, in a plenary session called "Free Enterprise in A Global Context," 13-year-old Craig Kielburger from "Free the Children" was chiding multinational corporations like Nike for using child labor overseas.

Was this the "Slave Labor" panel? A dirty look told me that I had asked the wrong question. Evidently it's politically incorrect to bring up slave labor issues, when mega-corporations move their factories overseas.

The New World Order's Ruud Lubbers, former Prime Minister of the Netherlands, reassured the young man that, "The World Labor Organization was created just for that purpose." And guess what? Nobody in the audience even snickered.

Later Gorby's favorite futurist Hazel Henderson herself spoke saying, "today we are rewriting much of that history." (Orwell would have been proud) and quoting more dubious statistics like "70% of Americans have been telling us they want an international tax on global arms sales." Her smooth serpent-like voice saturated the Ballroom berating everyone about how "the US should pay its dues to the U.N. to meet the needs of the 21st century." She was one slick mouthpiece and Gorby's admiration for her was obviously well founded.

Then there was four-star General Lee Butler, former Commander of Strategic Air Command. After a lifetime of being the Guy Who Would Push the Button, General Butler got religion (no, not literally) or came out (if you prefer) as an anti-nuclear advocate. Now that he's retired, Butler says, "I want to record my strong conviction that the risks entailed by nuclear weapons are far too great to leave the prospects of their elimination solely within the province of governments." That's code, by the way, for "forget about national sovereignty."

Oh no, the former Cold Warrior had seen the light. "There are steps which can be taken now, which will reduce needless risks and terminate Cold War practices which serve only as a chilling reminder of a world in which the principal antagonists could find no better solution to their entangled security fears than Mutual Assured Destruction."

And guess who's on the anti-nuke Canberra Commission that General Butler is fronting? Sure enough, there's unindicted war criminal Robert McNamara, prime architect of Mutual Assured Destruction. After a job as president of Ford Motors, McNamara became Secretary of Defense for Presidents Johnson and Kennedy, then become the head of the World Bank. Like Hollywood studio execs, failing upward is a given for Ruling Class technocrats.

It really makes you wonder. Are they against nuclear weapons because of a change of heart? Or because the Global Ruling Class has saturated the market with nuclear weapons and now it's time to sell so-called "non-lethal weapons" like mind control technology, pioneered by the CIA, DIA, NSA and DoD to keep the populations subservient — without the threat of blowing up the planet?

Butler sure loved to pontificate. "Such a world was and is intolerable. We are not condemned to repeat the lessons of forty years at the nuclear brink…The nuclear beast must be chained, its soul expunged, its lair laid waste. The task is daunting but we cannot shrink from it. The opportunity may not come again."

Then it was just like "We Are The World. Take Two." The Grand Finale was a Public Forum at Masonic Auditorium, moderated by BBC Anchor Tim Sebastian. The subject was "Global Security" discussed by Gorbachev, Jean Bertrand Aristide and Shimon Peres. When Gorby kept talking and talking, Tim Sebastian diplomatically allowed him to go on. Especially since Gorby emphatically stated, "I will not let you interrupt." It must have been like the good old days in the Soviet Politburo when appartchiks could drone on literally for hours.

Former Haitian President Aristide was on stage too. He looked (and acted) like somebody put a serious voodoo spell on him. Answering in a quiet simpering voice, it was bromide after bromide about "peace." Imagine Michael Jackson on bad drugs — without his eleven year old boyfriend. In the words of a BBC Radio newsman who interviewed him, "he was gone."

And then it was time for entertainment. John Denver came out and sang an old-time peace and love song. For the finale, he actually asked everybody to join hands and sing the chorus. And they did.

There was Gorby, the former Communist, holding hands with Shimon Peres, the former Israeli prime minister. It was a Globalist Wet Dream on stage.

But the Proles Still Walk. When it was over, I watched Gorby get in his black limo to drive the one and a half blocks to the Fairmont Hotel. And walking back from the Masonic Auditorium I found myself walking next to John Denver.

"What a photo opp," I said to him, but he was seriously noncommittal. So there we were walking together under a clear San Francisco blue sky. Just like the old days, the working class walks, I was thinking. The nomenclatura, the power elite, gets driven in limos. Yeah, me and John Denver — typical proles. Nob Hill. Hobnobbing with the New World Orderlies. What a concept.

In an era of planetary decentralization of power, the One World Government crowd has to come up with a new methodology, a "New Paradigm," to use current buzzword terminology. (Now I don't know about you but every time I hear the word "paradigm," I check my wallet to see if it's still there.)

And given the track record of corruption by politico-kleptocrats worldwide, it's time for the One Worlders to build a new consensus. After all it's still hard to keep order in the Global Casino (or is it Global Money Laundry?)

There's an old Communist Russian joke that comes to mind. "Where are you going in such a hurry?" said one rabbit to the other. "What's wrong with you?"

asked the second rabbit. "Haven't you heard there's a rumor going around that all the camels are going to be castrated?" "But you're not a camel," said the first rabbit. The second rabbit answered, "After they catch you and castrate you, try to prove that you're not a camel!"

And that was the agenda of the State of the World Forum, a network of power elite types and just plain folks seduced by the idea of peace, love, brotherhood — and, of course, "global" business.

The Ruling Class Gofers loved every bit of it, stage-managed as it was. And Gorby certainly followed the script.

After all, even Gorby knows there's no improv in the Geopolitical Theater.

BUSHWHACKED

Chapter 12

Up Against the Beast: High-Level Drug Running

Lawsuit Alleges FEMA Funded by Drug Profits

Speculation about the mysterious origin and funding of the so-called Federal Emergency Management Agency (FEMA) has continued for decades.

The history of FEMA as an illegal unconstitutional entity has been most recently exposed in an unprecedented lawsuit against the CIA and its alleged drug trafficking and money laundering operations.

In September 1998, a $63 million lawsuit (Case No. 98CV11829JLT) was filed by Massachusetts attorney Ray Kohlman on behalf of former Green Beret Bill Tyree.

Kohlman, a former legal investigator for attorney William Pepper in the Martin Luther King murder trial of James Earl Ray, filed a 101-page complaint on behalf of his client.

The suit, replete with five inches of affidavits and appendices, names the Central Intelligence Agency, former Massachusetts Governor A. Paul Celucci, former Massachusetts Attorney-General Scott Harshbarger, former CIA director and US President George Bush and self-admitted government assassin D. Gene Tatum as defendants in a far-reaching case involving US Government sanctioned drug smuggling, murder, and cover-up.

Bill Tyree is currently serving a life sentence for the murder of his wife — a case eerily similar to that of Dr. Jeffrey MacDonald, a Ft. Bragg doctor who was framed for the murder of his wife and children in the early 1980s.

"In the mid 1970s, while serving in Panama, Tyree and other Green Berets were led into Colombia under the command of Green Beret Colonels Cutolo and Baker to plant radio beacons, so that plane loads of cocaine could fly below Colombian and US radar and land undetected in Panama," writes Mike Ruppert in his newsletter *From the Wilderness*.

"Orders for these missions came from the CIA's Ed Wilson and Tom Clines," continues Ruppert. "Tyree had been a part of many secret missions and was losing his taste for it. His wife was keeping a diary [for which she was presumably murdered, after which the diary was confiscated and which later disappeared]."

"Five Special Forces Colonels — Cutolo, Baker, Malvesti, Rower and Bayard — have died under mysterious circumstances since. The heart of the Tyree documentation consists of an affidavit allegedly written by Colonel Cutolo who was also Tyree's commanding officer at Fort Devens, Mass. at the time of Tyree's arrest. Both were then with the 10th Special Forces."

"That fifteen page document gives precise details of CIA drug operations using Special Forces personnel. It also describes how Tyree was framed for the murder of his wife and how Special Forces personnel were used to intimidate and conduct illegal electronic and physical surveillance of anyone who might expose CIA drug dealing."

No Legal Funding for FEMA

According to the complaint in the lawsuit, "the Plaintiff [Tyree] alleges that the Defendants CIA and George Bush were negligent and failed at the conclusion of Operation Watchtower to monitor the post-Watchtower events and seek legal congressional funding for the origination of FEMA (Federal Emergency Management Agency), and this failure led to the concealment and cover-up of Operation Watchtower, written about in the diaries of Elaine Tyree, seized illegally and turned over to Colonel Carone and then to the CIA which ensured that the Operation Watchtower drug trafficking operation would remain covert, allowing the drug profits from this Operation to be used to circumvent Congress and fund FEMA and continue the pattern of criminal activity."

Colonel Carone, who died in 1990, was a CIA paymaster and Mafia-connected money launderer, who incidentally held the rank of full colonel in Army Intelligence. As Oliver North's bagman, he also couriered large amounts of cash in and out of the country.

According to former FAA investigator Rodney Stich, "Carone had complex relationships." In his underground best-selling book *Defrauding America*, Stich writes that "Carone was a member of the Gambino family, connections to other crime groups in the eastern part of the United States, a detective on the New York City vice squad, a member of the military and a CIA operative."

Stich writes that "Dee [Ferdinand, Carone's daughter] said her father was a detective and bagman in the New York City police department, collecting money that was distributed to captains and inspectors as payoffs for looking the other way where drugs were involved..."

"Referring to CIA-Mafia drug trafficking, she said she knew from what her father said that the drugs coming from South America, went to the Colombo, Genovesee and Gambino families, and that it was a joint CIA-Mafia drug operation under the code name Operation Amadeus. She said that during World War II, Operation Amadeus was involved in transporting Nazi officers from Germany into South American countries. According to her father's notes, Operation Amadeus split into several other operations, including Operation Sunrise and Operation Watchtower."

Tyree's lawsuit alleges that "to cover-up Operation Watchtower which was one of several illegal drug operations that produced a profit which was used in turn to help originate and implement FEMA violating: a. Separation of powers: the executive branch brought about an agency (i.e. FEMA) which has the authority to suspend the US Constitution, (e.g. further suspending legislative and judicial branches), but is vague in its verbiage as to what does constitute an emergency and fails to list what, if any duties the legislature and judiciary will have to perform if the US Constitution is suspended."

No Legal Standing for FEMA

Even though the origin of FEMA has remained historically unclear, Tyree's lawsuit alleges that FEMA, created by Executive Order, is illegitimate "since Congress had to approve FEMA for two specific reasons: (1) FEMA is a vaguely written Executive Branch created agency that has the power to suspend the US Constitution and put the legislative and judicial branches of government out of work; (2) FEMA is an Executive Branch creation that clearly affects all three branches of Government capable of silencing the voice of the people, (i.e. legislative) and the legal redress of the people, (i.e. judiciary)."

FEMA was allegedly created by Executive Order 12148 which became law simply by its publication in the Federal Registry. In other words, Congress was bypassed for FEMA's authorization as well as its funding. But if Congress never authorized the "agency," where do operational expenses come from?

Tyree's lawsuit alleges that laundered drug profits were the initial source of funding.

According to the lawsuit, "the Plaintiff alleges the Defendants CIA and

George Bush did intentionally engage in the complained of conduct herein to conceal: (1) the origins of FEMA and that profits from drug trafficking by the CIA were used in some part to originally fund FEMA and the drafting of the FEMA infrastructure."

In an even more astounding allegation, the lawsuit claims that Colonel Carone told the Plaintiff that "Colonel Ollie North worked on developing a plan known as FEMA, which would in an ill-defined national emergency, allow the US Military to take control of the United States to ensure National Security" and that Colonel Carone said that "FEMA" originally stood for "Federal Emergency Military Action" (i.e. Martial Law), but was retitled "Federal Emergency Management Agency" because it would be better received by the people of the United States.

The late Colonel Carone also claimed that "he took drug profits that were clean and laundered in 1982-1984 to the following: NSC — Colonel Oliver North who used the funds to create and develop FEMA." (p. 88)

Ollie North and FEMA

North's role in the creation of FEMA should be better known. Ben Bradlee, Jr., author of *Guts and Glory: The Rise and Fall of Oliver North* writes that "North's work for FEMA — from 1982 to the spring of 1984 — was highly classified and some would say bizarre. During that period, the *Miami Herald* reported that he was involved in helping to draft a sweeping contingency plan to impose martial law in the event of a nuclear war, or less serious national crises such as widespread internal dissent, or opposition to an American military invasion abroad."

"The plan — which also gave FEMA itself broad authority to report directly to the President, appoint military commanders and run state and local governments [Executive Order 11490] — ruffled many administration feathers," continues Bradlee.

"North would also play a role in helping FEMA stage a national emergency simulation exercise April 5-18, 1984... Rex-84 Bravo, authorized by President Reagan's signature of National Security Decision Directive 52, was predicated in his declaration of a state of national emergency concurrent with a mythical invasion (code-named 'Operation Night Train') of an unspecified Central American country, presumably Nicaragua."

"... Rex-84 Bravo was designed to test FEMA's readiness to assume authority over Department of Defense personnel, all fifty state National Guard forces and a number of 'State Defense Force' units which were to be created by state legislative enactments. FEMA would 'deputize' all DoD and state National Guard personnel so as to avoid violating the federal Posse Comitatus Act, which forbids using any military forces for domestic law enforcement…"

Colonel Carone also testified that "FEMA was one of those off-the-shelf creations that was funded through the giant black operations fund which came about from drug trafficking operations instituted by the CIA which Congress has no idea of and no control over," that "the FEMA Chain of Command, rules and regulations that he had seen violated the US Constitution, and actually established a succession to the Office of the President in the event of an emergency that circumvented the Vice-President and the Speaker of the House of Representatives."

Carone said "NSC used drug trafficking profits to start FEMA without congressional approval… a 1981 NSC Directive written by Frank Carlucci [states]:

'Normally a state of martial law will be proclaimed by the President. However in the absence of such action by the President, a senior military commander may impose martial law in an area of his command where there had been a complete breakdown in the exercise of government functions by local authorities.'"

"Colonel Carone said a literal interpretation of the 1981 NSC Directive was that local yokel national guard commander could institute martial law, and the actions of FEMA, without local citizens ever knowing how FEMA came to be, or what FEMA was originally intended to be about, would automatically be triggered without any type of presidential order… Congress doesn't even have the purse strings on this one. It's all from the Black Operations Fund which Congress will never force the US Intelligence Community to admit even exists."

None dare call it fascism, but due to this explosive lawsuit, the origin of FEMA and its illegal funding may finally be known.

The Great American Frame: Spooky Parallels between the Tyree and MacDonald Coverups

The spooks call it "limited hangout."

When criminals in government are about to be exposed, a story is concocted which uses some of the facts, mixes it with lies, and obscures the rest. This disinformation is then spread throughout the media, and *voila!* a cover-up is born. With Hollywood connections, a TV movie is produced. This new dose of fiction then becomes irrefutable "fact" in public memory.

There are significant parallels between the murder case of former Green Beret Bill Tyree and Dr. Jeffrey MacDonald. Both involve CIA-military drug-smuggling crimes and coverups. Both men were set-up and convicted. Both men have been languishing in prison for twenty years.

The story of emergency physician Dr. Jeffrey MacDonald, framed for the murder of his wife Collette and children Kimberly and Kristen in 1970, remains a tragedy. Author Joe McGinnis wrote a best-selling book *Fatal Vision*, which was made into a TV movie of the same name in 1984.

The real story is the frame-up of an innocent man who had powerful enemies, described in great detail by Jerry Allen Potter and Fred Bost in *Fatal Justice: Reinvestigating the MacDonald Murders* (1997, W.W. Norton & Co.) Errol Morris, director of *The Thin Blue Line*, writes, "if you think you know the Jeffrey MacDonald case from *Fatal Vision*, think again. *Fatal Justice* is the first account of the whole story." *Boston Phoenix* called it "a devastating rebuttal to *Fatal Vision*."

An investigator in the MacDonald case, former L.A. FBI Special Agent in Charge Ted Gunderson obtained a signed confession from Helena Stoeckley, the girl in the floppy hat, who told him that the group she was involved with "was active in an international drug operation that involved US Army personnel, including Army officers, police officers and at least two local attorneys" in the Ft. Bragg area. According to *Time Magazine* (January 1, 1973), drugs were being flown into the United States from the Far East in plastic bags in the body cavities of dead GI's.

Gunderson says members of this group "tried to shake down Dr. MacDonald because he was abusive to those who overdosed on drugs in the civilian hospital where he was moonlighting... The assailants [of MacDonald's family] were high on drugs and the situation escalated to the murders. Their intentions to shake down Dr. MacDonald were not known or approved by the leaders of the drug operation. When it was realized by the leaders that members of their network committed these murders, they were concerned that an investigation of the cult would expose the drug operations — thus the cover-up and 'framing' of Dr. MacDonald."

Gunderson himself has written *The Doctor Jeffrey R. MacDonald Investigation* that summarizes the facts. Evidence, like fingerprints, was intentionally destroyed by Army C.I.D. Other evidence like a bloody syringe, bloody clothing and boots were lost. More crucial evidence was never collected. Then allegations of FBI crime lab corruption surfaced through FBI whistleblower Frederick Whitehurst.

Michael P. Malone, an FBI forensic specialist, who testified in the MacDonald case was exposed by the inspector general's report. "Mr. Malone has indeed testified falsely and outside his expertise," wrote the *Wall Street Journal* (April 16, 1997). "In 1987 and 1988, Florida appellate courts overturned guilty verdicts — citing insufficient evidence — in cases in which Mr. Malone had testified for the prosecution," the article continued.

In addition, an internal FBI memo written in 1989 alleged that Mr. Malone had given 27 instances of false or misleading testimony in the 1985 proceedings that led to the impeachment and ouster of former US District Judge Alcee L. Hastings. Was it sloppy work or plain outright fraud? The evidence shows that FBI Crime Lab work can not be trusted. In MacDonald's case, Malone's testimony alone should have been grounds for a mistrial.

In *Psychic Dictatorship in the USA* (1995; Feral House), Alex Constantine also weighs in on the MacDonald case. "*Fatal Vision* is a political hit piece," he writes. "The paperback indictment of MacDonald has reinforced the public perception of MacDonald's guilt, and kept dormant one of the most unconscionable scandals in American military history."

"Three suspects in the murders have confessed," continues Constantine. "MacDonald's version of events has been confirmed by some 40 witnesses... *Fatal Vision* is myopic in its exclusion of any evidence that might clear MacDonald. McGinniss's claim to impartiality eroded completely in his flat refusal in 1980 to even look at the 1200-page report compiled by MacDonalds defense attorneys. The report, taken together with the sworn depositions of witnesses, press accounts and interviews with investigators combine in a case sharply at odds with the government's."

"MacDonald passed a polygraph," writes Constantine. "He submitted to five independent forensic examinations. The government's own lab specimens link Fort Bragg's body-bag [drug-smuggling] ring to the crime scene, including a long synthetic blonde strand corroborating MacDonald's contention that Stoeckley wore a blonde wig the night of the murders. A bloody syringe found in his home was 'lost' by the prosecution."

The case of William Tyree is just as complex, convoluted and byzantine. Tyree was in the Army Special Forces and also convicted of his wife's murder. However an *A&E* documentary called *Murder at Fort Devens* revealed evidence that he was also framed to conceal CIA-military drug trafficking.

Tyree says that drugs were flown into Panama as early as 1975, drugs which were subsequently shipped to the US via Mena, Arkansas, a state described as the CIA's own "banana republic."

According to Rodney Stich, author of *Defrauding America*, "the CIA utilized the Army Intelligence Agency in Operation Watchtower, which began in the mid 1970's. US Colonel A.J. Baker was ordered to oversee part of Operation Watchtower and turned the operation over to Colonel Edward P. Cutolo, who also commanded the 10th Special Forces based at Fort Devens, Massachusetts."

"[Cutolo] who had been ordered by the CIA to supervise Operation Watchtower, grew increasingly concerned about its flagrant illegality and conducted an investigation in an attempt to bring it to a halt," writes Stich. "Fearing he might be killed because of the investigation, he prepared a fifteen-page single-spaced affidavit dated March 11, 1980 describing the CIA drug trafficking and other activities…"

"Cutolo was killed as were several other people working with him to expose the drug trafficking operations…The affidavit described the installation and operation of the radio beacon towers [to guide airplanes bringing in drugs] and several of the drug flights in which he participated."

Relevant to the Tyree case itself, "The Cutolo affidavit described the killing of an Army servicewoman, Elaine Tyree, who had knowledge of Operation Watchtower which she described in her diary. To shift attention from the actual killer and his connection to the ongoing drug operation, the military charged Tyree's husband with the killing. 'It was too risky to allow a military court to review the charges against Pvt Tyree,' read the affidavit."

"At the first military hearing, the presiding judge found no reason to bind Tyree's husband over for trial for the murder of his wife," writes Stich. "This decision risked further investigation and possible exposure of the corrupt operation. Army pressure caused the county prosecutor to indict the husband for murdering his wife even though the army knew the actual killer was someone else."

"The Cutolo affidavit stated: 'On 29 February 1980, Pvt. Tyree was convicted of murder and will spend the duration of his life incarcerated. I could not disseminate intelligence gathered under Operation Orwell [a surveillance operation directed against US politicians] to notify civilian authorities who actually killed Elaine Tyree.'"

The A&E documentary *Murder at Fort Devens* featured Judge James Killian, who initially dismissed the case against Tyree, saying "I didn't believe a word the prosecution's chief witness said. He had the skills to do a decapitation." The judge was referring to Green Beret Earl Michael Peters, who was present when the murder was committed. Forensic evidence and witness testimony shows that Tyree was not present, and that Peters was most likely the killer of Elaine Tyree.

A new lawsuit on behalf of Bill Tyree has been filed by his attorney Ray Kohlman. The suit is seeking $63 million — $21 million for each year of incarceration and $42 million in exemplary damages. It also seeks an injunction against CIA from engaging in further illegal activities, as well as a new trial.

Bill Tyree, Dr. MacDonald and many others like former FBI Special Agent Richard Taus have been falsely arrested, convicted and imprisoned.

So what's new? Unlike the wrongfully imprisoned and recently released former Black Panther, Geronimo Pratt, who did 27 years for a murder he didn't commit, they are still political prisoners in the American Gulag.

It's called doing time for the CIA's crimes.

Secret History of America: Dead Men Do Tell Tales

The lawsuit by former Green Beret William Tyree against the CIA *et al* is a work of art, a masterpiece of legal reasoning, and an important historical source document.

Why? Because, for the record, it contains first-hand knowledge and revelations by the late US Army Colonel Al Carone of a far-reaching criminal conspiracy, namely US Government drug smuggling, money laundering, murder and cover-up. Carone's information corroborated with evidence by other sources reveals a dark history of the United States that has been neglected by mainstream historians and censored by the Mega-Media Cartel.

First, the lawsuit questions the constitutionality and legality of so-called "Executive Orders." According to the lawsuit, Executive Order #12333, for example, authorized the "privatization of intelligence and covert operations and permitted agencies other than the CIA to conduct 'Special Activities,' thus effectively opening the door, previously closed by [the National Security Act of 1947] to the White House National Security Council Staff or even private entities/assets, i.e. third party cut outs to carry out covert operations."

In plain language, this means that the CIA could subcontract or "farm out" their drug smuggling and assassinations to third party personnel and continue to enjoy their "plausible deniability," i.e. denying any knowledge or involvement with criminal activities.

According to the lawsuit, Bill Tyree claims his false imprisonment was due to the theft of his murdered wife Elaine's diaries, which contains evidence that would have exonerated him in his trial.

"Colonel Carone, either as a CIA asset/entity or as a CIA employee, did receive the diaries of Elaine Tyree in 1979," writes Tyree. "Colonel Carone became aware of the information that was listed in the diaries that related to Operation Watchtower and the illegal surveillance operation in New England/Massachusetts. Colonel Carone turned the diaries of Elaine Tyree over to the CIA for security reasons in an effort to conceal the drug Operation Watchtower and the subsequent surveillance operation that took place in New England/Massachusetts."

"Through Dee and Tom Ferdinand [Carone's daughter and son-in law] the Plaintiff [Tyree] learned for the first time in August 1995 that Colonel Carone had in fact been in possession of the diaries of Elaine Tyree and had subsequently traveled to Langley, VA to drop the diaries off at the CIA."

(The diaries of Mary Pinchot-Meyer, JFK's mistress and ex-wife of CIA operative Cord Meyer, also mysteriously disappeared following her unsolved murder in 1964. A book called *A Very Private Woman* (1998) by Nina Burleigh appears to be a cover-up (or at least a limited hangout) concerning the life and death of Pinchot-Meyer. Did she, like Elaine Tyree, know too much and more important-ly document illegal Agency "fun and games"?)

All Along the Watchtower: Bill Tyree's Story

According to his lawsuit, Tyree "took part in a US Army-CIA Operation Watchtower which brought cocaine out of Colombia into the US Airbase, Albrook Air Station, Panama, where the planes (not US Air Force Planes, planes of other Latin American countries and some unmarked airplanes) landed and offloaded the cocaine while the mission commander, Colonel A.J. Baker and Colonel Noriega, among others, looked on."

Tyree states "that in February and March 1976, a second and third Watchtower Operation took place under the command of Colonel Edward Cutolo and more cocaine was brought into Albrook Air Station, Panama. [Tyree] who was also involved in a non-volunteer capacity as Crew Chief on a US Army Helicopter saw CIA Officer Edwin Wilson, CIA Officer Frank Terpil, CIA Asset/Officer Colonel Albert V. Carone, and Israeli Colonel Michael Harari."

"In late 1976, Colonel George Bayard, US Army, CIA Middle East Expert, contacted US Army Special Forces Colonel Edward Cutolo and James N. Rowe and told them that Operation Watchtower was not a sanctioned US Congressional Operation and he had found out this information through a Middle East Intelligence contact associated with a bank known as BCCI."

"In 1977 Colonel Bayard went to Atlanta, Georgia to follow up on a lead and contacted Colonel Rowe from Atlanta. Colonel Bayard was murdered in Atlanta after he spoke to Colonel Rowe and that murder remains unsolved..."

"In October 1977, Tyree arrived at the 10th Special Forces Group Airborne, Ft. Devens, Massachusetts and the Group commander was Colonel John Shalikashvili."

In December 31, 1977, he married Elaine. She was an avid diarist who had been keeping detailed notes on all the illegal activities she was observing.

On January 30, 1979, Elaine Tyree was murdered. Judge James Killiam III entered a written decision that SP4 Earl Michael Peters killed Elaine Tyree and that "Pvt Aarhus assisted SP4 Peters in killing Elaine Tyree."

In a bizarre string of events, "on June 6, 1979, in an unprecedented decision from the Single Justice of the SJC, not only did the SJC strike down all criminal charges against Peters, but issued the order which forbids any court in

Massachusetts from issuing criminal process against anyone in the Elaine Tyree homicide unless authorized to do so by the SJC."

"After Erik Aarhus stood trial for the murder and was convicted and sentenced to life in prison, Tyree himself went on trial and was convicted without testimony of Erik Aarhus on February 29, 1980." A pretty good frame, if you can get away with it.

To Die For: Elaine Tyree's Diaries

In August-September 1996, former Army CID investigator Bill McCoy introduced Bill Tyree to Dee Carone-Ferdinand, the daughter of Colonel Carone. According to the lawsuit, after a two year long correspondence by phone, a stunning breakthrough occurred in the case when "Dee Ferdinand at a point notified the Plaintiff [Tyree] that she was the daughter of Colonel Carone and said: my father had the diaries that belonged to your wife Elaine. He went to Langley, Virginia to drop them off with 'The Boys.' That's what he said. I read some of the diaries, or at least the parts that my father showed me. I saw the photograph in the front of the diaries that was of you and your wife."

Unfortunately in 1997, CW4 William H. McCoy was found dead in his home in Fairfax, Virginia, and was immediately cremated before the medical examiner could determine the cause of death.

According to the lawsuit, McCoy told Tyree, "no matter what happens, if I die and you're not sure what I died from, have my family get an independent medical examiner to check me out. Be sure. Give me your word."

McCoy, after all, was concerned that people just seemed to drop dead after they learned about the CIA cocaine operation at Mena, Arkansas. Among the dead were Stanley Huggins, Kevin Ives, Donald Henry, Keith McCaskell, Greg Collins, Jeff Rhodes and Richard Winters. Or they got "suicided" — like writer Danny Casolaro, attorney Paul Wilcher and NSA Colonel Vince Foster. Etcetera. Etcetera.

Fighting Commies with Cocaine Profits: The Al Carone Story

"The CIA had predicted a large communist buildup in Latin America in the early 1970s," Carone told Tyree. "Operation Watchtower was initiated to preposition drugs in Panama/Central America from South America to fund covert actions against the predicted communist threat. The prediction became reality and the flow of cocaine into the United States increased as a result of the prediction. The American people wouldn't sufficiently fund a covert action anywhere following Vietnam for the amount of money which was needed. The cocaine couldn't be moved into the United States until an avenue was established that took the CIA out of the picture because the CIA was already busy fending off allegations of trafficking drugs out of Southeast Asia and Europe, and the CIA couldn't be tied in to the Latin America cocaine at all."

"Once Ronald Reagan became president," Carone continued, "his old-time friend William Casey, the head of the CIA, was able to convince him to sign Executive Order #12333 into effect which… took the CIA out of covert operations business, …authorized the use of private assets/entities to be used by the National Security Council to conduct covert operations including the drug [smuggling]… Allowing private assets and entities to do the dirty work meant the CIA could do whatever it wanted to do, in or out of the United States…"

In other words, EO #12333 essentially privatized CIA's drug smuggling, making the Agency even more insulated from discovery of its criminal activities.

"You had NSC staffers that were tied right into the drug trafficking themselves like Ollie North," Carone said, continuing his history lesson.

"Hell, his diary had everything in it. Between his diary and your wife's [Elaine Tyree's] diaries, the whole thing is blown. Totally compromised."

"I remember seeing him [North] write over 200 entries in his diary that related to major drug profits being used to buy weapons for the Contras," continued Carone. "The diary of Ollie North alone would prove what I've told you and show the violation of 50 USC, *403 and everything."

North's diary contained the following entry, "July 5, 1985 - $14 million to buy arms came from drugs." Unindicted drug kingpin Oliver North is still free, while William Tyree has served twenty years in prison. Why? Because corrupt officials in CIA, the Department of Defense and Department of Justice continue the cover-up.

Colonel Carone told Tyree that "Operation Watchtower provided cocaine that was sold to finance anti-Communist operations in Latin America because the US Congress has shut down general funding of anti-Communist activities in that area," while heroin trafficking by CIA in Southeast Asia was used to fight communism there.

Selling drugs to Americans to fight communism overseas has to be one of the biggest ironies of the twentieth century.

Carone also told Tyree that "he had delivered money to the Los Angeles based gangs, i.e. 'the Bloods and the Crips' which are among the most violent African-American gangs in the United States. He had delivered money to the gangs because they were on the CIA payroll under Executive Order 12333 which allowed for the CIA to hire outside sources to help the CIA perform their jobs.

He had delivered money to the gangs because they transported drugs across the United States, i.e., Atlanta, Norfolk, Philadelphia, New York and Boston."

Carone's revelations dovetail exactly with the in-depth investigations of Gary Webb in his book *Dark Alliance* (1998; Seven Stories Press).

In other information which informs recent American history, CIA operative Al Carone says that "George Bush was CIA prior to the assassination of John Kennedy in 1963" and that "the Governor of Arkansas that looked the other way at Mena [CIA's cocaine trans-shipping station] Bill Clinton was CIA back in the late 60s."

CIA agent Cord Meyer has often been named as Bill Clinton's handler, while the late Pamela Harriman has been cited as the proverbial "power behind the throne."

Green Berets – The CIA's Drug Running Gofers

Colonel Carone told Tyree "I've worked with Green Berets (Special Forces) all over the world... Most of the guys trained Contras in violation of the Boland Amendment at Special Forces 'A Camps' built on the border of Nicaragua and Honduras during the big buildup in the early 1980s. Hell, I saw the camps myself. A lot of the Green Berets from 7thSFG (A) were involved in the cocaine shipments that were brought into the 'A Camps' from Panama. These 'A Camps' were isolated. They were cut right out of the jungle in many cases with good runways."

"A lot of the Green Berets in Thailand for example helped with the drug flow," Carone continued. "These Green Berets knew that the deal was simple. Without drug profits, there were no Contras to train, as there was no equipment to train them with, as Congress cut off the funding."

"Without real world situations, everyone of those Green Berets knew that they would be sitting somewhere going through some boring routine with training. Many of them were either involved with drug shipments out of Latin America into the United States or simply looked the other way. And you know, the Green Berets out in the middle of nowhere won't tell on each other, as they have to depend on their teammates to survive."

George Bush, CIA and the JFK Hit

Carone also told Tyree that "he had taken money to a female named Ruth Paine in late 1956 on orders from William Casey [an OSS-CIA operative who was Director of CIA from 1981-1987]. Carone said that Paine was approached by the CIA to find and recruit an individual that was expendable with communist ties and some type of anti-American background…"

"Carone said that when Ruth Paine found the individual she notified her CIA contact identified as George DeMohrenschildt, who in turn contacted his CIA supervisor, identified as George Bush. Carone said that George Bush was the same George Bush that was CIA director. Carone said the individual located by Ruth Paine was identified as a Mr. Lee Harvey Oswald."

"FBI records/reports within 14 days after the assassination of President Kennedy will reflect that Mr. George Bush met with J. Edgar Hoover, as Bush was trying to ascertain what the FBI might have stumbled onto by mistake in regards to the Ruth Paine-Oswald connection."

The CIA's Global Money Laundry: Stephens, Riady, and BCCI

In his sworn testimony, Al Carone told Bill Tyree that "he was a paymaster for both US Military Intelligence personnel and CIA personnel when Tyree knew and worked with him."

"He [Carone] also worked as a representative of the Bank of Credit and Commerce International (BCCI) which he stated was a bank founded by the US Intelligence Community in part to finance Covert (Black) Operations worldwide without the approval of the US Congress."

"He was authorized to withdraw funds from First American Bankshares (aka BCCI) account #2843900, which he stated was a black operation fund unknown to the US Congress at the time." Moreover, Carone said that "he was the middleman between certain CIA factions and certain Mafia families that operated illegal enterprises in New York City."

"Carone told the Plaintiff [Tyree] that the CIA used BCCI, BNL, BCP and Intermaritime Bank to launder money for black operations worldwide and for the Mafia in New York City."

According to Tyree's lawsuit, "Colonel Carone said the military drug trafficking Operation Watchtower fit in the picture in the following fashion. Between 1971-72, BCCI was conceived and born primarily as a bank for the US Intelligence Community to go around Congress in funding so-called 'black operations.'"

"In December 1975, February-March 1976, Operation Watchtower took place that brought over 100 military-style cargo plane loads of cocaine out of Colombia into Albrook Air Station in Panama."

"In 1976, Arkansas businessman Jackson Stephens and Indonesian businessman Mochtar Riady formed Stephens Financial Ltd in Hong Kong which led to a meeting of Stephens and Riady with members of the BCCI."

"In 1977, Jackson Stephens invited BCCI into America and helped BCCI bring about the purchase of First American Bankshares, operated by Clark Clifford and Robert Altman."

How do these facts connect? Jack Stephens has been the financial backer of both the George Bush campaign and the Bill Clinton campaign for US President. The long and winding road of corruption has also led Stephens to purchase Alltel, whose subsidiary Systematics, used a version of the oft-purloined PROMIS software.

According to Tyree's lawsuit, "Jackson Stephens and Mochtar Riady were in business together and paid off politicians from Arkansas to look the other way and ignore the CIA cocaine operation at Mena, Arkansas. The Lippo Group, i.e. Mochtar Riady, had been involved with Bill Clinton since Clinton was Governor in Arkansas."

"Stephens, Riady and the CIA are in bed together," says Carone. "They own a lot of people. They have a lot of money. They get things done. I answer to Stephens indirectly. I answer to his money is who I answer to, and so does everyone else at the CIA that wants to get things done where Stephens has influence."

Just as Special Prosecutor Lawrence Walsh effectively covered-up the "high crimes and misdemeanors" of George Bush in the so-called 'Iran'- Contra Report, so Kenneth Starr has continued the cover-up of CIA drug trafficking with the Clinton-Lewinsky Sexcapades and the Clinton Impeachment.

FBI Agent Richard Taus Framed

When Long Island, New York based FBI Special Agent Richard M. Taus, a decorated Vietnam veteran, got too close to CIA drug-running, he was framed. Ironically imprisoned at "Clinton" Corrections Facility in Dannemora, New York, Taus is currently seeking an attorney to appeal his sentence.

How does it all tie in? Carone told Tyree that "you need to find out and uncover the business that involved Ollie North and George Bush called 'The Enterprise' as everything went through there."

According to Tyree's lawsuit, "Vincent Foster, a good friend of Governor Bill Clinton, often shuttled vast sums of money around the world that related completely to 'The Enterprise' formed by Ollie North and George Bush."

The Enterprise was also called "K Team." Taus has said that since his trial he has tried to "obtain records and files from the FBI concerning me, especially about my investigation into K-Team's involvement in the Iran Contra Arms Initiative. Finally in 1995, the Bureau acknowledged possessing 2,400 pages that mentioned the Irangate affair and my name — but I have never received them or any records on me — records that were used by the prosecution in my case against me, yet never shared with the defense."

Taus says that "it was my initial investigation into the organized crime case which evolved into the Pizza Connection Case that identified CIA involvement. And CIA's ugly head reared itself in many other FBI probes."

"I was convicted in January 1991, after a most unfair and outrageous county trial," writes Taus. "A CPL 330 motion was filed based upon a juror's undisclosed blood relationship to the District Attorney in Nassau New York and interview of jurors during the trial by investigating police officers as well as improper instructions to the jury by court officers, etc. The trial record shows judicial prejudice, prosecutorial misconduct, fraud, duress, misrepresentation, Rosario and Brady violations as well as numerous violations of my constitutional rights."

"I am seeking an aggressive and dynamic appellate attorney to handle my direct appeal in the 2nd Appellate Division, Brooklyn New York," writes Taus, adding "both my military and FBI records are impeccable. Given my former law enforcement background, I have done the legal research. There are only limited funds available for the appeal." (Richard Taus, 91A1040, LH, Clinton C.F., P.O. Box 2001, Dannemora, New York 12929)

CIA Coke: The Real Thing

The Big Media Cartel continues the cover-up of the CIA's criminal activities despite documented and cross-corroborated evidence detailed in books by whistleblowers Rodney Stich (*Defrauding America*), Michael Levine (*The Great White Lie*), Gary Webb (*Dark Alliance*), Celerino Castillo (*Powderburns*) and others.

In a book called *Compromised: Clinton, Bush and the CIA* (1994, S.P.I. Books), authors Terry Reed and John Cummings corroborate the Carone story in Tyree's lawsuit — a dirty and tangled web of drugs-and-gun-smuggling and money laundering in Arkansas during the late 1980s.

"The meeting had been called at Fort Robinson, an Army facility outside Little Rock, to get some problems ironed out," writes former CIA operative Terry Reed. "In addition to the governor [Clinton] and his aide, the guest list included Max Gomez [Felix Rodriguez], John Cathey [Oliver North], resident CIA agent Akihide Sawahata, Agency subcontractor Terry Reed and the man in charge, the one who would call the shots. He called himself Robert Johnson [It was CIA agent William Barr, later appointed US Attorney General by George Bush.] A lot of loose ends were to be tied up…"

"'Our deal was for you to have 10% of the profits, not 10% of the gross,'

Johnson sternly admonished Clinton. 'This has turned into a feeding frenzy for your good ole boy sharks. We know what's been going on. Our people are professionals. They're not stupid. They didn't fall off the turnip truck yesterday, as you guys say.'"

"This ADFA [Arkansas Development Finance Authority] of yours is double-dipping. Our deal with you was to launder our money. You get 10% after costs and after post tax profits. No one agreed for you to start loaning our money out to your friends through your ADFA so that they could buy machinery to build our guns. That wasn't the deal..."

"That's why we're pulling the operation out of Arkansas. It's become a liability for us. We don't need 'live' liabilities." (p. 234)

The long list of Clinton/Bush-related casualties is proof that live liabilities are definitely not on the CIA balance sheet.

Army Colonel Al Carone himself died on January 7, 1990 in Albuquerque, New Mexico. His medical records state "chemical toxicity of unknown etiology."

CIA cancer, anyone? Or is it, CIA — the cancer?

Dead Spooks Don't Lie

In the ongoing cover-up of the Bill Tyree frame, Ray Kohlman, Tyree's attorney, received a document called the Declaration of William Casey. In Kohlman's own affidavit, dated August 27, 1999, he states that "most of the contents of this affidavit can be proven" and that he "will testify to the contents of this affidavit in court."

Kohlman then filed the document in US District Court for the District of Columbia, November 8, 1999 as Civil Action No. 99cv2709, William M Tyree, Plaintiff v. Department of the US Army, Defendant. Judge Colleen Kollar-Kotelly entered a "Sealing Order" for the Casey Document marked "Top Secret." In a letter to this author, Tyree pointedly asks, "Why seal it — if it isn't authentic?"

(Please note the heavy irony and the specious reasoning of this dead member of the so-called "Greatest Generation," whose defense of his own criminality contains powerful insights into the aberrant psychology of the Ruling Class. The "Ends Justifies the Means" philosophy of the late former CIA Director William Casey also belies his jesuitical training and programming.

The following affidavit — Casey's rationalization of his heinous behavior and his cocaine trafficking, which he frames as a noble battle against the enemies of Western Civilization — should be required reading for every student of 20th Century History — and every student of psychopathology. Casey's *Apologia Pro*

Vita Sua is the classic defense of a world-class criminal.)

Declaration: I, William J. Casey, declare: I have found that freedom is a priceless commodity that demands constant vigilance to guaranteed [sic] its longevity.

I was assigned to the Office of Strategic Services (OSS, in London England during World War II. During that time I befriended a young German soldier named Gunther [Russbacher? He later became one of the key covert operatives of the CIA-US Secret Criminal Government, also called the Shadow Government]. I used Gunther and several other anti-Nazi German prisoners of war in OSS operations within Nazi Germany.

I knew this violated Geneva (War) Convention. I did not care. The Geneva Convention was but a set of rules governing man's atrocities committed in the name of political ideology. To wage war with rules is to prolong human suffering. Open warfare is the last resort of a civilized nation and must be used sparingly. Wars must be fought savagely utilizing all tools and tricks at hand. Gunther was a tool. Ignoring the Geneva Convention was the trick.

After I became Director of Central Intelligence (DCI) on January 28, 1981, I was approached and briefed by William Colby, former DCI. My history with Bill Colby is known. Colby notified me off the record of two operations he was still running in Latin America. Both operations were without the knowledge and consent of the United States Congress, President Ronald Reagan or even the United States intelligence apparatus. Colby identified the operations as "A-6" (RED MIST) and "A-7" (PROJECT SANDMAN). A-7 entailed smaller operations.

[Retired US Army Colonel William Wilson, a former Military Intelligence (MI) Officer who worked with the Office of the US Army Inspector General (IG) and who, like the late US Army Criminal Investigator William McCoy, also died under mysterious circumstances in November 1996, completed an exhaustive investigation of the Bill Tyree case, verifying the facts in the Cutolo document. According to Wilson's affidavit, he writes that "in the affidavit of June 6, 1996, at paragraph fifty five, I stated Mr. Tyree had been decorated in relation to the classified operations he participated in. Following the participation of Mr. Tyree in the Watchtower operation, he was called upon to serve his country in a variety of classified operations in Latin America, Africa and Pakistan. Our investigation found that these subsequent operations came under the general project referred to as SANDMAN. SANDMAN was a project of the United States Central Intelligence Agency (CIA). SANDMAN also involved soldiers of the United States military. The information about SANDMAN is limited. SANDMAN exclusively dealt with so-called "wet operations" (i.e. assassinations) and Mr. Tyree was involved in several assassinations that were verified by Special Forces soldiers we interviewed. This resulted in Mr. Tyree receiving a variety of decorations, which the US Army refuses to admit were ever awarded to Mr. Tyree."

Wilson also stated that "ironically during conversations I had with Mr. Colby, I learned that he had personally requested and attained a waiver be given to soldiers involved in WATCHTOWER and SANDMAN. One of those soldiers was Mr. Tyree. The waiver allowed Mr. Tyree to receive the decorations and Combat Infantry Badge (CIB) that Mr. Tyree was recommended for. The same decorations and CIB, that had to be sterilized from the records of Mr. Tyree. From my involvement in the CIA Program MK-ULTRA (Manufacturing Killers Utilizing Lethal Tradecraft Requiring Assassination), I was aware that waivers could be given in regards to meritorious action during the course of intelligence related operations." (Page 4 of Wilson Affidavit)

The Casey Affidavit continues: I was told that A-6 identified individuals and the build up of the communist threat in Latin America. Some intelligence collected in A-6 was used in TASK FORCE-157.

I was told that A-7 was "the Phoenix Program" of Latin America. It involved the assassination of the communist infrastructure throughout Latin America.

I was told that Colby authorized assets's [sic] involved in A-6 and A-7 to engage in narcotic's [sic] trafficking to finance both operation's [sic]. Colby engaged in similar operations's [sic] that I know of in Vietnam for the same reason.

Colby candidly informed me that he had prepositioned more than one million pounds of cocaine in Panama between December 1, 1975 and April 1, 1976. This was done with the aid of our gallant ally, General Manuel Noreiga. The cocaine was transported into El Salvador, Costa Rica and Honduras between 1976 and 1981. Colby now sat in front of me with hat in hand and requested my help in the delivery of the cocaine to the american [sic] market.

I was told that Colby was using a mutual friend of ours, Colonel Albert Vincent Carone, United States Army, Military Intelligence, to field A-6 and A-7. Al Carone is a charismatic patriot that General Joseph W. Stilwell introduced us to in late 1945. Beside the usual qualifications, Al Carone brought to the anti-Communist effort a direct connection to his longtime friend, Vito Genovese. Genovese was the head of the gambling and narcotics for the controlling mafia family in New York to which Al Carone was a made member. Carone is a friend of international fugitive Robert Vesco. Carone has several anti-Communist intelligence sources that include Maurita Lorenz, a friend of Fidel Castro. Al Carone is the younger brother of Dr. Pasquale Carone. Dr Carone worked for Central Intelligence on other matters.

Colby told me that profits from the propositioned cocaine would be laundered through Al Carone, the New York mafia and Robert Vesco, then redirected to the anti-Communist effort through Colby.

After discussion with Al Carone, I made the decision to bring the prepositioned cocaine into Mena airport, Mena, Arkansas. Central Intelligence has used Mena Airport on prior occasions. This time the cocaine is the tool. The trick was to ignore the law and avoid public scrutiny. We were helped in our efforts by William J. Clinton and William F. Weld.

By 1984 all prepositioned cocaine had arrived at Mena airport and additional cocaine sources were secured. Cocaine was being transshipped through Hangar Four and Five at Ilopango Airbase, El Salvador. My point man at Mena was Adler Berriman Seal (Berry [sic] Seal).

Bill Clinton has proved invaluable so far by containing the local law enforcement investigations into the intelligence activity at Mena. Bill Weld, as Assistant United States Attorney, was placed in charge of the Criminal Division of the Department of Justice. This was done so that Bill Weld could control investigations into Mena by federal law enforcement agencies. The placement of Weld has proved invaluable.

I ordered John Poindexter, Robert McFarland, and Oliver North to go outside normal channel's [sic] and use available assets, including the mafia, to ensure the arrival of the cocaine into Mena Airport. The arrival's [sic] occurred in no small part through the effort's [sic] personnel assigned to the National Security Agency (NSA) and Army Security Agency (ASA). The men and women of the NSA and ASA blinded early warning defense satellites and radar grid to enable the aircraft to land undetected at Mena Airport. The NSA and ASA operation's [sic] were SEA SPRAY and JADE BRIDGE.

I have learned that the course of the democratic struggle for Nicaragua and Latin America is beginning to swing in our direction I attribute this success to A-6 and A-7 which Bill Colby had the insight, precision and spine to carry out.

I take notice of the heroic efforts of Al Carone, Bill Clinton, Bill Weld, John Poindexter, Bud McFarland and Ollie North. Without these men, A-6 and A-7 would not have appeared.

Freedom is a priceless commodity. The amount of freedom you enjoy is a result of the amount of vigilance you invest.

[Please note the remarkable jesuitic casuistry, which possessed the man till he died.]

My actions may be recorded as criminal condemning countless american's [sic] to drug dependency. I don't care. All wars produce casualties. Generally the more violent the war, the shorter the length. My choice was either to stare down a protracted cold war guerilla insurgency in Latin America or use the means' [sic] available to finance and wage a violent war of short duration for democracy. I stand by my decisions. The tool is cocaine. The trick is to understand that the drug user had the freedom to make a choice. They chose the drug. I chose to use their habit to finance the democracy that all american's [sic] enjoy. To keep those american's [sic] safe from the communist threat knocking on our back door in Latin America. For a change the drug user will contribute to society.

I declare under penalty of perjury that the above facts are true and correct to the best of my knowledge and belief. Executed this 9th day of December 1986 in McLean, Virginia, William J. Casey.

BUSHWHACKED

Chapter 13

Mind Control Slavery for the New World Order

H IGH-TECH SLAVERY IS ALIVE and well on Planet Earth. Ever since World War II when the US Government's Project Paperclip sponsored the resettlement of about two-thousand high level Nazis in the United States, the technology of mind control programming has advanced rapidly.

"The Germans under the Nazi government began to do serious scientific research into trauma-based mind control," write Fritz Springmeier and Cisco Wheeler, authors of *The Illuminati Formula Used to Create an Undetectable Total Mind Controlled Slave*. "Under the auspices of the Kaiser Wilhelm Medical Institute in Berlin, Josef Mengele conducted mind control research on thousands of twins and thousands of other hapless victims."

Mengele, known as "The Angel of Death," was one of the approximately 900 military scientists and medical researchers, secretly exfiltrated into the US, where he continued his so-called "research" and trained others in the black arts of mind control. This work in behavior manipulation was later incorporated into the CIA's Projects Bluebird and Artichoke, which in 1953 became the notorious MK-ULTRA. CIA claims that these programs were discontinued, but there is no credible evidence that *The Search for a Manchurian Candidate* (the title of the definitive book by John Marks) was ever discontinued.

In fact, Captain John McCarthy, US Army Special Forces (ret.), who ran CIA assassination teams out of Saigon during the Vietnam War, has said that "MK-ULTRA is a CIA acronym that officially stands for 'Manufacturing Killers Utilizing Lethal Tradecraft Requiring Assassinations.'" Thus the CIA's official obsession with producing programmed killers through the MK-ULTRA program contained more than 149 sub-programs in fields ranging from biology, pharmacology, psychology to laser physics and ESP.

More recently new evidence points to the continuous use of so-called trauma-based programming techniques to accomplish the same goal. This includes the deliberate induction of Multiple Personality Disorder (MPD) in involuntary human subjects, in essence, human guinea pigs.

MPD has been reclassified by the American Psychiatric Association as Dissociative Identity Disorder (DID). The psychiatrists' bible, Diagnostic and Statistical Manual, (DSM-IV) characterizes it by "A. The presence of two or more distinct personality states, B. At least two of these identities or personality states recurrently take control of the person's behavior, C. Inability to recall important personal information that is too extensive to be explained by ordinary forgetfulness, D. The disturbance is not due to the direct physiological effects of a substance or a general medical condition." (p. 487)

No matter what name is assigned to the problem, however, to create this condition by conscious intent is an atrocity so depraved that trauma-based mind control programming remains the *defacto* Secret Holocaust of the 20th Century.

Known as the Monarch Project, it has been verified and corroborated by numerous survivors like Cathy O'Brien, author of *Trance-Formation in America*, Brice Taylor, author of *Starshine*, and K. Sullivan, author of *MK*.

No paper trail has been found which leads from the CIA's MK-ULTRA program to the Monarch Project — a catchword for mind control, which involves US military, CIA, NASA, and other government agencies.

Attorney John W. DeCamp's ground-breaking book about high-level pedophilia *The Franklin Cover-up*, also describes the sordid details of Monarch. "Drugs are not the deepest level of government-sponsored evil," he writes. "I think the lowest level of Hell is reserved for those who conjured up and carried out the 'Monarch Project.' 'Monarch' refers to young people in America who were victims of mind control experiments run either by US government agencies such as CIA or military intelligence agencies."

DeCamp's client, Monarch abuse survivor Paul Bonacci, has a story which parallels the experiences of O'Brien, Taylor and Sullivan — an extensive cross-corroboration of perpetrators and their methodology. It's simply "the production of a horde of children in whom the soul is crushed, who would spy, whore, kill and commit suicide," in the words of investigative reporter Anton Chaitkin, quoted by DeCamp in his book.

Recovering Monarch victims speak of ongoing trauma through "ritual abuse," also known as "satanic ritual abuse," because of the identifiable iconography of a belief structure associated with Satanism. By using drugs, hypnosis, torture, and electro-shock, the Monarch criminal perpetrators have produced new and succeeding generations of victims.

This is not science fiction, but science fact. MPD involves the creation of personality "alters," alternate personalities or personality fragments, which can be used for specific tasks — illegal activities like delivering drugs or other black market activities (mules), or messages (couriers), or killing (assassins). These alters, or soul fragments, are segregated and compartmentalized within the victim's mind by the repeated use of stunguns, drugs, and hypnosis which isolate the memories of their experiences.

An alter can be accessed by anyone who knows the "codes" or "triggers." These triggers which induce an altered or trance state in a programmed victim can be anything including telephone tones, nursery rhymes, dialogue from certain movies, or hand signals.

According to Springmeier and Wheeler, whose 468-page book has become a reference in the field, "the basis for the success of the Monarch mind control programming is that different personalities or personality parts called alters can be created who do not know each other, but who can take the body at different times. The amnesia walls that are built by traumas form a protective shield of secrecy that prevents the abusers from being found out and prevents the front personalities who hold the body much of the time to know how their system of alters is being used."

The mind control programming, however, has not worked according to plan. In fact, the perpetrators, in their arrogance and hubris, never dreamed that their methods could fail. The retrieval of survivors' photographic-like memories of actual abuse incidents including images, sounds, and smells constitutes a major exposure of human rights abuses.

More on Illuminati Mind Control

According to *Conspirators Hierarchy: The Committee of 300* author John Coleman, "the Illuminati is very much alive and well in America... Since the Illuminati is also known as Satanism, it must follow that the CIA was controlled by a Satanist while Dulles had charge of it. The same holds true for George Bush [a member of the Order of Skull and Bones]."

"Given the ghastly mind control experiments constantly being conducted by the CIA and its past connections to fiendish monsters like Dr. Campbell and Dr. Sidney Gottlieb, it does not take much to conclude that the CIA follows satanic roads," Coleman concludes in his monograph "Illuminati in America."

With regards to "the brainwashing capabilities of the Tavistock Institute as well as US Department of Defense projects like the Advanced Research Project Agency," Coleman writes that "the bottom line of the projects is mind control as predicted by the book *The Technetronic Era* by Zbigniew Brzezinski. The project goes by the name Monarch Program and it is a vast project involving not only the CIA, but the Army, Air Force and Navy with all of their skills and vast resources."

Sullivan's Travels

The horrific torture, sexual abuse of children and pedophilia, also called "satanic ritual abuse," has been a key component in the creation of mind controlled slaves.

Mind control survivor K. Sullivan has written an astounding book called MK, a fictionalized account of her life, which describes the world of multiple personalities. Sullivan, a programmed assassin and sex slave, says she was abused and raped by Robert Maxwell, Henry Kissinger, George Bush and Billy Graham among others. One of her controllers was deceased CIA spymaster James Jesus Angleton, who was a KGB and Mossad asset himself.

In a recent interview, Sullivan spoke about her background as a "family-generational slave" to the elite and about her father, now deceased, who was initially her primary programmer. His cover was a church-going upstanding citizen, a professional mechanical and systems engineer with a curious interest in robotics.

"There were a number of people who trained, conditioned, then broke my will, broke my psyche, and programmed me in different altered states," she said in a recent interview. "My father was the one who did me the most. He did it through terror. He did it through torture. He was a very brilliant man, and he seemed to enjoy doing it to me and other children."

Confirming that "he was horribly abused as a child," she continues, "I know that for certain. His father was a Welsh Druid, who had been sold as a child to a ship captain who brought him over to the US — at least that's the mentality in my family, for slavery of children to be OK. I heard this from older family members. They've never denied it. But my grandfather was a covert Druid as well. I'm sure he brought the religion over with him. One of the things he would do is go to the graveyard near his house and dig up bodies and take them in the basement and take them apart and have fun with them. And he also did rituals out in the woods sometimes at night. He would sacrifice babies. And I was exposed to that. And so I'm sure my father was too, which left him no other alternative but to become like his father."

And how is this behavior related to Satanism or is it just generational child abuse? "I think it's both," she answers slowly. "And what it boils down to is these people are doing illegal activities. Criminals tend to find criminals. They tend to gravitate toward each other. It's amazing how they can find each other out. My grandfather developed connections to the Mafia in our area. I understand it was the Colombo family. I don't know what he did exactly, but I do have one memory of riding in a cement truck where he and other drivers with cement trucks were using the cement from the trucks to bury several bodies. So I guess they just did whatever needed to be done. That was in New York and Pennsylvania. My father was an assassin as well as other things and these people really enjoy killing people. He killed people more for favors than for hire. He got to have as many kids as he wanted to raise."

Her father also had CIA and NASA connections. "The CIA work seems to be rather covert. He worked for Western Electric and later on for AT&T," she said. "I found out, since then that Western Electric has had very strong CIA ties. I have been able to go through some of his papers, since his death in 1990, and I have found on his desk calendar for that year that he had several contacts with NASA. Since then I have remembered that there were several facilities that he took me to that were NASA facilities. The NASA connections seem to be directly connected to the [Operation] Paperclip connection. The Nazis were brought into the country and then were integrated into the NASA structure after the war."

"My father, because of his Celtic background, had very low self-esteem," continues Sullivan. "Being exposed to some of these Nazi war criminals seemed to mean a whole lot to him because he had a mother that was German. Between the Celtic background and a German mother, these men built up his self-esteem as being Teutonic as far as being Aryan. He very much identified with them, and I think, from what I understand, he got a lot of his training especially from one man I knew as Dr. Schwartz. He had slightly wavy black hair and very dark eyes. He was slim. I can't say his height because I was just a child. He had a definite German accent. People called him Herr Doctor or Dr. Schwartz, one of the two. Sometimes he was called Dr. Black. He was a pedophile for sure and he was a very cold man. He liked to make kids think that they would feel safe with him, but he would do something that would upset the children and then they would be afraid of him after that."

Multi-Mode Programming

Sullivan says that she was used to both sexually service males and females in the Beta mode and to do assassination, bodyguarding and intrusions in hostage situations in the Delta mode.

And what is Alpha, Beta, Delta, and Theta programming?

"Alpha was the basis for all the other programs," she continues. "It seems to be where a lot of information was stored in my memory, in my mind, that was used by programmers to develop the other programs. It's where some of my more generic alter states were also stored. Beta was the sexual servicing part of me. They also sometimes called the alter state 'Barbie.' It was supposed to be named after Klaus Barbie." Barbie Doll, get it?

Survivors Cathy O'Brien and Brice Taylor were also subjected to Beta, or sex-slave, programming. They, like actress Marilyn Monroe, were called "presidential models," mind-controlled slaves for the use of high-level politicians. According to Springmeier, "in 1981, the New World Order made training films for their novice programmers. Monarch slave Cathy O'Brien was used to make the film 'How To Divide a Personality' and 'How To Create a Sex Slave.' Two Huntsville porn photographers were used to help NASA create these training films."

Sullivan recalls that "in that state I was used both as a child and as an adult in those alter states, and I had more than one. In those alter states I wold not resist. I had no anger. I was an absolute sexual slave and I would do whatever I was told to do."

Delta programming is military-assassin programming, which has trickled into popular consciousness through movies like *La Femme Nikita*, its American remake *Point of No Return*, *Telefon* and *The Long Kiss Goodnight*.

Sullivan herself says that "it was when I was used to do hits, kills, and also bodyguarding and hostage extraction. I had a great number of alter personalities that had specialized training and had different modes to do different things."

Why was the training kept separate for different alters?

"Part of it was so I wouldn't recall too much at any one time — if I did start to remember," she says. "And also because they hand-pick each part out for a certain type of situation. If you had a part coming out that was very loyal to people that that part was bodyguarding, you don't want that part going off and killing somebody. And you don't want a part that's specifically programmed to kill coming out and feeling sorry for the target. So you have to keep the emotions and the motives separate as well. And so that's why they had to have different parts."

Sullivan's description of Theta programming seems to correlate to the development and use of so-called extra-sensory powers and extra-physical abilities. "Theta was where they used — I don't like the word psychic because I think it's been so misused, but it's where they used thought energy. I just knew it as magnetic type energy from the individual to do a number of different things that they were experimenting with including long distance mind connection with other people — even in other countries. I guess you would call it 'remote viewing' where I could see what a person was doing in another state in a room or something like that."

"It was both actual programming and experimentation. Because what they did — they kept it encapsulated in several parts of me — several altered states. It was a lot of training, a lot of experimentation."

Theta programming also implies the use of thought energy to kill someone at a distance. "A lot of times I ran across other victims with Theta programming," Sullivan said in a CKLN radio interview. "One of the movie and book themes they used extensively was *Dune* by Frank Herbert. It won't be too hard to figure because what they taught us was that we could cause things to happen to other people. It was to build up rage inside. It would come out in a form of pure energy that would hit them... They had talked about people imploding internally in their digestive organs. I don't know because I can't see what goes on inside another body, but I do know that it does work."

The calculated admixture of doing good and evil seems to be a hallmark of the Illuminati methodology. It's as if they recognize, at a spiritual level, that all the horrible karma they create can be balanced by generous philanthropic gestures, for example, giving a billion dollars to the UN, or other feats of extraordinary compassion.

"Also, they tried to use me for hands-on healing because I had a grandmother who was a healer from Sweden," says Sullivan. "So they were trying — that was me and several other survivors I talked to since — to use them in that mode also. And hands-on healing means that you would focus electromagnetic energy into the other person's body."

Taylor's Ordeal

Another book called *Starshine: One Woman's Valiant Escape from Mind Control* by Brice Taylor, a pseudonym, was published in 1995. Being a "presidential model," she also says she had many experiences with politicians promoting the New World Order. "What it means [being a presidential model] is that your program is to have sex with presidents — and I did overhear this — that different politicians were encouraged to use CIA escorts for sex, so they wouldn't be in a vulnerable position if they ever disclosed any national security secrets to anyone on the outside or for blackmail."

"My daughter and I were programmed," says Taylor. "When somebody is in the Project like I was (and you understand the intergenerational nature) Bob Hope who was my family's 'owner' looked at me like his 'thoroughbred' — that's what he called me. And my daughter followed in my footsteps as a 'presidential model.'"

"I went to his [Hope's] place in Palm Springs. The programming was done at military bases all over California. My daughter Kelly and I were both taken to his parties in Palm Springs and a lot of other places."

And how many sex-slaves did he have?

"I know there were more than me because there were parties where there were lots of them — women and children and boys. In his house, there were lots of rooms so that if any of these guys wanted sex with children, they would go in and make their selection."

The question arises that if she was under mind control, how did she figure out that Hope was her so-called "owner?"

"I have a memory of how he actually purchased me," she calmly replies. "There were whole fashion shows of sorts where everybody there must have been under mind control. We were modeling casual clothes, then real dressy evening attire, and then there was a real sexual act."

Like a Miss America pageant?

"Yes, except I believe they were all mind-controlled slaves. I had a whole repertoire of dancing and acts that went along with that. And then Bob purchased me."

And how would she characterize this so-called New World Order?

"It is an attempt to bring in a One World Government in which elite families have things the way they want. Their belief was that the planet was overpopulated and that something had to be done — psychological and biological warfare. They considered mind control as a tool, their ace-in-the-hole, something really different that would act as an invisible weapon."

Adventures with Henry the K and "The Council"

In her recovery Brice Taylor also has memories of being used by Henry Kissinger as a mind-controlled courier. "If you program someone to have a perfect photographic memory and total recall, then you have the capacity to be able to deal with many different tasks and assignments simultaneously," she explains. "Henry Kissinger created a 'mind-file' inside of my head. I would be sent around to all these leaders to keep their data — on some of their projects or whatever their agenda was — sorted. When I was sent in, I would be programmed by either Kissinger or Nelson Rockefeller. This was in the mid sixties."

But who's running the "show"?

"I think there's this other layer that I call the 'Council' in my book," Taylor explains. "I know that this is a group of men that stand head and shoulders above even Kissinger and the Rockefellers. They have been genetically engineered in a way that they have..." she hesitates, searching for the right words, "different leadership abilities and that they are actually the ones running the plan."

They refer to themselves as "The Council"?

"Yes. When I was telling other people within the intelligence community about it, they confirmed that they had heard them called the Council. The CIA has all these mind control operatives that are working for the Government. Then there's the Council, which also understands about the mind control project. But the Council is not CIA controlled. They could take someone like myself and be able to debrief me to find out what my agenda was."

According to Springmeier and Wheeler, this could be a reference to the Illuminati Councils, which coordinate the implementation of policy on a regional basis throughout the United States.

So they knew the codewords or triggers to activate your programming?

"Yes. It was a terrifying thing to have it happen. I remembered when I was first recovering, a long time ago I kept telling my therapist that I had the sense that it was like no one was in charge of me. I had the sense that they could grab me anytime. They knew from my programming that they could try to access information. I even had people that knew I had the information but had a Mob mentality that would kick me and abuse me in order to get the information. They didn't realize that I was a sophisticated piece of mind machinery that they would have to have actual codes to access me. Even though they tried to beat me up, they weren't able to crack open the information because it was locked under program."

More Bad Memories

But how did she first figure out she was suffering from MPD and that she was a programmed multiple? "It started in 1985," says Taylor. "I had a very serious car accident in which my head went through the windshield. I began to have memory flashes like a memory bleed-through from one alter to another. I think what occurred was I began having access to both sides of my brain. Before, with all the sophisticated programming, half my brain was shut away from me. Now the neuron pathways had opened up because of the accident. I know of other women who have also had memories come back."

So a severe blow to the brain had broken up the programming? "Exactly," she said. "What happened is memories began coming back. I was in school working on my master's degree in psychology, when a flood of memories came back. I have a closet full of journals. I wrote down everything I was remembering. Once I got to a certain level, I had a lot of therapeutic support because every time I'd start remembering I'd want to hurt myself or kill myself. I lost control of my body in a car on the freeway in the fast lane one time as I was trying to really understand how programming worked. I was trying to understand from inside, a part of me was trying to explain programming to me and I was on the freeway in the fast lane and I could not move my body. It was terrifying. These are the kinds of obstacles I had to constantly fight."

"When I deprogrammed I literally spent two years in my bedroom drinking coffee just writing everything down," she says. "They programmed me with perfect photographic memory. When memories came back, like the ones with Kissinger, I not only could hear his words and his voice, I could smell his cigar. I could smell his farts. I mean I could hear and see as I remembered everything in my mind."

Working Through the Bush League

Taylor also has memories of being used as an informational courier by George Bush, Sr. "There are people like myself who were spending time with all the world leaders to give them information and bring information back. George Bush had a number in my head that was his personal post office box. Many major leaders were involved."

And what kind of information would be left in this box?

"Information about different strategies or agendas that they felt were important not to lose or mess up. It was like a reporting place where they could keep data and dates organized without anyone ever knowing that these things were going on at this level."

Like live-person voice mail?

"Henry [Kissinger] always said that a person's mind could be made into such a fantastic computer," she answers. "You know how Bob [Hope] was always connected to all the presidents. Well, because of him, I also was. I became like a major tool to bring in this New World Order — by aiding the global elitists with mind-files and having sex and delivering the messages."

"Bob Hope was blackmailing affluent people left and right at his parties. My daughter was being prostituted to different politicians by the time she was three years old. George Bush was one of them. I don't know if you heard this, but George Bush was so arrogant that he had a lot of children that were created and programmed to be presidential models purposely named 'Kelly,' so he wouldn't have to worry about getting the name wrong. And there are 'Kellys' that have been prostituted to George Bush, who is a pedophile, all over the country. Many are in institutions, or like my daughter who's in very serious condition. My daughter, for the most part, is now catatonic and drools much of the day. I have two others who have absolutely no clue that they are programmed. They have been programmed with the highest level programming on this planet. Kids are programmed as a 'human resource.'"

Coincidentally or not, Cathy O'Brien's daughter is also named "Kelly."

The Charles and Di Operation

"They collected research on the people they would target," says Brice Taylor. "I'll give you a very specific example of one I was involved in — the monarchy in England. Their strategy, with Henry Kissinger as their mastermind, was to be able to destabilize the monarchy in England — and any kind of government in any other country — so that when they came to the One World Government they wouldn't have a lot of stability or unity in the country to stop it."

"I was actually flown to England, but part of it was done here," she says. "The Rockefellers were in tight with the Royal Family and they would bring Charles and Di here when they were first married. They had a plan from early on. It may have even been before they were married; I don't know. They had a plan to be able to take these people and destroy their marriage in front of the public and make them look so stupid and bizarre that people would have no faith in this monarchy."

Was the whole disintegration of the Charles and Di marriage pre-planned and instituted as a public pageant?

"They had a whole agenda to promote Charles and Di," says Taylor. "They actually brought them here. They would put them up in a hotel somewhere and take the children to Disneyland where they would probably be programmed as well. I was pre-programmed by them to leave special things in their hotel room. They created a scenario where I would be used at times as a prostitute with Charles, although he was not that sexually oriented. But I would implant the agenda in him to creating in him certain attitudes about his wife."

"For instance, I would say 'I can understand you're such an incredibly intellectual man, and you're married to a woman who can only think far enough to worry about what her hair and her clothes look like.' Basically, they did this back and forth. I'd end up having sex with him and giving him all this information they programmed me to give him. Then I would go to Di and say to her — when Charles was somewhere else — 'I can understand how hard it must be for you to be with a man who's as not that sexual when you're such a beautiful woman.' I mean they just worked it. They had done so much research on their personality profile. And this was under the direction of Kissinger and Rockefeller."

More Celebrity Perps

Who are some of the other world perps that Brice Taylor was involved with? "Well, Frank Sinatra and his Mob. I don't know if he was a multiple, but he hurt me," says Taylor. "He was a perpetrator. Michael Jackson. I watched him be hurt and used in pornography as a child even in conjunction with Bob Hope and a lot of Hollywood people. There was a situation where he was performing with his brothers and they were hurting all of them. Sammy Davis Jr., Dean Martin — that whole Rat Pack were all involved. They were all perpetrators."

Taylor's Satanic Ritual Abuse Experiences

So-called ritual abuse is a constant in mind control survivors' experience.

"From the time you're born, you are subjected to physical torture," explains Taylor. "Near death drowning. Physical beatings. Sexual abuse. Drugging. All kinds of psychological tortures that create dissociative barriers. My father did that intentionally and he would name 'personalities.' He would make up names for them. My father early on created a personality called 'Laura' who was my school personality. There was so much abuse going on that there was no way I could have been functioning well at school without an alternate personality."

These rituals were used to intentionally traumatize the mind and the soul. But did the abusers ascribe some occult significance to it?

"My satanic abuse happened within a Baptist Church and a Catholic Church," says Taylor. "I was sexually abused in all of them, right within the church. They never worshipped Satan, instead it was a twisted perversion of Christianity. There were rituals out in the field, in the dark of night, with people's blood. Raping children. Having orgies. Killing. Cannibalism. All of that was done when I was really young. And as I grew older that kind of ritual seemed to stop and was intermittent as they started to bring in more of the electronics, more sophisticated programming which they would have done at UCLA or at military bases."

"It was very confusing. It was almost worse, because instead of saying Satan, they would say Christ. Because then when I would understand what had happened later on I would have been able to recognize it as satanic. It's even more satanic, I think, to do that kind of thing in the name of Christ."

"In my book I talked about one minister. After he sodomized me or used me to perform oral sex on him, he would say to me that I was going to hell for what I had just done; that I could ask God to forgive me, but that he would never love me. I believe that there are two levels of this where all these people that were doing these things were also in a generational ritual abuse system. I think that the mind control experts could then jump in and utilize these people who were already dissociated. I tell the therapists that I counsel 'don't get stuck on all these satanic belief systems. Just know that the reason it was done was to intentionally create the dissociative barriers which are needed for mind control.' They

would stick pins and needles in me all the time, in my feet, in my vagina, everywhere, and they would call on different forces."

The Satanic-Ritual-Murder Connection

Missing children, sexual abuse of children and pedophilia around the world
all point to the involvement of an organized network of high-level criminals who
covertly control the legal system. Former FBI agent and private investigator Ted
Gunderson agrees. He claims that "there's a considerable overlap from various
groups and organizations, but one of the driving forces is the satanic cult movement today."

In his video "Satanism and the CIA's International Trafficking of Children,"
he mentions the notorious black magician Aleister Crowley as the "inspiration"
of the current problem. "The Satanists have used his writings as a guide," he says,
referring to Crowley's *Magick in Theory and Practice*.

In Chapter XII, "Of the Bloody Sacrifice," Crowley writes that "it would be
unwise to condemn as irrational the practice of those savages who tear the heart
and liver from an adversary while yet warm. In my case it was the theory of the
ancient magicians that any living being is a storehouse of energy varying in
quantity according to the size and health of the animal and in quality according
to its mental and moral character. At the death of this animal, this energy is lib-
erated suddenly. The animal should therefore be killed within the circle [the
satanic circle] or the triangle as the base may be so its energy cannot escape."

"An animal should be selected whose nature accords with that of the ceremony. Thus by sacrificing a female lamb, one would not obtain any of the quantity of fierce energy useful to the magician who was invoking Mars."

"In such a case, a ram would be more suitable. And this ram should be virgin
— the whole potential of its original total energy should not have been dimin-
ished in any way."

"For the highest spiritual working, one must accordingly choose that victim
which contains that greatest and purest force. A male child of perfect innocence
and high intelligence is the most satisfactory and suitable victim." (p.94)

"We're talking about human sacrifice here," says Gunderson.

More recently the so-called "tradition" of human sacrifice has been promoted
by the late Anton LaVey, founder of the Church of Satan, who wrote in the
Satanic Bible, "the only time a Satanist would perform a human sacrifice would
be if he were to serve a twofold purpose; that being to release the magickian's
wrath in throwing a curse and more importantly, to dispose of a totally obnox-
ious and deserving person." (p.88)

Note the casual reference to murdering someone because he or she "displeased" the Satanist-black magician. Ding-dong, LaVey is dead, but his crimes live on. He's been named by several of his victim-slaves as a mind control perpetrator. After all, the late perp himself wrote in the Satanic Bible that "the ideal sacrifice may be emotionally insecure, but nonetheless can in the machinations of his insecurity cause severe damage to your tranquility or sound reputation."(p. 90)

The Satanists after all follow Crowley's injunction, "Do what thou wilt. That is the law." In other words, Satanists as gods themselves will decide what to do — bypassing God's laws, as well as the laws of men. It sounds like the *modus operandi* of the Illuminati. Try, if you can, to tell them apart.

Gunderson continues, "In my estimation, there are over 3 million practicing Satanists in America today. How did I come up with these figures? I have informants. For instance, in the South Bay area of Los Angeles with a population of 200,000, he told me there are 3,000 practicing Satanists. That is where the well-known McMartin Preschool Case took place. I have an informant in Lincoln, Nebraska. In Iowa City, Iowa, a town of 150,000 — 1,500 Satanists. It averages to about 1.5% of the population."

Gunderson asserts that "50,000 to 60,000 individuals are sacrificed every year. There are about eight satanic holidays." The sick joke of it all? The FBI keeps a count of stolen or missing cars, but has yet to keep a tab on missing children in America.

Crypto-Satanist in the FBI?

You shouldn't be surprised to know that FBI Supervisory Special Agent Kenneth V. Lanning of the Behavioral Science Unit of the National Center for the Analysis of Violent Crime denies the existence of satanic ritual abuse in his 1992 "Investigator's Guide to Allegations of Ritual Child Abuse."

Lanning's intellectual posturing and specious reasoning should be studied as a prime example of serpentine logic. His semantics are astonishing, as he claims that "the words 'satanic,' 'occult' and 'ritual' are often used interchangeably" and "it is difficult to define 'Satanism' precisely."

Maybe he should have asked Michael "Mikey" Aquino, founder of the Temple of Set, to help him out with his fantastic word puzzle problems.

Then Lanning frames the discussion of Satanism in "non-judgmental terms" writing that "it is important to realize that for some people any religious belief system, other than their own is satanic."

As Pilate asked, "What is truth?" Lanning asks, "What is Satanism?" He writes that at "law enforcement training conferences, it is witchcraft, santeria, paganism and the occult that are most often referred to as forms of Satanism. It may be a matter of definition, but these things are not necessarily the same as traditional Satanism."

In other words, he claims to know the difference between "traditional" and "non-traditional" Satanism — even though he denies its existence. A neat trick by the FBI shyster.

Then Lanning almost trips over himself, declaiming the impossibility of knowing the definition, dismissing satanic ritual abuse as a simple psychological problem — "Obsessive Compulsive Disorder."

Of course, if Lanning had taken the time to interview "true believers," he would know that Satanism is an actual belief system, based on the ritual performance of torture and murder to instill loyalty to Satan and in exchange for future rewards from the forces of darkness.

Lanning's denial — ignoring the evidence of mind-control atrocities and ritual abuse — is absolutely unbelievable.

Is Lanning then just a Crypto-Satanist? He's publicly denied it — and nobody has publicly "outed" him as one, but he didn't really have to bother.

His freedom of "religion" is supposed to be protected by the US Constitution, so he could be just a closet Satanist in the FBI, and it's nobody's business but his own.

Especially when he denies the existence of Satanism.

Fatal Justice Revisited

Private investigator Ted L. Gunderson was dragged kicking and screaming into the netherworld of Satanism, child kidnapping, drug smuggling, and other corruption.

Before he retired in 1979, Ted Gunderson was the FBI Special Agent in Charge (SAC), in Los Angeles. He headed the FBI office, where he had 800 men under him and a yearly budget of over US$24 million. Since then Gunderson's role as a private investigator and security consultant has led him to expose CIA drug dealing, child kidnapping and trafficking, mind control, and satanic murder-for-hire groups. He has also investigated many high profile cases like the Dr. Jeffrey MacDonald case, McMartin Pre-school case, Nebraska's Franklin Cover-up case, Oklahoma City Bombing case, Inslaw/Octopus case, and many other real-life criminal conspiracies.

"Shortly after my retirement, I was asked to investigate the Jeffrey R. McDonald case as a private investigator," says Gunderson. "He's a doctor who was convicted of murdering his wife and two children at Fort Bragg, North Carolina on February 17, 1970. I put in about 2,000 hours on the case. He had been convicted and sentenced to three consecutive life sentences."

"Much to my surprise, the evidence that I read, the information I developed, I've established beyond any question of a doubt that this man is absolutely innocent," says Gunderson. Jerry Allen Potter, author of *Fatal Justice*, agrees. His book is a powerful point-by-point refutation of Joe McGinniss's official cover-up book *Fatal Vision*.

"I obtained a signed confession from Helena Stoeckley, the girl in the floppy hat, for those who are familiar with the case," continues Gunderson. "She said Dr. McDonald did not commit these crimes. They were committed, she said 'by my satanic cult group. It was my initiation into the cult that night,' she said."

After a while Gunderson realized that the MacDonald case was a classic case of US government crime and cover-up. "She gave me detailed information about movements within the house. She told me she attempted to ride a rocking horse in the child's bedroom that night, but she couldn't ride it because the spring was broken. The only way she could have known that was to have been there that night."

"I submitted a 1100-plus page report in March 1981 to Judge William Webster who was then the head of the FBI with a personal letter to him and to the US Department of Justice. Much to my surprise, my 19 witnesses including Helena Stokely started calling me and telling me, 'Hey Ted, they're trying to get me to recant.' And I'm telling myself, 'That isn't the responsibility of the FBI. The FBI is supposed to gather information not destroy it.' And that was my first clue that we had a serious problem in that case and in the other cases I handled. I noticed in each instance that evidence was destroyed, lost, stolen, that there were strong indications of corruption."

"So I asked myself, 'What's going on here?' And over the years I started gathering materials. Up until about two years ago, I kept saying 'There's a loose-knit network operating in this country involving drugs, pedophilia, prostitution, corruption, etc.' From my research I'm convinced it's much more serious. It's much more than a loose-knit network. It is a conspiracy. And you know how the media goes after you when you use that c-word. And I'm going to prove it to you. By the way, this conspiracy involves pornography, drugs, pedophilia, and organized child kidnapping."

"My 'missing children' lecture documents that the Finders, an organization in Washington, D.C. is a CIA front," says Gunderson. "It's a covert operation involved in international trafficking of children." He is referring to a US Customs Service report, which states that the Finders case is to be closed because it is "an internal CIA matter."

That's an official way of saying "hands off."

Gunderson says, "These people, the satanic movement in the world, has set up preschools for the purpose of getting their hands on our children. The parents drop them off at nine in the morning and pick them up at night."

Far-fetched? Think again. In another quote from *The Law Is For All* by Aleister Crowley, he writes "Moreover the Beast 666 [Crowley's reference to himself] adviseth that all children shall be accustomed from infancy to witness every type of sexual act as also the process of birth, lest falsehood fog and mystery stupefy their minds whose error else might thwart and misdirect the growth of their subconscious system of self-symbolism."

Sexual abuse of children and mind control may be just a tenet of "faith" for the Satanist-believer-programmer. Or it may be symptomatic of a larger struggle on a cosmic scale. For instance, peering into the face of Absolute Evil, Dr. M. Scott Peck, author of *The People of the Lie*, writes that "at one point I defined evil as 'the exercise of political power that is the imposition of one's will upon others by overt or covert coercion in order to avoid... spiritual growth.'"

Psychologist Erich Fromm, author of *The Heart of Man*, proposes this struggle between Good and Evil as biophilia (the love of life) vs. necrophilia (the love of death.) "The necrophilous person is driven by the desire to transform the organic into the inorganic, to approach life mechanically as if all living persons were things," writes Fromm. "The necrophilous person can relate to an object — a flower or a person— only if he possesses it; hence a threat to his possession is a threat to himself... He loves control and in the act of controlling he kills life... 'Law and order' for them are idols..."

Sound familiar? In the end, mind control and ritual abuse may be the religion of the living dead.

Or it might be just another name for satanic imperialism.

Bibliography

Coleman, John. "Illuminati in America," (1992) World in Review, 2533 N. Carson St., Carson City, Nevada 89706

Constantine, Alex. *Virtual Government: CIA Mind Control Operations in America* (1997) (Feral House)

DeCamp, John. *The Franklin Cover-up: Child Abuse, Satanism and Murder in Nebraska* $13; (Second Edition, 1996) AWT, Inc., P.O. Box 85461, Lincoln, Nebraska 68501

Marks, John. *The Search for the Manchurian Candidate: The CIA and Mind Control* (1980) (McGraw Hill)

Mind Control Foundation Website: http://www.mk.net/~mcf

Mind Control Series (CKLN-FM)

Website: http://www.mk.net/~mcf/ckln

O'Brien, Cathy. *TranceFormation in America*, (1995) $20

Potter, Jerry Allen & Fred Bost. *Fatal Justice: Reinvestigating the MacDonald Murders* (1997) WW Norton Co, New York, London

Springmeier, Fritz. *Bloodlines of the Illuminati*, (Second Edition, 1999) $20; (Ambassador House, P.O. Box 1153, Westminster, Colorado 80030)

Springmeier, Fritz and Cisco Wheeler. *Illuminati Formula Used to Create an Undetectable Total Mind Controlled Slave*, (1996)

Stratford, Lauren. *Satan's Underground* (1998) $10.95; (Pelican Publishing Co. P.O. 3110, Gretna, LA 70054)

Sullivan, K. *MK* (1998) $18; K. Sullivan, P.O. Box 1328, Soddy Daisy, Tennessee 37384

Taylor, Brice. *Starshine: One Woman's Valiant Escape from Mind Control*, (1995) $20; Brice Taylor Trust, P. O. Box 655, Landrum, South Carolina 29356

Chapter 14

Monarch Mind Control Victim Awarded $1 Million

U S GOVERNMENT MIND CONTROL programs, like MK-Ultra and Monarch, directed against helpless victims — human guinea pigs — have been virtually ignored by the Big Media Cartel.

On February 27, 1999, however, US District Court Judge Warren Urbom found former Franklin S&L manager Lawrence E. King guilty of numerous crimes committed against mind control victim Paul A. Bonacci.

King, serving a 15-year sentence for his role in the theft of $40 million from Franklin, an Omaha, Nebraska credit union, was ordered by Judge Urbom to pay Bonacci $800,000 in compensatory damages and an additional $200,000 in punitive damages.

This legal judgment against a notorious perpetrator of satanic-ritual child abuse is unprecedented.

In the Memorandum of Decision, Judge Urbom wrote "King continually subjected the plaintiff [Bonacci] to repeated sexual assaults, false imprisonments, infliction of extreme emotional distress, organized and directed satanic rituals, forced the plaintiff to 'scavenge' for children to be a part of the defendant King's sexual abuse and pornography ring, forced the plaintiff to engage in numerous sexual contacts with the defendant King and others and participate in deviate sexual games and masochistic orgies with other minor children."

"He [Bonacci} has suffered burns, broken fingers, beatings of the head and face and other indignities by the wrongful actions of the defendant King," the judge declared. "In addition to the misery of going through the experiences just related over a period of eight years [1980-1988], the plaintiff has suffered the lingering results to the present time."

"He [Bonacci] is a victim of multiple personality disorder, involving as many as fourteen distinct personalities aside from his primary personality," wrote the judge. "He has given up a desired military career and received threats on his life. He suffers from sleeplessness, has bad dreams, has difficulty holding a job, is fearful that others are following him, fears getting killed, has depressing flashbacks, and is verbally violent on occasion, all in connection with the multiple personality disorder and caused by the wrongful activities of the defendant King."

Franklin Cover-up

Bonacci's lawyer, John DeCamp, has waged a long, lonely and expensive legal campaign in exposing crimes involving an international pedophile-pornography ring.

In 1991, DeCamp filed a 12-count suit in federal court, charging sixteen prominent individuals and institutions, including Lawrence E. King, *Omaha World Herald* publisher Harold Andersen and the Omaha Police Department with conspiracy to deprive Paul Bonacci of his civil rights. DeCamp's suit detailed slander, false imprisonment, child abuse, assault, battery and infliction of emotional distress suffered by Bonacci.

The complex case also involved high-level politicians, business leaders, judges and police officials with connections to the drug distribution-money laundering operation known as "Iran"- Contra which goes back to then Vice President George Herbert Walker Bush. Initially called "Operation Brownstone," it was a black-ops used to entrap and compromise politicians with underage boys.

DeCamp, a former Nebraska State Senator, even wrote a ground breaking book about the sordid history of the case called *The Franklin Cover-Up: Child Abuse, Satanism and Murder in Nebraska.*

Monarch Project

"The horrendous Monarch Project refers to young people in America who were victims of mind control experiments run either by US government agencies such as the Central Intelligence Agency or military intelligence agencies," writes DeCamp.

"The story told by Monarch victims — one of whom was Paul Bonacci — is that they were tortured for the purpose of creating 'multiple personalities' within them," DeCamp continues from his book. "These multiple personalities could then be programmed — as spies, 'drug mules,' prostitutes or assassins."

An article by Anton Chaitkin quoted in the book states that "professionals probing the child victims of 'Monarch' say there are clearly two responsible elements at work: the government/military, and cooperating satanic (or more exactly pagan) cults. These are multi-generation groups, whose parents donate their own children — who are proudly called 'bloodline' or simply 'blood' cultists — to be smashed with drugs and electric shock, and shaped. Other children are kidnapped and sold into this hell, or are brought in gradually through day-care situations."

"Paul Bonacci and other child victims have given evidence in great depth on the central role of Lt. Col. Michael Aquino in this depravity," continues Chaitkin. "Aquino, alleged to have recently retired from an active military role, was long the leader of an Army psychological warfare section which drew on his 'expertise' and personal practices in brainwashing, Satanism, Nazism, homosexual pedophilia and murder."

DeCamp's victory in court and the million dollar judgment is a vindication of mind control survivors Paul Bonacci, Alisha Owens and others who were falsely imprisoned to keep them from testifying against their abusers.

Police and FBI Cover-Up

According to the sworn testimony of Noreen Gosch, an activist on behalf of "Missing Children," whose own 12-year old son Johnny, a West Des Moines, Iowa paperboy kidnapped in 1991, was drugged and sold into prostitution and pornography, "there was no law on the books in Iowa or most any other state in the country specifying that the police would have to act sooner than 72 hours — even though we had five witnesses that could describe the car, the man and various details of the kidnapping. So I wrote the first piece of legislation which became the Johnny Gosch bill."

Gosch also alleges that the FBI was active in quashing a TV expose. "Just prior to the *America's Most Wanted* story going on the air... within a week or two of air time, the FBI in Quantico, Virginia contacted *America's Most Wanted* and told them to kill the story," Gosch continued.

"They did not want the Johnny Gosch story broadcast," she says. "The only reason the story went on is because John Walsh is a personal friend, and he stood up to them, and he said this story goes. This woman does not lie. I've known her for years. We're going with the story. You can fire me afterwards. We're doing the story. And they did the story. But the FBI tried to kill this story."

When DeCamp, the attorney, asked her if she knew why, she replied, "Well, of course. It would have opened up the biggest scandal in the United States, bigger than the Iran-Contra story."

The Satanic-Military-Mind Control Connection

Continuing her sworn testimony, Noreen Gosch spoke about "the MK Ultra program developed in the 1950s by the CIA. It was used to help spy on other countries during the cold war because they felt that the other countries were spying on us. It was very successful."

"...Then there was a man by the name of Michael Aquino. He was in the military. He had top Pentagon clearance. He was a Satanist. He's founded the Temple of Set. And he was also a very close friend of Anton LaVey [the late founder of the Church of Satan]. The two of them were very active in ritualistic sexual abuse. And they deferred funding from this government program to use this experimentation upon children where they deliberately split off the personalities of these children into multiples, so that when they're questioned, or put under oath, or questioned under lie detector, that unless the operator knows how to question a multiple personality disorder they turn up with no evidence."

"They use these kids to sexually compromise politicians or anyone else they wish to have control of," Gosch continued. "This sounds so far out and so bizarre. I had trouble accepting it in the beginning myself, until I was presented with the data. We have the proof. In black and white."

DeCamp asked her "you know that Colonel Aquino was drummed out of the military?"

"He was," replied Gosch. "But then there were no charges filed against him that stuck [the San Francisco Presidio child abuse allegations]... I know that Michael Aquino has been in Iowa. I know that Michael Aquino has been to Offutt Air Force Base [described by numerous victims as a center of mind control-ritual abuse]. I know that he had contact with many of these children."

Bonacci's Story

One of the most heart-rending parts of the court transcript is the testimony of Paul A. Bonacci, the mind control victim-survivor, on whose behalf DeCamp sued Lawrence E. King.

Bonacci testified that King took him on many trips to Washington, D.C., Kansas City, Chicago, Minnesota and Los Angeles, where he prostituted the kidnapped and drugged youngster to the rich and famous — and depraved.

Bonacci said that "one person I'm not afraid to talk about because Larry King always said him and this guy were on opposite ends of the field because this guy was a Democrat and Larry King was a Republican... And this guy — every time I see him on TV, my wife knows my hatred for him... His name is Barney Frank."

When asked if he had "relationships" with him, Bonacci replied, "In

Washington, D.C. And also I was sent to a house, I believe it was in Massachusetts in Boston where I believe it was his house because there's pictures on the wall with him and different people and stuff, that he had met I guess, but it was in his basement."

Suffering from Multiple Personality Disorder, currently called Dissociative Identity Disorder (DID), Bonacci testified that as one of his alters called Wesley, he lured Johnny Gosch into the van when he was kidnapped.

"I went up to him, asked him [Gosch] a question," said Bonacci. "At that point he was close enough to the car where Tony [another kidnapper] had pulled up in the van and they pushed him in the car and they had a rag with chloroform in the bag that they had us stick over his face. And then put it back in the bag after he was out... We drove several miles... we met up with a station wagon and a van several times."

After switching vehicles and changing direction, the kidnapping of Johnny Gosch was over.

More Chilling Memories

When the judge asked Paul Bonacci if Lawrence E. King ever sexually abused him, he answered "Yes, he did on numerous occasions." How many times would you estimate, the judge then asked. "Probably a couple of hundred. Within all of the different personalities. Beginning at the time I was approximately 12 or 13 years old. Up until I was about 17 or 18."

And what was his primary duty, according to directions he received from Mr. King, asked the judge. "It depended on what was needed," replied Bonacci. "Most of the time it was to compromise politicians so he could get whatever he wanted from them... If they wanted to get something passed through the legislature or whatever, he would put some people that were against it in a compromising position, by using us boys and girls."

And how often was he used at these "parties" in Washington?

"Kind of hard to say," replied Bonacci. "Because there were times when there would be four or five in a night. And I hardly knew, I didn't know most of them. But probably a couple thousand times."

New Ramifications

Since the judgment in favor of Paul Bonacci contradicts the previous findings of the US Attorney, Nebraska Attorney General, and the entire judicial system regarding the "Franklin Cover-Up," DeCamp has issued an open letter challenging the verdicts of the last ten years of court battles regarding this case and its principals.

DeCamp wrote that "I believe that the US Attorney has no choice but to either charge the witnesses with perjury having testified under oath in a federal court... or the US Attorney has an obligation to investigate further into the Franklin saga and reopen matters."

"This time there are pictures [tens of thousands of pornographic photos taken by Rusty Nelson]," continues DeCamp. "This time Rusty Nelson [King's former porno-photographer] exists and testified completely contrary to Chief Wadman's testimony under oath to the legislature. This time Noreen Gosch validated the credibility and story of Paul Bonacci... At a minimum some Federal or State authority has an obligation to reopen the Alisha Owen case."

Alisha Owen, another mind control victim, was sent to prison for 15 years for refusing to recant her testimony against her abusers, namely former Omaha Police Chief Wadman.

Despite this victory, the mind control cover-up continues — as long as Alisha Owen and others remain in prison. And the Monarch Program? As more and more survivors appear and give eyewitness accounts of mind control atrocities, these outrageous human rights abuses — the Secret Holocaust of the 20th Century — will finally become common knowledge.

Chapter 15

Al Martin: The Man Who Knows Too Much

A L MARTIN IS THE MAN WHO knows too much. About government fraud at the highest levels. About Iran Contra. And about the conspirators who still continue their dirty work.

He's a self-described fourth level "player," just below George and Jeb Bush, and he has first-hand knowledge of the dirty deals and scams that never stopped.

Why is this story still important? Because these frauds are ongoing (they just roll them over) and they continue to cost taxpayers billions of dollars a year.

In the past, Lt. Cmdr. Al Martin (U.S. Navy, Ret) has testified before Congress for the Kerry Committee and the Alexander Committee, which investigated the illicit deals of so-called Iran-Contra.

Al Martin's memoir, *The Conspirators: Secrets of an Iran Contra Insider*, is an astonishing true crime story that has been too hot for prime time. In fact, it's an unprecedented exposé of high-level government crimes, coverups and scandals.

The book includes eye-witness accounts of US Government-sanctioned narcotics trafficking, illegal weapons deals, and an epidemic of securities fraud, real estate fraud, banking fraud and insurance fraud by high-level government perps.

These criminal perpetrators are members of the cryptocracy, those who rule from the shadows of government. In his landmark historical study, *Operation Mind Control*, author Walter Bowart describes the cryptocracy as "a secret bureaucracy still supported by all the power of the federal government, but which operates outside the chain of government command." Former Assistant

Secretary of State Elliott Abrams called it "a shadow government in the United States," or in Al Martin's words, it's a "Government Within a Government, comprising some thirty to forty thousand people the American Government turns to, when it wishes certain illegal covert operations to be extant pursuant to a political objective."

Bowart describes the cryptocracy as "a technocratic organization without ideology, loyal only to an unspoken, expedient, and undefined patriotism... Its funds are secret. Its operational history is secret. Even its goals are secret."

Because of what he's experienced, Al Martin has been in hiding, a whistle-blower targeted by these very same bureaucrat-perps.

Secret History of Iran-Contra

"Iran-Contra" itself is a euphemism for the tremendous fraud perpetrated by government criminals for profit and control. Offhandedly, this inaccurate term entered history as shorthand for the public scandals of illicit arms sales to Iran coupled with illicit weapons deals for Nicaragua. The real story, however, is much more complex.

When George Bush, Bill Casey and Oliver North initiated their plan of government-sanctioned fraud and drug smuggling, they envisioned using 500 men to raise $35 billion.

When Iran-Contra finally fell apart, they ended up using 5,000 operatives and making $350 billion in covert revenues to fund their illegal secret operations.

One of Al Martin's primary roles was as a fundraiser for the bogus "War Against Communism" in Nicaragua. His expertise as a finance specialist served "The Cause." That's how Oliver North called his "Enterprise" of raising cash for secret illicit operations.

After he retired as from the Navy, Al Martin's life went into the fast lane as a black ops specialist and Office of Navy Intelligence (ONI) officer. In his memoir The Conspirators, Al Martin tells the facts that have been ignored or covered-up for over 15 years, ripping off the covers of the sleaziest secrets of the Washington power-mongers.

The book contains material never released before, like 1) The National Programs Office (NPO) and Operation Sledgehammer, 2) Oliver North: The Money Laundering Drug Smuggling Patriot, 3) "Do Nothing" Janet Reno and Iran-Contra Suppression, 4) Classified Illegal Operations: Cordoba Harbor and Screw Worm, 5) The Don Austin-Denver HUD Fraud Case, 6) Insider Stock Swindles for "The Cause," 7) US Government Narcotics Smuggling & Illicit Weapons Sales, 8) The Chinese Connection: US Weapons Scams, 9) The Real Story of Operation Watchtower, and 10) Bush Family Corporate, Real Estate, and Bank Frauds.

Because of his failing health, Al Martin has decided to go public and tell the whole story of the Iran-Contra Conspiracy. His book is an unprecedented revelation of the secret world of the US Shadow Government, a first hand account of his own personal involvement with Iran-Contra scams

Since he worked directly with members of the Bush Family and has personal knowledge of their criminal activities, Al Martin states unequivocally that both the Republican and the Democrat Parties were complicit in illegal fundraising and money laundering. In fact, he is so blasé about high-level corruption that he refers to it casually as "How the Real World Works."

His book *The Conspirators* is a secret history of the 20th century, an expose of unbelievable proportions, an uncensored version of what really goes on in the back rooms of realpolitik brokers and gofers.

Al Martin tells the facts and names names, which no one has dared write or publish before. He describes the hidden side of Washington in a story of true conspiracy that is breathtaking in its sweep. If you can imagine a system in which corporate and government insiders use the US Government, its agencies and programs as their own private piggy bank (a criminal and privatized "public sector," if you will), you can understand the all-pervading levels of corruption and criminality that thrive in Washington.

In a recent interview, Al Martin decided to share some of his knowledge of this covert world of global fraudsters, unsuspected by most of the inhabitants of Planet Earth.

Lawrence Richard Hamil: International Man of Mystery

At a meeting with General Richard V. Secord and government-sponsored con man Lawrence Richard Hamil, Martin was briefed about Iran Contra operations and allowed to view CIA white papers on "Operation Black Eagle," code name for the illegal program of narcotics trafficking, massive fraud and weapons deals.

"Hamil was the type of guy who had a big ego, and he liked to impress people," says Martin. "I thought he was trying to impress me because of the level of his access, but it was much more sublime than that. He knew that later on these documents would become increasingly valuable as Iran-Contra would start to fall apart."

The documents he showed Martin revealed an operation that was basically government-sanctioned fraud, a "license to steal," as it were, in other words, a government-protected racket.

"Hamil was a master of 'The Game,' one of the best in the United States," Martin says. "He's one of the best political manipulators behind the scenes to ever come down the pike. He is not just a simple con man, a government-connected swindler and money launderer, as people seem to think. He was very deeply involved in all sorts of political deals at the same time. In late 1984, Hamil undertook a separate operation. He began dispensing money to House and Senate Republicans, and I don't think anyone else knew this."

The payoffs and systemic corruption were just "business as usual," according to Martin. "you have to look at the states where Hamil did a lot of business. Not only are they states controlled by Republicans, but they are also states where Hamil passed out a lot of envelopes. Illinois, Tennessee, Kentucky. On three occasions, I met then Governor Thompson of Illinois. We met him and his aide several times, in the bar at the Whitehall Hotel in Chicago [to pass envelopes of cash to him]. Also to the governor of Kentucky, Martha Collins."

You've heard of COD (Cash On Delivery), but to maintain this level of fraud requires CIE. That's Cash In Envelope.

Al Martin's Covert Ops Career

And how did he start? "I was in the Naval Reserves for a long time," he continues. "How I actually got involved was in 1975, with an old chum of mine George W Carver III, son of George W. Carver Jr., one of the then Deputy Directors of Intelligence for the CIA. He was DDI on their Central and Southern Desk. Actually I volunteered for ONI [the Office of Naval Intelligence.] I went from being a lowly 'G' (G's were essentially citizens who kept their eyes and ears open) They weren't looked at as particular assets or resources. Apparently, I did a pretty good job.

"We were in Peru," he continues. "At the time the country had a military dictatorship and its political line was officially pro-Moscow. There were about 4,000 so-called Russian advisors in Peru at the time. Peru has always been a problem for Washington because of the number of Russians in the country. The Russian military presence increased for another two years until the installation of civilian president Bernando Terry. In 1975, my function was to simply keep an eye out on any movement of Russian troops."

So did he realize that Peru would become a staging area for CIA cocaine production and trafficking? "I didn't notice any organized effort in narcotics trafficking when I was there," he replies. "But I knew the CIA Deputy Station Chief in Lima at the time, the famous 'Buzz' Barlow, Eugene 'Buzz' Barlow."

"As you well know, the Tingo Maria area of Peru became a focal point of cocaine processing," I pressed on. "That wasn't until after the Russians were kicked out," he answers. "The only thing the CIA seemed to care about at the time was perpetually subverting Soviet interests in Peru and continuously attempting to establish a narcotics base of operations as it were. But the Russians would continually frustrate that. They [the Agency] wanted to establish a network of narcotics traffickers within Peru who would cooperate with the Agency."

Was CIA looking forward to a time when the Soviet presence would be gone and they could step in? "They were trying to build a network," Al answers. "That was already in the process, when I was there in 1975. I lived in Central and South America from 1975 to late 1979 — early 1980. Then I became involved in smuggling American Express cards into Argentina. I also became involved in circumventing the Dominican sugar embargo of 1981. That's how I first met Hamil, from weapons sales to Argentina during the so-called Falklands War in 1982.

"As you can imagine, the CIA could not be put in the political position of helping Argentina during the Falklands War. The American Express Card Affair in Argentina and the subsequent subversion of the Dominican Sugar Embargo were CIA-instituted. Through the operation in Argentina, I also met the famous Carlos Cardoen, the Chilean arms merchant. That was simply business.

"In my service career as an active officer, I was never involved in anything covert," Al continues. "That came later. Also there has never been a whole lot of interagency cooperation. There has never been a truly joint operation between the CIA and ONI. I know people like to say that, but the only people the CIA wouldn't step on to accomplish their aims was ONI. They would easily subvert an FBI or DEA investigation, but never ONI, because they were frightened of them."

In his book, Al writes, that contrary to popular belief, ONI is the most powerful US intelligence agency.

"The ONI already had a deep existing covert illegal structure. They had a mechanism before the CIA even existed. They had contacts in foreign intelligence services and in foreign governments that the CIA never could have hoped to obtain.

"Also ONI controlled its own assets, which the CIA had to build from scratch later on. The CIA can't control any of its own assets domestically because it's against the law for it to do so, thus the ONI is obviously in a superior position. For instance, you don't see an airfield that says 'Owned by the CIA' on it in the United States. The ONI doesn't have any such restrictions because it's part of the US Navy.

"ONI is where the real deep control is. It's where the real deep secrets are kept. That was what ONI always did the best. Keeping secrets. Accumulating secrets. Warehousing secrets for the purposes of control."

When I asked him what secrets? he replied, "One thing I can tell you is the

ONI was instrumental in dethroning former Mexican President Louis Portillo. Portillo got very friendly with George Bush and the CIA, and ONI had never aligned with the Bush faction. I know what people think, but that's not true. From what I can tell, it has never been aligned, but has always been hostile to that Eastern Country Club Bush Cabal and their friends in the CIA. The Bill Casey faction is the George Bush-Allen Dulles Faction.

The principals of the ONI faction are "people that you wouldn't know. Admiral Anderson. Admiral Garrett. Their power comes from the fact that they're not known. Their names wouldn't really mean anything, therefore, they can act in such a behind-the-scenes fashion — much more than the CIA. It's because of their established structure. They're very deep in old contacts. They've simply been around longer than the CIA. They are able to blend overt and covert operations in the same breath because they are essentially not a covert agency like the CIA. It allows them great cover to operate in the open."

Offshore Money Flows

"Follow the money" has always been an imperative in understanding the covert flow of revenues from the US "offshore," to tax-free jurisdictions where bits and bytes of monetary transactions can be hidden from public scrutiny.

For instance, so-called "Dutch Sandwiches" are well-known in certain well-heeled circles, including movie moguls like Saul Zaentz, recording impresario and *Amadeus* and *One Flew Over the Cuckoo's Nest* producer. The novel *Black Money* by Michael Thomas also deals extensively with them, as well as other arcane money laundry techniques.

When asked about them, Al laughs knowingly. When pressed further, he replies, "A Dutch Sandwich is a certain exotic money transaction. What allows it to exist is a peculiarity in the Dutch legal system and Dutch banking laws. You can retain a lawyer in the Netherlands for offshore trusts in the Netherlands Antilles, and you can give the lawyer exceptional power. He also has exceptional protection from Dutch law, as long as that lawyer is a Dutch citizen. If he is outside the Netherlands, then he can break certain financial laws with impunity. What you're talking about [Dutch sandwich] has been used in the past for the flow of monies. In Hamil's personal address book, he always had a bunch of names of Dutch law firms in Amsterdam and the senior law partners in those firms. I still have those names."

And where did the money from rich Republican donors go?

"The money went in two different directions," Martin answers. "Hamil had to pay some of the money over to Oliver North and Richard Secord. Otherwise he wouldn't have been allowed to operate. I know what the arrangements were with me. I imagine he had other arrangements with them. I know one of the principal accounts he used to pay into was the account of International Industries S.A. of San Jose, Costa Rica, which was an account controlled by Oliver North and Richard Secord. This very account, as a matter of fact, became public during the Kerry Committee Hearings of 1987. It was one of the principal accounts North used to launder money through.

"Surprisingly enough, from what I could see, North operated through very few accounts, of which Intercontinental Industries SA happened to be a big one.

He also operated through Secord's accounts. Secord had longstanding accounts and the names are quite famous. Stanford. Stanford Technologies Overseas. Stanford Exports Overseas. During Iran-Contra, when it came to the money end, anything with the word 'Stanford' in it was controlled by Richard Secord."

Another prime way of hiding the flow of money was through the use of tax-free foundations, designated 501c3 entities, by US tax code.

"That was a whole separate diversion scheme instituted by Senator [Jesse] Helms in collusion with Oliver North," Martin continues. "Money could be raised through a 501c3, then made tax-exempt for a seemingly charitable or innocuous purpose. Even political monies can be raised through tax-exempt organizations, and this is a quirk in the law — as long as they support a charitable purpose. This is when North came up with the idea of setting up all those medical clinics. He wanted to set up a string of medical clinics in Guatemala and Mexico. It was those medical clinics in concert with his partner Dr. Louis Oschner of New Orleans. He's a very famous name in covert circles. He was a longtime friend of Bill Casey. I don't know exactly what their relationship was, but North went to Oschner to set up a series of medical clinics. Supposedly tax free charities would fund these."

The entire Contra Clinic fable was a great cover story. "The real purpose of these clinics, by the way, was to treat Contra wounded because they didn't want a lot of Contra wounded coming to the United States for medical treatment and the obvious questions that would be raised. Therefore, North came up with this idea much closer to the scene, ostensibly for the purpose of treating Contra wounded. Of course, the reason it didn't happen is because there wasn't that many Contra wounded because they never engaged in any pitched battle with the Sandinistas. There were very advanced plans made and certainly a lot of money was raised. The clinics were never established, but a lot of tax-free money went into them."

The Brady Bond Scams and the Masters of Fraud

Al Martin has plenty of behind the scenes information about the career tracks of government insiders like Frank Carlucci, Richard Armitage and their Blackstone "investment" group.

Because of Blackstone's involvement in many high-level high-profile frauds like the Russian Bailout and the Mexican Bailout, one could assume that the company itself was a CIA "cut-out," an actual propriertary of the Agency.

"No, it's not," says Martin. "They're just sympathizers. They're an asset of the agency. They're not a cut-out. They're just one of the legion of financial companies, mostly domiciled in Washington or northern Virginia, which the CIA turns to, on occasion, to launder money, or for some other illegal purpose."

And who gave them the green-light to go to Russia for the post-glasnost scams?

"You're talking about long established relationships that probably existed since the 1950s. Assistant Secretary of State Richard Armitage and National Security Advisor Frank Carlucci were not young in the mid 1980s," answers Martin.

"They had been involved with their Blackstone Investment Group, and they have other partners, originally Assistant Deputy Secretary of Defense Richard Stilwell, the son of the famous General Stilwell. Stilwell himself was a retired Major General. Stilwell was also very close to Armitage, Carlucci, and Pete Peterson.

"There was a whole cabal of these guys," Martin continues. "They had been involved in all sorts of stuff for a long while. For instance, when we were bailing out the Mexicans in 1994, the new covert thing became to commit frauds in Mexico, against the Brady Plan, not the Brady Bonds themselves, the whole plan of using Brady Bonds to back up Mexican debt. There was a window of about a year, when you could commit fraud against the Bank of Mexico and other Mexican companies. You would buy essentially worthless Mexican bonds, and you could give a Mexican company in a file drawer a face lift, and then you could get Brady Bonds in exchange for them, which were backed by the US Government.

"Or, to back those up, to securitize essentially worthless Mexican corporate securities — you could take a security that was essentially worth two or three cents on the dollar and make it suddenly worth thirty or forty cents on the dollar in the marketplace. The only thing Brady Bonds are is a collateral guarantee.

"A Brady Bond is essentially a strip-down, what's called a strip or a stripped down US Treasury bond that essentially guarantees the ultimate mature capital value of a note. It does not however guarantee the interest of that note. It only guarantees the return of capital."

For the record, the underwriters of these bonds were powerhouse investment banking firms Goldman Sachs, Shearson Lehman and Merril Lynch. "They were making the one and a half point concession fees on the bonds and they were known as the primary dealer of the bonds," Martin says.

Likewise the so-called Russian Bailout followed a similar scenario. "Follow the money, and it will lead you to the new fraud," instructs Al Martin. "The Blackstone Investment Group, even before the Mexican loan deal, was 'in the bag' as it were. Blackstone immediately set up an office in Mexico City because it knew that where there was fraud, there was money to be made. You see it three years later in 1997 when Blackstone set up an office in Mexico."

Likewise there was massive trading activity in the Far East, where the bottom-feeder investment bankers, would arrive to pick up "distressed assets," defaulted stocks and bonds for pennies on the dollar. "That was early in 1998 before things fell apart," says Al Martin, "because they knew things were going to fall apart.

"The Carlyle Group, which is Frank Carlucci, and the Blackstone Investment Group are virtually one and the same. Two different names, but they are virtually the same organization," he continues. "All they do is ride the crest of the waves of various frauds from country to country. Before the so-called Global Financial Crisis of 1998, Blackstone and Carlyle suddenly opened up an office in Jakarta. They didn't have an office in Jakarta before because they were very friendly with President Sukarto. Sukarto gave them all sort of inside capabilities to short, or sell short, the Indonesian rupiah which nobody really had the ability to do because the currency wasn't particularly liquid. They do on a large scale on a multi-billion dollar scale what Richard Hamil does on a multi-million dollar scale.

"They actually purchase a security, let's say US Treasury Bonds, one security with their own money. They then use that security and hypothecate it ten or twenty times to all different types of transactions. Now that kind of fraud is not particularly hard to commit, particularly if you have a trust company under your control or a trust company that's willing to play ball with you. It isn't that hard to take the same asset and pledge it twenty times."

Because bank officers don't do due diligence or what? I asked. "You have to understand that the securities don't move anyplace. They're just pledged. They're usually just held in an account in a securities firm."

And one bank won't tell another bank that these assets have been pledged and there's no way of finding it out? I pressed on.

"Not if you got people willing to play ball with you," Al Martin replies. "The people willing to play ball are the security firms in the United States which have long-standing relationships with, not only the CIA, but also this little Eastern

Country Club Cabal, as I call it. The firms that have had longstanding intelligence activities and illegal relationships with wealthy Republicans would be undoubtedly Goldman Sachs and Merril Lynch."

You could call them the Insiders' Insider Deals. "Look where Press Secretary Regan came from," Al Martin points out. "He was the chairman of Merril Lynch."

The Harken Energy Fraud

In his online column, "Behind the Scenes of the Beltway, (http://www.almart-inraw.com), Al Martin has written that "you have to look at the entire Bush Family in this context — as if the entire family ran a corporation called 'Frauds-R-Us.' Each member of the family, George Sr., George Jr., Neil, Jeb, Prescott, Wally, etc., have their own specialty of fraud.

"George Jr.'s specialty was insurance and security fraud. Jeb's specialty was oil and gas fraud. Neil's specialty was real estate fraud. Prescott's specialty was banking fraud. Wally's specialty was securities fraud. And George Bush Sr.'s specialty? All of the above."

In this context, the infamous Harken Energy Fraud takes on new meaning as a multi-generational family of fraudsters, using high-level insider contacts, are able to manipulate stock prices for their own profiteering.

"Harken was one of those deals that was a combination fraud as well as a manipulation," says Al Martin. "There's different types of fraud when you get into securities. When George Jr. was put in charge of Harken Energy by his father [George Herbert Walker Bush], he essentially took it down the tubes. You have to realize that every business that George Jr. has ever had has failed. That's the man's business record."

Inquiring minds want to know — was it deliberate? "It was a deliberate act by the old man, knowing that his son would take it down the tubes because the son's incompetent," Al Martin replies. "George Bush, Sr. and James Baker and Senator Tower would heavily short Harken stock. I have a list of everybody because I was one of them but to a much smaller extent. Harken stock was trading at 7-3/4 or 8, when George Jr., was put in charge of it. A year later, the stock was trading at 1-1/8 bid, 3/8 offer. They pumped the stock back up through a lot of bogus press releases and by using essentially worthless leases in Bahrain and essentially worthless South American oil leases and through sympathetic geologists making them appear to be really worth something and making it appear that Harken's about to make a strike when in fact it's all made up. It's all fictitious. And through carefully crafted broker releases and broker statements and press releases, you can pump the stock back up. This has happened sixteen times to my knowledge. Harken would get pumped back up from the dead, from say a buck, buck and a half, back to seven, seven and a half, then it would get dumped again. Originally George Jr. had control of the company. He stayed on the board."

The Hidden Side of Barry Seal

The notorious Barry Seal was a legendary CIA drug smuggling pilot, but there was another side to this 20th century government-pirate (or privateer), which Al Martin reveals in this interview.

"Barry Seal was extensively involved in all manner of fraud," says Al Martin. "His principal partner was after all, Larry Hamil. Hamil had an equal relationship with Barry Seal. Barry provided seed money to set up fraudulent oil and gas and real estate limited partnerships for Hamil. Hamil later profited from them. Hamil would allow Barry to use these limited partnerships for Barry to launder his money through.

"It was a laundry situation. Barry would provide the seed money perhaps a million dollars or whatever to establish a fraudulent limited partnership, then Barry would use that limited partnership to launder money in lieu of a fee. That was his return."

Was it to launder Seals' money or CIA revenues? "From what I could tell it was for Seals' own money, not an Agency thing. But where Seals' own money stops and the Agency's monies begins, (the percentage or whatever deal they had), I'm not familiar with that. I just know what Seals' relationship was with Hamil. Before I mentioned Triton Energy, one of Hamil's oil and gas frauds that he set up in conjunction with Seal.

"It was a scam, but Barry wasn't really interested in the point of it being a scam. What attracted Barry about it was Hamil's ability to launder money, to hide money, to move money, and since these were fraudulent, since they were all set up under temporary corporate names, it was easy to disguise everything when it all fell apart."

BUSHWHACKED

Chapter 16

Interview with Al Martin (Part 2)

DESCRIBED AS THE "HIGHEST-RANKING DEFECTOR of a major crime family since Joe Valachi" (that's the Bush Family, of course), Al Martin, author of *The Conspirators: Secrets of an Iran Contra Insider* brings unprecedented insights into the machinations of the Ruling Class and, as he so aptly puts it, "How the Real World Works."

Broken PROMIS

Describing the infamous so-called "Inslaw Affair," the subject of congressional hearings and several high-profile legal cases, Al Martin says that the oft-purloined software called PROMIS, initially developed as a highly interactive database by Bill Hamilton and his company called Inslaw, was sold and resold by government insiders to line their own pockets.

"Bill Hamilton developed the PROMIS software originally," says Martin, "but he wasn't smart enough to market it with a trap door. That was his original problem. The trap-door concept came up later on, and it wasn't his idea. Other people saw that the software could be easily encoded with a discreet backdoor. Essentially he got the whole thing taken away from him."

The software was ostensibly created legal cases. However with modifications like the Trojan Horse trap-door, PROMIS would allow secret unauthorized access to any computer system. Likewise the software could track financial dealings — within banks, within institutions and within individuals' private accounts. In essence, the extortion possibilities — as well as insider trading knowledge — would become virtually limitless.

In other words, intelligence and banking records accessed through a Trojan Horse trap-door would give the proprietor of the software unimaginable powers.

"I don't know what the capabilities of the software are," Al Martin continues. "I know where the software went. This is the famous Canadian angle, which involved two agents from the Canadian Royal Mounted Police. They were the ones who handled the physical transfer of the software itself to Israel."

The PROMIS software was stolen from Bill Hamilton and the INSLAW company by Dr. Earl Brian, a member of President Ronald Reagan's so-called "Kitchen Cabinet," as affirmed by a federal judge who ruled that the software was stolen by the Department of Justice [In Re Inslaw, 885 F.2d 880 (D.C. Cir. 1989)].

And what was the agenda?

"As far as I know it was simply money," replies Al Martin. "The Department of Justice got hold of it first. They were essentially co-opted by the Department of Defense, who in turn were co-opted by the CIA. The CIA also saw the possibilities with this software for a trap door. The Israelis wanted it, and the CIA saw that they could work out a deal with the Israelis to make a couple of bucks. They needed some intermediaries and they used the Canadians as intermediaries."

The SDI ("Star Wars") Scam

U.S. Government officials have never had any intention of defending or protecting the United States or its citizens from missile attack, according to Al Martin.

"The Strategic Defense Initiative [nicknamed 'Star Wars'] was just another scam," he flatly states. "If I could give credit to anybody, it wouldn't be [Bill] Casey [the dead CIA director] because Casey was actually out of the picture by then.

"This would have been about 1987," Al Martin continues. "I think the guy that first came up with it was Jack Verona, the head of DARPA [Defense Advanced Research Projects Agency]. He was interested in doing it because he knew that DARPA was going to get a big budget cutback after 1987. He had to come up with some idea to keep DARPA's hand in. I think he was the one who originally came up with the idea that 'hey, we can put these models together, and we can make sure enough information leaks out to the public and the press (who always cooperate with us in fraudulent Department of Defense dummying up testing) and we'll make the Russians believe it.'"

The Star Wars Scam was tied into several agendas.

"Verona's idea was taken [then President] Ronald Reagan and [the Vice President] George Bush — more so George Bush who understood it right away for what it was. He knew that now there could be fresh hundreds of billions of dollars in deficit spending out of the Department of Defense to fund essentially fictitious projects that didn't exist for which there would be no accountability, which means that all the money could essentially disappear through the cracks — as it always has in the past.

"This is what sounds conspiratorial — but it really isn't." he continues. "The reason why it isn't conspiratorial anymore is because of the activities of the Reagan-Bush Regime. They were a little more open about it because it had been done before: hundreds of billions of dollars of essentially redundant, useless, surreptitious, or fraudulent military projects that don't work, which go to fund this entire Military-Industrial Complex. This is the money that gets kicked back to Republicans. It works all the way around. Also through these corporations — money can get bled out for all sorts of black operations of other agencies of government. There is, for example, the famous E-Systems Look at the number of retired admirals and generals on the Board [of Directors]. That'll tell you something.

"E-Systems has been used for a long time for the illicit transfer of weapons," he continues. "It's a publicly traded company and one of the largest defense contractors in the nation. Some deals are on the up and up, and some aren't. You get a company like that which already ships an awful lot of electronic military product, and it's easy to disguise other [illegal] product with that product. When you have a customs service, that is sympathetic, or is told to look the other way, and always does as it's told, anything is possible. You have to realize that a lot of times the 'destinations' are not the 'end users.' They're simply way-points."

The Mysterious CZX

"Then there was CZX, which was a narcotics operation — but there was also a lot hidden in CZX," Al Martin explains.

CZX is an abbreviation for "Casey-Zumwalt-X-Files Productions Limited."

"Ostensibly it was just another narco-operation with a bunch of airplanes and some hangars and a run-field," he continues. "Why CZX became interesting or important is because CZX is one of the few things you can point to which is a definitive crossover link between CIA and ONI [Office of Naval Intelligence] operations. Hence CZX's operations, like Southern Air Transport's or Southern Air Transport's affiliate Polar Air Aviation and Southern Cross, an airline with a long history of affiliation with the CIA, you also find CZX Production facilities at airfields and companies like Evergreen Airlines, for instance, with longtime affiliations to ONI."

"The X-Files refers to the list of the 'secrets,' the secret names," he explains.

When asked "What secret names?," Al Martin says, "No way."

Refining the question as "not the names themselves, but what do the 'secret names' imply?," Al Martin says, "You have to look at the timing. CZX was formed at a time when Casey was dying and Zumwalt wasn't far behind. There had to be a repository for the 'names' for a time after these guys had gone, the names that had to be gotten out of their respective agencies. The names, dates, transactions, records, corporate names, bank names. These were the deepest of the 'deep files.'

"This was a way to safeguard these files for the next generation of 'mischief-makers,' he explained. "And they did that under the guise of operating what was quote 'just another CIA/ONI dope operation.'"

It should be noted that this could certainly be considered "conspiratorial," if he's referring to the trans-generational preservation of these kind of records.

"It's for the next generation of control, for mischief-makers, those in the shadows," Al Martin explains. "People know who Casey was [CIA Director and top-level Shadow Government Insider] and certainly understand who Zumwalt was."

For the record, Zumwalt was a US Navy Admiral responsible for murdering his own son.

Al Martin replies, "That's still clouded."

When asked, "What's clouded about it? It's a clear fact," he concedes, "Yeah, well I know."

After all, Zumwalt gave the order for Agent Orange to be dispensed in Vietnam. The son suffered and the son died.

"Well, yeah I know," he says.

It was actually very straightforward.

Al says, "And everyone felt sorry for him at the time."

"For the old one or the young man?" I laughed.

"For Zumwalt, senior."

Anatomy of the Shadow Government: Restricted Access Groups

During the criminal government activities now known as "Iran Contra," Shadow Government Insiders (those who were "in the loop," so to speak) protected themselves and their covert and illegal activities by using so-called "Restricted Access Groups."

"'Restricted Access Group' is civilian code, which usually refers to one ranking member of one agency office or department that is involved in an overview, or some sort of interconnected superceding group," Al Martin explains. RAG groups — RAG-1, RAG-2, RAG-3 — all existed during Iran Contra. RAG 1 was the highest level. It involved the Vice President [George Bush Sr.] who was ultimately the head of all Iran Contra operations.

"One of the decisions of Operation Black Eagle was that Iran Contra operations would ultimately be consolidated under the office of the Vice President — because it is generally thought of as a pretty safe place. The Office of the Vice President doesn't get a lot of attention.

"George Bush was head of Restricted Access Group 1, which also involved Frank Carlucci as the National Security Advisor. Richard Armitage was a member of it, and so was Lawrence Eagleburger, then Under-Secretary of State and Casper Weinberger, the Secretary of Defense. These groups exist for the purposes of coordinating covert and illegal activities."

When asked about the "compartmentalized" nature of the RAG Groups, Al Martin replies that "it's not really compartmentalized.

"'Compartmentalization' is too narrow a definition because it implies that something is set up to compartmentalize information which is not the primary function of a RAG Group The primary function of a RAG Group is to coordinate inter-agency involvement in something that is illegal, covert and surreptitious."

Project Reassurance

"Project Reassurance" was a program initiated by the Iran Contra players to convince those who were involved that they would not be hung out to dry, but would be "taken care of" financially for their covert and illegal activities on behalf of the State.

And that's how Al Martin got snookered by Oliver North…

"This was the infamous Thursday meeting in December 1985," Al begins his recollection. "Beginning in January 1985, I had retained Steve Dinnerstein, the renowned private investigator, essentially to document my own operations, whom I was meeting, telephone calls etc. I did that because I figured, correctly so, that at some point I was going to be made a scapegoat and I wanted a second party involved who could verify what I had been involved in, what I had done, and also to chase down Larry Hamil — to exert pressure against Larry Hamil for monies he owed me after Larry and I parted ways in January of 1985. (See *The Conspirators* by Al Martin, Chapter 11, "Lawrence Richard Hamil: The US Government's Con Man")

"One of the things I kept doing was pressuring [Richard] Secord and by extension [Oliver] North all through 1985 about Hamil. I kept pestering them about it. Dinnerstein kept burrowing in deeper and deeper into Iran Contra and by the end of 1985, he was probably the civilian in the United States who was the most familiar with what Iran Contra was all about. He was in a tremendous position by the end of 1985.

"This all culminated in a meeting at North's request in the famous Denny's Restaurant on Biscayne Boulevard on 36th Street, which is where everyone met. It was diagonally right across the street from the old FBI building. It's where all the spooks and the FBI and everybody in Miami met — at this one Denny's.

"Anyway a meeting took place and in this meeting, I was promised $200,000 which was essentially the money Hamil owed me plus the money I was out of pocket because of my retention of Steven Dinnerstein."

So North knew about this "invoice," this money that was owed him?

"North knew what I was owed. Hamil was, after all, one of North's paymasters. Of course, North knew exactly what it was. I had had communications with North throughout 1985."

Enquiring minds would want to know — why was there this hesitation, this reticence, this prolonging of paying a "simple" invoice?

"I really don't know," he replies, "but I kind of do know. The reason is that I pressured them so hard that I actually in March 1985, I had gone to the FBI, the Miami Field Office, and talked to a field agent who was on the outside — not on the inside circle."

And was this a *faux pas*, a false move on Al Martin's part?

"The reason I did it was on purpose," he replies. "It was to shake them up. It sure did shake them up, but unfortunately it was probably a little too much at the time. And that's probably what delayed everything — is that I pushed them too hard. I made a lot of noise in 1985."

And was that when he crossed the line from the "asset" column to the "liability" column?

"Not completely," he replies. "But I was certainly put in the suspicion column. I did not cross over into the 'liability column' until after the very end of December, the beginning of January 1986. And what gave me that indication was this meeting North wanted me to set up with Larry Hamil in my office wherein they wanted to retrieve documents from Larry Hamil and pay him some money and pay me. When that didn't take place, I kind of figured that was the end for me. And it was. And the effort to deny me and to discredit me started shortly thereafter.

"Remember this was all prior to 'Iran Contra' falling apart," he says. "They couldn't pres me as hard as they wanted to because they knew by this time, 1986, that judges in Miami and Washington were getting very leery about granting the government's repeated requests for 'closed door trials.' They kept seeing all this stuff about Central America and then 'closed door trials.'"

But wouldn't they have to control only three or four judges in DC and so on?

"They had to control judges in Miami, in Atlanta, in New Orleans, every-place where there was an Iran Contra operation," Al replies.

And "problems" were popping up everywhere and they weren't able to control the situations?

"The real thing they weren't able to control by then was the media," Al Martin continues. "By the end of 1985, the media was pretty well into this thing. National networks started to have people with camcorders showing up at Southern Air Transport's operations at Miami International Airport. The cat was already getting out of the bag by the end of 1985, and everyone was getting nervous. It really is a testimony to [CIA Director Bill] Casey's know-how and North's sheer tenacity, which kept the thing going for another eleven months. It really should have fallen apart by the end of 1985.

"North promised to pay me $200,000 which was essentially what I was owed and out of pocket. North wanted to stop me from pressuring him all the time. Plus he wanted to get Dinnerstein out of the picture because Dinnerstein was finding out too much."

What's still incomprehensible is why didn't they just pay Al Martin off and get him off of North's back. That part is still not understandable.

Al Martin replies, "I know. And that is what has frustrated me all this time."

It seems like such a piddling amount — relatively speaking.

Al says, "Hey, pal, don't tell me because frankly I do not know. I could speculate, but I do not know for sure. I would speculate that by the middle of 1986, part of the problem might have been that every agency thought I was someone else, other than who I really was. It's not that I had a bunch of different aliases. It's really the places that I would be seen at. I would be oftentimes seen on the weekends at the Czechoslovakian Club in Miami.

"Counterintelligence agents of the FBI CI-3 would come to visit me in April of 1985," he continues. "CI-3 is Counter Intelligence Level 3. Or so they called it, even though they couldn't find a counter in a room full of intelligence.

"The real problem, and the problem why I think I haven't been dealt with till this very day — is that they weren't able to pigeon-hole me. And that was the real problem. I had to me put into twelve different cubby-holes."

But Oliver North could have straightened that out, couldn't he?

"I don't think so — because North himself didn't know who I was. North himself would get conflicting reports. I started to play the game... What I did... the mistake I made was playing the game too hard, too early on.

"What that means is I played the game too hard when they still had pretty good control of what was going on. In February, March, April of 1985. Had I waited till February, March, April of 1986 to do what I did a year earlier, I'd be sitting in my chalet on Lake Geneva right now.

"I was exerting too much pressure and making people too nervous too early in the game — before it was really falling apart," he says. "But the government was able to keep it going. I'm sure George Bush thanks his lucky stars to this day that it fell apart in such a way that the government was able to control the falling apart. They were the ones who collapsed it. It wasn't the media, or Congress, or anyone else that did it. It was the government itself. They pulled the plug out, when the pulling was good.

"What I mean is that I probably started playing the game a little too hard, a little too fast and loose in 1985, and I started to be seen in places that were not directly related to any Iran Contra operation. Or anything that I was supposed to be doing.

"It was a conscious decision on my part to do that for two reasons. Number one, I did it to confuse and to obfuscate — a job, that looking back on it, I have learned subsequently and heard from others — I did *too* well. By the end of 1986, I had twelve different agencies of the government thinking that I was twelve different people. And that is one of the problems — why I have not been dealt with in all these years — the way others have been — and have not been paid what I have been owed is because people in this business, particularly those who run things, when they can't pigeon-hole you, they have a real hard time with you."

And that was the fallout from Project Reassurance. "It didn't come to pass — when North asked for a meeting the following week in my office (and obviously they meant for it to happen because they gave me such elaborate detail}. They wouldn't have given me such elaborate detail, if they didn't think the meeting would take place. I was told exactly who would attend. I was even told that there would be two briefcases there, a black one which would be for Hamil and a smaller brown for me. I was even told that when the meeting was over, I was to have my own office swept and closed the same day."

So who queered the deal so to speak?

"Hamil found out what the intent of the meeting was fifteen hours before the meeting was to take place."

Which was to take care of him and liquidate him?

"Yes, and that's what put the kibosh on it. He was supposed to appear. There would be me, him and five other individuals. Most of the others were prominent CIA-connected Bay of Pigs types of Cubans that Hamil knew. What was supposed to happen is that Hamil was supposed to deliver certain sets of documents to me. I was given parameters as to what these documents would contain. I was given sort of an outline of what to look for on certain pages. I was given key words to look for. They didn't give me any explanation of what the documents were, but I kind of guessed that it was all these materials from CIA operations manuals. That's what I assumed from what they were saying. I was given verification page numbers.

"I was supposed to verify the documents. I was supposed to give Hamil the black briefcase, which I was told by North would contain four million dollars in US currency. But that wasn't my concern. They just told me that's what it was. And Hamil was going to walk out. And they knew that Hamil would leave from the front entrance of the office building because the office didn't have any rear parking areas. And there was only one place for limousines to park, and that was in front, and Hamil always traveled by limousine.

"So Hamil somehow found out. I never had any contact after this time with Oliver North. It just ended — flat. They didn't inform me that Hamil found out. Dinnerstein found out that Hamil had found out because Dinnerstein called him. He said that I know that I'm being set up and you know they're setting me up. Dinnerstein immediately called me and told me the whole thing's off because Hamil s found out what this is all about. I never received any contact after that from Oliver North."

"In other words, they just scratched the whole thing, which was too bad. because I was looking forward to going to St. Martens. I was supposed to leave for St. Martens that evening. I was going to get to stay in one of our safe houses which is still in business today on the island."

And what happened to Hamil?

"He still lives in Florida. The State of Florida has him officially declared dead which isn't true. I know some other states do. Jackson State Memorial Hospital dummied up documents a couple months ago to claim that he died. There were documents dummied up in Virginia. They made it appear that Hamil was buried at Arlington National Cemetery, though in fact he wasn't."

And how did Al Martin "get religion," regarding all these activities which had been performed under the guise of "patriotism" or "doing your duty" or "service to country"? What was the turning point?

"The turning point came probably in 1985," he explains, "when Hamil and I separated. When I finally came to the realization (and perhaps I'd realized it earlier — that we were doing was all wrong. I had always... You tend to blend it together in this business, whether you're a patriot or not because what you do all your life is illegal. If you were like me and all your adult life, you had never done anything legal..." His voice trails off.

Then there would be no "line" to cross?

"The moral aspect of it dulls a little bit because you're constantly justifying it — your own actions — by what your superiors tell you, that you are committing illegal acts, on behalf of the interest of the nation or the security of the nation.

"This is more of an intelligence 'community' mindset that when you're young you are brought up into this thing under the notion that you are protecting 'national security' or those times 'fighting communism' — and that went a long way. Then suddenly as you get deeper and deeper in, you find out you're having to justify more and more what you're doing. And it gets to the point like it did with me in 1985, when you finally say, 'how much justification is there'?"

When did this realization hit him?

"People want to make me out as a hero but that is not the reality," he says. "I could make myself out to be the hero, that I was sucked into this and I believed what my superiors told me."

That's Oliver North's line.

"I could say that and it isn't true. Just like what Ollie North says — it isn't true. It's — how do you say it? You put it on a scale. It's weighing your illegal activities versus what the outcome of what that is. And the outcome of that is 'the fight against communism' or the supposed 'security of the nation.' It's trade-offs. And how many trade-offs do you make?

"It's like the conversation I had with Oliver North once. I know where he's coming from. I mean this guy was prepared to have one citizen liquidated to keep something quiet or ten thousand, he'd say. 'It's all just semantics and numbers.' And I understand the mentality. Those are the real zealots. But guys like me… after so many years in it, you get to the point and you say to yourself of what you've been involved in, what you've seen, what you've heard, what you've known others have been involved in, and you think — how far does this thing go? How many billions must the American people pay? How many thousands must be liquidated to maintain the deniability of others?

"It comes down to yourself. I'll tell you a movie parallel that's the best parallel that I could ever think of, in terms of people like me, particularly after you get to a certain age. *Three Days of the Condor.* When Robert Redford, towards the very end of the movie, just after Max von Sydow, the CIA shooter has killed the deputy director and they're walking out of the house, and von Sydow says, 'You've got to go. You've got to leave the country. There's nothing left for you here anymore.' And Redford says, 'What would I do?' And he says, 'Come with me. I'll help you. I'll get you into my business.' And Redford says, 'I don't think I could do that for a living. And von Sydow says, 'Of course, you could. There's no politics. There's no East or West. It's just yourself.'

"What happens is your moral compass gets subverted because you tend to live very well when you're involved in the next covert illegal operation of State. You get to live very well. Private jets. Limousines. Thousand dollar bottles of wine.

You get very easily seduced by that kind of lifestyle, but it's meant to be that way. That's part of the excuse that you can use to justify it. It's part of the perks. Intelligence people are treated so generously so they don't think about the moral implications of what they're doing.

"That's the long and short of it. And they're supposed to be given, though Iran Contra changed this mold, lifetime guarantees when they're washed up, when they're done psychologically. You notice that in the intelligence community, there is no retirement age."

The crux of the matter is betrayal. The old adage of "no honor among thieves" must be amended. There's no honor among spooks either.

BUSHWHACKED

Chapter 17

HUD Fraud: A How To Guide

A L MARTIN, AUTHOR OF THE CONSPIRATORS: *Secrets of an Iran Contra Insider*, was involved in what he called the "money" side of Iran- Contra. In this interview, he reveals the techniques used to defraud HUD, the US Department of Housing and Urban Development.

"What we did was called the classical Section 8 Frauds, which was using Section 8 (low-income) housing as a fraud. " he begins. "This was done throughout the 1980s. During 'Iran-Contra,' it was one of the classic ways *visavis* real estate to commit fraud against HUD. The Section 8 Housing Act was used because of the extraordinary tax benefits that were offered. These included accelerated write-offs, accelerated depreciations, and extra-ordinary cost accounting. An invest-or could easily leverage it to a two-to one write-off. HUD allowed this purposely because the original concept was to entice people to invest in Section 8 housing deals.

"The government was, therefore, very generous in tax write-offs.

"How you commit a fraud is by buying a piece of 'busted out' HUD Section 8 property. 'Busted out' property is real estate that was previously in a HUD deal, then went down the tubes, and got 'busted out.' HUD puts it back on the market again for virtually nothing. They're just looking for someone to pick it up. These were low income housing that were built in blocks of 200 to 300 units.

"Then a limited partnership would be formed, whose primary function would be to buy out this busted out property," Al Martin continues. "Obviously by this time the property would be completely run down and completely dilapidated (for what might have been the fourth time) because the piece of property might have been re-picked up, re-picked-up, re-picked up — three or four times."

Syndicating the Scams

According to Al Martin, there weren't any companies that were very prominent in fraud, except some of the smaller securities companies like Atlantis Securities, Singer Island Securities, Marcos Securities, Balfour McLean Securities. "These were all nickel and dime security companies, and they were all located in Denver," he says. "This was after most of them were consolidated under the National Brokerage Group, when Dick Brenneke was put in charge of it. Blinder Robinson was his major partner in the National Brokerage Group. That's when the fraud got organized — through these nickel and dime securities firms. What I mean is organized fraud within the 'syndication' of limited partnerships. 'Syndication' is the proffering of a limited partnership, or the syndication of a deal. Syndicated means it's spread out over many firms. You have one firm that puts the deal together. Then you have co-sponsors or co-underwriters, which are three or four other firms that get all the commissions on a concession basis, which is called a 'take-down' fee. They are committed to 'take down,' that is, purchase so much of the product for retail resale on a mark-up basis. The co-syndicators or co-managers get the concession fee.

"It doesn't have to be real estate limited partnership. It could also be a stock offering or anything else. We're just talking about the route by which all securities are sold.

"Here is the bottom line. Normally this would be done in thousands or tens of thousands of units at a time. This was the way that HUD sold the stuff off. You would take a group of busted out Section 8 property that existed in inner cities around the United States. It could be anywhere in the United States, within certain inner-city areas. Busted out deals are defaulted loans."

Were they "rolled over" by the same cast of players?

"Sometimes the people would default," Al explains. "The people who put the deal together the first time would then default, change the name of the corporation they were doing business as, and pick it up the second time and commit the same fraud twice. You could do that over and over again. I hold the record for doing that, I think, through our series of limited partnerships we formulated in 1985 in Miami that was known as the Blackbird Investment Group — 'Blackbird' being named after Richard Secord."

Al laughs when he says, "I think I hold the record for picking them up, bust-ing them out, defaulting, and re-hypothecating the same 360 units in the Overtown section of Miami a total of sixteen times."

The Condo Block Scam

"That's one type of scam. We used to call it the old Section 8 Scam," says Al. "Now what Don Austin was involved in was another type of thing altogether. [See Chapter 6 of *The Conspirators*, "The Don Austin Denver HUD Fraud Case."] That was what we used to call the old Condo Block Scam. That meant buying blocks of defaulted-on condominiums townhouses, semi-detached units, which would be sold off in enormous quantities. Twelve thousand units. Eighteen thousand units at a time. Usually it would be within the same state because the prior syndicator, which had busted out or defaulted would normally only do stuff in the same state because they didn't have a sufficient management team to manage property all over the country.

"What guys like Austin would do is pick up 'busted out' condo block properties very, very cheaply," Al continues. "Let's say places that originally sold for between $69,000 and $89,000 retail would be picked up for $24,000 each.

"These were purposeful frauds. It wasn't that someone did this legitimately, then made a business decision that it wasn't worthwhile or they were losing money.

"Austin was involved, although Austin was not a scamscateer," Al explains. "His partner was. He was involved in the 'legitimate' end of the condo block trade with HUD — buying the busted out HUD properties en masse, getting them refinanced, putting a little bit of money into them, and then selling them off, auctioning them off again, and then trying to make a spread of maybe five or six thousand dollars a unit. He would take the property and kick up the appraisal a little bit, which wasn't hard to do. He would get enough money from a bank or a short term lending institution or sometimes even from the government itself.

"Sometimes you could borrow money from the SBA or SBGC to pick the property back up again. It depends on how HUD classifies the property. You give them a little bit of a face-lift. You'd put maybe three, four or five thousand dollars per unit into them. Then you'd re-auction them, or you would break them all down individually, or by buildings, and you would get a group of realtors involved to sell them off at auction. That's generally how it worked.

"In other words, they would be sold off at auction to other real estate investors who didn't buy them by the thousands, but could buy them by the hundreds, who would then in turn resell them to someone who could buy ten, twelve, fifteen, fifty units, wherein they ultimately would be retailed out. You'd have to pay insurance. What got Austin screwed up was the problem of paying the insurance on the mortgage that HUD was guaranteeing."

The HUD Insurance Scam

"Don Austin was the victim of a tertiary type of scam known as the old HUD Insurance Scam," Al continues. "This is an indirect type of scam perpetrated on HUD. You apply to become an insurance agent or an insurance collecting agent of HUD. Then HUD farms that stuff out individually. Anyone can apply and become a subcontractor to HUD as long as you have a Regulation 202 and a Regulation 212 insurance license. Anyone can apply to HUD to set up a company to collect insurance premiums for HUD mortgagees. What you simply do is you don't pass along the money to HUD."

Al laughs again. "That's pretty simple. I mean it's the simplest type of scam in the world. You collect insurance premiums from mortgage holders from HUD mortgages, and then you simply fail to pass the money along. With HUD's book-keeping system the way it was, you could perpetrate this scam for two or three years — before HUD even noticed that the insurance payments weren't being made. And then even once they did know, you could make a ten percent payment, and you could blame it on your own internal company problems and pay a small penalty and interest on the insurance due and then keep the scam going for another twelve months."

According to Al Martin, this was a common type of fraud, called the HUD Insurance Bust Out scheme. These have been going on since HUD began in the 1960s.

The HUD "Candy Store"

"HUD has always been a cash cow — both for regular and government-connected scamscateers," Al Martin continues.

"The volume of fraud committed against HUD would always spike during illegal covert operations of state. HUD was always considered to be a 'candy store' by the CIA, its hangers-on and its minions in the shadows — like me and the Oliver Norths of this world. You could essentially defraud the government of resources and use those resources to sustain an illegal operation of state."

How complicit are HUD commissioners in this? Do they know what's going on?

"Of course they do," he replies. "They're all political appointees."

So they know what a mess they're inheriting? Then the question arises, why would a guy like Jack Kemp agree to be in charge? Was he blackmailed, for example?

"You have to remember that was a different ball of wax," Al replies. "Jack Kemp wasn't really brought in to run HUD. He was brought in to quiet everything down. He was a cover-up guy. One way to find out about HUD and its history is to look at the series of directors it has had. You will see that a director it had during an illegal covert operation of state, wherein fraud was being committed against HUD pursuant to the sustenance of said illegal operation would continue for three or four years, until the operation broke out and became public. After that, a political appointee would be brought in to clean up HUD. This happened during the Reagan-Bush Administration and during the Carter Administration."

And why did Denver become such a focal point in the fraud?

"Because that's where HUD is located," he replies. "HUD has an enormous regional operation in Denver, and Denver is also the head-quarters for all the 'busted-out' properties. The re-circulation of busted out stuff goes through Denver. All national 'busted-out' stuff goes through their Denver office."

In other words, the entire operation of the resale of defaulted HUD properties was set up using a "systems" approach to make it as easy to defraud the American tax-payers as possible.

"That's why Denver became such a center of HUD fraud," Al explains.

"You might think that California, Florida, and Washington, DC proper-ties would be dealt with regionally, but that's not correct."

Al Martin says, "Nothing works on a regional basis with HUD. It all works on a national basis. You see, HUD is divided into departments. They have one department that handles all 'busted out' and default-ed properties. The compartmentalization was deliberate. None of the other departments talk to one another. Like all federal agencies, the right hand seldom knows what the left hand is doing.

"What the public was told was that Jack Kemp was brought in as a 'clean-up man,'" says Al. "He was actually brought in as a PLC-er, (pronounced 'pilker') or Political Liability Control Specialist. Just look at what Kemp would be brought into. Besides any official titles he had, Kemp was brought into the Department of Defense as a 'cleanup guy' and into the Department of Justice as a 'cleanup guy.' But he was just another PLC, as we used to call it.

"Cisneros was actually supposed to clean up the liability and straighten the place out, but he didn't do anything. There really was nothing he *could* do. He was just like Samuel Pierce. There was nothing he could do either. These guys are appointed as directors of HUD, and when they get there... In some cases they're quite naïve like Samuel Pierce was… I think he actually thought that the place was a *legitimate* operation."

It makes you wonder how many of these guys are chumps. "Well, Samuel Pierce was certainly a chump," says Al.

You'd think a guy like that would do a little bit of due diligence before accepting such a position.

Al replies, "On the surface, Washington makes HUD sound wonderful. And he was a black guy. And HUD originally was formed to help the black community, but what Pierce didn't realize is that HUD isn't even a legitimate agency. It doesn't even perform the function it's billed as performing. It is simply a huge morass of fraud.

"HUD was established because of the Civil Rights Act of 1964. It builds millions of low-income housing units. It's just that the nature of HUD (certainly by the time I was in the picture) had changed. It became less about building low income housing units and more about the commission of fraud to provide covert revenue streams for other illicit operations of state. Obviously the people doing that became very rich."

The Country Club Scam

"Look at Larry Hamil, for instance, who did probably some of the largest HUD fraud deals ever committed," Al continues. "What Hamil did was another type of HUD fraud, which was often referred to as Country Club HUD Fraud.

"HUD not only finances residential units (actual residential construction) but, in the 1980s, it began financing a lot of other projects, including building upscale country clubs and even theme parks," Al continues.

"Clearly HUD began to expand its mandate and began getting involved in the luxury end of the market. And that's where a lot of fraud was committed. Hamil's specialty was community development fraud. He would purchase property, but he would only make a down payment. He would never close the transaction. A section of prime land that was going to be cleared to build a gated community. Very popular in Florida. You have mixed single family, mixed condo, mixed townhouse, all built around the golf course and the clubhouse. Hamil would get his hands on the land, but not actually close the deal. He would make it appear that he owned the land. That's very easily done with some false deeds. False deeds are very easily obtained in this country, particularly if you have friends. Hamil had people on his payroll working in various registries of deeds. That makes it real easy.

"Hamil would then get HUD loan guarantees to build out the whole development. He would then borrow the money. Of course, the bank would let you borrow only so much at a time. He would build three or four model units. He would build a selling office. He would have elaborate plans drawn up of what it was going to look like, beautiful color inlaid details and everything. Very well done. Very slick promotion.

"Then he would go to banks separately with his HUD and SBIC (Small Business Investors Corporation) guarantees. There are so many lending agencies that get involved in this that it is literally mind-boggling. He would go in with these HUD guarantees to get short term bridge funding for the construction of the units or the construction of the clubhouse. Then he would just have the foundation laid.

"What he would do is called a 'Progressive Fraud.' He would keep borrowing, borrowing, borrowing and hypothecating — on a scale-up basis to complete every phase of the development. At the end, he would start taking money from individuals to secure their choice lots. He would build in a scarcity factor, a premium factor. He'd say, 'You have top pay $1,500 earnest money in order to secure your choice lot.' And that would be another scam.

"Then he'd package up the whole scam and go to a bunch of banks in New York or Washington. It's not hard to borrow money and make it appear that you haven't done so, that the item you borrowed against is not encumbered. That's very easy to do particularly when you're dealing in the world of guaranteed bridge loans and blocked funding from government agencies like Small Business Investors Corporation."

And how do bridge loans work? "HUD will guarantee bridge loans to a certain number of millions of dollars. SBIC would guarantee them up to a million dollars. SBA guaranteed them up to a million dollars. You form a corporation — like Hamil did. You noticed Hamil's were always Gulf something — Gulf Coast Investment, Gulf Coast Realty, Gulf Oil and whatever. Then what-ver that corporation was going to be doing, you would simply make arrangements with SBA. You'd make the appropriate SBA filings and the appropriate SBIC filings. The appropriate OIDC filings. Hamil would always have a branch in Europe. That was so he could get OIDC money. You could get another million and a half dollars out of OIDC (Overseas Investors Development Corporation). And, then of course, OPIC is another part of it." "The bottom line was that you could borrow money from government agencies in order to commit a fraud against another government agency," explains Al Martin, "Namely HUD.

"You could then re-hypothecate that to make it appear that your net assets were more than they were, to drain more money out of the same government lending or guaranteeing agencies that you went to before. And you could go back and forth like this almost endlessly. Then you could back it all into a public shell

— or a securities deal. Sell it out as a limited partnership for the fourteenth time. Then you could collapse it. Then you could buy it back and re-syndicate it. Bury Rule 144 paper through offshore banking syndications. In other words, you could take one fraud, as Hamil used to be very good at…Hamil was one of the masters of the 32nd Degree Fraud. And he's one of the very few masters that exist, I think. The 32nd Degree Fraud is where you take the initial cooperation you're going to commit the fraud to, then commit a compounded fraud to the 32nd degree, 32 times, on a compounded basis."

Literally thirty two times? "Yes," he answers. "By this time, you have every government lending agency, every state lending agency, every bank sucked into the deal, every security firm sucked into the deal, investors sucked into the deal, offshore banks sucked into the deal, offshore securities firms sucked into the deal. And it's all the same deal. You can start like Hamil did with that Destin Country Club Development deal, which I mentioned in the book. That started from a corporation, which Hamil funded with $20,000. Eighteen months later, he had pulled $118 million out of various US corporations, lending agencies guarantee agencies, guarantee lending banks, quasi-banks, securities firms — all based on the same fraud."

Larry Hamil: Super-Fraudster

And where did Hamil learn to do these scams?

"I don't know," Al answers. "We had found out that the guy's got a criminal record that extends back to the 1960s. He was committing fraud pretty early on, considering the guy wasn't born until 1944.

"I think he learned it by being around it all his life. That's the way most of us learn our trade. You don't learn it in school. His father Harry was the senior Department of Defense analyst in their Central and South American desk for years before he retired. Because of that, Hamil got introduced (when he was young), to a lot of shadowy types around the Department of Defense. His sister Nancy worked for the National Security Agency for a number of years. As a matter of fact, she was the personal secretary to three different directors of the NSA. It was because of his family's connections. His cousin Ron was the police chief of Falls Church, Virginia, which was a police unit very closely connected to the CIA And I think that being around these people over the years, he simply picked it up."

Real Estate Fraud (Boom)

The real estate boom in Phoenix, Arizona can also be traced to the large-scale frauds of the 1980s and 1990s.

Al Martin agrees. "Lincoln Savings and Loan took advantage of the real estate boom of the 1980s. That was Charlie Keating's bank. They did the Phoenician, the McLaren Ranches in Phoenix, the Sunshine Community Development. They syndicated a lot of real estate deals. Then there was Fife Symington, the former governor of Arizona. He actually committed fraud against Lincoln Savings & Loan. He had his own real estate company and, using false appraisals, he pumped up real estate values — just like everybody else was doing. The problem was that when the real estate market came tumbling down in the late 80s, guys who didn't have enough cash or hadn't sold enough property early enough, were up shit creek. And Fife was one of them. Another governor of Arizona, Evan Mecham, was also involved in real estate fraud. Governors of Arizona were like the governors of Louisiana. It was almost expected.

SEC: Complicit with Fraud

Asked if he ever had to travel to Denver, the proverbial capital of HUD fraud, Al Martin says he didn't have to.

"When the fraud was getting to the point when it was 'going public' through some sort of securities deals, the due diligence meetings would usually be in Miami because all the Denver penny stock firms had offices in Miami. Miami and all of Florida, of course, is a well-known place for fraud," he answers.

And how was the SEC, the Securities and Exchange Commission, typically handled by the fraudsters?

"The SEC had absolutely no idea what was going on," says Al. "Either they had no idea, or they were told to look the other way. I knew the local SEC commissioner in Miami. It was Charlie Harper, and Harper would make recommendations. They had to look at all the deals that passed through Miami as a region, even the shell deals and the fraud deals. The only thing that Harper would do is bump it up the line to his immediate superior, George Weiss, who eventually became the Customs Commissioner of the United States."

So the implication is that SEC would be told that these deals with Hamil were politically protected deals. "On the field-office level, they wouldn't know that," he explains. "On the regional level, all the SEC stuff would go back to SEC in Washington for review. In some cases, the regional or local commissioners would make a recommendation that a prosecution be started, but they couldn't do anything without the approval of the SEC in Washington. That's where the political control was — at the very top of the SEC."

From time to time, there are high profile prosecutions that take place, with all the attendant publicity in all the typical financial publications. It's hard to understand, however, how and why certain individuals are prosecuted and others are not. Are they simply committing "unsanctioned" frauds?

"Sure," Al replies. "Like the William Irwin case in 1985-86 in Miami. That was an enormous prosecution of this kind of securities fraud, but most of the securities fraud prosecution you saw, particularly in those years, were people who were not 'connected.' They were not on the inside. They were just, as Charlie Harper used to say, regular 'garden variety' scamscateers. They didn't have government connections."

The Truth Shall Make You _____ *(Fill in the Blank)*

"In the past, I've talked about George Bush Sr.'s famous quote that 'truth will get you broke — or dead,'" Al Martin continues.

"This is something that Jeb Bush said to me. I didn't dare say this before, but I'm going to say it now. I'm just coming out and saying it. This is something Jeb Bush once said to me. I went to Jeb Bush's office in February 1986. This is when Jeb was in the real estate business in Miami. He had a company called Bush Codina Realty. He had an office upstairs in a building on 1390 Brickell Avenue.

"The reason I was there was my attorney Von Zampft had sent me to talk to Bush about my upcoming grand jury testimony," Al says. "Bush was telling me that it was all arranged, that Ed Meese himself is going to call my lawyer and tell me what to say. Because, by this time, the deal that I had with Ollie [North] about the money that Ollie had promised me wasn't forthcoming, I had intimated to Bush at that time that I just *might* tell the truth.

"And he looked at me. This is Jeb. And Jeb is tall. He's about six foot three, and he's dark-haired and blue-eyed. And I've sat next him over the years, so I know. When Jeb lies, the top of his forehead starts to flush and turn red, and little beads of sweat form under his hairline. That's how you could always tell the guy was lying. Even to this day, when you see him on television giving a speech, you'll see the little beads of sweat, when he starts to lie. And he gets flushed at the top of his forehead.

"But he said something to me, warning me about telling the truth. He said, 'The truth is useless. You have to understand this right now. You can't deposit the truth in the bank. You can't buy groceries with the truth. You can't pay the rent with the truth. The truth is a useless commodity that will hang around your neck like an albatross—all the way to the homeless shelter. And if you think that the million or so people in this country that are *really* interested in the truth about their government can support people who would tell them the truth, you got another thing coming. Because the million people in this country that are truly interested in the truth don't have any money.'

"And then he repeated Oliver North's famous words, 'The truth is a useless commodity.'

"Oliver North used to say this all the time, that the truth is counter-productive to the individual telling it and is, therefore, ultimately a useless commodity."

So this interchange obviously made a profound impression on him — this entire incident?

"Obviously it hadn't," Al says laughing. "Look at the way I've lived my life since..."

"I knew it would be a tough row to hoe.

"You know what Richard Secord used to say about the truth? He'd be half in the bag, and I'd be sitting next to him at the Turnberry Club in Miami. He'd be drinking with Jimmy Langdon, the president of Southern Air Transport [the infamous CIA proprietary]. They used to laugh about the truth. Secord used to say that 'people who tell the truth wind up living in broken down trailer parks in South Florida, or Arizona or New Mexico, while people that don't tell the truth wind up living in $800,000 colonial-style suburban ranches in Silver Springs, Maryland — with condos in the Bahamas.'"

It's understandable. Secord just doesn't want to see himself in a maximum-security prison.

BUSHWHACKED

Chapter 18

True Stories from the Scam Business

I
N THIS INTERVIEW, AL MARTIN, author of *The Conspirators: Secrets of an Iran Contra Insider*, talks about the heyday of stock scams and other frauds during the late 1980s and 1990s.

Referring to the many limited partnership scams then prevalent, he says, "You didn't sell this stuff to little old ladies, and mutual funds didn't make markets in it. You sold it essentially to people who thought they were smarter than you — doctors, dentists, lawyers, and people who could afford to drop fifty or a hundred grand and not worry too much about it. They did it out of their own greed. They think they're smarter than you are, and they think they know what they're doing. And we'd fuck them — just to teach them a lesson."

"The game was confined to a relatively small set of players," he continues. "There were some Joe Six-packs, who would spread the tip around at all the local bars. Then a lot of the Joe Six-packs would be buying a hundred shares at three dollars a share, and they ultimately had to sell the stock at fifty cents a share. So what? They lose a couple hundreds bucks a share. But that's the way it always was. There was a code of honor about this business."

The Pump-and Dump Stock Frauds

Then came the stock frauds called "Pump-and-Dumps," in which the price of a stock was pumped up and then dumped by insiders, who knew when to sell out, while the uninitiated were left holding the proverbial bag.

"It began to fall apart, it began to change in the late 1980s," he continues. "When Bush got into office after 1988, 1989, then you started to see the big pump-and-dump deals. The first big pump-and-dump deals were the publishing companies. Harcourt Brace Jovanovich, before it was broken up. McMillan, before it was broken up. That was a nice pump-and-dump scheme. Those deals then started to get into the billions, the low billions admittedly. They were being controlled by the big players, main street market makers, like Merrill Lynch, Goldman Sachs, Hutton.

"The scam was constituted because you had a fake buyer. It would always be some syndicate of buyers, but the buyer wasn't actually genuine. What would happen is that a bid would come out, like it did for McMillan, and then there would be a lot of rumors. What they did is they flooded the market. I don't know who was behind it, but I got the stock tip from a lawyer who worked for Bush. That's how it came my way. They involved a lot of Canadian broker firms in it. You'll see when there's a Bush presence in a stock fraud, one of the keys to look for is a lot of Canadian involvement. I'm not talking about the stocks. I'm talking about brokerage firms and market makers. Look for a lot of Canadian involvement. Both the Vancouver and Toronto exchange. There were a lot of scams there. Then they told people they cleaned up their act. They made a giant effort to clean up their act, and they got a lot of good publicity in financial publications. The only thing they did, though, is they started to dress their frauds in Brooks Brothers suits – not quite to the Armani levels yet, but...

"Look at the time that Bush was in power and Joe Clarke was in power in Canada. At that time, there was a lot of collaboration in the commission of fraud. A lot of people wanted to make money, and you see how many boards of directors of Canadian firms Bush was on, or Henry Kissinger, or any of the Old Gang. This Canadian Connection is actually better known by the Canadian people than it is here. There has been a lot more written there than here."

Tele-Communications Stock Scams

And after the publishing industry what was the next industry segment that got bushwhacked, so to speak?

"Publishing was the first one," says Al, "then they went on to the telecommunication deals, when the big multi-billion dollar telecommunications companies began to get formed in the late 1980s. When Time merged with Warner Brothers. Then there was Viacom — Sumner Redstone's deal, when Viacom merged with Qualcomm, which in turn merged with Liberty. That was a three-way merger done in 1992. What they did is they artificially suppressed the shares of Liberty. It was an interesting deal the way it was structured. Liberty had Class A and Class B shares. They finagled the bagel by suddenly issuing a lot of Class A shares. The long and short of that deal was that Diller made about a billion dollars in Qualcomm. It was Qualcomm that got pumped. All the Bushes, all the normal gang made out on it."

Soros and His Insider Stock Scams

"John Malone was Liberty Media, and TCI was a subsidiary, which then broke apart, when they did a spin-off of it. It's like AT&T did a spin-off of Lucent. That's where George Soros made billions — in that Lucent deal. He was one of the biggest investors. Soros knew it was going to be a good company. Soros isn't any great investor or particularly uncanny. Soros knew that since AT&T made the deal so rich, they gave a lot of licensing contracts to their own spin-off, contracts which they shouldn't have given them.

"Lucent went from fifteen or twenty dollars to a hundred — pretty quick. This was unusual for what was supposed to be a more bread and butter technology company. They gave them royalty revenues on patent products, which they shouldn't have. Then when Lucent was climbing from twenty to a hundred, AT&T was declining from sixty to twenty.

"Soros knew what the deal was on the inside. He owned a big piece of it from the get-go. The deal was purposely played down. It wasn't popular. The stock wasn't even fully subscribed , when they released it out of syndication. What Soros did (and it wasn't the first time) — his traditional trick on an IPO that he knows is going to be a good deal, he purposely puts out the word (and his word means a lot on the Street), that this deal sucks, whilst at the same time, he's buying it. Traditionally, that's how Soros operated."

European Bank Scams

"After the publishing and communications deals, you started to get a lot of the European bank scams in the early to mid 90s. These were the next ones in the pump-and-dumps. Credit Lyonnais. Banque Paribas. Even Union Bank of Switzerland. They pumped them up. There was a lot of politics. These were banks that were on their last legs. So much fraud had been committed against these banks that they were on their last legs. Yet when they began to pump them, as the net capital of these banks was slipping into the minus column, the shares were reaching all-time highs in the marketplace."

And the suckers were...?

"There were a lot of European buyers, of course. And a lot of American mutual funds had Banque Paribas and Credit Lyonnais as part of their foreign holdings.

"You have to remember that George Bush was the single largest mover and shaker at Banque Paribas and Credit Lyonnais for a very long time because the Bushes financed so much of their fraud through Credit Lyonnais, Caribbean subsidiaries of which were the most commonly used offshore accounts during the Iran Contra period," explains Al.

And how did the scams work?

"What the Bushes did is they often used these banks to re-hypothecate a fraud," says Al. "When they had to bail out of a previously committed fraud, when they were up against it, they used these banks to do it. They used them to collateralize the loans, since the paper generated from the fraud wasn't worth anything. This is the old Bank of Greece Connection. What they would do is use a lot of stand-by letters. In Bush Fraud, you would see an extensive use of LCs (standby letters of credit), which are in fact bogus. This is one of the easiest ways to commit fraud, by the use of standby letters."

And nobody does due diligence?

"It's the name of the ultimate lending institution that guarantees the item," Al explains. "But standby LCs were used extensively in the late 1980s and even beyond for the commission of fraud — because a standby LC hardly cost anything. After all, it was a 'standby' instrument, which means it cost virtually nothing. It didn't cost the bank anything to issue it, and it cost the purchaser very little."

"There are two types of LCs: standbys and full faith. Full faith means 'it's good.' Period. It's a full-faith credit instrument. What they would do is this — George Bush was very influential at the Bank of Greece for a number of years, particularly when Andreas Papandreou was in power, before he was finally kicked out and charged with fraud against the Bank of Greece. That included illegal currency transactions and so on. It turned out that the National Bank of Greece under Papandreou had issued ten thousand times its capital in letters of credit."

And how were they used in the scams?

"They would be used to collateralize loans from other institutions," says Al. "What would happen is you could do that with a standby loan, because very simply put, you take a standby LC and use it for collateral at another lending institution. Then, the only way that institution looks to that LC for money (and the way the deal has to be written) is if you default on the LC. All standby LCs eventually become full faith and credit instruments, what becomes known as 'full faith' letters of credit."

It should also be noted that these were the European banks, which pumped millions and millions of dollars into Hollywood movies. Film production money was flowing fast and furious at the time. A lot of movies must have been made using bogus LCs.

Al agrees. "Oh sure, they were," he answers. "That was a very common way to finance movies, when studios didn't have the money to finance them. Instead of kiting checks, they would kite standby LCs."

Scams With Prestigious Bank Names

"Nothing like the good old trusty LC from Barclay's Bank — of Guernsey and Jersey," Al laughs. "A lot of times what would happen is that fraudulent banks would be formed with exactly the same name as legitimate banks. That was a common way. And in the due diligence departments of a lot of banks, nobody would bother to ever look at them. They'd say, 'Oh, it's Barclay's Bank,' and that's all. It would be put in the Barclay file, but it wasn't the same Barclay. In very small print, it would say 'Barclay Bank of the Guernsey and Jersey Isles.'

"This was the famous Barclay's Bank Trust Scandal by Phil Davis, the famous Barclay's scamscateer," says Al. "Phil Davis was the guy who first formulated the Barclays Scam of the late 70s — using LCs to commit fraud. He was a swindler based in the Guernsey Islands and he set up offshore banks there. For years, nobody really understood what he was doing. Ultimately he defrauded about 1,400 international banks out of two or three hundred million bucks, which was a sizeable fraud in those days.

"He did it by playing a shell game with offshore banks issuing LCs," says Al. "He even formed one bank which people thought was in Wisconsin. It was called the First National Bank of Montserrat, which happens to be a city in Wisconsin. But then it was followed by the letters WI, which people assumed was Wisconsin — instead of West Indies."

"This guy was a smart guy, but he was greedy, and that's what ultimately brought him down — his own greed. He started selling bogus cashiers checks — and that's what took him down. He was crafty as hell about it — like the First National Bank of Montserrat, WI. Banks all over the country in the United States cashed these things. They'd look up in their registry table and find that there really was a First National Bank of Montserrat — in Wisconsin.

"Phil got a bunch of people to pass the checks and he got a cut out of everything. He had professional check passers and they were good at it. That's what they do for a living. But I remember a lot of banks got stung with them. It was always thousand dollar amounts, nothing really big, nothing that would raise eyebrows. But he passed a ton of them.

"He even copied Citibank at one time," Al continues. "Instead of Citi, he used City. He even had First National City Bank of Plymouth, Virginia. Of course, there is a real town, and there is a First National City Bank there. Again, it wasn't Plymouth, Virginia, though; it was Plymouth, Virgin Islands. It's right on the border. Because of its jurisdiction, you could put down VI or VA. It's actually in the Antilles. So it's actually Plymouth, Virgin Islands/Netherlands Antilles. He had the same logo of the bank. The checks looked wonderful. He had routing numbers that were genuine. The reason he got away with it for such a long time is that they had a hard time prosecuting him. He had the actual routing number of the bank he was duplicating, but the account number was an actual account number of this offshore bank. This offshore bank was real — real to the extent that it had an external wire transit number. It actually had collateral banks in the United States with small accounts, but of course, not enough to cover the amounts. They only had about 1/100 of the amount of the checks.

"That was one reason he was able to get away with it. He used the transit number of the bank he was carrying and the secondary five-digit code was the actual code of his bank and the next three-digit code was the code of his corresponding bank within the United States. What happened is that it got the Federal Reserve all screwed up trying to clear the checks. The Fed would be sending these checks everywhere, trying to figure out which bank would make good on them."

Phil Davis – Scammers Hall of Fame

"Davis was one of the earliest and more sophisticated scamscateers," recalls Al. "In the early 1980s, this guy Davis had the Federal Reserve and the Comptroller of the Currency all tied up in knots. They'd keep sending them to sixteen different banks before they found out they weren't worth anything.

"Davis could keep a bank check literally floating for six months. In the Fed, it gets cleared by transit, and the transit number directs the Fed as to where the check goes next. So it would just go from one bank to another bank to another bank (and offshore jurisdictions take ten to twelve days longer); then it would go to Mongolia or some other crazy place; then it would go to Vanuatu on its way back and then to the Barclay's Bank of the Kingdom of Tonga before it made its way back to Wisconsin. Then the bank in Tonga didn't know the difference. Here's how they did it. In some of the smaller jurisdictions, Davis had these people in his pocket. He was bribing them — for instance, let's say, the Tongan Comptroller of the Currency. He would send the check back — the wrong way. But this guy was great. There was a bank called the First Commercial Bank of Ulan Bator. He had some of the greatest 'banks' going."

The Offshore Tax Shelter Cattle Scam

"Davis also financed a huge tax shelter-cattle fraud in the Guernsey and Jersey Island," says Al. "And you can imagine how stupid the people were who invested in it — if you know how small Guernsey and Jersey Isles are. Guernsey is only about three square miles, and Jersey isn't much bigger. The Cattle Scam was done under the old F1 agricultural deals, in which the IRS used to allow offshore tax shelters for cattle depreciation. Davis didn't know anything about cows, but he claims that we've got 500,000 cows ready to go in Guernsey. And you couldn't even fit 500,000 cows on Guernsey (unless they were all on top of each other). But people didn't know, and nobody ever bothered it check it out. These were limited partnerships for 'tax-advantaged investors in foreign cattle operations,' which the IRS allowed. That's where a lot of those Costa Rican coffee and macadamia nut scams came from in the mid 80s. They called them 'offshore agricultural exemptions.' It could only happen in certain qualified nations. It was rather esoteric. All of the Hawaiian macadamia nut limited partnerships in the 80s were formed under the same act — and they were all scams.

"Some of the scams this guy Davis pulled off were absolutely out of this world.

And they were so stupid. Anyone that bought them had to be pretty stupid."

And what happened to Mr. Davis?

"It got so hot that by the early 80s, Davis was wanted by every single jurisdiction on earth — and then some. He never knew when to quit. I know he was eventually caught and worked out a deal. He got a thirty-year sentence, but I think he only served about thirteen years of that."

Astro-Scams and Beyond

"This was the guy that came up with the original scam of selling property on the Moon and even on Mars," says Al. "He sold deeded property rights on Mars. He had another Astro-Scam, where he was supposedly building rockets, so you could have your corpse shot up into outer space. Some people apparently like that idea. Or you could supposedly have your ashes scattered in outer space. He was also the founder of the cryogenics scam in 1979. The Bristol Research Cryogenic Institute. That was his deal. It was a little tiny office the size of a broom closet in Bristol, England."

This guy definitely earned his place in the Scamscateers Hall of Fame.

"This guy was one of the greatest scammers to ever come down the pike," says Al Martin. "He sold postal addresses. He did the university scams, diploma mills scams. This guy was into everything.

"Davis was smart. He would do what Hamil would do. [See Chapter 11 – 'Lawrence Richard Hamil: The US Government's Con Man' in *The Conspirators: Secrets of an Iran Contra Insider* by Al Martin]. When he got absolutely cornered on something, he would pay it off because this guy was dealing with such numbers that if he got pressed for a couple million bucks or go to jail, he's going to come up with a couple million bucks. He was very elusive. He had warrants out for him everywhere, but he traveled under a fake passports.

"He was very proud of telling this story in the end, when he was in court in London. When the judge asked him how many fake passports did he have, he said, 'Well, Your Honor, there are currently 143 nations in the world and I have 143 passports — not including my Lunar and Martian passport.' But these passports were genuine. They weren't fake. He would simply buy them, or do whatever it takes, buy a post office box in Upper Volta, or whatever was necessary. What would happen when he'd go from country to country, since these passports were legitimately obtained, they would have to go through extradition proceedings and a lot of paperwork to try to get the authorities of that country to arrest him. And he had informants everywhere. He always knew what the opposition in law enforcement was up to. He could go to one country and stay ten days. Then before the paperwork could be done and they could find him, he'd be in another country."

It seems that guys like that typically would have their outpost on a boat. The founder of Scientology, L. Ron Hubbard (allegedly another ONI operative) comes to mind. His so-called Sea Org, or Sea Organization, was based on a luxury yacht, which plowed the seas out of the jurisdiction of any country.

"That's where Davis lived — on a 112 foot ship," replies Al. "When you're in international waters, you're not completely untouchable but a country that wants you has to go through the Admiralty Court in London, and then notice has to be issued to all other signatories of the International Maritime Admiralty Agreement, and it's a very cumbersome process. My own attorney did some of that work. It would take at least thirty days to get a warrant to nab somebody in international waters and by that time they would simply duck into the coastal waters of some country. The United States and Britain are maybe the only two countries in the world, which will just grab somebody illegally. So what you do is you try to avoid having your big beefs in countries that kidnap people."

The Law Enforcement "Retirement" Program

Al recalls another story about the way that Florida police and federal agents would get their self-created "retirement pensions." A private investigator he knows "was partners with a guy by the name of Bill Venturi, a former City of Hollywood, Florida police detective, who retired on a disability after he confiscated a briefcase containing $400,000 in cash."

"It was a drug arrest which never made it to the police station," says Al. "He just kicked it under the bed when nobody was looking. He said that was commonly done in the 1980s. That's how guys retired. They'd be screwing around with this disability retirement, and they didn't want to give it to them, so they'd say 'Hey, I'll make my own.'

"The way he tells the story is funny as hell," says Al. "He was the first cop on the scene. The briefcase was on the bed, and he didn't know how much was in it. He just knew it was full of money. He threw it on the floor and got it about three quarters under the bed. When his partner arrived, he just gave the thing a little tap underneath the bed. And they're searching the room, and he says, 'Oh yeah, I already looked under the bed, but I didn't find anything there.' Then, of course, everyone was arrested, and the place was sealed up with police tape. When everybody was gone, three or four hours later, he came back and just retrieved the briefcase. He didn't even have to wear gloves because his fingerprints were going to be there anyway. But he was so blatant.

"This kind of corruption in the 1980s was so common that the cops and FBI agents, Ernie Jacobson, Tommy Sullivan, all these guys that would get involved – they didn't even try to hide it," says Al. "This guy Billy was probably in his mid to late 30s at the time. And he's finally getting a disability of $42,000 a year. He lives in this little $79,000 condo in Emerald Hills in Hollywood. Then suddenly he goes over and buys a house for $279,000 in cash. In cash. And nobody asked him any questions about where he got the money. He went to the same bank everybody else did. It was finally shut down from money laundering. It was called the People's Bank in Hollywood, Florida. It's where all law enforcement, involved in corruption, including the Broward's Sheriff office and Nick Navarro, laundered their money, all at the same bank. They had big American flags in front of it and it catered to law enforcement. That was their thing and that's how they advertised it. I remember the bank's advertisements. We're the Patriotic Bank. We launder money the old fashioned way," Al chuckles.

"The owners were a little marginal, but they were Republican," he continues. "That's why they stayed in business for so long — if you were Republican, and if you were connected, and if you gave part of the proceeds to the RNC, or some offshore account controlled by the RNC, or GOPAC. You were guaranteed protection. You could commit scam after scam after scam, as long as you kept it cool and didn't rip off a lot of old ladies. You keep ripping off institutions, not a lot of individual investors. As long as you were donating a third of the proceeds…"

That's called "tithing," isn't it?

"Yes, as long as you were giving the Republican Party its tithe money, you were all set," Al says. "If you try to tell people that — 90% of the people in the country wouldn't believe it. But I lived it. This is the way it was."

And why does he think people won't believe it?

"This is what I hear on the radio shows a lot, particularly the Republican-type radio show. 'Oh, well, the Democrats did the same thing, and they're all corrupt.' No, that's the Republicans who try to lay that idea on everyone. If the people really understood of how little consequence the Democratic Party is — as a party… They are virtually meaningless."

Steve Dinnerstein, a Florida-based private investigator, also has a lot of good stories. Al says, "He worked on a lot of cases in Miami and Fort Lauderdale, a lot of big drug and weapons cases. Lots of times, he'd get pushed out of the drug and weapons cases because the CIA was involved in the case somehow. He'd be pushed out. He'd be told to get out of it."

As in, "Don't follow this or else?"

"If it was a CIA deal, everybody knew to stay away from it," Al explains. "They weren't subtle about it. This all exists within a certain world, within a certain community. It's a subculture that the public at large doesn't have any idea really exists."

The Mob Pushed Out by Government Criminals

When asked about the presence of the Mob in Southern Florida, Al says, "By the mid 1980s, the Mob had gone out. They didn't have the power any more.

"Meyer Lansky was the pioneer of all the offshore stuff. But he was long gone by this time," Al adds. "You didn't have a lot of Mob connections or cross connection between Mob and Government that you used to have. The Mob simply didn't have the juice anymore.

"The Colombians had largely pushed the Mob out of their traditional areas," he continues. "The mafia had been reduced from the enormous presence it once had in Florida. It had been pushed out of the narcotics business altogether, though it still had some gambling operations. Even organized prostitution was falling apart. They still had loan sharking. They were still pretty strong in that because it served a purpose, but the Mob was disappearing from the scene. A lot of construction firms were involved with the Mob, involved in nickel and dime kickback schemes with state and country bureaus, but it was hundreds of thousands, not millions. The only reason they were tolerated was because they would be used for cash in a hurry. If you had to swing a deal, they were there."

When asked how Jeb Bush was positioned in Florida, Al says, "That wasn't hard to do. He used, what was at that time a 90% fiercely loyal Republican Cuban minority, to springboard himself into politics."

And was this George Bush Sr.'s doing? "Well, sure. George Sr. was always popular with the Cubanos."

And with regards to positioning a Bush in a strategic state that has a great influx of drugs? "In terms of Iran Contra operations, sure," says Al. "That's why there was the installation of the Vice Presidential Task Force on Drugs in Miami in 1983 — to prevent any more embarrassing force-downs of 'authorized' narcotics traffic.

"Texas at the time was a big marijuana state," Al continues. "But you did not have the quantity of cocaine being shipped through Texas — not like Florida. Florida was THE cocaine market, probably followed by New Orleans. There was a lot of narcotics distribution points in Texas, New Mexico and Arizona, and this is where you get into the involvement of the ONI (Office of Navy Intelligence).

"There was a lot of involvement of ONI in narcotics trafficking in what was known as the Western Corridor because they had the facilities to do it," he says. "They had a lot of air facilities. They controlled Evergreen Airlines out of Oregon. That was a big regional cargo carrier at the time. They also controlled a big trucking company in Phoenix, Arizona."

CIA vs. ONI

Was there rivalry between the CIA and ONI in their narcotics trafficking and distribution?

"Sure, there was," he answers. "The rivalry was always contained, because from my perspective the ONI, for a long time, was allowed the wholesale drug business in the Midwest and Desert Southwest, and the CIA had wanted the big retail markets on the West Coast. The ONI literally got what was left over.

"After Iran-Contra, you started to see more articles being written about ONI involvement in drug trafficking in the West," he continues. "There was a lot written about it in the media. Then, when Gary Eitel filed that lawsuit against Evergreen, alleging what I just said, he did a pretty good job in proving it. He had the resources to keep the lawsuit outstanding for a very long time. He drew attention to it and that's what finally forced Evergreen into bankruptcy. He was just trying to prove that Evergreen Airlines was a proprietary of the ONI and what ONI had been doing with it. Just like Southern Air Transport, Evergreen filed for bankruptcy. It has since reorganized, but it's just a shadow of its former self.

"There were so many scams," Al Martin concludes. "It's like Jeb Bush used to say, 'So many scams. So little time.'"

BUSHWHACKED

Chapter 19

Not Just Another Lone Nut:
The Passion of Richard Belzer

A CCORDING TO RECENT SURVEY/POLLS, nearly 70% of the American people believe that JFK was murdered by a criminal conspiracy — not by designated patsy Lee Harvey Oswald. They also believe that the Warren Commission Report on the JFK Assassination is an elaborate and not-so-clever hoax.

Actor-author Richard Belzer agrees.

In fact, his whimsically titled book *UFO's, JFK and Elvis: Conspiracies You Don't Have To Be Crazy to Believe*, is a great overview of the ludicrous albeit amusing flaws in government cover-up stories, officially part of the Authorized Version of History.

The facts are on his side, despite the Government-Media's disinformation on some of the most important unanswered questions — "Who Killed JFK? And Why?" and "What about UFO's?"

Belzer, best known for his role as John Munch on the NBC-TV series *Homicide: Life on the Street* and the spin-off *Special Victims Unit*, is also an accomplished comic with his own brand of edgy politically incorrect humor.

Known as an eclectic reader, Belzer says in a interview, "I used to read Steamshovel Press — when I could find it. I started years ago and always looked for it, but I haven't seen it lately."

His reading diet also includes *Prevailing Winds, the Nation, New York Times Washington Post, New York Post, USA Today, International Herald Tribune,* and the *Wall Street Journal*.

And what does he like about Steamshovel Press? (http://www.steamshovelpress.com) "You know — the alternative press that's willing to go where the mainstream press doesn't go — I'm attracted to that," he says.

Listing Steamshovel Press in the book's bibliography as one of the primary sources of alternative news and commentary, Richard Belzer praises the pioneering work of publisher-editor Kenn Thomas, saying, "I like their take on things, their openness. They've done some good work on the Kennedy stuff. Things you can't find in too many places."

Kenn Thomas is the author of many ground-breaking books, including *The Octopus* (Feral House) and *Moray Island UFO* (Feral House).

Referring to his own book, Belzer admits, "These are subjects that I've been interested in and fascinated by for many, many years. I would often go on about them at lunch or dinner, with my friends and family. It seemed that I had all this information that was so compelling and not generally known. Being in the position I'm in now where I'm kind of known, I felt compelled to get it out and drive the rest of the world crazy — not just my friends."

And did his friends say, "Oh, Richard's just ranting again," or what?

"Some of them were very intrigued and they were educated by it," he continues, "and others are still skeptical. There's a wide range of reaction to this material, and that's what intrigues me. I mean, there are people who absolutely refuse to believe the truth when its presented to them irrefutably, and that really fascinates me about human nature. You know, when really smart people just can't accept the reality of something, it's just amazing."

Is he referring to his friend and neighbors?

"Yeah, famous people and unfamous people and fans and people from all different disciplines and walks of life have varied takes on stuff that I have found to be true," he says. "Another reason I wrote the book — it has such a big bibliography — is that you don't have to make anything up. The reality is so fascinating and compelling and strange and funny. I don't need to invent any new theories. It's just my take on things that are in existence."

So who's the book written for? Belzer's book, after all, can be found in the "Comedy" section of bookstores.

"It's written kind of tongue in cheek," continues Belzer, "and it's unusual. It's a hybrid animal — let's face it. It's history, journalism, comedy. In addition to being for the choir, those who don't need to be converted, it's mostly for those people who have established points of views and aren't aware of information that's in the book and then they get turned around. That's happened to me a lot. I did a ten-city book tour and met some people along the way who were totally convinced that there was no conspiracy. After reading my book, they admitted that they changed their mind. And that's incredibly satisfying."

Were these readers *Homicide* fans or his stand-up comedy fans?

"I've been around for such a long time, so [I have] a lot of different fans for different reasons, a combination of people," says Belzer. "Some people were into this stuff already and didn't need to be converted, but there's a lot of information they didn't know. A lot of these books on UFO's and JFK are very dry. You have to wade through a lot of stuff. I felt that there are so many titillating things that you could give some of the highlights of these two worlds and conspiracies. It was exciting to me to finally concretize it and put it down on paper."

And how did he personally get interested in the JFK Hit?

"When it first happened, like most people, I didn't think there was any conspiracy," replies Belzer. "Then things started happening like the Mark Lane book, *Rush to Judgment* and then you had the Garrison Trial [of Clay Shaw in New Orleans]. Bobby Kennedy was assassinated. Then [there was] the Watergate break-in. It just seemed that the same cast of characters started showing up every time America did something dirty."

Belzer's right. It's like the motto of the CIA was — "So many hits, so little time."

"It got to be a cumulative thing and kind of galvanized in the late sixties," he continues. "And then when Watergate happened, we realized that some of the same people involved in the Bay of Pigs invasion were involved in the Watergate Break-in. That was another Wake Up Call."

And why did he throw Elvis into the mix, since it could be argued that it actually puts the book in, well, a kooky light?

"Well," he hems and haws. "I thought it was explained in the first chapter when I say that George Bush, when asked about JFK and was there a conspiracy said in response, 'Yeah, and some people believe Elvis is still alive.' It's a way for the mainstream to marginalize serious research into JFK and UFO's."

But does he realize what it does to the book by its title?

Belzer replies cautiously, "Underneath it says 'Conspiracies you don't have to be crazy to believe.' I'm sorry it has that impact, but I think that people will pick up the book just out of curiosity and discover that it's not by any stretch of the imagination marginalized."

A better title might have been, "UFOs, JFK and No Elvis," I said — but he got the point. So did he ever do a standup routine on "The JFK Hit" like Lenny Bruce's infamous "Neckrophilia Routine"?

"I did an HBO special," says Belzer. "I sang a song about it and did the Gerald Ford thing which is in the book about the single bullet. I also did a song called

"Eleven Miles an Hour," a song by Don Was. Belzer proceeds to sing a couple verses, a song which ends with the memorable line, "Eleven miles an hour. Lead fell like a shower at eleven miles an hour.

"I love standup and occasionally I do charity shows to get back up on stage. There's nothing like having immediate response in a live audience — the dynamism and immediate feedback. I miss it. I do, once I'm onstage.

"I started as an actor," he says. "Most standups [comedians] do standup and then go into acting, but I started in a movie called *The Groove Tube* in the early seventies. Then I started to do standup in 1972. I started acting in 1971."

The most notable thing about *The Groove Tube* is that it preceded *Saturday Night Live* type satirical sketches — but in feature film format. Belzer's role as a paranoid marijuana dealer still withstands the test of time. And his comedy is definitely in the same class as the politically incorrect humor of Lenny Bruce, Mort Sahl, George Carlin and Jackie Mason.

"We have a house in southwestern France, which is an idyllic lifestyle," he continues. "Long meals and walks. Visiting ancient places. Being in nature. Totally opposite of the United States.

"My wife visited some friends about twelve years ago," he says. "We found this house that was for sale and got a loan from a French bank. Now we're renovating it. We've been going there every year for about ten years — during hiatus in spring and summer."

And does he live in R. Crumb country?

Belzer says no, adding that the famous cartoonist Robert Crumb "gave a book of his drawings to a guy and the guy gave him a villa in southern France. He's a few hours away from me. I've never met Robert."

And what's on the horizon for the future?

"I'm doing the show [*Special Victims Unit*] and I'm getting ready to write another book, *Richard Belzer's History of the World*. I'll start at the beginning of recorded time to the present day. One of the chapters is going to be "What's with the fucking Germans anyway?" about the history of Germans. Then there will be the real history of the United States — the real history of certain things in archaeology that are true that aren't generally known and things that throughout antiquity that weren't generally taught in schools but are true and helped really shape our history. History very often is propaganda of that particular culture and not what really happened.

"History is conspiracy by definition," says Belzer. "People conspire to do things to change events."

The prevailing paradigm taught in schools, however, is the Accident Theory of History. This Belief System teaches that events just happen by accident — all kinds of random unconnected events. Those who recognize that events are shaped by the movers and shakers behind the scenes are derided as conspiracy theorists.

"I think it's naive to think that things are that random," says Belzer, "especially now when so many things can be controlled by technology."

For instance, according to Professor Antony C. Sutton's book, *America's Secret Establishment*, the origins of both the American Psychological Society and the American Historical Society lead to the same group — a Yale secret society called Skull and Bones. Today, the funding and control mechanism of so-called historians and psychologists is clear. Those who mold public opinion and the perception of history must toe the line regarding what's acceptable and what's not. It could be argued that this in itself is a *defacto* conspiracy.

The passion of Richard Belzer is his desire to show people an alternative view.

"I really feel compelled for some reason to present in an entertaining fashion some of the serious truths of our existence," he says. "Other people apparently don't have the time or inclination.

"I'm an actor. I'm crazy. I'm obsessed, so I have the time to study this stuff. I'm fortunate that I'm well known enough so I can get published. I feel that at some modest level I'm doing journalistic historical research which I'm sharing."

The reception he's gotten with his book has emboldened Belzer to write more.

"I originally wanted to do a history book," he says, "so this is something that's been on my mind for a long time. The success of this book will just make it easier to do the next one. This one is doing very well. It's still selling and I got a lot of great reviews. I'm really flattered about how well it's been treated and how little ridicule and vilification have occurred. Whoever's read it can see that this is serious research — though its treated sardonically."

And is he going to write about fun stuff like secret societies in his history book? "Well, yeah, that's a part of who we are and particularly in American history, everyone involved in fomenting the Boston Tea Party had just come out of a Masonic lodge. There are all kinds of connections with the historical role that secret societies play. Virtually every power player belongs to organizations that are not generally known. Some are covers for other things."

Maybe he should apply for membership in the Council on Foreign Relations. He could join other CFR members who are media luminaries: Diane Sawyer (ABC), Dan Rather (CBS), Tom Brokaw (NBC), Daniel Schorr (NPR), R. Emmett Tyrrell (American Spectator), Bill Kristol (Weekly Standard), Leon Wieseltier (New Republic), Lewis Lapham (Harlers), William F. Buckley Jr. (National Review), or Joe "Anonymous" Klein (Newsweek).

"To apply — that's not a bad idea," Belz answers. It's unclear if he's serious or not.

Send him an app. Maybe he needs a sponsor too, like membership in an exclusive golf club or co-op.

Richard Belzer is also working on a documentary film of his book tour. "I filmed my tour, so I'm doing a movie like Michael Moore did [*The Big One*]," he says.

"We're editing that now. I took a film crew with me. I got great stuff from all over, some of the [book] signings. We interviewed scholars, historians and doctors. People who were in my audience came up. Lyndon Johnson's mistress — we got her on film telling a story of how Lyndon told her it was the CIA and the oil millionaires who killed Kennedy. And I got it on film and got a release from her. I got doctors' autopsies and photos.

"I also have footage of UFO's given to us by people in Sedona, Arizona. Really great compelling footage. I have footage of black helicopters. I have some great stuff. There's already an interest in it. It'll be the same title as the book. So it's going to be really exciting."

Richard Belzer's enthusiasm is infectious. His comedy CD, *Another Lone Nut*, is a great example of the adage that comedy is simply tragedy after some time has passed.

It's about time. Since 1963, the JFK Hit has been a relatively taboo subject. Using humor to puncture the conspiracy and its cover-up by the Government-Media, Richard Belzer is the epitome of politically incorrect black humor.

Besides it's Official. Even comedian Chris Rock endorses Belz as "the greatest black comic."

Yuck. Yuck.

Chapter 20

New! Improved! Manipulation!
An Interview with Douglas Rushkoff

E VEN THOUGH DOUGLAS RUSHKOFF'S *Coercion* is really about mind control, he never mentions it. But this is, after all, his most subversive book. Rushkoff has been billed as "a brilliant heir to [Marshall] McLuhan." And as the author of *Media Virus, Cyberia, Playing the Future*, and the novel *Ecstasy Club*, Douglas Rushkoff has been in the avant-garde of media analysis for many years.

Coercion is a fascinating book about the technology of sales and media manipulation. Using personal anecdotes, Rushkoff shows the reader how to sell anything to anybody — and how to resist.

His conclusion? The powerful techniques of coercion — from Carnegie's classic *How to Win Friends and Influence People* to Neuro-Linguistic Programming (NLP) to the diabolical CIA Interrogation Manual — have poisoned our lives. All personal interactions, from our daily workday encounters to our most intimate relationships, have been tagged, even perverted, by the meta-language of "sales."

In other words, the manipulative power of advertising and commercial programming has exacted a devastating social cost on our lives. And the coercive strategies of the Mega-Corporate Capitalist juggernaut are effectively ruling the planet.

Cult Branding

When asked about the controversy surrounding his book, Rushkoff replies that good reviews were plenty — but only the *Wall Street Journal*, the bastion of corporate consumerism, dismissed it.

"That was my only really negative review [*the Wall Street Journal*]," said Rushkoff. "The real way that Corporate America will squash this book, if they have any intention to do so, is by ignoring it, not by making it controversial. The amazing thing in that [Journal review] was they really attempted to reconceptualize the book as conspiracy theory.

"[They wrote] that I was making wild speculative allegations against the advertising industry, whereas that's not what I was doing at all," he continues. "What I actually did — and it was painstaking to do so — was keep myself from making conclusions. Instead, I just reported the scenes and experiences I had — working as a consultant to the top ten advertising and public relations firms in the United States.

"I was working with one firm that was doing focus groups with cult members about how they got pulled into their cult and what the cult did… They interviewed some people from Scientology. Some of them were still in. And [they interviewed] those who were in cult-like organizations like Amway or Hells Angels."

"Or Microsoft?" I added… "Just kidding."

"Well, they didn't," said Rushkoff. "[They wanted to] find out what these different organizations had in common in the hopes of then applying these techniques to brands."

"Wouldn't a typical Microsoft employee be a possibility for a focus group like that?" I asked.

"Yes, but I don't think that Microsoft is quite as engineered in a cult way," replied Rushkoff. "I mean they actually interviewed Apple users because there was a cult-like appeal to that brand. And what does that have in common? They're not saying that cults are all evil necessarily, but they are cults. People have irrational devotion to brands, ideas, organizations."

Not unlike Windows. Maybe.

The other Doug — Doug Coupland wrote about it in his parody called *MicroSerfs* — I told him. That ties in somehow, doesn't it?

"I mean it does," said Rushkoff, "but I didn't write about it. I didn't really think about it that much. Corporate cultures exploit certain family dynamics in order to gain loyalty, for sure."

But there are cult-like characteristics to any so-called "corporate" so-called "culture," I insisted.

"Right," he agreed, "but they're a little less applicable to advertising a brand because you've got all the people working in one place. You can use architecture and employee policies, stock reimbursement and things like that, to create a cult atmosphere, whereas a brand like Apple or a group like Harley Davidson riders, or even Scientology are spread out over a much wider geography. The loyalty is created using techniques that are not really dependent on everyone going to the same place at the same time. You have to create a set of aspirational goals and so on.

"For the ad agency — I made a presentation to them on what all the cults have in common," continued Rushkoff. "How do they work? Why do so many seemingly intelligent people get involved?"

And what was the purpose of the research?

"They were looking for ways to apply the techniques of cult indoctrination to 'cult brands.' They're called 'cult brands.' In other words — how to take a brand and have an off-the-shelf set of rules that they can apply. If a client comes in and says, 'We want our brand to be a cult brand,' they say, 'Well, this is how to do it.'

"Then they use the twenty steps or stages that I came up with and outlined in the book. I came up with a step-by-step how-to [guide to] increase someone's loyalty to one brand and hatred of all others."

So clients actually went to this agency and specifically asked for a cult brand? Or did it develop out of his work?

"It was more of something that the advertising agency wants to be able to offer. And it's part of four or five different things that they use. They already use 'media viruses,' which is from a book I wrote on how to launch an idea through the media and use secondary media to spread the idea, rather than money."

And how was the "media virus" concept applied by the marketing wizards to get us to buy stuff?

"A media virus is basically an idea that's wrapped in a shell," explained Rushkoff. "The shell is what allows it to be spread through the media. The shell of a media virus is something that generally breaks a rule of media in order to get attention. So then the idea, or the brand, or whatever you want to spread, can go along with it.

"I wrote a book called *Media Virus* and then lo and behold! we started seeing advertisements like Calvin Klein's campaign that pictured young adults. There was a little carpet with wood paneling behind them [while they were] answering weird questions to an off-camera voice. That was supposed to look like young people auditioning for porn films. And after a few weeks, as that aesthetic was discovered, there were all these news stories about it. Then Calvin Klein took those commercials off the air, but they ended up getting more media about the advertisements than they could have ever possibly bought. Because it became an actual 'news story.' We started seeing these ads on every news show. And even though it was scandalous, it ended up perpetuating this image of Calvin Klein jeans and underwear as subversive and countercultural and daring.

"So it actually helped his brand. So things like 'media viruses' which I thought were cool countercultural media weapons, ended up being used by Madison Avenue as an advertising tool."

I reminded Rushkoff that the same thing happened to the guy he himself marginalized in his own book. Historically, the Canadian media professor named Wilson Bryan Key, author of *Subliminal Seduction*, was also discredited and attacked by the Ad Agency Establishment.

"Right," he said. Even though Key's books were pooh-poohed and are now being used in media classes and advertising courses, Rushkoff doesn't "believe" in subliminal manipulation.

"The thing is and the reason why that's not really dangerous is because the techniques that he believes he uncovered don't actually exist," insisted Rushkoff. "They weren't actually in practice," he claims — with no evidence, it should be noted..

Stunned, I asked him, "You're saying that the technology for putting electromagnetic frequencies on a carrier wave don't exist?" The standard techniques of using carrier frequency waves and adding other audio or visual information has been well-researched. The result is not obvious to the conscious mind, however, but has been fully imprinted on the subconscious.

"You're saying that technology does not exist?" I questioned him further.

"I'm saying that I've worked in the deepest, darkest conference rooms and back rooms of the world's leading public relations firms, US government and advertising, and no one, or anyone I've run into, has ever heard of or used those techniques," he stated flatly.

As if they'd tell him, I thought to myself — a "mere consultant."

"But you asked them and they denied it? Or what are you saying?" I pressed on.

"I'm saying that I've watched the inception, creation and execution of hundreds, perhaps thousands of advertising and public relations campaigns, and in none of them was there a process in which pictures were imbedded with phalluses, or with the word 'sex,' or commercials in which carrier frequencies had hidden messages. None of it."

"And you think you would be privy to that?" I asked him.

"Yes," he answered. I said, "Why is that?"

"Because I was working side by side with the people who were responsible for making the most coercive style advertisement and public relations campaigns known to man. I was in the state of the art companies where this is done. And I was treated as one of them."

Subliminal Media Technology

With all due respect to Douglas Rushkoff, the technologies of subliminal manipulation have been documented by N. F. Dixon in *Subliminal Perception* (1971) and Wilson Bryan Key in *Subliminal Seduction* (1973).

With an introduction called "Media Ad-Vice" by media guru Marshall McLuhan himself, Dr. Key's book as well as his subsequent titles, *Media Sexploitation* (1976) and *The Clam Plate Orgy* (1980) are well worth reading.

For those who think they think for themselves, another highly recommended title is Key's book, *The Age of Manipulation: The Con in Confidence, The Sin in Sincere* (1989). Key's description of subliminal manipulation technology used in advertising and the media is a classic.

Dr. Key writes that "high-tech mass persuasion has achieved levels of sophistication far beyond what most individuals imagine. Most still desperately cling to the delusion that they think for themselves, determine their own destinies, exercise both individual and collective free will (the great myth that underlies democratic ideology); that advertising works in the interest of the consumer; and perhaps the greatest self-deception of all — that they can easily discriminate between fantasy and reality."

He also describes "audio-visual techniques through which subliminal information can be communicated, hidden from conscious awareness, that appear frequently in ad media," and explores the fine line between fantasies, realities, and mythology, as well as the psychology and physiology underlying our basic perceptions of the world.

Key then goes into great detail on psychological manipulation through symbols and stereotypes, as well as the prolific use of sex and death images in advertising, most commonly in liquor and cigarette ads, but also for products like margarine, salad dressing, and chewing gum.

After reading the book, you'll be able to find the phallus in the Chivas ad.

Or the female genitals in the Betty Crocker cake mix ad. (They're illustrated in the book.)

Then you can meditate on why you didn't realize that the Michael Jackson song *Beat It* is a masturbation fantasy. Jackson's music, after all, could be his way of introducing children to pedophilia as an "alternative lifestyle." After all, he's revealed himself quite thoroughly through his music. He bragged that he was not only *Bad*, but also *Dangerous*.

[Another pop culture artifact showing just how subliminal advertising is done can be seen in the film *Agency* (1981), starring Robert Mitchum as a sinister ad executive.]

Media Manipulation

When Rushkoff said he worked with the most coercive agencies, I asked him how he would characterize those?

He replied, "Hill and Knowlton" [the notorious and well-documented CIA front].

[Incidentally, this PR firm was instrumental in swaying public opinion to support the illegal Gulf War by spreading disinformation that Saddam Hussein's soldiers were taking babies out of incubators in Kuwaiti hospitals and letting them die. It was a strategic lie concocted by Hill and Knowlton as a rationale for unindicted state criminal George Bush Sr. and his so-called "Gulf War."]

What kind of technology or methodology does that describe? I asked Rushkoff.

"The kinds of methodologies are much more basic than you would think. Using Neuro-Linguistic Programming. Cues in advertising copy. Using hypnosis techniques in hand to hand sales. Using presumptive language in attempting to close a deal before it's closed." Which is standard sales stuff, I added.

"The darkness is not these bizarre secret hidden techniques. If anything… the only place I've seen them used is in non-lethal weapons technology by the Defense Department. By focussing on those, we end up really missing what's actually going on and how dangerous what's happening in front of our faces really is. Things as simple as collaborative filtering online. Websites will look at the things you've bought and then compare that with things other people like you have bought in order to make recommendations and pull you more towards certain kinds of purchases than you might have done otherwise."

Which is the front-end page of Amazon.com, I said.

"Yes, essentially," he agreed. "It's really much simpler than all of that and when you live in a world — when even mentioning that you've been a part of an advertising agency developing 'cult-branding' techniques is so hard for people to believe — there's really no reason to get into stuff that no one's actually witnessed."

And you had experience with so-called non-lethal weapons technology? I asked him. "Those are things ranging from using low-frequency [electromagnetic] waves in battlefield situations to intimidate your enemy to using smells. There's a lot of scents now that chemo-reception scientists have figured out make people upset and make people intimidated."

Acting with emotional triggers, so to speak?

"Right," he said. "And those are real, and more than enough to talk about. I've seen them being [used in field test situations] or read research reports about them being used. I've interviewed people in the military who have used them. I've read the public relations materials — bill collection agencies that use pheromones in the ink in collection letters."

The Cult of Consumerism

Rushkoff is adamant in his stance. "One of the least empowering positions one can take is that there's this big conspiracy of people doing these nasty things and we're just these helpless Pavlovian humans. The fact is we're not. We actively participate in these things. The way we participate in them now is by buying into the idea that more money and more possessions are going to make us happy, that we need to work more days every week.

"It's very simple stuff," he continued. "And the way to break free of these kinds of programming is much simpler than people give it credit for."

And what does he recommend?

"For example, the Sabbath," said Rushkoff. "It was invented, maybe four thousand years ago, by the Hebrews — the idea of taking one day off a week, when you don't buy or sell anything. When you don't consume or produce. Where you basically accept that you are sacred — just the way you are. That's a very powerful thing to do. And 'they,' whoever they are, can't stop us because we have religious freedom in this country. That puts us in the same camp as the Moral Majority, God bless them, who are, for better or for worse, protecting certain kinds of religious freedoms."

There's no doubt about it — the coercive techniques of advertising and sales which Rushkoff enumerates in his book diminish people's awareness of the sacredness of their lives, reducing them to a materialistic level of consumerism.

"All coercive techniques involve, on one level or another, frightening, or threatening, or intimidating a person, so that they move into survival mode," said Rushkoff, referring to the responses of the so-called reptilian brain.

"If you think about Maslow's Hierarchy of Needs, it's how a person develops. When you move up into really higher causes like love, like community, like self-actualization, other things begin to matter. When you are intimidated, either by a salesman, or by a commercial, or by an architecture, or by a cityscape, or by a policeman — whoever intimidates you — you are thrown back into a survival mode."

Describing the bottomless pit of Desire, Rushkoff said, "If you already have all the things you need to survive, all that does is it puts you in consumption mode.

So the kind of consumption that we see in America now is really just an exaggeration and an inappropriate exercise of our survival instincts. If you've got an OK house, an OK car, you have a place for your family to live, they have a school to go to, and they have food on the table, now you're going to want to work more and buy more and participate more, so you can get a bigger house with a bigger yard, and a bigger security system, and more stuff."

And that's exactly why Rushkoff has been perceived as a threat to the promotion of "consumer culture."

"Well, right," he answered, "because the maintenance of the consumer culture, the maintenance of what we're calling the 'GNP' really, the maintenance of a growth culture depends on more people buying more stuff in less time.

"The only way to get more people buying more stuff in less time is to get them to buy more stuff they don't actually need. And that requires creating needs or creating a sense of needs. And the way you create a sense of constant need is make people feel they're under a sense of constant stress — of losing what they have, of not being strong, or powerful enough. Their dick isn't big enough, Their land isn't big enough. Their job isn't important enough."

[Note: Rushkoff should examine in greater detail the UK's Tavistock Institute methodology of using stress and media as psychological warfare against a targeted population, in this case, the residents of America.]

It can also be argued that the advertising-driven corporate culture exported from the United States is the *defacto* plague of globalization, or globalism, or globaloney. Popularized by gofers of the New World Order like New York Times columnist Thomas Friedman, author of *The Lexus and the Olive Tree*, it is a prime example of promoting global consumption to the exclusion of spiritual needs.

In fact, Rushkoff has eloquently explained why his latest book is a threat to the unthrottled growth of Mega-Corporate Consumer Culture.

If he was used to consulting with ad agencies, then he's endangered his livelihood in a sense, I noted.

"One way to look at it is that I'm endangering my livelihood," Rushkoff answered. "Another way to look at it — which I get a lot — is that I'm a hypocrite, that I'm trying to sell books. And that if I'm selling books — why am I exacerbating the same problem?"

People have actually said that to you? I asked. "Oh yeah, all the time. Actually I'm not a communist. I do believe that people should be able to have jobs, to make money and sell things. What I don't like is when people and companies coerce people into buying things they don't need. In other words, when you suspend somebody's ability to make a rational logical decision because you want them to buy more stuff — I question an economy that depends on this kind of expansion."

Then I told him that what I really liked about his book is that he explains the different techniques and uses anecdotes to draw the conclusion that we're actually poisoning our interpersonal relationships by using these manipulations.

Rushkoff said, "What happens — and that's really why I try to steer clear of so-called 'conspiracy theory' — paranoia is our enemy. Paranoia puts us in a confused, scared, survival state. A paranoid person is going to be sold more easily than a non-paranoid person. That's why paranoia sells so well. Paranoia is used to sell Y2K products. If you're a paranoid conspiracy theorist, you're going to buy the full survivalist kit. You get your house out in the middle of nowhere. You get your guns. You get your wells. You get your generator. You know how much that costs? A lot."

So everyone's greatest enemy is fear? "When a person is isolated and tense, they're more easily manipulated," he said. "And they're more easily manipulated because they're in survival mode. And survival mode is more like instinctive reaction, impulsive reaction, rather than a considered one. The fact is that we're human beings and what makes us better — dare I say better? — than the animals is that we can actually conform nature to our designs — to a higher moral and ethical standard than nature follows."

Future of the Internet

Much has been said about Rushkoff's disenchantment with the way the Internet has become a controlling, rather than an empowering tool.

"I believe that the Internet can still be an empowering tool," he said. "People can express who they are through a computer and a phone line. People can share information with people around the world. People can join discussions. People can self-express and form communities. I think that opportunity is being missed as our entire culture seems bent into turning the Internet into an electronic strip mall and to use the tool of technology, to use the vast processing of our computers, in order to entrain us to purchase more things in less time."

And what is his vision of moving the Internet into a broadcast medium?

"I don't think it became a broadcast medium," Rushkoff answered. "I think it went from a telecommunications medium into a direct marketing platform, which is actually worse. If it turned into a TV, it would be just innocuous, a potential opportunity missed. Now that it's being turned into a direct marketing tool, it's actually further exacerbating the problem of a consumer culture.

"We are automating the process of coercion, so now we don't even need a smart person to figure it out. Computers using a shotgun approach are trying everything they can to get us to buy more stuff. They're just following their programs."

And how does Rushkoff cope with it? How does he disentangle himself from this robot-control buy-sell mechanism?

"I don't use the web," he admitted, "Or very infrequently, because I don't like what's there. I know that almost every website you go to is working to push you towards the 'buy' button somewhere. And I don't want to be in that environment. It's a private space, not a public space. It's like walking through the mall, and I don't want to be there, so I don't use the web.

"I use e-mail. Because more and more of the world we live in is commodified, more and more of it is in the control of advertisers, of marketing, more and more of public space is being privatized, I take my one day off when I don't deal with that. That's the only thing I've found that I can do, and as I do that, I find my mindset shifts a little bit. I get shifted out of survival mode and into enlightenment mode, if you will."

When asked if he's still "consulting," Rushkoff said, "No, not at all."

Is it fallout from the book? "I can't bring myself to do it," he answered. "I only did the consulting, as research for the book. In 1994-95 — back when the people I was consulting to weren't doing anything mean. They just wanted to understand what the fuck was going on. And that's what inspired me to write the book. Then I found out they were using what I was saying to retool for the electronic age. So then I figured, I'm going to go and see what's going on, to see the worst of the worst, find out what they do and write a book about it.

"I was offered $20,000 to go for one day to do a consult for an ad agency, and I said no — which is a frightening thought. I mean, talk about survival instinct. Twenty thousand is a lot of money, especially when you're just going to be a writer again."

And how did the book *Coercion* originate? "I wanted to see what was the current state of the art. I wanted to see where we were in the coercion arms race.

"I was hoping that I would find out that I was right all along and that the tools of new media have empowered us to see through the coercive techniques. And instead, what I found out was that for a year or two, we were breaking free, but that now advertisers and e-commerce people have taken it back. They've moved to the next version."

Surprised? "It's not like I've had a reverse course. I haven't at all. I've been fighting and arguing for and envisioning the very same thing. It's just that the world has changed. The Internet's a different thing than it was in 1994.

"My internet experience originated in 1988. I had written some books in 1994. This is my seventh book [*Coercion*]. I wrote some other books about the Internet, but they were much more positive." And idealistic, I might add.

"In those books, I espoused the belief that we were breaking free of coercion.

People weren't going to be able to do mean things to us anymore and that's no longer the case."

And where is it heading? I asked him. "I think people are starting to get annoyed, and I think that coercion is being done so rapidly, so blatantly, and so transparently that people are seeing what is the root cause of it."

Rushkoff points to a new trend — how marketers deal with consumer over-dose to coercion by promoting instead a "return to the basics."

"TimeWarner is coming out with a new magazine called *Simplicity* which is for the simple-minded return- to-simplicity ethics, so it's possible that it'll be marketed straight back to us, but it's possible that we'll see that too. I think people are just tired."

And how about TV? Do people watch TV in New York? "New York is an expensive place," he answered. "You've got to earn a lot of money to live here. People have different attitudes. How do people relate to the issues we talk about? It's not really so much about television, as it's about the stock market and their brokers. If they're watching TV, they're watching CNBC to see if the Dow or the NASDAQ is going up or down. And there's a lot of that. It's very money-centric."

And what's the reaction of his friends to the book?

"Some of them are kind of libertarian," answered Rushkoff. "Anybody who's made a ton of money off the Internet, who was kind of a cool pot-smoking person before has to become a libertarian. A libertarian is someone who believes that free market capitalism is the only thing that matters — as long as someone's making money. So they become people who believe in the economy. Period. It becomes their new religion. They read their Ayn Rand books."

So they go from making a ton of cash to becoming an Ayn Randist or an Objectivist? "It's been a trend for the last five years in San Francisco and New York," he said.

"I never knew where they all came from," I confided.

"They're very vocal," he said. "John Barlow. Mike Godling. And it's very hard. If you get a job at an Internet company and you have vested stock and you have the ticker on your Windows desktop of the stock that you're working for, you're really plugged into it.

"It's really simple. Get all your employees in there. Give them some stock. Get the stock ticker on there. If they're working for TimeWarner, they want the TimeWarner stock ticker to go up. And they make that go up by getting more advertising, by nice stories about Microsoft. So all these people are pro-Microsoft and anti-government. That's how it happens."

And what are some other memes that Rushkoff would like to see propagated?

"I'd like people to take more time. Before you buy something, picture yourself with that thing, and ask do you really want that? Before you take a job, before you do something at work that you think might be mean to someone else, think for a second — do I really want to do this? It's a matter of thinking before we act. The internet and our very fast-paced culture is asking us to make impulsive reactions to things.

"What I'm arguing is that impulsive reactions are very often not the most conscious ones. I'm telling people to bring back consciousness into what they're doing by taking a conscious pause. Experience 'buyer's remorse' before you buy — rather than after."

The Buddhists call it Right Mind, I tell him.

"It's hard," said Rushkoff, "especially when it's Now Or Never — Now Or Never... You don't lose those opportunities."

"If they say Now Or Never — just say Never."

Chapter 21

The Montessori Legacy: An Interview with Dr. Elisabeth Caspari

I magine having lived in three centuries... Dr. Elisabeth Caspari has actually done it. Born Elisabeth Getaz on September 6, 1899 in Chateau d'Oex [pronounced "day"], a Swiss mountain village, Dr. Elisabeth Caspari now lives in the mountain village of Emigrant, Montana, just north of Yellowstone National Park.

Dr. Caspari is, by all accounts, the oldest Montessori teacher in the world and one of the last living students of the famous child education revolutionary Maria Montessori herself.

"You were a Montessorian before we met," Dr. Caspari recalls Montessori telling her in 1939. It's a compliment which underscores her longstanding commitment.

Having earned a Doctorate in Music and Pedagogy, Dr. Caspari established her own flourishing school of music in Switzerland in the 1920s.

Married to Charles Caspari, an engineer, in 1930, she continued her spiritual pursuits through their mutual interest in comparative religion.

True Adventures in Tibet

At the invitation of Mrs. Clarence Gasque, the Casparis left Switzerland for a tour of the Himalayas in December 1938 — just before the start of World War

II. They planned a trip to Tibet with stops in India and Kashmir, proposing to study Buddhism and make a pilgrimage to Mount Kailas, the sacred Tibetan mountain.

Their adventure continued as they traveled through the Himalayas by caravan, which included 12 servants, 112 ponies, plus guides and drivers. After their stop in Leh, which, at 11,500 ft., is one of the highest cities in the world, they continued travelling through a desert plateau on the way to Himis.

Later at a Tibetan monastery reception, a local librarian and two monks approached their party. They were carrying Buddhist books made of sheets of parchment sandwiched between two pieces of wood and wrapped in brocade.

The Europeans were astonished when the monk unwrapped one of the books and presented it to Mrs. Gasque saying, "These books say your Jesus was here."

This reference to Jesus and the time he had evidently spent traveling as far east as India and Tibet stunned Madame Caspari.

In fact, Dr. Caspari's recollections of her adventures can also be found in a book called *The Lost Years of Jesus* by Elizabeth Clare Prophet (Summit University Press)

Dr. Caspari then remembered her childhood Sunday school Bible verses, "And there are also many other things which Jesus did, the which, if they should be written every one, I suppose that even the world itself could not contain the books that should be written."

The astonished women examined the parchment — even holding the rare manuscripts in their own hands.

Could it be true? Dr. Caspari wonders to this day about the meaning of that encounter. Was Christ really in Tibet two thousand years ago?

To this day Dr. Caspari believes that the lama had no ulterior motive in presenting them with the manuscripts — only a sense of spiritual kinship with souls who had come so far to study the path of the Buddha.

After their tour leader Mrs. Gasque took the last plane to Europe, the Casparis found themselves stranded in India. War had come, but they had the good fortune not to be imprisoned. Since Great Britain controlled India and the Casparis were Italian, they could, of course, have been considered "enemies" and sent to an internment camp as many others were.

The Casparis, however, had found a home and jobs in a mission school nearby.

During that time, Dr. Caspari met Maria Montessori, the famous child education pioneer, and she continued to work closely with her for four years. It was a momentous and life-changing experience. At the end of this period in her life, Dr. Caspari had rededicated her life to what she calls the Montessori message.

Remembering Montessori

Still in awe of her legendary teacher, Dr. Caspari recalls in a recent interview that "Montessori herself had a degree in medicine. Then she got a degree in psychology, so she understood the mind. Then she got a degree in philosophy. And then she got a degree in anthropology, so she had a very scientific background."

Dr. Maria Montessori was the first woman in Italy to receive a medical degree from the University of Rome. Initially she taught brain injured and handicapped children. She did so well in fact, that these "disadvantaged" children were able to score as well as so-called normal children in exams.

Then Dr. Montessori's techniques evolved into an entire educational system to help children learn how to learn by themselves. Specially designed teaching materials are now used to develop a child's practical living skills, language and math skills, motor skills, as well as increasing self-awareness and building confidence.

"The little babies in the cribs will become the men and women of tomorrow who will change the world, Montessori told me," says Dr. Caspari. Then she asks rhetorically, "What can we do to help? Montessori said what I am bringing is help to Life."

She also recalls that Montessori "didn't like the word 'method'" — as in Montessori method. Dr. Caspari affirms that "it *works* because it is a principle of education — not a method.

"Why does it work? It will work tomorrow because it is based on a principle not a theory. And principles are eternal," Dr. Caspari continues. "She [Montessori] didn't bring theories. She brought principles. They always work — with the poorest children of India and the richest children in New York."

Still a fervent promoter, Dr. Caspari says "our children read before they go to first grade. Montessori said the right age [for optimal teaching] is from four to six. Because when they try to teach reading later, they [the children] don't have the enthusiasm."

Always thinking of the future, Dr. Caspari says, "Our time is come. It's wanted everywhere. I have three cities in Australia that want me to teach them how to give courses, and two in India which train doctors in healing that want to teach child education."

Celebrating Her Birthday

Dr. Caspari's 100th birthday party, held in Bozeman, Montana's Baxter Hotel ballroom, was a celebration of her life. Many notable educators from around the country came to honor Dr. Caspari with reminiscences of her love and her far-reaching work.

These included Bill and Beverly McGee, Alexander Montessori School, Miami, Florida, Dr. Feland Meadows, President, Pan-American Montessori Society, Patty Tepper-Rasmussen, President of the Montessori Society, Mary Ellen Maunz, Montessori International, and Anita Wolberd, Montessori Garden School, Emigrant, Montana and Co-founder, Caspari-Montessori Institute.

Janet Nielsen of Minneapolis recalled how her mother and Dr. Caspari had started the Wee Wisdom Montessori School in Unity Village, Missouri. Ms. Nielsen remembers it as "a small but wonderful place, alive with peace and understanding. Her [Dr. Caspari's] classroom was always a place of joy.

"We see how she leaves her signature on our lives," she says. "Dr. Caspari is a jewel without price."

Montessori educator Jim McGee recalled how he and his wife had asked Dr. Caspari to conduct a teacher-training course at the Alexander School in Florida. The first time he heard her lecture, he says, "I was really awed and impressed."

"The crowd was very educated and sophisticated," McGee continued. "When Elisabeth delivered a lecture, she produced true believers."

He called the Casparis "Montessori apostles" — not Montessori gypsies — as they were known for their constant travel, conducting Montessori teacher training courses throughout North America.

Dr. Meadows himself started a Montessori school in Mexico for his own children in 1970. Then in 1972, he traveled to Palo Alto for a conference called "Cosmic Education," where he met Dr. Caspari and invited her to Mexico to train more teachers. Persistent in his pursuit, he asked the Casparis if they could come in February, then June, then Christmas.

Dr. Caspari was working in Florida at the time. She rebuffed him saying, "I'm not a bird on a branch." Finally relenting, the Casparis arrived in Mexico City in 1973, their car trunk full of Montessori materials.

"I see you do the real thing here," Meadows recalls her saying after she walked in to his Montessori classroom.

Both Casparis worked as a team, training Montessori teachers wherever they went. Charles was a qualified engineer and linguist yet he would say, "My profession was getting in the way of my vocation."

Montana-based Caspari-Montessori Institute co-founder Anita Wolberd also speaks of the future. She is promoting a Montessori teacher-training program as a job training alternative for young mothers. By teaching their own children in a Montessori school setting, she says, women can become self-sufficient, working as professional teachers even as they stay with their children.

The Caspari Legacy

Dr. Caspari is still thinking ahead. She says, "We want to build a center here [in Montana] the Montessori Center of Paradise Valley. And the world will come. it's going to bring a lot of people."

In her life so far, Dr. Caspari has trained hundreds of Montessori teachers in California, Kansas, Missouri, Florida, South Carolina, Montana and Mexico.

"Montessori said we have to go higher to the Spirit. That's the whole secret of her work," says Dr. Caspari, who radiates peace, but is still reluctant to rest on her laurels.

Mentally sharp and still acutely aware of current world events, she says, "That was Montessori's secret. She was very humble, in spite of her degrees. She gave credit to the highest, in other words, to God."

A deeply spiritual person herself, Dr. Caspari is a real-life visionary whose grasp has not exceeded her life.

Her friends and neighbors affectionately call her "Mother" Caspari.

Still upbeat and always optimistic, she reminds everyone that "people in the Old Testament lived until they were 300."

Dr. Caspari remains a precious treasure to many generations.

(Dr. Caspari can be reached by mail at P. O. Box 933, Emigrant, Montana 59027 or by e-mail at ecaspari@prodigy.net.)

BUSHWHACKED

Chapter 22

The Prophet of Cyber Grunge:
An Interview with William Gibson

W RITER WILLIAM GIBSON HAS SEEN the future — and it is Grunge. High-tech. Lo-tek. Artificial Intelligence. Nanotech. Sentient Holograms. Corporate Assassins. Drugs. Hustlers. Low-Life Proles. More Drugs. Filtered through Nightmare Noir. Reframed by the Bad Karma-Mojo of pop culture icons William Burroughs, Phillip K. Dick and J. G. Ballard.

As Gibson himself admitted during a cameo appearance in the cult TV serial *Wild Palms*, he's been credited with inventing the term "cyberspace" — and "they won't ever let me forget it."

Since his first novel *Neuromancer*, HyperNow has been extrapolated to a Surely More Decadent Tomorrow. And Gibson's Future still occupies a grotesque and detailed universe of doom and gloom, tinged with GeeWhiz, Flash and Buzz.

In a strange anomaly — or is it synchronicity? — Orwell's Novel of the Future — *1984* — was published in 1948. It described then current off-the-shelf technology — Big Brother's blueprint for the world after World War II.

Gibson's *Neuromancer*, on the other hand, was published in 1984 — the year of Orwell's Big Bad Promise.

With a slight southern twang in his voice, Gibson spoke from the Beverly Hills Four Seasons Hotel in an interview by phone.

Gibson in Movieland

So what did he learn from the experiences of working on the movie version of his short story *Johnny Mnemonic*, (1995) a film starring Keanu Reeves and directed by artist Robert Longo?

"That really, really large sums of money, like multiples of millions, have their own peculiar momentum," he answers hesitantly. "People talk about having control and losing control, and I look at that very differently now.

"In terms of practical application, I don't think I'm going to know until I get there," he adds cryptically.

And there were no obvious "lessons" after he passed through the experience?

"Only that it's all a lot more serious a business than you can imagine before you've actually been there," says Gibson, alluding to the prototypical shark-like behavior of studio executives and others in the entertainment "industry."

Johnny Mnemonic was shot in Canada — in part because of tax incentives for investors. "I was there on set in Canada quite a bit," says Gibson. "Considerably more so than a screenwriter ordinarily would be. Because of my relationship with Robert Longo and also because the script was changing as it was shot."

And who was responsible for that?

"I was responsible," admits Gibson freely. "It had to do with how we started. We started with a modestly budgeted independent film." Initial estimates held the budget at one to three million. Then the inflation began.

"I wasn't very concerned with that at the time," he says. "I think the top end might have been seven or eight [million] which wouldn't have been a very big deal.

"We started with an actor who wasn't (on the day we signed him) a movie star. When we started with Keanu [Reeves], *Speed* had not been released. And Keanu was not a star in the way he was after *Speed* was released. So Keanu's suddenly bankable status as an action star definitely put a spin on what was happening, and it got us a gradually expanding budget. And it also got us in TriStar's pocket because of the escalating budget.

"So what we wound up with, in the end, I've always said that it's what you would have gotten if the studio had recut David Lynch's *Blue Velvet* and marketed it as a mainstream detective story."

Was there a lot of editing after it was "in the can" — more or less completely shot?

Trying to be diplomatic, I said, "There were a lot of controversial aspects to it. It got dissed pretty regularly."

"It might not have been dissed if you'd have the film that I wrote and Longo shot," says Gibson. "It got so radically reconceptualized that when I watched it

202

for the first time, [I said] 'Oh my God, it doesn't make sense.' To some extent, it had been intentionally a comment film, a very alternative sort of SF film, very self-conscious about its genre in an ironic way. When the frame for that was lost — it got lost after the last cut — they recut it to their specs."

So was the *Johnny Mnemonic* experience somewhat of an abortion — with the sense of loss and what could have been?

Gibson remains non-committal. He says simply, "It was a learning experience."

And whose idea was it to cannibalize the "Bridge" (a future squatters version of the famous San Francisco hallmark) — from *Virtual Light* and put it in the film?

"That was mine," Gibson admits. "At the time, I didn't think that I'd have a chance to do anything else. I saw *Johnny Mnemonic* as I wrote it, and we shot it as a collage of a lot of things. It was about a particular kind of science fiction. It's not about *Virtual Light*, but about that sort of environment. The set that Longo constructed was stunningly great, and the cut that emerged — you scarcely get any sense of it. It was probably one of the most beautifully realized science fiction sets since *Blade Runner*. Really really great. And as we shot it, the film made considerably more use of it, but it did not make it to the screen."

So was Longo's and Gibsons "vision" not the same as the "suits," the studio execs and the producers? Or what happened?

Gibson answers tentatively, "After a certain point, the suit who was most supportive of us throughout the process — he would speak to my position by saying, 'At this point, I have to speak for the members of our audience who are "Gibson-challenged"' — and at that point I knew that I was in trouble. This guy was saying that whatever it is you're laying down here, bud, they ain't going to get it. He was just doing his job."

When asked about the film directed by Abel Ferrara, *New Rose Hotel* (1999), also based on another Gibson short story, he says, "*New Rose Hotel* was a really interesting film. I had absolutely nothing to do with it, so it was as a film, one that you'd expect from Ferrara.

"Probably it would give some people pause," says Gibson. "It's really interesting because it's ostensibly a science fiction film, ostensibly a genre film, but it pays less attention to doing that than any genre film ever made — which I though was quite admirable. It's completely about character and the metaphorical nature of the world these guys have. They say it's the future, but it's really a world that consists of airplanes, hotel rooms, boardrooms, and brothels. That's it."

Sound like the basic LA lifestyle.

Asia Argento played the girl. "Asia's hot enough in that film to fry a dozen eggs on the street," says Gibson. "She's really, really terrific. And on the basis of that role, she should get a lot of work. That is one funny sexy girl."

Maybe she'll get out of that Italian horror genre thing. "Well, she was born into that. You know, her dad Dario Argento, is the grand master [of Italian horror.]"

"Ferrara has a tiny stable, maybe two who do all the screenplays," he continues. "You can't go too far wrong with a film that stars Christopher Walken. It's a very interesting piece of work. It's ferociously idiosyncratic."

(For the record, *New Rose Hotel* is unwatchable. The script is virtually nonexistent. The acting is tiresome improvisation by Willem Dafoe and Chris Walken, who seem to be amused, smirking at the latitude given them by director Abel Ferrara, who has directed otherwise exquisite films like *King of New York City* and *Body Snatchers*. Produced by indie veteran Edward Pressman, *New Rose Hotel* is clearly without *any* redeeming social or artistic value. In other words, if this movie wasn't made specifically to launder drug money, somebody lost a great opportunity.)

Gibson and the New Millennium

In the book, *All Tomorrow's Parties*, there's an overwhelming sense of some kind of "expectation," but it's cryptically very nebulous and amorphous.

Since the book is about "the end of the world as we know it," what kind of feelings does Gibson have about the new millennium?

"The millennium is just a Christian holiday," he replies, "but the peculiar spin that's been put on that is that, as a species, we have this other consciousness, that we're nearing some sort of cusp, something really big is changing.

"Most people haven't really thought about the word 'modern' and what that actually means," he continues. "If you use it in the sense of an academic historian, the Elizabethans were Early Modern. 'Modern' has been going on for a really, really long time. My hunch is that we are really Late Modern, and I think we haven't really decided what we're going to call the next thing. Some people call it Post Modern for want of a better term, and that's what Post Modern really means.

"I think that we're there," says Gibson. "That causes us to experience what literary theorist Frederick Jamison calls the 'Post-Modern Sublime' which he says is characterized by the simultaneous apprehension of dread and ecstasy. I think that what I'm really writing about is 'Dread&Ecstasy R US.' I get you to sit still for it because I say, 'relax, it's the future; it's just the future; it's not happening now,' but actually it *is* happening now. Science fiction is always written about the day in which it was written. When you go back and read old SF, it's never about the future, which you are living in when you are reading it. They never get it right, and neither do I."

All Tomorrow's Parties implies or infers some kind of Change (of Consciousness or something bigger, more momentous, all-enveloping, or all-encompassing) a Change to something that hasn't been seen before.

"I think it's what T. S. Kuhn called a Paradigm Shift," says Gibson. "He's a historian of scientific revolutions and how the world really works, changes, all the pain and friction that happens in humanity when it changes. I think we're going through a whole bunch of paradigm shifts right now, as we find our way to what the new paradigm is going to be. And it's going to be someplace where everybody is going to be sitting around looking back at us the way we look back at the Victorians. The Victorians were complex, and in many ways weirdly like us. They were very techno-stressed people. In a way, they weren't really playing with a full deck. They didn't know about the unconscious, for instance. They're not like us. Whoever our descendants are — sitting up there in the future — they're looking back at us saying, 'They were very interesting people and they went through some interesting stuff, but they didn't know about _____ (fill in the blank).' And I can't fill in that blank."

Globalist Technology Rules

Gibson's novels extrapolate the fast-moving worlds of biotech, life extension and artificial intelligence into the darker regions of the imagination, a soulless netherworld of spiritual emptiness in the midst of material abundance.

It seems that Gibson takes for granted that "Science Marches On" regardless of the cost to human rights and values, making moral or ethical implications a moot point. Is that really the way he feels about it?

"What's happening is that emergent technology is driving social change," he answers. "That's what's driving it. Because it's driving the market, we're living in the triumph of global capitalism, so emerging technology is driving social change. It's not legislated into existence. It's brought into existence by creativity and markets."

The fact that it could be driven by globalist mega-corporate cartels, which control resources and capital, somehow escapes Gibson.

"Or sheer clout of power?" I ask. "Are you familiar with what are going to be massive anti-globalism demonstrations in Seattle at the end of November 1999? Are you familiar with that at all?

"No," Gibson answers. "There's going to be a World Trade Organization meeting with hundreds of groups from left and right that will be demonstrating and protesting in the streets," I tell him. "Five thousand teamsters bussed in. Environmentalists rappelling off of skyscrapers."

"Sort of like protesting the New World Order?" asks Gibson.

"That's right," I say. "It's interesting because it's a coalition of people that are saying to global capitalism, 'enough is enough' — this runaway technology etc. must be stopped and reassessed."

"I don't get how they think they're actually going to stop it," says Gibson. "The nature of this protest is that it's out of control. Some of the more sensitive theorists — my friend Kevin Kelly comes to mind — have pointed out that it actually works."

"What works?" I ask.

"Emergent technology emerges best when it's out of control," he continues. "The internet is the classic example because no government on this planet would have given permission to build that. No way."

Gibson's statement belies his ignorance of 20th century history — DARPA and the US Department of Defense were the progenitors of what has become the World Wide Web as well as the infrastructure of the Internet.

"They would not have ceded that degree of control," Gibson continues, "and in fact they have probably, to some extent, planted the seeds of their eventual withering dissolution."

Dumbfounded, I ask him, "You really believe that?"

"They're going to have to play a cleaner game of pool from here on in because no government can control its citizens' access to free information. Not now. You just can't do it. It's not working."

Gibson had obvsiously never heard of Brain Quig whose website http://www.dcia.com has been hacked badly for several years. Slashing, trashing and crashing a site that's inimical to Big Government corruption — that might be the wave of the future.

Gibson remained nonplussed. "What surprised me about the Internet emerging as it emerged," says Gibson, "after *Neuromancer* — not that *Neuromancer* made it emerge — I expected it to emerge as primarily a corporate/military realm. That's the way it's depicted in *Neuromancer* but it emerged as a more populist, democratic, non-hierarchical thing, which is way more interesting."

Gibson obviously never heard of the draconian information scooping technology of the Echelon spy satellite systems.

"I've been working with Chris Cunningham, a young British director who hasn't done a feature [film] yet. So I've got another director [like Robert Longo] who hasn't done a feature yet. He's done a bunch of brilliant brilliant videos, some really great television commercials. We're at the stage now of discovering what our mutual creative language might be."

Gibson himself, however, has no aspirations to direct. "Having seen what it takes, I just think now that I like having a life," he says. "That [directing] has to be the hardest job that I've ever seen anyone do — even directing a television episode."

Referring to future garage-moviemaking, he adds that "if it becomes an inexpensive and leisurely activity in the evolution of digital cinema, maybe I'll do that in retirement."

Gibson — The Future Artist/Writer

When asked if he feels like he has to produce his work in a certain style, a style to which his readers have become accustomed — like the doomed artist Jean-Michel Basquiat, for example, who was forced to use certain iconographies because of his market value, Gibson is unequivocal — sort of.

"That which doesn't grow — dies," he answers. "If I was only in this to make a buck, I would be gearing up to strip mine my own earlier work and giving you fifteen volumes of young Molly Millions and how she got her fingernails.

"God forbid, if I was old enough and sufficiently artistically corrupt, you might see it. I've seen it happen to better men than me. I hope I have the courage to change."

And how would it feel if he did something radically different? How would it be received? Does he have it in him? Is that even an option?

"I think [Bruce] Sterling and I did it to an extent with *The Difference Engine*," replies Gibson. "The result of that was that a certain percentage of my readership probably enjoyed it, and others said 'what the hell was that about? I didn't get it.' And there's this other interesting contingent who came in and said, 'That's the best thing you've ever done? When are you gonna do something else like that?'"

The writing of *The Difference Engine* had its own methodology and rules, according to Gibson. "It was a full-on literary collaboration. We wrote it together," he says. "We actually could have done it by e-mail if we had e-mail, but it predated e-mail for both of us so we did it with floppy disks."

Gibson describes this work as an evolving piece of art. "I could tell you the actual rules though it's a little complicated. The only hard and fast rule was that the text as it existed on this increasingly thick stack of floppies was the text. Neither of us had absolute carte blanche to change anything in there. But neither of us was allowed to go back to any previous version or ever refer to any previous version of the text.

"That's what it had to be, if it was going to be anything other than a cheap sci-fi novel," Gibson continues. "That's the way we had to do it. I would write a chapter, send it to Bruce. Bruce would get it and he'd change anything in there

207

he wanted to, add a little more and send it back to me. I would start at the beginning and change anything I felt like changing, add a little more and send it to him.

"It took about two years to write. It was a very, very labor-intensive piece because when you do alternate histories you have to go and learn real history. And it's very demanding that way. So we were doing a lot of reading and lot of research all the way through it — and sort of keeping our selves in this Victorian mind space.

"By the time we were a third of the way into it, it was as though the book was being dictated by this third party — whom neither of us had met and neither of us had particularly liked. If we wanted to have a book that was real, we had to go where the author was taking it."

Channeling *The Difference Engine* does sound like hard work. And where was it going?

"It was very Victorian in its pace," Gibson explains. "It didn't move. It moved like a Victorian novel — like Benjamin Disraeli on crack [?]. A very strange piece of work. It's the only book of mine, if I can call it that, that I would go back and read for my own enlightenment. I would go back to it and see what that 'guy' who didn't exist wrote."

Channeling may be a very accurate description after all.

"William Burroughs wrote about it," says Gibson. "He called it the 'third man syndrome.' He was fascinated by literary collaboration. He said all good literary collaboration generates a literal third entity out of the personalities of the two writers. And as the third entity takes over the book, the writers don't feel that kindly disposed toward this poltergeist narrator they've created unconsciously.

"I think Burroughs was probably thinking of his work with Bryon Gysin. A lot of what Burroughs did was a kind of collaboration anyway because he would cut up other people's text and collage them in. Sterling and I were doing that too, although the stuff we were cutting up was hundred year old tabloid reporting, Victorian pornography, and Victorian pulp fiction."

So did Gibson and Sterling actually use Burroughs' well-documented cut-up method? "We did it in a sense," he says, "but the difference was that with word processing, we had a power tool. A lot of my technique, my solo technique, owes quite a lot to Burroughs' cut-up technique, but with word processing, I've got it sort of automated and I can spray paint the scene and alter it."

Gibson describes his writing methodology. "I'll find a piece of text somewhere, a description of something, a piece of technical literature, and I'll drop it right into the mix, but with cut and paste, I can sort of dither the edges, as they say in Photoshop and tweak it a little bit, file the serial numbers off, and wind up with something that's sort of disturbing, but a little more realistic than I might have come up with."

This faceless geekish descriptive writing actually has a name. It's called "technical writing."

"Right," says Gibson, "that's what J. G. Ballard calls 'invisible literature.'" This is the "literature" of commerce, the so-called "sales literature," ad copy, spec sheets, white papers and bureaucratese reports.

The Singularity of the Sixties

Before William Gibson became a famous author of outré science fiction, he left the United States for Canada. It was during the Days of Rage against the Vietnam War.

Reflecting on his personal history, he says, "I went there [Canada] and then I wasn't drafted. I don't know why. I suspected they knew I was there."

In retrospect, Gibson says, "It was never a legal problem. I stayed there and I got into it. It [Canada] became where I lived. I had the emotional experience, which was pretty heavy. I didn't hang out with the draft dodger community when I was there because it was too depressing. A lot of those guys were clinically depressed and very disturbed by what had happened to them. There were a lot of suicides.

"They [draft-age young men] were totally traumatized by having to leave under these bizarre circumstances [the Vietnam War]." he continues. "Their families had disowned them. The emotional tenor of the times was actually difficult to connect. It was very heavy for some people to have a kid who would refuse the patriotic obligation to serve. It's different now. Whatever happened changed that.

"I went there to evade military service," admits Gibson, "but I never had the really hard decision of having gotten the [draft] letter and saying should I go back, or should I stay here? I guess I kind of went sideways, and I got lost in the paperwork for which I'm really grateful."

Gibson's bio reads, "He spent his childhood in southwestern Virginia, attended a boys' boarding school in Tucson, and decamped at age nineteen for Toronto intent on avoiding military service and experiencing the historical singularity recalled today as The Sixties."

Now he states simply, "We definitely hit one. A singularity in the sense of a black hole. We hit something in our social history and all went down it. Everything on the other side of it has been very different than it would have been if we hadn't. Because we went down it — that's the nature of what we are. It's not easy to get a handle on it. There's a passing awareness that it really really changed a lot of things."

Would he liken it to the paradigm shift he mentioned before?

Gibson gropes for words. "There's a much broader palette of colors in the world."

So it comes back to the issue of drugs and their consciousness changing *modus operandi*?

Gibson hesitates. "Maybe that was central, but in a way, drugs were a metaphor for the actual experience [of the singularity]. The actual experience was societal, but drugs gave you an excuse for having this societal experience."

Drugs, Conspiracies and More Drugs

One of Gibson's characters in *All Tomorrow's Parties*, Laney, was given drugs as a human guinea pig for the government. These drugs changed him, enabling him to have so-called extra-perceptive abilities. He's the one who eagerly awaits the "Change of the World As We Know It."

During the interview with Gibson, former math professor Ted Kaczynski, in prison for the Unabomber bombings, came to mind. Interestingly enough, he was also dosed with drugs in Harvard, as a "volunteer" for a government drug-testing program, according to *Nation* columnist Alexander Cockburn. This is one of the subterranean historical trends they don't teach in High School History — the covert experimentation by military-intelligence agencies on an unsuspecting population.

"Yeah," Gibson laughed. "I'm sure it happens."

When I told him that it seemed to be like a reality bleed-through from his subconscious, he said, "I've read about that stuff."

In fact, he agreed that the Sixties Singularity, as he called it, was a paradigm shift that included the entire world — from overt hedonistic drug taking by a self-medicating population to the covert experimentation by the CIA who introduced and distributed LSD throughout North America.

Gibson agrees. "The CIA predated a lot of the civilian stuff. There's a great book, *Storming Heaven*, and it lays this stuff out. As usual, it's a lot more fuzzy and multiplex than the conspiracy theory version.

"People like conspiracy theories," Gibson maintains, "because they present a sort of comprehensible universe and consequently I always think *all* conspiracy theories are cop-outs to comfort."

And what "conspiracy theories" come to Gibson's mind?

"Everything from 'who killed Kennedy' to the 'Trilateral Commission,'" he replies. "Anything that is a conspiracy theory that purports to explain everything. I think that's why these things are popular. They're inherently comforting.

"My take on that stuff is that any depiction of the real nature of history that

I can get my head around can't be true," Gibson concludes. "If I can get my little mammalian brain around a theory of history, it's got to be woefully inadequate to describe reality on the face of it. I'm thinking of the short-form MK-Ultra, aliens are stealing our genetic material... Or the 'Freemasons run the universe' kind of thing."

Gibson knows. He's written for exploitation TV shows himself, most notably *X-Files* and *Harsh Realms*.

Conspiracy theories, after all, are just more entertainment.

Conspiracy realities, however, are still not quite ready for prime time.

BUSHWHACKED

Chapter 23

Spiritual Wickedness in High Places: An Interview with Malachi Martin

EVER SINCE NIMROD AND THE Tower of Babel, the Power Elite have never given up on their feverish dream of One World Government. "Former" Jesuit Malachi Martin's novel, *Windswept House* (Doubleday/Main Street Books), offers a lurid behind the scenes look at a cabal of Vatican insiders who want to use the Roman Catholic Church as a foundation for a politico-religious New World Order.

The plot of the novel involves a group of Church officials who scheme with a group of likeminded corporate executives to manipulate the Church into a ready-made infrastructure for a One World Religion — a universal umbrella for everybody from Episcopalians to voodoo practitioners.

The new ecumenicalism is clothed in Globalist garb. The agenda includes promoting issues like population control, environmentalism and secular humanism, which the plotters hope will eventually lead to the complete secularization of religion.

The most outrageous and controversial premise of the novel — described in great detail in the prologue — is that a ceremony was performed in the Vatican in 1963 — an occult ritual which enthroned the fallen archangel Lucifer as the head of the Roman Catholic Church.

Does Dr. Martin believe that this enthronement actually took place in his novel, which could liberally be described as a *roman a clef*?

"Yes, it did," he says emphatically. "Beyond a shadow of a doubt in my mind. But now the place, time, hour etc., are all obfuscated to protect the guilty and save the innocent."

Was it common knowledge in the Vatican at the time? "Not common knowledge," explains Martin. "But I found out about it by being a member of the Vatican circles that learned these things. It's like everything else. I'm sure there are people floating around Washington, and they know an awful lot about what's going on. Someone says, 'how do you know that'? Well, it's just... we know it."

The story of *Windswept House* continues in present day Europe as an international group of conspirators spanning Church and State plots One World Government on behalf of Lucifer. So are readers to infer that no matter what happens, the Pope and the Church hierarchy are bound to serve the fallen angel?

"No," explains Dr. Martin. "What it means is that for the moment, Lucifer the biggest archangel, the leader of the revolt against God, has a big in with certain Vatican officials. Enthronement doesn't mean that he rules. It means that they did their best to put him there. The ideal would be to have their man as Pope. In that case then Satan would be enthroned."

The book goes on to describe how two brothers, one a priest and the other an investment banker, grapple with these awesome consequences as pawns in the game. Meanwhile the cabal of Globalist-oriented Vatican officials and European-based internationalists try to corner the Pope into voluntary resignation so that they can get their man in the Chair of Peter.

This theme coincidentally is also the basis, albeit in non-fiction form, of Martin's book *The Keys of This Blood: Pope John Paul II Versus Russia and the West for Control of the New World Order.*

The upshot? One World Government is a fait accompli, he infers. What Dr. Martin calls the "millennium endgame" is a competition for a new global hegemony by the key Globalist players. What's interesting is that the novel appears to be a seamless transition from his previous non-fiction work. The reader then is put in the position of concluding that the New World Order is a done deal, that a One World Government is here and now and, as the expression goes, it's all over but the crying.

But you wouldn't expect Globalist agit-prop from a former Jesuit. Or would you?

And Who Is Malachi Martin?

Author of 15 books on religious and geo-political topics, Malachi Martin is highly regarded and respected as a world-renowned scholar.

Trained in theology at Louvain, he received his doctorates in Semitic

Languages, Archaeology and Oriental History. He subsequently studied at Oxford and Hebrew University in Jerusalem. From 1958 to 1964, he served in Rome, where he was a close associate of the Jesuit cardinal Augustin Bea and Pope John XXIII, as well as a professor at the Vatican's Pontifical Biblical Institute.

Malachi Martin is the author of many best-selling books including *Vatican*, *Hostage to the Devil*, *The Jesuits*, *The Final Conclave*, and *The Keys of This Blood*. Also he was a Roman Catholic priest of the Society of Jesus until 1964 when he left the Jesuits. Why? "It was a grave decision," he says. "I could see the way the Church was going, the way churchmen were going in their decisions and all the anchors I had for morality and zeal were being undone. Then when the Vatican Council started in 1962, I could see the way the flow of opinion was going in the Vatican by a group of cardinals from Belgium, Germany and France. They were maneuvering the Church into totally new ecclesiology. I couldn't accept this."

As an advisor to three Popes, Dr. Martin has had his fair share of *romanita*, that uniquely Roman methodology of connivance and power politicking. "I started off as an advisor on Judaism," he continues. "I was trained in Semitic languages and I spent a year and a half studying the Talmud... Then my superiors in Rome also found that I understood Judaism very well. They wanted someone to explain it, since they were studying the whole question of Jewish-Christian relations. So I was drafted into helping with that."

And the outcome? "They produced a document in which they sort of absolved the Jewish people of the death of Christ."

Based on his research? "No, not on my research," argues Martin. "I was only a cog in the wheel. I didn't agree with the final document either. It went too far. And then there were conclusions about the need for Catholics to study Judaism and get to know them better."

So this was the ecumenicalization of the Church that was going on?

"That's it in one word," concurs Martin. "And I couldn't agree with the total effect of all that because I thought they went too far."

Dr. Martin was also involved with Vatican intelligence. What did he do? "Just assessing things in Israel, whatever anti-Christianity there was amongst the Israelis. There was and still is. And what was the position of the Arabs. I used to live in Jordan and Lebanon and Egypt. I knew those places very well and could assess the position of the Church and the various Christian communities."

The many-talented Dr. Martin is also known as a practicing exorcist and has even written a book about the subject called *Hostage to the Devil*.

He says he came up against evil as a force in the world in an uncontrovertible, undeniable way in his first exorcism.

"I was in Cairo and it was evil," Dr. Martin recalls.

"You know you only have to enter its presence, or for it to enter your presence to know that you are in the presence of something which is summarily evil.

"It's invisible. You can't see it. But you know it wants you dead. Dead. Dead. And in a horrible way," he repeats in a droning, hypnotic voice. "It's touching your very bones by its presence."

So how does he explain the phenomenon of demonic possession? "Free will," says Dr. Martin. "For the first time in the work we have been doing for thirty-one years in this corner of the globe, during the last ten years or so, we have found young men and women thirty-somethings or twenty-somethings coming forward and saying, 'Listen, I made a pact with the devil. I wanted this woman. I wanted this man. I wanted this job. I wanted this money. I wanted this, this, this, and I made a pact and he gave it to me and now I can't get free of him. He dominates my will. Please liberate me.' And then people get to it by means of things like a ouija board or by spiritual seances or channeling."

Malachi Martin is also known as a serious scholar of apocryphal writings, having authored a book called *The Scribal Character of the Dead Sea Scrolls*.

(As an impressive mark of his erudition, Malachi Martin even knew about the alternative Abraham and Isaac story in one of the so-called Pseudepigrapha, the Book of Jubilees. In this unsanctioned version of *Genesis*, Abraham is commanded to kill his son, but not by God. Instead it is Mastema, a fallen angel known as "The Accusing Angel," as well as the Tempter and Executioner, who tells the Hebrew patriarch to do the dirty deed. To his credit, of course, Abraham doesn't slaughter his firstborn. When asked why the *Genesis* version omits details of the fallen angel Mastema as the instigator of Abraham's test, however, even Malachi Martin admits ignorance.)

The Globalist Imperative

Like the prissy intellectuals of the 1930's enamored by National Socialism (as well as the more "erudite" Fabian Socialism), the current *fin de siecle* version of internationalists are likewise paving their own road to a Globalist hell with good intentions.

Using the Hegelian model of history, first there was Capitalism (thesis), then Communism (antithesis), and now there's Corporate/State Socialism, also called "the New World Order" (synthesis), risen from the ashes of the Cold War and the formerly "competing" ideologies.

International socialism (or Globalism) is, in fact, the trendy philosophy for the end of the millennium. In his book *Megatrends 2000*, Olympian futurist John

Naisbitt calls it "free market socialism," a hybrid economic system that combines welfare state policies with multinational corporate business on a global level.

Globalism, however, as a secular religion, has a dogma all its own. Its primary belief system is based on the notion that the usefulness of the nation-state is over. In other words, national sovereignty is a thing of the past and a One World Government is inevitable. But... this effort must be couched in cryptic language for the unwashed masses. Otherwise they'd get too upset.

Globalist spokesman Zbigniew Brzezinski, former Columbia University professor, President Carter's former National Security advisor, and founder of the Trilateral Commission spoke at the Gorbachev Foundation's State of the World Forum in 1995, "We cannot leap into world government in one quick step," he said. "[It] requires a process of gradually expanding the range of democratic cooperation."

In plain language, he means that people must be further indoctrinated, programmed and brainwashed.

Eurocrat Jean-Marie Guehenno hints at this global hegemony or one world totalitarianism calling it an "empire without an emperor." Guehenno wrote *The End of the Nation-State* (1995), which was called *La fin de la democratie* (*The End of Democracy*) in the original French version. Since nation states are obsolete, he claims, "'Wise Men' capable of thinking through the finite world that has become our common lot" must be entrusted to guide us into what he calls an "Imperial Age." Presumably Guehenno counts himself as one of the ranks of "The Wise Men."

Most striking though is a chapter in Guehenno's book called "Religions without God," which evokes the image of the humanist shaking his fist at an empty sky. The ultimate reduction of this conundrum for the internationalists is to hint at a "global politburo" to run the world as posited by Paul Mazur in *Unfinished Business* (1979).

According to Dr. Martin's nomenclature, there are more than one kind of globalist. Guehenno is one of the Transnationalists — bureaucrats who believe that Globalism is based on "the development of new and ever wider interrelationships between the governments of the world."

On the other hand, the Internationalists are "individuals who operate from a power base of finance, industry and technology." Together these groups are the Globalists, the social engineers conniving for the convergence of East and West in the so-called New World Order.

Luciferian Geo-Politics

For a Churchman, Malachi Martin shows a remarkable familiarity with

Luciferianism, a belief system which holds human wisdom, or secular humanism if you will, as its paragon and the fallen archangel Lucifer as the Prince who will rule the world.

Readers of *Windswept House* are given the impression that the old traditional Catholic Church is good because the protagonists, Christian Gladstone and his mother are defending it, while we know that the Church has been dedicated to Lucifer. Faced with these two alternatives, the conclusion is that the Roman Catholic Church run by Lucifer is good — a classic (and incredibly sophisticated) double bind, which is constantly reinforced in the reader's mind throughout the 646 pages of this monumental novel.

"Well, the Church itself has not been given to Lucifer," argues Dr. Martin. "He was enthroned in the Vatican by Vatican officials. That doesn't mean he possesses the Church yet. The Church, anyway, is an ambiguous term because it either means the actual physical bloc of churches, convents, libraries, academies, parish houses and cathedrals, the physical plant. Or it means the group of faithful in the state of grace whether they are alive in Purgatory or in Heaven. That is the body of Christ.

"There has always been, since the fourth century, this organization set up by the Emperor Constantine. But that is not essential for the Church. The Church can exist without it. So that mystical body of Christ has not fallen into Lucifer's hands. The organization to some degree has. That's the difficulty."

What about the book putting his readers in a double bind? You're presented with two choices only. Either A. The Luciferian-controlled Roman Catholic Church. Or B. The Luciferian-controlled New World Order. So where does Malachi Martin find himself?

"The New World Order is definitely won by Luciferian believers," Dr. Martin answers. "There's no doubt about that."

And then he starts to rationalize their *modus operandi*. Remember he's a Jesuit, and Jesuits are thoroughly trained in advanced casuistry and other forms of specious reasoning.

"But these are men who came to be and are in their actions at least, humanitarian and philanthropic. They want to wipe out hunger and disease. They want to limit the population of the world. They believe the world is headed for mass starvation. They also want to enter into education. They would like to have an alliance with the Roman Catholic Church and with another pope. This one — they know would stand in their way in regards to population control because he is deadset against abortion, contraceptives, genetic engineering."

And what about "The Process" he refers to in his book?

Dr. Martin replies that it's "the 'Luciferian Process' of secularizing every religious mind so that the common mind today would be one which regarded the earth as a planned paradise to be built up. There is no God above the skies, no heaven, and there is no hell beneath the earth. It's complete secularization."

But do the Luciferians have a timetable?

"We are now according to the official doctrine of the Luciferians in what they call 'the Availing Time,'" he answers. "They have a tradition that in these years they can avail of the time to install the Prince, who is Lucifer, as the greatest power on earth in charge of human civilization and adored by men."

And to what end?

"To exalt the power of Lucifer. That is the end in itself. It's the Luciferian purpose. If they don't do it in these years, then it is put off *sine die*, without resolution. They are very keen on getting it done."

And what are the next steps in this "Process?"

"The purpose is to secularize education completely," continues Dr. Martin. "And to eliminate from considerations of life and death — medicine, sociality, finance, birth, development etc., to free that of any religious presumption whatever. To free it from the superstition of religion so that man is dealt with scientifically and humanly. And that is 'the Process.' 'The Process' is to make the human mind accept that... 'The Process' is whereby all education, primary secondary and higher, college university and all public activity is completely rid of all religious presumptions.

"There is a layer of Satanism, of Satanist ritual which prepares people for perfect Luciferian adoption. They have covens and sacrifices and rites. The Luciferians have no rites, you know."

So dabbling with Satanism in these rituals leads to a different form of "commitment" which is Luciferianism?

"It is a preparation for Luciferianism and there are reversals sometimes," claims Dr. Martin. "You will find a crowd of Luciferians having a satanic ritual as a reminder of things. But they have all passed through in a sense and that involves three things: the infliction of pain without flinching, the infliction of death without flinching, and the use of fire."

Windswept House: The Message and Its Subtext

In *Windswept House*, Christians and Luciferians clash over the carcass of the Roman Catholic Church. It's a controversial and provocative story, a political thriller with metaphysical implications. It delves into the depths of treachery, intrigue and Machiavellian politics at the highest levels of the Church. As a fact-based novel with frequent lengthy asides on real historical geopolitical events like the fall of the Soviet Empire and the Helsinki Accords, *Windswept House* is a vehicle for one simple message — the New World Order is here and now.

While a group of cardinals scheme to force the Pope to resign his office so they'll be able to install a man who will do the Luciferians' bidding, a priest, Christian Gladstone is called to Rome. Cardinal Maestroianni, a power player and one of the leaders of the cabal, enlists the priest to poll bishops regarding closer ties with the European Economic Community. In fact, however, the Cardinal is assessing the timing for a conclave in which the Slavic Pope would be forced to resign because he has become a stumbling block in the Luciferians' plans.

From the business side, Paul Gladstone, Christian's brother and an expert in international relations working at a Globalist law firm, is also unknowingly recruited to bring the Luciferian plan to fruition. When the brothers find out they are both being unwittingly used in the schemes of the Luciferians, they join forces. Christian then must reach the Pope to tell him that he is being manipulated to abdicate the Chair of Peter.

Will the Pope resign? Will he exorcise the Church in time?

The subtext? It doesn't really make a hell of a lot of difference.

The Future of the Church Militant

In his novel *Windswept House*, Malachi Martin expostulates his readers regarding the reasons why the so-called "Slavic Pope" (Pope John Paul II) is so ineffectual. But what is the Pope's agenda as he sees it?

"I think that from the very start John Paul II for whatever reasons, has sought after one thing and one thing only," says Dr. Martin. "The formation of what now appears to be in his mind, a universal assemblage of Catholics at the core; grouped with them the Protestant denominations, sects and churches; grouped around them believing Jews, believing Muslims, believing Hindus, believing Buddhists. And that would be a universal religious assembly that could have a powerful dynamic kick in civilization and in solving the problems of men and women today. That is the only thing you can really say this man has sought heart and soul and body with all his travelling. When he went to churches all over the world, member churches of the Catholic Church in all the countries, he was bolstering the reputation of the papacy and he was speaking Catholic dogma, Catholic belief, and Catholic morals. But in reality he was reaching out to everybody. He wanted to make friends with everybody."

And what about the widespread homosexuality, pedophilia and satanic rituals in the Church, common knowledge he avers known to all Vatican insiders? Since as he wrote Christ is no longer honored in the tabernacle, what does he think will happen?

"Once the tabernacle is emptied of Christ's real presence, then the Church ceases to be holy and therefore it's going to be entered by the opposite power, Lucifer," says Martin. "And this is taking place now. Not widespread, but it is taking place. There's no doubt about that."

It's the End of Religion (As We Know It).

So will the Church fall on its own? "It's disintegrating slowly," says Martin. "As an organization, it's being marginalized sociopolitically and culturally. And religiously, it's weakening and decaying, obsolescing…

"If you look at any country today there are three identifiable components of that State. One, the government. Two, there is industry. Third, there are what we call NGO's, the non-governmental organizations. That's everything from Mothers Against Drunk Drivers to the Catholic Church. And they're just simply lumped together, voluntary associations with as much power as they can grasp but of no special importance. Now fifty or seventy years ago, when an ethical or moral question arose, people and governments looked to the churches. Now they don't any longer."

And there's yet another sensitive question. Something doesn't add up. Malachi Martin is supposedly a priest. He's supposed to fight evil. Yet his book *Windswept House* is clear evidence that he's thrown in the towel.

"Well I don't see evidence of having thrown in the towel," protests Dr. Martin. "Because there's a lot I'm being made to pay for, in the sense that the writer obviously likes and reveres this Pope even though he disagrees with him. The writer also believes in the Blessed Sacrament. He believes in the Pope's infallibility. He believes in salvation. He believes in hell. He believes in the evil of the devil."

You might even believe that a recitation of beliefs actually means something. So why doesn't *Windswept House* end with Christ Victorious in the book?

Does Dr. Martin believe that the Luciferian forces have won already?

"No. No. No," Dr. Martin protests again. "This is an interim book. It ends in a big doubt — everybody waiting."

This must be what they call the "European ending," open-ended and with many options, as opposed to the "American ending," where all the loose ends are tied up.

Then the interview shifts into "The Devil, Er, I Mean the Editor Made Me Do It."

"The publisher said, 'Listen the story isn't finished yet,'" says Dr. Martin. "I had a lovely glorious ending. I had a vision. I had a marvelous thing over the Alps. He cut it out."

This was an actual editorial decision? "Yes," says Dr. Martin.

But with all due respect, it almost sounds like Luciferian tampering. Not that anyone wants a saccharine ending. So are readers to conclude that the Luciferians won because of the passivity of the Pope in defending the Church?

"Well, they haven't won yet," says Dr. Martin on a slightly upbeat note. "We're waiting for this man to do something. He's the Vicar of Christ. I know I'm defending him but…"

"Readers who call me or write me say, what do we do now? I say, read my next book," he continues.

With Martin's passing on July 28, 1999, that helpful hint or fatherly suggestion seems to be a moot point.

"So perhaps editorially," he concludes, "it was the right decision, but religiously it was the wrong decision. I don't know."

It's been said that "By their fruits, ye shall know them." Malachi Martin's assent to the so-called "Process" is the tangible "fruit" of his final book called *Windswept House*.

Is the novel a prophecy? Or is it just a warning?

In any case, the New (Luciferian) World Order that Malachi Martin describes puts a religious spin to the whole so-called "Process" of history.

It's also clear — *Windswept House* is a Luciferian masterpiece.

Chapter 24

Secrets of the Bush Crime Family

ESPITE THE GOVERNMENT-MEDIA'S coronation of George W. Bush as the next US President, skeletons keep rattling in the Bush Family closet. Most recently it's been the Secret Bush Brothers Video, which allegedly shows George Jr. and Jeb with a formidable quantity of cocaine — an allegedly controlled substance.

According to LAPD whistleblower Michael C. Ruppert, the Drug Enforcement Agency has in its possession a video of George W. Bush and Jeb Bush flying in to Tamiami Airport outside of Miami, Florida "to pick up a couple of kilos of powder for a party." (*From the Wilderness Newsletter*, PO Box 6061-350, Sherman Oaks, CA 91413).

Ruppert heard about it from Terry Reed, author of *Compromised: Clinton, Bush and the CIA* (1994). "I was with Terry recently at a public speaking engagement where he reminded the audience of a little passage from his book *Compromised*," writes Ruppert. "In that passage he describes how Barry Seal had told him that he had 'insurance' in the form of proof that the Bush Boys were doing heavy drugs."

"Thanks to the 'uc,' as undercovers are called, Barry Seal and Terry Reed were sent on a drug sting to meet some wealthy Texans," writes Ruppert. "It turns out that the wealthy Texans were George W. and Jeb Bush who flew in on the family owned King Air to pick up the cocaine themselves. Hidden DEA cameras filmed the whole incident, including the tail number of the aircraft and both

Bushes participation. According to Reed, nobody knew in advance who the buyers were."

In a hair-raising finale to the story, Reed states that he has both the tail number of the aircraft and the DEA case file number, "and he strongly suspects that tape to turn up during the 2000 presidential election." Don't hold your breath.

Getting the Dope on Bush

Former CIA operative Terry Reed had worked closely with the late Barry Seal, a notorious drug smuggling pilot who also worked for the CIA.

In his fascinating book, *Compromised*, co-written with veteran journalist John Cummings, Reed describes a conversation he had with Seal about his 'insurance' aka blackmail, in case the Bush Crime Family Syndicate would try to double-cross him.

"Ever hear the old expression, it's not what ya know, it's who ya know? Well, whoever said that just hadn't caught the Vice President's [George Bush Sr.'s] kids in the dope business, 'cause I can tell ya for sure what ya know can definitely be more important than who ya know,'" bragged Seal to his buddy.

Reed was incredulous. "Barry, are you telling me George Bush's kids are in the drug business?" he asked.

"Yup, that's what I'm tellin ya. A guy in Florida who flipped for the DEA has got the goods on the Bush boys. Now I heard this from a reliable source in Colombia, but I just sat on it then, waiting to use it as a trump card if I ever needed it. Well, I need to use it now. I got names, dates, places, even got some tape recordings. I even got surveillance videos catchin' the Bush Boys red-handed. I consider this stuff my insurance policy," said Seal.

"It makes me and the mole on the inside that's feeding the stuff to me invincible. Now this is real sensitive shit inside of US Customs and DEA and those guys are pretty much under control. It's damage control as usual. But where it gets real interesting is what the Republicans will do to the Democrats in order to dirty up the people who might use this information against Bush."

Hinting at a high-level Mob War between the Bush Family and Clinton's Dixie Mafia, Seal told Reed that "he was on a secret mission by none other than the Agency [CIA] to sort of dirty up some people real close to the Governor [Clinton].

"Now I had been working on this through Dan Lasater," continued Seal. "Now Dan's a good ol' boy and all that, but he's gotta drug problem and he's got the balls to be stealin' from the Agency too."

Balls? Imagine stealing cocaine drug profits from the CIA.

When Reed questioned him about the duffel bag Seal had taken to Skeeter

Ward, Seal said, "Let's don't call it cocaine. Let's call it neutralizing powder. Least that's the way the Bush family saw it. This is just one family warrin' against another. Just like the Mob."

Reed claims he found these revelations "disquieting." Seal tried to reassure him by saying, "Terry I told ya when I met ya. I'm in transportation and I transport what the government wants transported. In this case, the Republicans...the Bush family... wanted some stuff transported into Mena and into Arkansas that would end up in the noses of some very prominent Democrats."

Seal was later assassinated. The cover story involved some "Colombian" hit men.

Federal Assets Beware

More corroboration of Bush Crime Family shenanigans comes from former FBI asset Darlene Novinger.

It's a tough life to work for the Feds, after all, especially if you expect *not* to get stabbed in the back.

Rodney Stich, in his 1994 edition of *Defrauding America*, writes that Novinger was a "former FBI operative, [who] reportedly discovered during an FBI investigation that Vice President George Bush and two of his sons were using drugs and prostitutes in a Florida hotel while Bush was Vice President.

"She reported her findings to FBI supervisors and then [was] warned not to repeat what she had discovered," continues Stich. "Novinger had been requested to infiltrate drug trafficking operations in South America and the United States. She was pressured to quit her FBI position; her husband was beaten to death; and four hours after she appeared on a July 1993 talkshow [Tom Valentine, Radio Free America] describing her findings (after she was warned not to appear), her father mysteriously died. A dead white canary was left on his grave as a warning to her. After receiving death threats she went into hiding, from where she occasionally appeared as a guest on talk shows and called from undisclosed locations."

Presumably the long arm of the Bush Crime Family Syndicate has kept her in hiding ever since.

According to Stich, in the 1998 edition of *Defrauding America*, Novinger was a former investigator for the Federal Crime Task Force working with the FBI in an unofficial capacity. She was recruited as an undercover operative, and she had the authority to investigate and report criminal activities, but not the power to arrest. She was not paid a salary, either, but received periodic payments based upon assets seized or the value government agents placed upon their information.

Her success led her to be assigned to Atlanta where she was involved with "an investigation that revealed a large drug operation involving a powerful Lebanese drug trafficking family living in luxury in Miami and Jamaica," writes Stich. "It was called Operation Nimbus and it involved the Smatt family, headed by William Smatt, related to the Lebanese Phlangee group."

Most importantly, Novinger said "the investigations showed that the drug trafficking operation involving the Smatt group also implicated Vice President George Bush and his son Jeb."

In fact, it can be argued that there is an important strategic value in having the two Bush Boys — Jeb and George Jr. — positioned as governors of Florida and Texas. These two states happen to be the primary drug trafficking portals into the country.

Stich writes that "the irony of this discovery was that George Bush was the head of the South Florida Drug Task Force. The investigation also discovered that Bush was being politically corrupted and blackmailed by drug traffickers who knew of the vice president's involvement in these criminal activities."

After submitting her report to the FBI concerning Bush's involvement, Novinger says that orders came from Washington to stop the entire investigation and destroy all reports.

Stich adds additional corroboration of Bush Crime Family drug trafficking.

"Before Operation Nimbus was shut down, veteran US Customs investigator, Joe Price, had filed similar reports involving high level drug trafficking, including the George Bush involvement," writes Stich. "After Price had filed his report in September 1983 concerning Bush's involvement in drugs, supporting Darlene's reports, FBI arrested Price on false narcotics trafficking charges."

Note to all US Federal employees — report a crime, go to jail.

So-called "misprision of felony" (Title 18 U.S.C.* 4) is a cruel charade. The law states that "whoever, having knowledge of the actual commission of a felony cognizable by a court of the United States, conceals and does not as soon as possible make known the same to some judge or other person in civil or military authority under the United States, shall be fined not more than $500 or imprisoned not more than three years or both."

Fighting Against the Bush Crime Family

One of the most outspoken anti-Bush Crime Family activists is private investigator Stewart A. Webb. He claims that the Bush Boys — George Jr., Jeb and Neil — as well as George Bush Sr. are implicated in many top-level criminal activities.

Webb, a political whistleblower on the highest levels of federal fraud, has been investigating government corruption since 1986. He has produced a series of videos called "Corruption in High Places." Webb has also uncovered key evidence linking government officials with illegal drug smuggling and money laundering, as well as data on the Savings & Loan Scandal of the 1980s, in which an estimated $1 trillion was stolen from the American people.

In his research, Webb also discovered the connection between the so-called HUD scandals in which over $50 billion was stolen in US Department of Housing and Urban Development fraud and the Junk Bond Scams/Loan Swaps of Michael Milken, Larry Mizel and Charles Keating (The Daisy Chain) which claimed over $6 billion.

Since then he has been a prime source of information to Rodney Stich, author of *Defrauding America* (1994, 1998), Pete Brewton, author of *The Mafia, CIA and George Bush* (1992), and Jonathan Beatty, a senior correspondent for Time Magazine.

"The news articles that Mr. Webb contributed to exposed a pattern of illicit political influence in Denver and led to the indictments and subsequent convictions of several businessmen," wrote Beatty.

Reporter Sarah McClendon wrote in her Washington Report (December 24, 1991) that "Stew Webb cannot lay his head on a pillow at home because he must keep running from the FBI which wants to jail him for talking publicly how private industry was involved in raising money for covert action by the CIA and also how Bush friends in Denver are involved in using government housing money for developments and profitmaking."

Webb has pursued justice in a system in which key government officials and judges have been compromised through bribery and other scandals.

It's gotten real up-close and personal since Webb's former father in law, Leonard Y. Millman, a prominent Denver businessman, has blocked access to Webb's own daughter.

Webb claims to have evidence that Millman (MDC Holdings, National Brokerage Companies) has been one of George Bush's primary money launderers for the last twenty years. His fight for a Grand Jury demand has been suspiciously stalled.

In a letter to US District Court Judge Richard P. Matsch, Webb writes that he has "a Justice Department Assistant Inspector General who is prepared to act in our behalf to assist in the Grand Jury investigation. Other government agents are willing to help. A dozen secret witnesses can be selected from more than 200 potential witnesses. They will testify about Leonard Y. Millman, Larry Mizel [MDC Holdings], Norman Brownstein [NSA attorney; Director, MDC Holdings] and others involved in an ongoing criminal enterprise."

The Brownstein Connection

Webb has been tangling with some serious players. Brownstein, for example, is chairman of the board of Denver law firm Brownstein, Hyatt, Farber and Strickland P. C., "the state's most politically connected firm," according to Denver, Colorado's *5280 Magazine* (April/May 1998).

"Just how influential is Norm Brownstein?" asks *5280*. "When Brownstein visits Capitol Hill, US Senators follow him down the hall. Ted Kennedy calls him the '101st Senator.' Bill Clinton takes his calls... Brownstein operates at the national level where he is considered to be one of the country's top five fundraisers."

In Pete Brewton's groundbreaking exposé *The Mafia, CIA and George Bush*, Brownstein is named as "one of the most influential political fundraisers in Colorado." He was a member of the board of directors of the infamous MDC Holdings from 1980 to 1989 and paid $492,000 in 1986 and $280,000 in 1987 for his legal work.

"MDC Holdings is a large Denver based home builder and residential developer headed by Larry Mizel," writes Brewton. "It has gained notoriety in the savings and loan debacle for its dealings with Michael Milken, Charles Keating's Lincoln Savings, San Jacinto Savings and most of all, Silverado Savings, the Denver S & L where Neil Bush, the President's son sat on the board of directors."

Brewton writes that "as a lobbyist, Brownstein has worked for the junk bond industry, including many companies that issued bonds through Drexel Burnham, and he has also lobbied for savings and loans, including Imperial, that had large junk bond portfolios."

Brownstein also lobbied for Lincoln Saving, controlled by CIA operative Charles Keating, who raised money to buy Lincoln from Michael Milken.

The Grey Men's Empire

Webb also claims that the Bush Crime Family Syndicate — he calls them "The Grey Men's Empire" — is responsible for high level national corruption that includes illegal drug smuggling, arms smuggling, money laundering, insurance fraud, savings and loan fraud and murder for hire.

The sons of George Bush, Webb claims, are also co-conspirators in this interlocking series of scandals. Texas Governor George Bush Jr., for example was heavily involved with Little Rock, Arkansas based Worthen Bank as well as Stephens, Inc., billionaire Jackson Stephens' financial holding company which was a front group for the entry of BCCI into the United States.

George W. Bush was also implicated in an insider trading stock scandal involving Harken Energy. Bush was a member of the Harken board of directors when the company signed a lucrative contract for the oil drilling rights off Bahrain.

How and why Bahrain gave this unknown company oil drilling rights in exchange for a new airbase to be built at American taxpayer expense is a story in itself.

Bush suspiciously cashed out before the Harken stock took a tumble.

According to Webb, "George Jr., Jeb and Neil Bush were all party to the crimes involving drugs and gun money laundering through Silverado Savings in Denver. They were all aware of 'Poppy' George's schemes using CIA, Israeli Mossad, Homestead Air Force Base and Mena, Arkansas to import drugs and ship weapons."

In the biowarfare-treason department, "Jeb Bush controlled the shipping of 18 types of chemicals shipped to Iraq through Leonard Millman's National Gulf Stream Aviation warehouses at Boca Raton Airport," says Webb. These chemicals are now being reported as responsible for Gulf War Syndrome currently killing Americans who served in the Gulf War.

More Criminal Conspiracies

Webb's investigations have uncovered many criminal conspiracies, which continue to be conducted under the auspices of what has been called the Shadow Government — the so-called national security and "intelligence" agencies. These include illegal covert drug smuggling, weapons dealing, and money laundering — operations which have their deadly roots in the World War II era of the Brownshoe Boys of the OSS/CIA.

Harassed, falsely arrested and imprisoned numerous times, Webb filed a Demand for Convening a Grand Jury in 1997 "to investigate crimes concerning Racketeering Influenced Corrupt Organizations (RICO) and continuous criminal enterprises, high treason, narcotics trafficking into the United States of America, theft of over $1 trillion from US Government and obstruction of justice' naming among others George Bush."

According to Webb, George Bush has bragged that "as long as we keep food on their table, gas in their gas tanks and a roof over their heads, we don't have to worry about the BUDsters."

The arrogant Bush calls the people "BUDsters." It stands for Broke, Useless and Depressed.

That's quite a joke coming from the former head of the CIA. After all, the "Boys" in the Agency refer to themselves — without any irony — as "Criminals In Action."

The Control Files — Blackmail of US Congressmen and Senators

Federal whistleblower Stewart Webb remains adamant in his outrage at the epidemic corruption in the highest levels of government, especially in the US Department of Justice.

"There is no party line difference," says Webb. "There's this group of criminals — and there's a woman in the White House, Hillary Clinton — who are screaming about Democrats — when in fact she herself was involved in the blackmail of Democrats. The highest echelons of the Democrats and the Republicans are both involved, and they have conspired in the elimination of good honest people in government. Also the control that they have in certain judicial districts is incredible. I've been told by Justice Department officials that Denver, Colorado was the most corrupt judicial district in the country because of the control that 'the Boys' had."

And who are "the Boys"? "The Boys" are the spooks and criminal elite who constitute the Shadow Government of the United States. The late journalist Danny Casolaro called this criminal network "The Octopus." It includes federal judges, attorneys, politicians, bureaucrats, current and former high-ranking military officers, as well as CIA, NSA, and other intelligence operatives.

The intelligence agency assets and covert operatives are part of a spook faction called Pegasus. This super secret group, which includes whistleblowers Gene "Chip" Tatum and Gunther Russbacher, conducts assassinations, drug trafficking and money laundering under the cover of "national security," continuing the criminal operations of the OSS-originated "Super Program" and the "Brownshoe Boys."

Webb tries to explain the complexity of this organized crime hierarchy which has infiltrated the federal government and which, in many cases, cannot be distinguished from the government itself.

"These are the players, and here's how it works," he says. "First there's General Richard Secord, Leonard Millman, Neil Bush, Jeb Bush, Hillary Clinton, Jackson Stephens and Jonathan Flake of the CIA. Those were the ones who were in charge of what they called 'The Control Files.'

"What happened was that they got the files from the CIA on the congressmen and senators... The alliance started with Secord, who was running the Iran-Contra operation, making sure there were weapons and guns — all part of the Denver equation as well. They did a lot of securities fraud and banking fraud on behalf of the Denver boys." [Stew is referring to the failed S&L's, HUD scams, and other real estate development subsidiaries used to launder money in the Denver area.]

At least since 1981, this organized crime group had established conduits for sending arms south into Latin America and drugs north into North America, then laundering the drug profits through Wall Street, banks, S&Ls, as well as real estate deals, often involving HUD low income housing and mortgages.

"Later in 1993, when they supposedly stopped funding the contras, they changed the name to Operation Black Eagle," Webb explains. "That's when they really went ballistic and started stealing from America wholesale.

"There was Hillary Clinton and the Rose Law firm, a CIA proprietary, and also Webster Hubbell, who's been indicted and jailed. [Hubbell was the former No. 2 at the Justice Department, used to run interference on any investigation that got too close]. He was the former Assistant Attorney General under Janet Reno. And there was Vince Foster [another Rose Law firm/intelligence operative] who had been killed. The car that drove off the body [of Vince Foster] had Denver ties. That was the Hensel Phelps construction company. The car license was RCG702, a yellow pickup truck with Arkansas tags that belonged to Hensel Phelps.

"Hensel Phelps was taken over back in 1992 by three Denver-connected people, including drug money launderer John Dick," Webb continues. "Clinton allowed the drugs to come into Arkansas. His partners were Dan Lasater and Jackson Stephens [the infamous financier of both the George Bush and Bill Clinton presidential campaigns]. Gene Tatum called it the 'Three Legs of Iran Contra' — Arkansas, Colorado, and Ohio."

Gene "Chip" Tatum, a CIA operative, helicopter pilot, mortgagee banking scamster and government assassin, was part of Pegasus, the *defacto* Bush Crime Family hit squad. He was often used to deal with uncooperative partners in crime. His work, of course, was also done under the cover of "national security." According to his own testimony, Tatum was "tasked" (gotta love those euphemisms) by George Herbert Walker Bush to eliminate Texas billionaire Ross Perot. When he refused (purportedly because Perot is a US national), Tatum and his wife were prosecuted under phony charges and falsely imprisoned. According to recent reports, Tatum is offshore enjoying the fruits of a deal he made to remain silent.

The Real Banana Republicans

"Ohio was Carl Lindner's Chiquita Banana," Webb continues. "He laundered part of the money from the drugs and so did Millman in Denver. The money went north. Millman then reinvested the laundered money into real estate, the 'Grey Men's Empire.'"

According to Pete Brewton, author of the groundbreaking expose *The Mafia,*

CIA & George Bush (1992), "allegations of CIA connections to Lindner waft around him, but nothing has ever been proved. One interesting link was Lindner's purchase of United Brands, which as United Fruit worked hand in hand with the CIA in the overthrow of the Jacob Arbenz government in Guatemala in 1954. In February 1984, Lindner's American Financial Corp increased its ownership in United Brands to 45.4 percent from 29.3 percent.

"Lindner's spokeswoman said that Lindner had never had any relations with the CIA," writes Brewton. "But Lindner does have a relationship with former CIA Director George Bush. The corporate recluse is one of Bush's biggest campaign donors... During the 1990 summit with French President Francois Miterrand, Bush held a press conference in the backyard of Lindner's Ocean Reef house."

In his book, Brewton also ties drug trafficker Jack DeVoe in with Lindner. "DeVoe used the Ocean Reef landing strip to fly much of his cocaine from Columbia," writes Brewton. "The exclusive Ocean Reef Club is owned by Cincinnati billionaire Carl Lindner, the secretive, security-obsessed, semi reclusive, Baptist corporate raider and major Republican donor.

"Lindner, who had been Michael Milken's biggest and most respected client, started out in the milk business and gradually expanded into other areas," continues Brewton. "His business empire includes the insurance and financial services company American Financial Corporation, Chiquita Brands International (formerly United Brands and before that United Fruit) and PennCentral, which bought Marathon Manufacturing from Walter Mischer and Mischer's close partner Howard Terry in 1979."

Infamous CIA scamster-lawyer Charles Keating represented Lindner in Cincinnati. Then Keating quit his law firm and went to work for Lindner as executive vice president of American Financial. In 1976 Keating moved to Phoenix to take over Lindner's home building company American Continental Homes. Keating bought the company and changed the name to American Continental Corporation.

Continuing the trail of the money-laundering story, Webb says that "it went directly from William Kennedy, the other Rose Law Firm partner (nobody talks about) who's in prison for twenty four years in Lompoc Penitentiary in California. He laundered the money on behalf of Rose Law Firm through M&L Business Machines in Denver, which was a cutout for Millman. M&L ended up in trouble. Because they had so many loans out from Capital Fed in Aurora, Colorado, Capital Fed itself collapsed.

"Beside laundering M&L money for Rose Law Firm, William Kennedy was also involved with the blackmail of public officials and payoffs through Boulder Properties, including US Attorney Mike Norton."

How Corporate-Government Criminals Work Together

And what was the transfer mechanism to pay off Norton?

"There was an attorney from Boulder, Colorado called Tom Berg," explains Webb. "He was also the one who laundered the money for a guy by the name of Macy — of Macy's Department Store — at the time when Mr. Macy was under bankruptcy. In order to bleed Macy's Department Store and make it look legit, they made it look like they kept paying millions in attorney fees. That's how Macy himself drained his own company.

"Norton was paid off through artificial M&L front accounts," continues Webb. "In other words, they would put money in an artificial name into investor accounts with M&L. Then they would shove the money overseas. They were setting up offshore trusts and laundering it through the Bahamas, then over to the Isle of Jersey.

"The M&L Business Machines corporate attorney was Norman Brownstein. M&L laundered money for US Attorney Norton, who actually had me under a false warrant," Webb continued. "He also laundered the money for Bob Pence, former special agent in charge of the FBI, who covered up for them in the 1970s-80s. He was the guy who was running the covert operation for the CIA to get me arrested.

"They laundered the money of Charles Keating and Lincoln Savings into M&L and then into an account for M&L called Realty Holdings, Inc. in Denver. Realty Holdings, Inc. today owns massive amounts of shopping centers all across the United States, especially in Las Vegas, Colorado and the West Coast. Bribes were also paid to public officials to hide their identities. Real Corp Realty, they called it.

"There are two components — Rose Law Firm launders the drug money into M&L, while they were paying public officials," said Webb. "At the time the Attorney General for the State of Colorado, Gale Norton covered it up. [Other corrupt deals like] the Denver Airport and Silverado and all that stuff was in the limelight. Gale Norton was covering it up because one of her assistants at the AG's office told me that she was rewriting the reports. They even came up with the idea how Gale Norton got paid. She was resistant to them in the beginning.

"The way they got her? Mike Norton kept telling her she'd better play ball. They got legislation passed to allow four attorneys to be put on the payroll. She was getting salaries of four nonexistent attorneys supposedly working in the basement. The checks got delivered to M&L in an account for Gale Norton.

"When she left, Gale Norton went to work for the Brownstein law firm," says Webb. "And one of Brownstein's attorneys became the Attorney General for the State of Colorado. The typical revolving door scenario."

Then Gale Norton was named the US Secretary of the Interior in the Bush Jr. Administration.

"Also they laundered the money for the FBI agent protecting them, Bob Pence; US Attorney Mike Norton; and Colorado Attorney General Gale Norton (no relation). They also laundered money for local District Attorneys, as well as DA's and US Attorneys out of Phoenix.

"They laundered the bribes for an SEC attorney named Joseph Dougherty. He was a contract attorney from Philadelphia who was supposed to go after 'the Boys' and investigate Charles Keating. Dougherty delivered cash to M&L on behalf of Charles Keating to hide the money."

The Boulder Properties Scam

"'The Control Files' means that once they compromise you, they own you for life," explained Webb. "Or they get you jailed.

"M&L suddenly ended up in bankruptcy court, while they're laundering money for the Boys," says Webb. "All these records were sealed, so nobody could get to them. As a result William Kennedy ends up in jail. At the same time, they worked the deal against the congressmen and senators they didn't have under control — special key Committee member such as Chuck Schumer on the Judiciary Committee, who has since become a rabid anti-gun advocate."

According to Webb, the Boulder Properties Scam compromised Congressmen Stephen Solarz, Ron Dellums, David Boren, Bill Alexander and Charles Schumer among others.

"Here's how they worked the deal against Schumer. The blackmail came through what they called 'Boulder Properties Ltd.' This is how they did it. Whitewater Development had loans at three banks — Madison Savings, Twin Cities Bank of Little Rock, Arkansas, and Beach Federal of Arkansas. Twin Cities Bank was used as a front for the Rose Law Firm. The CIA broke the bank. Before the bank finally went down, there was an operation set up in which the bank was used to send letters to senators and congressmen, whom they wanted to target. Letters said that real estate limited partnerships were available. They called them 'Marine Research and Development Corp.,' [Florida Governor] Jeb Bush's front. They told them that 'you should invest in this deal, that you can make high returns on your money, and get tax breaks and so on with the 1981 Recovery Act. Many of these congressmen and senators were foolish enough to do it. They had cash, and they were looking for tax breaks. They kept getting bombarded by these letters, so they took the chance.

"It was a simple $3000 investment. All of a sudden, their investment went to a $20,000 profit in 6 to 9 months. And that was the bait and switch. All of a sudden they're getting a $20,000 check on a $3000 investment. They thought 'hallelujah' this is the greatest thing ever. This is legit. I got huge profits. I got a tax write-off. The whole bit.

"Then all of a sudden, right after they get their check, they get a letter from Twin Cities again. We have another legitimate real estate deal for you to invest in, Boulder Properties Ltd. So they all put their money back in to Boulder Properties. Guess who financed Boulder Properties? Silverado Savings and Loan."

Silverado, which later collapsed, was the notorious CIA money laundry front, which had Neil Bush on the Board of Directors as window dressing.

And who was the mastermind behind this Control Files scam?

"Originally it was [General Richard] Secord," says Webb. "He was given the Control Files by George Bush. They told him who needed to be under control, that they didn't have under control, and the ones they had not blackmailed."

And why was this so important to the Bush Crime Family?

"They [these legislators] were chief [Congressional] Committee members, involved in congressional investigations having to do with House banking and stealing from S&Ls or they were key Committee members dealing with [Department of] Justice involving the appointment of prosecutors and so on. Or, they were involved in Housing, where they steal on a constant basis from HUD. Or they were involved with Foreign Affairs — shipping biological and chemical agents [overseas]. So they had to have control of them.

"They were planning ahead in case something would happen, they would have control of these congressmen and senators," explains Webb.

"They targeted these legislators. Arkansas Congressman Bill Alexander, who was sucked into this deal, later filed a lawsuit against Twin Cities bank. Alexander also ended up as co-counsel for Terry Reed in his lawsuit against them for guns and drugs. Bill Alexander doesn't know — and still doesn't know — how he got sucked in and set up. He just knows he's got a lawsuit. He knows he was targeted. He knows he was cratered. He had a 28-year record in Congress with an impeccable reputation for being honest. The reason he got cratered was because he was looking at the guns and drugs situation in Arkansas. They called it the Alexander Committee. It was a Congressional enquiry in 1990-1991. He took statements under oath from CIA operative Heinrich Rupp, CIA operative Dick Brenneke, CIA operative Gunther Russbacher and others. They testified in these secret inquiries about guns and drugs in Arkansas. And that's the reason they had to take Bill Alexander out. They had him co-opted with the Boulder Properties Scam.

"And here's how Leonard Millman fits in. Millman and his boys in Denver were in control, since MDC Holdings, Inc. owned Silverado. So Millman threw in a bunch of his old properties — rundown properties he no longer wanted — and bare land, whose value was overinflated and made it look like it was worth a lot more than it was. They falsified financial statements on junk apartments, HUD properties they stole. Then they falsified financial statements, so it looked like the deal was producing income. They pulled the money out of their bank Silverado in order to make the loan.

"They kept the partnerships alive. They had Boulder Properties I, II, III — up to thirteen or fourteen of them. One was designed for Bill Alexander and anybody else who would scream about guns and drugs. One was designed for HUD. One was designed for banking [committee] members.

"When the time came that Alexander, as an example, started inquiring into the situation, all of a sudden the plug got pulled. The partnership was no longer was valid. It was in trouble financially, so each partner had to come up with $10,000 a month each — to meet their obligations.

"It was all planned that way. So all of a sudden this guy's pumping out ten grand a month out of his pocket — that he can't afford. And that put him into bankruptcy. They used that against him in the election, saying 'look, how can this person represent you who's in bankruptcy personally; how can he even manage the money of the country?'

"And that's how they did it. They put him in a financial squeeze," says Webb.

According to Webb, they got Schumer through his wife. "Schumer didn't even do that. He was an attorney and he was going to fight them. You know how they got to him? They got his wife a job. Remember the House Post Office scandal. Check kiting. Selling coke over the counter. They gave her six months probation. They set her up. And that was the final blow — when Schumer turned on key congressional investigations. That's the way the game is played — the basic blackmail.

"It was Millman's personal and other MDC properties they threw into the partnerships. And it was Hillary Clinton's law firm, the Rose Law Firm, that wrote the original partnerships. They did the original paperwork."

The Bill and Hillary Story

"So you have two known Republicans — Jeb Bush and Neil Bush — along with Democrats — Hillary [Clinton] and Jackson Stephens — all involved and all in bed together, blackmailing United States Congressmen and Senators through Boulder Properties," Webb continues.

"You've also got Hillary Clinton again, laundering money through the Rose Law Firm [a CIA proprietary operation] the drug money that M&L was laundering and the bribes and payoffs of the people protecting them — United States Attorneys, judges. prosecutors, etc."

The story of the compromise of Bill and Hillary Clinton should be better known, since the Monopoly Media Cartel has never told the real story.

"Bill McCoy gave me all the details," said Webb. The late Bill McCoy was a former Army CID investigator who was mysteriously killed in 1997.

"They used Clinton as a Vietnam protester in London. His handler was London CIA Station Chief Cord Meyer. Mary Meyer was his wife. She was killed after she was found to have had an affair with [U.S. President John F.] Kennedy. That embarrassed Meyer."

Wholesale US Government Corruption

"They paid off FBI agents, FDIC inspectors, IRS agents, and they paid off three judges," Webb says, continuing his litany of high crimes and treasonous activities. "Public officials were paid with condos in Vail, Colorado. They controlled Judge Sherman Finesilver, who was part of the Shamrock Overseas Disbursement Company. He was paid through Richmond Homes, a division of MDC Holdings, through a United Bank account in Denver. He was paid for construction supplies like plywood and insulation on houses for Richmond that were never delivered. In other words, they made it look like he was paid for items which were delivered, when in fact they weren't.

"Another judge — Judge Zita Weinshank got paid through condos given to her in Vail. She was given an MDC transferred property into her name for ten dollars. They also set up artificial names and corporations.

"Judge Nottingham was the same judge they used to control the M&L Business Machines testimony by the president of M&L Business Machines, Robert Joseph. His testimony was that M&L was a huge money laundering operation. That was grand jury testimony, which became public record in May 1994. A reporter with the Rocky Mountain News interviewed Joseph, who told him that M&L was involved in a money laundering, not a check kiting, scheme.

"U.S. Attorney Mike Norton was protecting him. He had taken bribes and had laundered his own bribes through M&L investor accounts. He said this wasn't money laundering, that it was check kiting [the cover story]."

Since then Sherman Finesilver has retired. Nottingham is still a judge and Zita Weinshank is still a judge.

Anatomy of the Bush Crime Family

"Secord was the controller who worked directly for George Bush," explained

Webb. "When Secord gave orders, everybody knew they came from George Bush. Stephens was the money guy and financier. Millman was the money launderer. Hillary and the CIA's Rose Law Firm set things up. Jeb Bush was primarily into the drugs. And Neil was primarily into the money laundering. As an example, Jeb Bush's partner Ron Morales got busted under the DEA's Operation Desert Fox, the largest cocaine bust in US history that never hit the news. They estimated that he had imported over 400,000 tons of cocaine and marijuana in his operation over a period of ten years. They brought it into Colorado. They brought it into West Texas and then it was delivered in about eighteen semi rigs to Colorado. That's where a lot of the arms were being shipped out of."

Arizona-based investigator Brian Quig also figured prominently in exposing the guns for drugs network of the Bush Crime Family. His website is called DCIA, or Decentralizing the CIA, a great repository of secret US history of the late 20th century (http://www.dcia.com).

"Quig used to be an investigator for the Assassinations Subcommittee," says Stew. "Then he ended up going after Keating and Singlaub. General Jack Singlaub, who ran the Mena drug operation, was silently in charge. His office was right across the hall from Charles Keating. And the other guy [in the office] across the hall was Walter Bush, the nephew of George Bush. So Quig was over there, digging in the trash and finding notes from the Secret Service being sent to Singlaub."

Criminal Cover-up at the Department of Justice

One of the most notorious and successful DoJ cover-up artists is Lee Radek, chief of the ironically named "Public Integrity" Section of the Criminal Division.

Radek's adeptness at stalling Bush/Clinton Crime Family investigations is a matter of public record. His ability to hide government corruption has elevated the art of criminal cover-up to a science.

For instance, when the Landmark Legal Foundation asked for an inquiry into campaign corruption, Radek wrote this weaselly reply — "An inquiry into this matter is already underway within the Defense Department, to which Justice Department will defer until such time that a prosecutive opinion is sought concerning any potential criminal violation."

On February 28, 1997, when US District Judge Falcon Hawkins of South Carolina issued an 86-page order rebuking the Justice Department and the FBI for their phony sting operation, which destroyed the South Carolina Legislative Black Caucus and led to the impeachment of former federal judge Alcee Hastings, Lee Radek was specifically singled out for censure for what was described as "a pattern of outrageous judicial misconduct" and "appalling and egregious prosecutorial misconduct."

Judge Hawkins called the DoJ corruption "repetitious, flagrant and long standing... amounting to a pattern of misconduct." Likewise other permanent DoJ bureaucrats like John Keeney and Mark Richard have been instrumental in institutionalizing DoJ crimes and cover-up. Coincidentally, Mark Richard has recently been reassigned overseas.

In a December 21, 1997 article called "Public Integrity?," columnist William Safire called for an Independent Counsel to investigate Radek for covering up the Clinton campaign corruption scandals. Radek even went to court to impede prosecution of high officials under investigation. "Specific information from credible sources — an Independent Counsel and a District Attorney — support a charge that Radek may have violated Section 1505 of the Criminal Code, 'Obstruction of proceedings before departments, agencies and committees,'" wrote Safire. "Section 1505 makes it a felony to try to 'influence, obstruct or impede the due and proper administration of the law...' [The Department of] Justice cannot credibly investigate itself."

In other cases of illegal campaign contributions in the 1992 and 1996 elections, the investigation of Jorge Castro Barredo was taken away from prosecutors in the Southern District of Florida by Lee Radek and the Public Integrity Section, so that the statute of limitations would expire. It did, and the case was effectively killed.

More evidence of DoJ obstruction of justice includes the Charlie Trie fundraising scandal. According to a Washington Times story by Jerry Seper, "Senate panel to probe FBI's lost Trie notes" (9-28-99), "Justice Department lawyer Laura Ingersoll who headed the campaign finance probe blocked their bid for a search warrant to stop the destruction of evidence by Charlie Trie and his assistant. Miss Ingersoll and her boss Lee Radek, head of the department's Public Integrity section, refused for four months to allow agents to ask a magistrate for a search warrant after a 'trash cover' investigation showed financial business and travel records were being destroyed... Mr. Thompson said he believed Miss Ingersoll had been set up as a fall person. 'I don't think a lot of this necessarily has to do with her. I think she was just doing what she was told by Mr. Radek.'"

Likewise the investigation into the Buddhist temple fundraiser, attended by Al Gore where illegal contributions were laundered, was halted when Lee Radek ordered California Assistant US Attorney Steve Mansfield to stop his inquiries. Mansfield was told that an independent counsel should handle it. The investigation stalled while the nuns destroyed evidence even while admitting that it was to protect Al Gore.

Secrets of the DoJ "God Squad"

"When an IRS sting got too close to one of the Boys' money laundry operations, M&L Business Machines in Denver, the DoJ's Lee Radek reportedly made a secret settlement with Larry Mizel, Phill Winn, Norman Brownstein and others for a whopping one billion dollars," says Stew Webb.

Lee Radek and the DoJ's Public Integrity Section have so much power in obstructing justice and directing (or quashing) "investigations" that it's referred to as "The God Squad."

Before the Bush presidency, there was no centralization of federal prosecution. In other words, before a federal case was filed, the FBI would do an investigation and if there was enough evidence, it was sent to the US Attorney for prosecution. The Department of Justice had ten offices in the country with a Federal Racketeering Division, which dealt specifically with these types of cases.

Not anymore. Today's justice system works like this. Before a federal case is filed, the investigative reports go though the local US Attorney's office which forwards it to Lee Radek's God Squad, which then determines whether the case warrants prosecution or not. "Radek is responsible for steering certain investigations into a dead end and otherwise making secret deals with criminals to avoid prosecution," Webb contends.

"Lee Radek and the God Squad — the Public Integrity section of the Department of Justice — is supposed to be the watchdog," says Stew. "When Janet Reno talks about how she has confidence in the 'Public Integrity' Section, that they can handle any prosecution that needs to be done, she means the protection of the corruption in Justice."

Of course, the highly publicized INSLAW affair must figure prominently. The DoJ theft of the PROMIS software, a highly advanced interactive database which could track cases and cross-reference them to prosecutors, defendants and attorneys must have been extremely useful in derailing "sensitive" cases.

According to Webb, M&L Business Machines, a corporate-shell money laundry front for the Denver Connection, had offshore trusts, REITS and other companies to disguise the origin of drug profits and other funds stolen from scams like ongoing HUD mortgage fraud.

MDC Holdings Inc., which had around $12 billion in assets, was run by Leonard Millman, Larry Mizel, and convicted HUD figure Phil Winn, former ambassador to Switzerland appointed by George Bush.

Even CIA asset Eugene Hasenfus, whose plane crashed in Nicaragua during the Iran-Contra era, had paychecks from M&L. Other covert operations were run out of HUD, where financing, enforcement and regulation authority also provided the perfect cover for money laundering.

SECRETS OF THE BUSH CRIME FAMILY

"Radek came out of the CIA counsel, I believe, in 1977 and 78," continues Webb. "His underling — the Assistant Inspector General was David Mann, who also laundered his bribes through M&L Business Machines. Mann, by the way, was US Attorney Mike Norton's direct boss."

Pennsylvania Senator Arlen Specter, inventor of the Warren Commission's goofy Single Bullet Theory ("a single bullet went through President John F. Kennedy, then zigzagged into Texas Governor John Connally, got tired, decided to take a nap, then landed on JFK's stretcher") has also been linked to these scandals and corrupt activities, says Webb.

"Specter was involved with Mizel and Millman in a company called International Signals and Control in Scranton, Pennsylvania," he says. "There was a guy by the name of Jacobs, who went to prison because of their Iran-Contra activities. They were shipping missiles and component parts to Iran and Iraq. And Specter never went to jail. Millman and Mizel had ownership of the company."

World-Class Criminals Rule

If the Bush Crime Family has infiltrated and subverted the federal government to this extent, then the legitimacy of the State itself falls into question.

Retired US Army Brigadier General Russell S. Bowen in his book *The Immaculate Deception: The Bush Crime Family Exposed* (1991) wrote that "scandalous intrigues, outright deceptions and downright lying have been the continuing modi operandi of the Bush clan. They have an unmatched and unprecedented history of self-aggrandizement. They have dimmed the dream of their country. That will be their dubious legacy..."

And now that George Bush Jr. has grasped the ultimate prize, this "Super Program" of organized white-collar crime is positioned to move to the next phase. In essence, the Family That Preys Together Gets the White House. And more.

Unchecked, unprosecuted and unconvicted — the rise of the Bush Crime Family marks the beginning of a New Age of Global Caesarism.

This real-life criminal conspiracy is the consolidated piracy of the New World Order itself. Its prophet, George Herbert Walker Bush, declared the New World Order as a rationale for his criminal military action during the Persian Gulf War.

None dare call it Global Fascism, but this overworld mega-corporate oligopoly working with underworld organized crime syndicates is the *defacto* Ruling Class of Planet Earth. It still remains the greatest threat to freedom.

BUSHWHACKED

Chapter 25

True Stories from the 4th Dimension: An Interview with David Morehouse

I N A TOP-SECRET HIDDEN LOCATION on a US Army base, men and women working for the CIA prepare to "fall" into the Fourth Dimension. It's an all gray room, walls, carpet, furniture, everything. Baroque music plays while they recline, relaxing, preparing to enter an altered state of consciousness. What they're about to do is access the time-space continuum in a technique known as "remote viewing." When the brain registers the theta-wave state on the monitoring equipment, they are ready to "jump into the ether" in the words of David Morehouse, author of *Psychic Warrior: Inside the CIA's Stargate Program* (St. Martin's Press).

Science fiction? Not at all. This is advanced technology pioneered by esteemed scientists, laser physicists like Dr. Targ and Dr. Puthoff at the Stanford Research Institute in the 1970s. More recently, the program was developed by the US Government's Central Intelligence Agency (CIA) and the Pentagon's Defense Intelligence Agency (DIA).

This top-secret psychic-warfare program was called by many names: Project Scanate, Grill Flame, Gondola Wish, Center Lane, then Operation Sunstreak, and finally Operation Stargate. Morehouse's controllers euphemistically described it as an "intelligence collection method."

Bypassing internal bureaucratic and Congressional oversight, they were called "Special Access Programs" or SAPs. They compartmentalized all activities, which might put the Pentagon in a bad light, as well as providing a rationale for "plausible denial." Interestingly enough, this cellular approach to organization has been used successfully by intelligence agencies, terrorist organizations, crime syndicates, as well as the Communist Party in its heyday.

Mapping the 4th Dimension

The ability to access the heaven worlds and other dimensions has been the gift of David Morehouse's life. Likewise, it has been his bane or curse. Why? Because he also has the ability to access what could accurately be called "hell," a netherworld containing the most sordid episodes in the history of mankind.

For example, as a training exercise, Morehouse was sent back to the Dachau death camps of Nazi Germany in the 1940s. Imagine what that was like. Morehouse had to live with the vivid memories and sense impressions of his experience for months thereafter.

So how does remote viewing work? How do you tap into the unconscious mind, the time-space continuum?

According to David Morehouse, remote viewing is "the learned ability of travel from the physical dimension to a target regardless of its location in time and space. When you're moving backward in time, you're travelling through the ether and you're actually tapping into the unconscious mind. I have always referred to the unconscious mind as the time-space continuum; essentially it is part of, or one and the same as the ether."

So is the ether the medium upon which you travel?

"No. It's a misnomer," continues Morehouse. "You're not really travelling. It's perhaps more like folding space. You are travelling, but you're not moving. Does that make sense?"

Well, not really. Something is going somewhere, you would think.

Morehouse again tries to explain. "If you have access to the unconscious mind, you have free range of the time-space continuum. You are collectively tied into all humanity, or the whole universe, or perhaps other universes and other dimensions. Jung and Sheldrake labeled this the 'collective unconscious.' At the same time, it has an individual aspect that is willing and wanting a connection with the conscious mind."

One of the biggest problems in communicating this experience seems to be the relative inadequacy of language. In other words, how do you express 4D concepts, experiences and phenomena in 3D language?

Obviously a new nomenclature is needed which can a represent a reality that is beyond the box of ordinary three-dimensional consensus reality.

So then what is the difference between an altered state and a so-called normal state?

"We're conversing in beta state," says Morehouse. "When you lie down tonight, you'll drop down into alpha. Then you'll drop briefly into a theta-wave state. In theta wave state, it appears that the conduits become open. It's called the 'thought incubation state,' a time when that limen which separates the conscious mind from the unconscious mind becomes thinner. The 'limen' is just a word to describe a plane, or a separator, or septum between states, but nobody knows what the unconscious mind truly is."

"The altered state is an extended theta-wave state, meaning the stage where the limen becomes transparent," continues Morehouse. "Another way to describe it is that doors or conduits begin to open and sensory data from the unconscious mind begins flowing uncontrollably and randomly. The difficulty is not in opening the conduits. That, in retrospect, becomes relatively easy. The difficulty is in teaching the conscious mind to translate — without analysis or packaging. The unconscious mind, playing the role of the individual self, that is your personality, carries in data from the collective unconscious and begins to sling it in. Because it wants to establish a connection with the conscious mind — all sorts of data relevant to the time-space continuum envelops your conscious mind."

It sounds chaotic and random.

"It is chaotic and it is random," Morehouse affirms. "It's the conscious mind that focuses primarily downward into the physical. I've found that the time-space continuum is a four dimensional existence, whereas the conscious mind is in a three-dimensional existence."

"The four-dimensional world is something I can't even begin to describe. It's an Omniscience, an Omnipotence, an Omnipresence, All-Seeing, All-Knowing Existence. If you exist in a four-dimensional world, then you truly become God-like."

Listening to someone talk about these experiences becomes like grasping at the ungraspable.

"We are all — you, I, all of us — connected in the unconscious at a level we cannot see," says Morehouse, sounding more and more like a mystic. "When I was growing up, I remember the times when I went to church. I would hear them talk about God as being in all places at all times, dwelling in your heart, and watching over everyone, omniscient, omnipotent, omnipresent. How can that happen? I always wondered. It's impossible. Remote viewing revealed an explanation. It doesn't take place in the physical dimension. It takes place in the four-dimensional world."

Remote Viewing: A How To Guide

So how do remote viewers access the Fourth Dimension?

"The methodology is rather complex and intensive. It begins with what we refer to as 'the cool down process.' The process is really nothing more than perfecting a personal ritual that allows you to achieve the theta-wave state," says Morehouse. "We were taught to go into a place we called 'sanctuary.' It was a place in the ether where you go to gather your bearings, to acclimate yourself. Each individual viewer created his own sanctuary. For some viewers, it was some sort of a garden, or a safe house, or a safe place."

"For me, it was a transparent box in space," continues Morehouse. "In the total blackness of space with stars all around. When I was in there, nothing could harm me."

So what did you visualize in that box?

"My conscious mind, what I projected out. I visualized it as an apparitional self, a phantom self. It looked like a human form, only a light-radiant, transparent self. Then I would begin what I call the descent into the target area, and that became a nomenclature that was widely used throughout."

And this is what was called "falling into the ether" or "jumping into the ether?"

"I stepped out of 'sanctuary,' and I stepped into a vortex," says Morehouse. "A tunnel of light would slowly begin to materialize as I prepared myself in the center of the floor of 'my sanctuary.' And when I was ready, I would step into the vortex and I would fall. I accelerated faster and faster and faster, until I hit some sort of a membrane. And then I would punch through into the target area."

"I often used to get vertigo. I would fall head first with my arms out, and I would accelerate until boom! I would punch through."

And what was happening in the gray room at this time?

"They were monitoring bio-signs. They recorded your sessions with audio and video equipment. They had low light cameras. They videotaped your sessions. They wanted to know everything that was happening."

And you could hold a conversation?

"You could talk to them, and they could talk to you," says Morehouse. "In coordinate remote viewing, it was a very disciplined structured regimen. You can be in a theta-wave state but you remain conscious throughout the process. You could sketch on paper. You could write down your perceptions. You could answer questions from the monitor."

"In the hybrid and experimental technique called 'extended remote viewing,' you begin the same way. Your task could be to 'access the target and describe the event taking place.' But you have the encrypted coordinates. Most remote viewing sessions last an hour or an hour and a half. Extended RV sessions can last two to three hours."

So what actually happened when Morehouse "fell" into the ether during a dissociative episode, when he was not "in control," pulling off to the side of a road while driving, as he described in his book?

"My analysis is that once you open the conduit, it's like trying to shut the flood gates on a dam. There's always spillage or leakage. There's always something there that never closes completely. I think there are a number of conduits that never close. When you're normally under control, you have the ability to recognize what's happening and you can put it in check right away, then you're okay. Mel Riley [another remote viewer and a former colleague of Morehouse] was interviewed on television, and he said, 'I always have channels open. Always.'"

Morehouse agrees.

"A way to describe it is that a remote viewer always has one foot in the conscious matrix of the mind and one foot in the unconscious matrix and what, where, and how he perceives the world around him will depend on what foot he stands. And you can metaphorically jump from one foot to another and back again almost without knowing it. Mel was better able to keep his balance because he grew up with it. His first experience with it was at age 11, so he grew up with this special gift. So did Ingo Swann. I didn't start out with this ability. I didn't want this ability. A gunshot wound made this happen to me."

And what can keep the conduits closed down?

"There are physiological remedies for this," says Morehouse. "They're antipsychotic medications like Haldol or Loxitane. We have lots of mental straitjackets. Then you walk around in a cloud, and you don't know your own name, but you don't have a dissociative disorder. And you don't step into the ether unwillingly.

"I think there are a lot of people who are diagnosed schizophrenic who essentially have conduits open into the unconscious. They have data flowing at random without their having any control, ability to interpret or understanding. Outwardly they hear voices. They're unwittingly tapping into another dimension. God only knows."

So how do hallucinogenic drugs relate to this phenomenon? After all, taking drugs has been described as "taking heaven by force."

"Chemical inducement of an altered state is in my opinion simply the chemical opening of conduits," says Morehouse. "The problem is that you never learn to do it on your own. You never learn anything from it because you never have any control while it's happening. You don't have the ability to master it. You're just on a joy ride. I think the mechanics are the same, though, and you just go on the magical mystery tour."

The Holographic Model of Reality

New models of "reality" have to be introduced in order to correlate the evidence gathered by remote viewing and other extraordinary phenomena.

For instance, according to alternative science theoretician Bruce Cathie, "a rough analogy of physical existence can be made by reference to a strip of motion picture film. Each frame or static picture on the filmstrip may be likened to a single pulse of physical existence. The division between one frame and the next represents a frame of anti-matter. When viewed as a complete strip, each frame would be seen as a static picture — say, one at either end of the strip — then the past and the future could be viewed simultaneously.

"However, when the film is fed through a projector, we obtain the illusion of motion and the passage of time. The divisions between the static pictures are not detected by our senses because of the frequency or speed of each projection on the movie screen. But by speeding up or slowing down the projector, we can alter the apparent time rate of the action shown by the film..."

In the 1970s, a radically new theory of consciousness was proposed by Stanford neurophysiologist Karl Pribram and University of London physicist David Bohm, a former protege of Einstein and a world renowned quantum physicist. Briefly stated they had come to the conclusion that the universe itself may be structured like a hologram, a kind of image or construct created at least in part by the human mind.

As described in Michael Talbot's book *The Holographic Universe*, they considered another way of looking at the world — "Our brains mathematically construct objective reality by interpreting frequencies that are ultimately projections from another dimension, a deeper order of existence that is beyond time and space: The brain is a hologram enfolded in a holographic universe."

Talbot's book is an invaluable introduction to the paradigm. This model also shows the interconnectedness of the so-called physical and metaphysical worlds, how various non-physical phenomena and states of consciousness, mystical states of awareness, out of body experiences, and near death experiences, can co-exist and interact with one another.

Even prophecy or forecasting the future can be described using this model *vis a vis* Putthoff and Targ's precognitive remote viewing experiments. In other words, "a view of the future as a hologram that is substantive enough for us to perceive it but malleable enough to be susceptible to change." Ingo Swann speaks of the future as "crystallizing possibilities."

Relating to Morehouse's description of accessing the fourth dimension through remote viewing, the late Itzhak Bentov, author of *Stalking the Wild Pendulum*, described the relationship between normal vs. expanded states of consciousness as a constant "on-off" process, in which time spent in our "solid" reality as opposed to other realities is like fine tuning the frequency dial of consciousness.

Other Models for ESP

Morehouse's description of remote viewing also correlates to the Buddhist term siddhis, or powers, which includes clairaudience, clairvoyance, even precipitation of matter from the ethers. Christians have called them the "gifts of the holy spirit," spiritual gifts given as a grace of God.

"Yes, I don't disagree," he says. "It's a gift, but by the same token, I think there must be a reason why we're not born with it."

Some Christians disagree with his advocacy of teaching remote viewing techniques. "Their position is that I'm teaching the black arts, and we shouldn't be doing this type of thing," says Morehouse. "I don't disagree that there is a dark side to this, but in the coming millennium we are eventually going to be in somewhat dire straits. We are going to be confronted with very difficult choices. If you knew that people with you are good people, would you not want them to be counted as warriors that serve God with you? Would you not want them to be armed with these powers?"

So do other so-called extrasensory powers like clairvoyance or telepathy come with this ability for remote viewing?

Morehouse replies that "what happens is that these are all words which describe the perceptions of individuals who have conduits open. The hardest thing is for the conscious mind to develop this ability. It's a learned or practiced skill to interpret the data presented to it by the unconscious mind. As the unconscious mind travels backwards and forwards on the time-space continuum, it throws back raw data without analysis. It wants to develop a dialogue, but the dialogue development has to come from the conscious mind. We have to consciously interpret, not analyze, what we're given by the unconscious mind. It's learning how to live with that still small voice within yourself and learning to interpret it correctly."

And what is that "still small voice?" Is it the voice of God? Or the voice of the Holy Spirit?

"You have to learn how to interpret it, how to speak that language," says Morehouse. "Your conscious mind can very successfully shut out the Holy Spirit."

This could be what Christians call the "carnal mind," the rational logical mind that breaches no intuitive sensitivity.

And what is the difference between out of body experiences and remote viewing techniques?

"We tried to develop the ability to provoke an out-of-body experience," says Morehouse. "There was actually experimentation done in developing protocols in developing OBE remote viewing. Remote viewing is just opening conduits. An out-of-body experience is an actual separation of the spiritual body from the physical body. And this did not take place in the remote viewing.

"When you tear the spiritual body from the physical, what does that mean? It's harmful. That means that you leave the physical body open. When the spiritual body is gone it leaves the physical body open to whatever chooses to inhabit it. We're not talking about levels of consciousness. We're talking about spiritual separation. The spiritual body roams around and it's not under control. It's like a balloon floating in a hot breeze. It goes wherever the breeze will carry it, and God only knows what makes up that breeze."

What about the idea that this spiritual body is the responsibility of every individual, that karma can be made and destructive things can be done because the body is not in control?

"I agree wholeheartedly with that," says Morehouse. "In fact I know that it's true. The physical body is never left in remote viewing. There was always contact, but the physical body begins to manifest the physiological signs of what the projected consciousness is experiencing in the target area."

So what was the term for this projection of consciousness into the target area if it wasn't a body?

Morehouse says, "It's called bi-location. It's folding space, folding time and space. It's like bringing the event to you without ever going to the event if you tap into it. It's omnipresent while traversing back and forth on the time space continuum. What does it mean? It means you're everywhere at the same time. So the only way you can be everywhere at the same time is because everywhere is where you are. So folding space is the best analogy I can think of — like a accordion that folds in on itself, where you don't move. I was taught to believe that it was like the pages of a book, of an encyclopedia. There are planes that are separated, yet they're connected by the spine of the book. The spine of the book corresponds to the unconscious."

Reality (Time) Bites

In his book *Psychic Warrior*, Morehouse writes that "the past is locked and the future was like an untethered fire hose rocking and swaying, constantly changing."

So can past time be changed to affect future time?

"If you went back to look at it, it's like pulling up that event as if it were a slide and stepping into it, reliving it completely... emotionally, aesthetically, physically. You are there in apparitional form, but you aren't really there at all. What you are experiencing there are the physical perceptions of temperature, sound, sight, smell and taste. Plus you take it a step further in the unconscious mind on all the intangibles, the aesthetic impact, the emotional impact. You feel the pain of the people. You feel all things. Why? Because you are looking at it from a four dimensional perspective and in translating it as quickly as the mind can operate back to the conscious mind puts it into physical terms. So you're experiencing it and it can take a definite toll on you.

"For instance, go to 1945 and step into Ground Zero Hiroshima. You can pull that event up and step into it and all the torment of souls being torn from their bodies, all of the horror relevant to that event lives on. You can step back there and experience it."

So this is a record that remains forever and ever?

"The past remains, but it's locked in that part of the time-space continuum," explains Morehouse. "You can step in and experience it, but you couldn't, for instance, go and kick someone in the shins, or perhaps push Adolf Hitler off the speaking platform, so he breaks his neck. You can't affect anything. You can't do anything there except be there and observe and gather information."

Accessing The Cosmic Memory Bank

And this is where physics and metaphysics collide. Morehouse's description of remote viewing sounds very similar to accessing what has been called "Akashic Records." Akasha is a Sanskrit word, which means "primordial substance."

According to *Supermemory* authors Ostrander and Schroeder, "this cosmic data bank of the totality of universal happenings was conceptualized as being recorded on a 'subtle ether,' a kind of invisible, all-pervading medium through which 'kasha' or the visible light passes throughout space as a manifestation of vibration."

In other words, like a 4D cosmic camcorder, the holographic record of each instant on the time space continuum is captured and held there forever.

A book called *The Human Aura* carries a very apt description of this phenomenon, which clearly resonates with Morehouse's descriptions.

"It is of utmost importance that the student understand that there is a process whereby every observation of his five senses is transmitted automatically to subconscious levels within himself, where by inner hieroglyph, events he has witnessed or matters which he has studied are recorded; thus the entire transmittal of data from the external world to the internal lies in the Akashic records of his own being. The process of recall, while quite involved from a technical standpoint, is almost instantaneous. Out of the storehouse of memory, man quite easily calls forth these treasures of being. Unfortunately, not all events are benign; not all recordings are example of perfection."

Akashic records, then, are "all that transpires in Matter is recorded in Akasha, etheric energy vibrating at a certain frequency so as to absorb, or record, all of the impressions of life."

Here is another definition of Akashic records — "the recordings of all that has taken place in an individual's world are written by recording angels upon a substance and dimension known as Akasha."

"Akasha is a primary substance; the subtlest, supersensuous, ethereal substance which fills the whole of space; energy vibrating at a certain frequency so as to absorb, or record, all of the impressions of life. These recordings can be read by those whose soul faculties are developed."

Edgar Cayce, "The Sleeping Prophet," is said to have contacted these records when he went in his "sleep" to bring back astonishingly precise information about the past, including historical details relating to people and events during the time of Jesus, for example.

Cayce's work also delivered specific prescriptions for diseases as well as the reasons why. Authors Ostrander and Schroeder write that Cayce's amazing gift "overshadowed the arresting fact that he could so easily dip into an unseen information bank and bring back provable data."

It would also stand to reason that details of historical events could be accessed in an attempt to discover what really happened — especially in events of criminal conspiracy, negligence and subsequent cover-up.

Like, for example, what really happened to TWA Flight 800?

The Secrets of TWA Flight 800

"It was like turning part of a 747 into a microwave oven."

That's how David Morehouse explains what happened to the TWA Flight 800 after he delivered a remote viewing report for CBS News, which was never aired.

"We originally started at the request of a producer at CBS to work in consonance with them to investigate the downing of Flight 800," explains Morehouse. "We used a team of six remote viewers. After having gone back in time and looking at the event, five of them did not say that a missile struck the aircraft, but said that it was an energy beam or a light beam, and the aircraft exploded. It was a light beam that could not be seen by the human eye. It was a high-powered microwave."

"We did a thirty-two page report for CBS on it, a lengthy investigation. We used a law enforcement liaison officer who was a retired US city cop. I was interviewing PhDs who owned patents on things like fiber optic cables and microwave technology."

"It goes right back to the CBW thing in the Gulf War [the cover-up of chemical biological warfare by the Pentagon]. The first thing that came out of the Navy was that 'we had no exercise going on, none whatsoever.'"

"I saw the message from the Department of the Navy to the FAA (Federal Aviation Administration) which said that from this time to this time, which was a time window that included the departure time of Flight 800, there was an exercise going on."

"The microwave — we think did it — was built by Phillips Laboratories. It's about the size of a small truck, and is capable of producing 1.4 gigawatts, a billion watts of power in a concentrated stream of electrons that are guided by a self-generated electromagnetic field. The footprint of this particular weapon can be adjusted up or down to accommodate the target. They can crank it down to a footprint the size of a basketball. They can expand it out to a footprint the size of a football field. Of course, the more you disperse the electrons, the less effective the beam is, but it's still pretty nasty stuff."

Morehouse, of course, had to deal with the usual denial. "The executives at CBS said, 'we don't have anything that has that kind of range.' It's like the PhD who installed microwave dishes around New York and New Jersey told us, that when the guys that work on the Empire State Building go out on a platform to change the lights for Christmas, they wear flash bulbs in their pockets. The reason is because of the radiant microwave energy from all the dishes and power mounted on the building. When they get closer than they're supposed to be, it pops the lightbulbs. That's how much ambient radiant energy is coming out of those dishes. If you were to stick a frozen chicken on the end of a fiberglass pole and suspend it in front of a microwave dish, faster than you could blink your eye, it would be charred black."

"Because of all the microwave dishes, the building next to the World Trade Center had the top twenty floors surfaced with a special film coating on the windows to reflect the microwave energy. All the employees in the building had been complaining of ringing in the ears and headaches.

"We went through this analysis. We looked at the message traffic. There are seven military operational or warning areas off the coast of Long Island. Of those military operational areas, three out of four of them were active. They were joined together into an operational area that was code-named Tango Billy by the

Department of the Navy. This was an open source message — the Navy just informing the FAA that these warning areas are off the coast. When those warning areas are active, the Navy tells the FAA.

"The FAA establishes what is called Flight Corridor Betty. I interviewed at least a half dozen TWA pilots who said 'yes, that's right, I've flown Betty many times.' They go to a VOR in New Jersey. They break a hard left and they fly an outbound radial to pick up an inbound radial on the Nantucket VOR. They hit the Nantucket VOR, break right and head for the European theater. But they fly through an invisible tunnel in the air called a 'flight corridor.' It's supposed to be a safe corridor and they stack the aircraft in this corridor. Aircraft going north-south, aircraft going south-north. So Flight 800 was in Flight Corridor Betty. It was late. The FAA doesn't notify the Navy that 'we have aircraft late on takeoff or anything else.' There was also the USS Normandy [an Aegis Class Missile Cruiser] thirty-five nautical miles away from this area called Tango Billy, which was ten or fifteen miles off the coast of Long Island.

"There is also Brookhaven National Labs, which was formed in the early twentieth century by Nikola Tesla. It's a miniature version of Los Alamos. There are people out there with Gamma clearances. There is a nuclear power plant and particle colliders there. The Governor of New York is trying to close it down because of all the radiation seepage in the water that is poisoning the people. New York is supposed to have the highest cancer rate on the East coast. There is also a top-secret naval weapons testing facility adjacent to Brookhaven National Labs. In fact they share the same fence line. This is a completely sterile naval facility, an airfield with no airplanes visible during daylight hours because everything's locked up in the hangars. At night they roll it out and test it and do whatever they do.

"From this facility, they were trying to shoot out over the water into Tango Billy and with a high powered microwave weapon kill a test drone Tomahawk missile which was fired from the deck of the USS Normandy. When that missile was fired, which we believe was the flame the witnesses saw, they saw a drone climb, level off, and head for Tango Billy. What happened next may never truly be known but our evidence indicates that the drone missile climbed and put Flight 800 between it and the gun target line. Flight 800 was in the gun target line. When you're testing weapons, it's an automated target acquisition device or worse yet, manually acquired and fired.

"So you have some guy, and he looks at a blip on the radar screen, knowing that he just got 'Launch' confirmation from the USS Normandy. He sees that blip which is now really two blips — the Tomahawk missile and Flight 800. He presses a button that fires a high powered microwave weapon.

"We presented all the evidence and the facts. We had satellite imagery that was purchased from the French. We had autopsy data from the French, testimony from Suffolk County medical examiners, where guys had inadvertently revealed the fact that they had seen a flight attendant who had a piece of metal fused to her back. That doesn't come from an explosion. That comes from high-energy microwaves, which superheat metal and burns it into human tissue. It fuses it.

"Government medical examiners were cutting open cranial cavities. They were removing brains. They were dishing out eyes. They were doing all this because microwaves aimed at humans takes out all the ocular neural networks first. It fries the brain and it fries the eyes. It hits the spinal fluid and the blood and the marrow of the bones. It boils the blood. In fact it actually gels the blood. This sounds very gruesome, but, according to several medical personnel, it happens so fast that the brain doesn't even have time to register pain. You're dead instantly.

"Did it hit everybody in that plane? No. What it did, we think, is that it hit center of mass, which would have been under the left wing, directly into the fuel tank in the belly of this thing, right near the galley. What it did is it fried all the analog circuitry in this aircraft because high-powered microwave weapons have an electromagnetic pulse effect, which means that they destroy solid-state circuitry. So everything inside this 747, all digital readouts and gauges are all fed by analog circuitry. That's why according to our sources, all the digital readouts in the cockpit were frozen in time. And that's why the black boxes, which were recovered had no recordings whatsoever. All the recordings were eliminated, zeroed out. That's why they didn't come back with anything on the black box. There was just white noise.

"When it was a deceleration injury, like the plane that crashed in the swamp in Florida, we could listen to what the pilot said right up the point when they went into the ground.

"Why would this be covered up? If a missile had shot an airplane down, rest assured that the Department of Defense would have said 'damn, we're really sorry, we did a missile test' and paid off the surviving family members. They would have apologized. However, what really happened was Les Aspin, Secretary of Defense for the Clinton Administration told the American people in 1993 that 'we are now at the end of the Star Wars era.' That is a direct quote from him. What he was saying is that we no longer need this defense, thus ending a ten year long debate about whether it was smart, safe or feasible for us to put space-based weapons platforms in orbit around our planet — lasers, microwave or otherwise. He was deceiving us because we've now spent an estimated 358 billion dollars developing weaponry of this nature, that is Star Wars technology.

"What was going to happen four months after Flight 800 went down? The President was vying for his second term in the November election. This would have been the perfect stake in his heart if the wrong people got hold of it. They would have said 'you told us in '93 when you took office, you liar, that you weren't doing this anymore. Now you are. You've been doing exactly what you promised not to do.'

"After the elections in November '96, on the pages of Armed Forces Journal International, we proudly displayed the new airborne laser system which is a 747-400, outfitted with a chemical-oxygen-iodine laser. The entire first class section is all target acquisition and tracking while the body houses the laser generating equipment. We're going to build seven of them, so we can fly at 45,000 feet and have a range of 380 nautical miles, and we'll be able to burn a hole in whatever — somebody's head, another tank, an airplane. It's up there to allegedly protect us from inbound intercontinental ballistic missiles at the boost or post-boost phase. Seen any of those flying over us lately??"

So Who is David Morehouse?

No ordinary whistleblower, David Morehouse, author of *Psychic Warrior: Inside the CIA's Stargate Program* is an accomplished military professional. In addition to a distinguished service record, he holds an M.A. degree in military art and science, as well as a Ph.D. from LaSalle University.

He's also the author of a book called *Nonlethal Weapons: War Without Death*, and is a highly decorated and respected third-generation army officer. Commissioned as an infantry second lieutenant, he went from officer school to Panama, where he was a platoon leader, general's aide and a company commander of the Army's only separate Airborne Rifle Company and attained the rank of major.

After spending time in the Army Rangers, he left in 1987 for a series of highly classified special access programs in US Army Intelligence Support Command (INSCOM) and the Defense Intelligence Agency.

While in Jordan on a routine training operation, he was accidentally shot in the head, or more accurately in the helmet. His extrasensory abilities were opened up, and this seemed to precipitate recurrent episodes that could be called "psychic." He then became a prime candidate for induction into the top secret Operation Stargate, a joint DIA/CIA program at Fort Meade, which utilized "remote viewing" as an "intelligence" operation.

During his military career, Morehouse won numerous meritorious service and commendation medals, as well as paratrooper wings from six foreign countries.

After he left the Remote Viewing Program in 1991, he was assigned as Battalion Executive Officer to the 2nd Battalion, 5065th Parachute Infantry Regiment of the 82nd Airborne Division serving as second in command of over 600 paratroopers.

Soon after, Morehouse decided to expose the Stargate operation and its technology with the hope that the potential beneficial and peaceful uses could be brought to the public. However, when he tried to get out of the program, Morehouse realized that getting out of a covert operation is not as easy as getting in. Getting out alive, in fact, became his ultimate survival exercise.

What happened? In order to discredit him and his exposé, the Army tried to court-martial him with trumped-up charges based upon unsubstantiated allegations. In December 1994, he resigned his commission.

The Life of a Whistleblower

So what happens to whistleblowers in the US Government?

In the case of David Morehouse, false charges were filed against him. The tires on his car were "cut to blow," slashed to cause a crash at freeway speed. He and his family were harassed by anonymous phone calls. Phone conversations were bugged. His house was filled with carbon monoxide gas in a bizarre and suspicious incident. His daughter almost perished from the poisonous fumes. Morehouse's real life story takes another weird turn as he describes it in his own words.

"Some months ago, I had a call from the woman doctor thanking me for changing the direction of her life. She said that because of me she was forced to leave government service, but now she's happy about it. This is a doctor who had eighteen years in the service."

"They ordered her to diagnose me as a paranoid schizophrenic and delusional. She refused to do it. Then diagnose him as a malingerer, they told her. She refused. She was a tenacious psychiatrist, the head of the ward."

"She stood there the day they strapped me to a gurney and put me in a plane that took me six hours away from my family, down to Ft. Bragg where I sat in a facility, which could do nothing for me — by design. I had to go to alcohol abuse classes, though I wasn't an alcohol abuser. I was given a Dixie cup of medication twice a day to keep me in a stupor."

"They finally removed me from my support group. They took me from my family in an effort to isolate me. Now instead of my family driving fifteen minutes to come to the hospital, I was in Ft. Bragg, North Carolina six hours away from them. They would dress me up, drug me and take me drugged into the courtroom for Article 805 hearings, where I would stand up and almost fall over. I couldn't even hear. It was like standing in an empty water tank and hearing people talk. And they made me endure that. The Army's final *coup de gras* was to require me to write the Family Caring Manual for the 82nd Airborne Division."

Then an orchestrated campaign to discredit Morehouse was started — writing anonymous letters to his book publisher and the movie production company that bought the rights.

Morehouse cites a handwritten note that was to coordinate the attack. "Here's the book. Here are the damaging documents. They may not be interested in what we have to say, but they may not be able ignore the avalanche of attack. Avalanche of attack. This is a quote from the note. That note was written by Major Paul Smith, a former remote viewer for Stargate — also the man who threatened Morehouse in Walter Reed Hospital."

CIA Harassment and Disinformation

After his decision to go public, David Morehouse was subjected to plenty of CIA harassment and character assassination. One of the primary character assassins was a man named John Alexander, the subject of a glowing report in *Wired Magazine* in 1995.

"Depending on who you talked to, John Alexander was, early in his career, a special forces officer in Vietnam," says Morehouse. "He commanded a Montagnard battalion which essentially meant he advised them. Somebody else would say he was a member of the Phoenix Project in Vietnam [the notorious CIA assassination program]."

"When he came out, he worked with the intelligence community and he never left. So this is a Special Forces guy who crossed over into the intelligence world and never went back. He's been connected with the Company [the CIA] for a very long time."

"I met him through Ed Dames who was his friend. John Alexander lived in Santa Fe, New Mexico and often met with Ed Dames there. Ed Dames was convinced that there were aliens underground in New Mexico. And so began an abuse of tax dollars — buying plane tickets to Albuquerque whenever he wanted."

"Ed Dames was part of [Operation] Torn Image, and he would fly out there allegedly to conduct business in support of his mission. He would meet with John Alexander who would hand him a photograph and ask him to do some remote viewing."

"With the exception of Jim Schnabel and Ed Dames, John Alexander has no friends in the remote viewing community. Most people think he's a shyster, except for guys like Russell Targ and Hal Puthoff, who are still drawing government paychecks. They were both laser physicists, the original takers of Central Intelligence Agency money to work for remote viewing projects."

"Three guys accessed the Freedom of Information Act before my book came out — John Alexander, the retired colonel still working for the CIA, Jim Schnabel, and Joe McMoneagle. Except for Joe, they actively went after me. They posted my name and social security number on the internet. They publicly called me a criminal, taking unsubstantiated allegations from the government and posting them on the internet."

Have they done this to anybody else? "Not to my knowledge," says Morehouse.

Military Intelligence: Attack of the Oxymorons

"There are reams and reams of documents which show that this phenomenon exists," says Morehouse. "A great deal of it is classified. Ed May claims that he has it all. He's a physicist who heads up the Cognitive Sciences Research Laboratories. That's a research facility for remote viewing and other paranormal phenomena dealing with human potentials of the mind. He claims he's not on the government payroll, but he still carries a top secret security clearance."

Continuing the CIA-orchestrated harassment, Ed May brandished documents at Morehouse prior to a talk show on which they would both appear. He subtly threatened Morehouse against reopening his court-martial case claiming the Government would re-open the prosecution as well and pursue the case all over again. According to Morehouse, Ed May clearly stated that this time the government wouldn't stop the proceedings for a resignation.

May also allegedly told Morehouse that "there are people out there who can get to you."

"Such is the case with all these guys: Jim Schnabel, John Alexander and Ed May," says Morehouse. "Ed May works for the CIA. He told the producer of the Gordon Elliott show that he was heavily involved in the military remote viewing program. The truth is I never saw this guy or heard his name while I was working there."

So does this mean that the Central Intelligence Agency is taking so-called proprietary information about remote viewing, developed with taxpayer money, and trying to privatize it, to kick back a revenue stream from it?

That's what allegedly happened in the INSLAW affair in which Bill Hamilton's PROMIS software was stolen from his company then handed out to foreign spy agencies so the CIA would have a backdoor into their computer database files.

According to Morehouse, "for three weeks Program Director stood at that shredder shredding documents when General Soyster, Commander of the DIA ordered an investigation, after the remote viewing program was transferred form INSCOM to DIA. Members of the unit were livid because the Director was shredding the history of the organization."

Hey, what's the big deal?

Lots of CIA files have been shredded. Reported known cases range from Oliver North's Enterprise notes to the CIA's MK-ULTRA files.

More Shaky Agents

So why did it get so personal? "You have a credible third-generation Army officer whom superior officers labeled as 'destined to wear stars' someone who came out of a Ranger battalion and stepped into the intelligence community," says Morehouse referring of course to himself.

To undermine his credibility? "Yes, fabricating stories about me and my wife for instance," continues Morehouse. "There isn't an author around who spends days, literally days, posting user groups. There were hundreds of postings made by Schnabel. Then John Alexander got into the fray and started doing the same thing. Then they started writing anonymous letters to Interscope, which bought movie rights to the book, and St. Martin's Press, the publisher."

"Then there's the case of Paul Smith, quoted as saying this to a reporter: 'What I told Dave is that if he would stop talking about the unit, we would get him a medical discharge.' Paul Smith was no longer working as a remote viewer from the unit but still working for DIA in some sort of capacity."

So why did it take so long for Morehouse to resign?

"I thought, and my defense team told me we could face the charges and beat them," he says. "We looked at everything the government had. I didn't know we would be ambushed with the other charges. Until I got the phone call one night from a brigadier colonel friend of mine who said, 'You still have friends. We're holding the door open, but we can't hold it open forever. This is bigger than us. You better get out.' That was the first clue that I had about their scheme. I had nobody who investigated on my behalf, yet the Government had the entire Criminal Investigation Division coming down on me. They looked at every fragment of my past. They interviewed every person they could find who ever knew me. Why? Because I was getting ready to tell a story about a top-secret government organization and nothing more."

"If it was Ed Dames," Morehouse begins. "How hard is it to discredit a guy who stands up and tells people that pregnant Martian females are coming out of the ground?

"But when you have a guy with an illustrious career and a family and kids and is moving on the fast track, when that guy comes out and says, 'I have an ethical and moral problem with what you're doing here.' You've got to attack this guy at his roots, at his family. They sent anonymous phone tapes in the mail to my wife and kids. They sent unsigned love letters to my wife from various locations in the US.

"They were recording my phone conversations. They wanted to undermine my support group. They want your family to disown you. They want to isolate you. The classic character assassination tactics. Because you can't fight the fight by yourself. But my wife stood by me. My father stood by me tearfully as I tendered my resignation. My father who fought for this country in two wars, hates the US Government and the military [for what they did]."

Viewing the Ark of the Covenant

Psychic Warrior details many of Morehouse's encounters with legendary and historical events. For example, when he describes remote viewing the Ark of the Covenant in his book, he calls the relic itself a "dimensional opening."

"When I came out of the ether I explained what I had seen to the program director," says Morehouse. "When I researched the theological background behind the Ark of the Covenant, it was clear to me that it was a part of the Temple in the wilderness that was carried around by the Israelites. They put the Ark of the Covenant in the inner sanctum, also known as the Holy of Holies. Those who entered into the inner sanctuary, the high priests, actually tied ropes on their ankles so they could be pulled back.

"It was the conclusion of the remote viewing community that this was in fact a conductor or convector of some sort. It was something that channeled power to form some sort of a portal or opening into a four-dimensional world, which is where the Creator dwelt. The high priest was stepping through the portal into this four-dimensional world."

And what about free roaming in the fourth dimension?

"That was called an open search — where you were told to go where the signal line takes you, analogous to standing on a platform at Penn Station in Manhattan and jumping at whatever train was rumbling by and going where that train takes you. You don't know where you're going to go or where you're going to end up. It can be very frightening; sometimes it's instructional; sometimes it's just magical."

So has Morehouse seen anything of any significance?

"I've just had the realization that we are not alone," he says. "I never saw God or Christ or Buddha. But I can tell you that there are other worlds and other civilizations and planets. It's all out there. Other dimensions. It's not simply what exists in our physical dimension, in our physical universe. There are other portals that lead to other universes, and there are universes upon universes. It's limitless, infinite. It's staggering."

There is a common misperception that remote viewing entails out-of-body or astral travel. "We were trying to develop OBE-RV, out-of-body remote viewing," says Morehouse. 'What we found was that we lacked the ability to make the separation occur at will and then control the separated body.

"Remote viewing was not based on the work of Robert Monroe. It was based on a very disciplined protocol developed at SRI in part under the direction of natural psychics like Ingo Swann, Pat Price, and Uri Geller. Uri Geller was heavily involved in the developing of these protocols at SRI. He has not ever really been given full credit for it. He was probably the best natural psychic they had there... in my opinion."

If this gift comes from God, then who is trying to control it and use it for negative purposes, i.e. the abuse of it by the military and intelligence agencies?

"I struggle with that question everyday," says Morehouse. "I don't know if the Military-Industrial Complex is doing this out of pure ignorance. If they're stumbling about like a bull in a china shop out of pure ignorance or whether they do it out of some deep-rooted sinister backdrop or foundation that makes them want to be able to use this to manipulate humanity.

"The only evidence I have is that I know that there is an enigma out there. I know that there is something that is larger than life itself which attempts to dominate and control all humanity.

"So if I find the answers, I'll talk about it because that's my calling now and my election."

Angels

Did Morehouse ever encounter what could be called "enlightened beings"?

"I had my experiences with what I call my angel. I also experienced beings from other worlds that had the Christ consciousness. I never saw Jesus Christ or Buddha. They were very benevolent, loving, enlightened, radiant individuals.

"While standing in their presence, you feel nothing but the presence of Good and a great warmth. They would recognize or acknowledge your presence, but they would never interact with you. They never guided you or directed you. Your remote viewing monitor would say, 'Approach them; attempt to engage them in conversation; ask them a question; ask them who they are.' They would politely smile and walk away. They recognized us as intruders yet harmless.

"According to my father, this particular angel watched over him in WW II and Korea. All my life he never shared this with me — not until I thought I needed it. When the Government assault was under way and I was crumbled under the pressure, my father calmly and somberly announced that he was passing on the protection and legacy of his angel to watch over me."

Demons and Possession

Had there been any occasions when Morehouse felt threatened, when he thought he was going to die?

"I felt frightened on several occasions when I encountered what I came to call lesser beings or demons," replied Moorhouse. "They're people who look just like us. They are very friendly and they smile. They want to engage you in conversation but the instant you realize what they are, they attack you — not physically but emotionally and spiritually.

"In an incident described in the book, I was held upside down by my ankles and I thought they were going to kill me. They clutched at me and pulled me back in the circle. I was screaming at the top of my lungs. The next thing I remember, the monitor who was watching me, was talking me back, bringing me back to the physical. In retrospect, nothing could possibly have happened to me but I feared for my life. I think there was a real danger in this attack at a four dimensional level. They know what frightens you. They amplify your fears. I think there are elements of the dark side that exist for the express purpose of attempting to inhabit the physical. They want to possess the physical body, to take you over for a brief period of time."

So how about channeling? Does that mean that entities can possess physical beings?

"Any channeler, for example, J. Z. Knight, will tell you that Ramtha possesses her physical body," says Morehouse.

"On the other hand, if you're a medium, you have the ability to listen across the limen and translate the message."

Regarding channeling and tarot cards, the attitude at the CIA seemed to be "look at what we're doing. Who are we to say that this has no merit?"

In fact, Morehouse says that "the chief scientist of the CIA, Dr. Jack Verona, a physicist, used to come in twice a month for personal readings from one of the channelers working for the program."

Just think. He could have saved all that taxpayer money. He should have just called the Psychic Hotline.

Gulf War Crimes

One of the most dramatic and shocking episodes in *Psychic Warrior* is a remote viewing mission Morehouse did near the end of the Persian Gulf War. At that time, three independent remote viewers, including Morehouse, were sent to the Gulf. Morehouse himself got an order to move to a 550 feet elevation and 20 miles north of where he landed. About an hour later, in the midst of intense smoke and fires near the oil wells, Morehouse spots a "smaller silver object in the sand, I think I see something unusual, a small canister it looks like stainless steel." (p. 168).

Morehouse writes, "Suddenly it all seemed clear to me. The DIA wanted to make sure that a chemical or biological agent had been released on US troops but they didn't want anyone else to know… once the use of these unconventional weapons had been confirmed, the DIA could start the cover-up so the American people would never find out."

Historian Antony Sutton, author of *America's Secret Establishment*, writes in his monthly newsletter *Phoenix Letter* that "one needs to read these pages [of Morehouse's book] carefully. It looks as if DIA knew where the canisters were to be planted. This confirms the report that CBW [Chemical Biological Warfare] was a joint US-Iraqi operation aimed at US troops."

Sutton also points out that "not only did the Iraqis use chemical biological warfare agents on US and allied troops, but the equipment was supplied with the knowledge, assistance and financing of the West.

"What the Pentagon is covering up is that CBW agents were legally exported to Iraq by the Bush Administration," writes Sutton. "The license was granted by the Department of Commerce for anthrax and an agent called mycoplasma incognitas. Mycoplasma was made in Florida and Texas and tested on death row inmates in Texas. This was reported to the press by Senator Donald Riegle of Michigan and ignored by CNN and the other networks." (February 9, 1994)

Morehouse agrees. "I found early on that you can't trust the network media in the United States to present truth. They're part of the problem because they're owned by defense contractors for a reason. The 900 billion dollar a year global defense industry is going to control that which can do them the most damage — truth in the media. They know that the media can sink them, so what do they do? They own the media."

Sutton continues his analysis by concluding that "the scandal and cover-up is that the supply of CBW weapons to Iraq implicated the Bush Administration, much as Prescott Bush, father of George Bush, was implicated through Union Bank in the buildup of Hitler in the 1930s."

Like father. Like son.

Like traitors.

Gulf War Crimes Cover-up

Sutton, author of many books including one about the former Soviet Union called *The Best Enemy Money Can Buy*, asks, "Why the cover-up? Morehouse believes that the US Government did not want to take care of thousands of military casualties. We suggest another reason. We have a report that the US allowed export of these agents to Iraq knowingly and even some members in the Government had investments in the firm making these for Iraq.

"Recall that no credible enemies are left for the military-industrial complex which General Eisenhower warned us about to use as a claim for large defense expenditures. Then the entire picture comes together... Then you see why *Psychic Warrior* is a key piece in the puzzle back of Desert Storm. An artificial war against an artificial enemy. Why? Because you can't have a defense budget unless you have a credible enemy. If no enemy exists, you make one."

Rodney Stich confirms these allegations in his monumental encyclopedia of US government crimes and cover-ups called *Defrauding America*. He writes in great detail in an entire chapter called "Bank of Lavoro and Iraqgate," about the scandal in which the Banca Nazionale del Lavoro (BNL), through its Atlanta branch, was used to loan over five billion dollars to Iraq just prior to the Gulf war.

Stich writes that "in November 1989, White House officials guaranteed the payment of loans made by banks to Iraq for the purchase of US farm products under a program run by the US Agriculture Department's Commodity Credit Corporation. The approval provided that US taxpayers would indemnify the banks lending money to Iraq for the purchase of US food supplies if Iraq defaulted on the loan payments...

"These loans made possible the war capability for Iraq to invade Kuwait. In effect the US taxpayers through their leaders made possible the terrible bloodshed in the Gulf War... Some of the money furnished by the United States was used to purchase poison gas that was used on Iraqi Kurdish villages, much of it purchased through Cardoen Industries in Chile, a CIA asset. Cardoen supplied considerable war materials to Iraq under the guidance of the CIA."

Regarding the Gulf War oil well fires, Morehouse wrote that "every soldier downwind of those fires must have inhaled the toxin." The implications are clear. The so-called Gulf War Syndrome is a direct result of this exposure. The Department of Defense knew about them and remains liable for the thousands of cases of veterans contaminated by this chemical biological warfare.

And what does Morehouse think about it now?

"I think about it everyday," he says, his voice dropping. "We know that we were being manipulated to 1. being able to confirm, and 2. confirm it in any record where anyone could go back to it. They denied it. They said it never happened.

"In time they said there might be something to it, that maybe we blew up one chemical dump. Then they said it was two chemical dumps... The problem is that the American people continue to forgive this sort of betrayal. They ignore it and thereby forgive it and so they set the stage for it to happen again. They stood there, men who knew and bald-faced lied to us and said it never happened.

"General Powell went before Congress and fervently denied that he had any knowledge of it or that he had any evidence of it, which is again 'plausible denial.' because nobody briefed him on it.

"The CIA was keeping track of all the wind charts pertaining to this theater of operations. Let me tell you something. In eighteen years in the military, I never once turned to the CIA for a weather report. So why is the CIA telling us that the downwind messages showed this and this?

"Are we so stupid that we can't see that these guys are concerned about what's going to be revealed in time, that they've jumped in to level the playing fields. They're in there BS-ing and lying right and left, day in day out."

Antony Sutton is unequivocal in praise of Morehouse and his book. He writes that "*Psychic Warrior* is one book that you should read. Not only will it open your eyes to the strange new technology we outlined, but it will make you disgusted with a Pentagon whose main interest appears to be to keep its Washington generals in luxury and golf courses, while it can't keep its planes in the air. Yet DoD has time to persecute an officer who truly served the United States."

Gulf War Crime Victims

David Morehouse tells heartrending stories about visiting Gulf War veterans in the hospital, the actual victims of this criminal conspiracy by the Department of Defense.

He talks about "a Navy corpsman in the Gulf War who's wasting away. All he can do now is blink his eyes. He contracted ALS, perhaps from exposure to a biological agent. He's dying, but he's hung on four years longer than he's supposed to have. He can't speak. He can't swallow. He's fed through a tube that goes directly to his stomach. It's a horrible agonizing death, but he maintains his sense of humor. He's very very upset with our government and the military-industrial complex, the President, with everybody."

So years after the Agent Orange scandal of the Vietnam War and other documented atrocities committed by the US Government against its own armed forces personnel as well as its citizens — testing bacteriological warfare, testing radiation, testing the effects of syphilis on untreated southern US black men, etc.

etc., it still doesn't end.

"They just do it over and over again," says Morehouse. "The whole thing is to put time and space between you and the event, between the politicians and the generals. They don't want their legacy destroyed. They want to march through time, clean and pure. When the people plagued by this mishap are dead, buried and forgotten, then we'll see our President in the year 2020 apologize for poisoning the troops in the Gulf War."

Criminal conspiracy at the Pentagon?

Sure, but just you try to litigate.

Psychic Assassins

An unconfirmed story about the US military's use of psychic assassins has been circulating for many years. According to the story, former Soviet dictator Yuri Andropov was actually killed by a team of remote viewers trained in directing energy at persons targeted by the CIA.

When asked about the use of psychic killers by the military, Morehouse was reluctant to answer, but verified that these operatives were referred to as "remote introject assassins," by General Stubblebine.

The King Hit

Fall guy James Earl Ray was sentenced to life in prison for the killing of famed civil rights leader Martin Luther King Jr.

His lawyer William Pepper, author of *Orders to Kill*, will be presenting new evidence in court — remote viewing data by David Morehouse on the assassination of the 60s era icon.

So who killed King?

Morehouse says "these were contract yobbos, low level CIA contract operatives who did it. US Special Forces sniper teams were also present, several of them who came out of the assassination school at Fort Bragg, North Carolina. They were always deployed in areas where riots were taking place or expected to take place. They had a hit list, a sequential hit list of people they were to take out. That was common operation protocol in the 60s.

"Every time there was a civil disturbance, these sniper teams were deployed and given encrypted orders that told them who and what. They had a standing list of people to hit. They would receive information that would say 'do it' or 'don't do it.' And if they did it, they had an egress route out of the area. Or a potted plant, people who would pick them up.

"The soldiers who were given charge to do this perceived individuals like

Martin Luther King (and others who provoked rioting and unrest on college campuses against the American Government) as Enemies of the State."

So what can attorney William Pepper do with Morehouse's remote viewing report?

"If it's good enough, he's going to take it to court as evidence and use it," says Morehouse. "His argument is that the US Government used this as an intelligence collection tool for twenty years.

"It's going to be admitted as evidence, verifying the information gathering methodology. He will say, 'Look, a military remote viewer has brought this information back and it was collected using existing and verifiable military technology.'"

Morehouse admits, however, that "what Pepper's trying to do is fight an uphill battle."

The Future of Warfare

Morehouse's new book is called *Nonlethal Weapons: War Without Death*. According to Morehouse, "conventional weaponry is designed to kill. The new hybrid conventional weaponry is designed to maim. Non-lethal weaponry, by this definition, must be anti-materiel and not anti-personnel.

"The book takes a very philosophical approach to the concept of non-lethality. It talks about what conventional weapons have done in this century — taken the lives of 170 million innocent human beings' lives. Doctors, lawyers, professors, housewives, children, not warriors, 80 million of them were summarily executed for their refusal to participate, and that number continues to grow exponentially. Less than 250,000 of those lives were taken through nuclear weapons.

"In the post Cold War era, the military-industrial complex has spent an inordinate amount of time on the disarmament and the abolition of the nuclear arsenal, unscrewing five nuclear warheads so we can pat ourselves on the back and say what a great job we did, while in the meantime we've spent 900 billion dollars plus last year to build and market weapons of death and destruction. So it's a shell game.

"The conclusion is that we're in a new strategic era at a crossroads of human history. We have to make a decision. Are we going to continue to build weapons on an ever-increasing scale? Or are we going to evolve to an era in which we retool the entire defense industry to outfit ourselves with weapons that preserve human life but yet destroy the war machine of a belligerent, thereby eliminating a belligerent's ability to wage war.

"We have that technology to 'kill' the tanks themselves. This is the premise. The nature of man will never change, and therefore the nature of war will never change, only the way in which wars are fought will change. All the so-called Star Wars technology, the electromagnetic pulse weapons, are lethal high tech conventional weaponry. That's all it is."

Morehouse continues with his analysis saying that in the book "it takes twelve truly non-lethal technologies and it templates them over fictional scenarios that contemplate current world events — Bosnia, Somalia, etc."

So the military-industrial complex has to be called for an accounting? "Exactly, that's what has to happen," says Morehouse. "We have to become more well-read on these issues. That's why the book creates this vision. Here's the scenario with conventional weapons and here's what happens if we inject a non-lethal form of technology.

"I saw this tested at Dugway Proving Grounds in Utah. It's called an anti-tank shroud round. Milliseconds before it impacts, it sends out a white hot plasma jet-stream which precedes the impact of the round and bores a hole through the armor faster than the speed of sound and spews molten metal into the interior of the tank which turns everything inside the tank into Jell-O. That's how Iraqi tanks were killed in the desert.

"What the shroud round does is that milliseconds before it hits it explodes into a wire reinforced polymer film that envelops the tank like an octopus envelops its prey. It shorts out everything. This polymer instantly wraps and shrinks down. They called it a shrink wrap round.

"The polymer's collective strength blew the hydraulics on an M-60 tank as it tried to traverse the turret. It seals all the lids shut. The wire shorts out the communication."

So why haven't they been bragging about it? "Because," explains Morehouse, "the 900 billion dollar a year military-industrial complex, these greedy war mongers, who build and market weapons to third world countries, don't want it.

"War is pure commerce and economics. You can't expect those who are in the business of building weapons of mass destruction to entertain notions of retooling the industry to build weapons on the opposite end of the spectrum. It's too cheap.

"Plus if you start saving lives and killing equipment, then you force diplomacy to take its rightful place as the tool of conflict resolution in the new millennium. So you start to screw up this perpetual market of death and destruction.

"We now have members of Congress who have appropriated billions of tax dollars as welfare for arms manufacturers. So when a manufacturer makes them and sells them to some third world tyrant who can't even afford to buy powdered milk for the babies starving in his country, but he buys twelve jets that he can't afford. So who pays for them? The US taxpayer. We now pay the weapons manufacturer, the arms dealers. And we pay that tyrant's bill when he defaults."

269

Morehouse has a point. This *modus operandi* has certainly worked for every single military conflict in the twentieth century. The Gulf War was only the latest scam to generate profit streams for the arms manufacturers and their bankers, as well as get rid of excess population, i.e. "cannon fodder" (military personnel) and "useless eaters" (non-revenue-producing, resource-depleting people).

Remote Viewing as a Public Service

So what's in the future for Psychic Warrior David Morehouse?

"What I've been working on is Remote Viewing Technologies, a private company involved in information and training seminars for remote viewing techniques," replies Morehouse. "Thus far we have not taught anyone in the private sector, only people in the commercial sector and law enforcement. We've been training police officers in remote viewing because they can readily make the transition. Trying to look through the eyes of a dead man for an hour and a half, that is not as disturbing to a cop as to a layman. Police officers seem to have this jaundiced view of the world anyway. If they're working homicide detail, they have a tendency not to get as unraveled or upset." However, video training and audio training cassette tapes will be available in the near future from another company called Nemesis Productions.

"Nemesis Productions will be involved in corporate training and lectures on R&D, as well as on individual and corporate motivation. This is for scientists and engineers to help them get an additional intuitive edge in their research projects.

"It shouldn't be difficult dealing with hard science folks. Validation for these phenomena was done by Dr. Russell Targ and Dr. Harold Puthof, who were laser physicists working for Stanford Research Institute. They took the extreme scientific approach to the exploration of remote viewing. They certainly weren't going to do anything to tarnish their scientific reputations so they followed strict scientific methodology in validating and evaluating what goes on. Their charter from the US Government was to essentially validate it. That's what CIA and SRI do. They tell us whether it works or doesn't. Their pay wasn't cut if it didn't work.

"Project Scanate not only accepted, but proved, the existence of the ability of the human mind to transcend time and space. Could they ever explain how it happens? No, they could not. Could they show empirical results about how it works? Yes, they could."

So what's being done with this technology as a public service so to speak?

"Probably the only two people that are spearheading that is Lin Buchanan and myself. I formed a company with police officers called Remote Viewing

Technologies. Lin has what's called the Assigned Witness Program. Remote Viewing Technologies has been working several cases in New Jersey and several cases in Baltimore. We're getting ready to train a large number of officers in New Jersey, and we've already trained seven police officers in Minnesota.

"The law enforcement agencies, the chief of police, the detectives — everyone has welcomed it with open arms. As long as they understand the need to keep a perspective on it and they know the Three Cardinal Rules of Remote Viewing must always prevail.

"One: it's not 100% accurate, never has been, never will be.

"Two: you can never trust the results of any single remote viewer operating independently of other remote viewers. Therefore you cannot task yourself. That's the problem that Courtney Brown and Ed Dames have run into. They front-load themselves. Courtney Brown sits downs and says 'Hale-Bobb object following. Describe.' It violates all the cardinal rules of remote viewing. There's no blind or double blind. If you task yourself, you step into the world of analytical overlay or the process of imagination. It's the same protocol violation that Ed Dames, who is not a remote viewer, falls into.

"Three: Remote viewing is not a stand-alone endeavor. It's always in consonance in the intelligence community with other 'collection platforms.' In law enforcement, it's always used with other investigative methodologies."

For the Benefit of Humanity

David Morehouse, author of *Psychic Warrior*, should be commended for his courage in exposing the secrets of the 4D world and bringing remote viewing out of the intelligence closet into mainstream awareness. Being a whistleblower can be the ultimate challenge. At great sacrifice to his family as well as his own life, he has endured unimaginable trials, tribulations, and harassment by the CIA and its stooges. And, despite an organized campaign against his work, he has withstood this barrage of disparagement and attack.

The importance of remote viewing should not be underestimated. Just as tapping into the internet can potentially deliver information faster, quicker, and easier than physically going to a library, so remote viewing has the potential to revolutionize access to historical records and other information inaccessible to the five senses.

Without a doubt, the twenty-first century will require new abilities and talents. Remote viewing and its ancillary skills, so-called extrasensory perception or paranormal powers, could in fact be crucial in the survival and evolution of the human race.

Bibliography

Constantine, Alex. *Psychic Dictatorship in the U.S.A.*
Chapter 2: "Blue Smoke & Lasers: SDI as a Cover Story for the R&D of Electromagnetic/Cybernetic Mind Control Technology"
(Feral House)

Morehouse, David. *Psychic Warrior* (St. Martin's Press)

Ostrander, Sheila and Schroeder Lynn. *Super-Memory: The Revolution* (Carroll & Graf Publishers)

Stich, Rodney. *Defrauding America* (Diablo Western Press, P. O. Box 5, Alamo, California 94507; 800-247-7389)

Sutton, Antony C. *America's Secret Establishment* (Liberty House Press, 4400 Loma Vista, Billings, Montana 59106)

Chapter 26

Spooks, Whistleblowers and Fall Guys: An Interview with Rodney Stich

"**A**FTER CLINTON WAS ELECTED President of the United States, his administration and its Justice Department halted all investigations and prosecution of the crimes related to Inslaw, October Surprise, CIA drug trafficking and money laundering, BNL, BCCI and Iraqgate," writes former US Federal Aviation Agency (FAA) investigator Rodney Stich in his monumental book *Defrauding America*.

"Clinton had much to hide when he left Arkansas to assume the presidency of the United States," Stich continues. "His misuse of government facilities and power to feed his sex drive, his use of drugs, his cover-up of the CIA's unlawful arms shipments from Arkansas and related drug trafficking, were crimes. The mysterious deaths, killings and beatings of people possessing information that would expose these corrupt activities added further to Clinton's problems. He certainly needed a thick armor of protective officials in government. Fortunately for him, the US media kept the lid on these major crimes."

That must be what they mean by "don't ask, don't tell."

Stich's book, *Defrauding America*, is a classic study of the secrets of twentieth century history. It contains hard evidence of state-sponsored terrorism by the US government. In fact, the cross-corroborated testimony of over three dozen federal agency whistleblowers contributed to the never before revealed information in this astounding book.

Does CIA Stand For Cocaine in America?

In a chapter called "Evidence on Top of Evidence," veteran FBI Special Agent Richard M. Taus recalls uncovering and reporting evidence of CIA drug trafficking by a group called the "K-Team."

According to Stich, "the K-Team had a front operation with the patriotic sounding name National Freedom Institute and called its operation the 'Enterprise,' the same that repeatedly surfaced in the Iran Contra congressional hearings... Taus's team discovered that that K-Team was a CIA operation and that it was engaged in drug trafficking, looting of savings and loans, and activities related to what later became known as Irangate and Iraqgate."

Another of Stich's informants, Gene "Chip" Tatum confirmed these allegations. He was the helicopter pilot who actually ferried Oliver North, Felix Rodriguez (aka Max Gomez) and William Barr (attorney of the CIA's Southern Air Transport and later George Bush's US Attorney General) in Central America.

Tatum describes one meeting to "determine where over $100 million in drug money disappeared on the three routes from Panama to Colorado, Ohio and Arkansas. This theft was financially draining the operation known as the 'Enterprise'... The first call was made by Fernandez to Oliver North, informing North that 'the money loss was occurring on the Panama to Arkansas route, and that means either Seal, Clinton or Noriega.'"

No honor among thieves, since not only CIA pilot Barry Seal, but Arkansas Governor Bill Clinton and Panama's General Manuel Noriega were *all* under suspicion of skimming George Bush Sr.'s cocaine profits.

And here's how the Dixie Mafia and the Yankee Mob work together, according to Gene "Chip" Tatum.

"Fifteen minutes later the portable phone rang and Vice President George Bush was on the line talking to William Barr," continues Stich. "Barr said at one point, referring to the missing funds, 'I would propose that no one source would be bold enough to siphon out that much money, but it is more plausible that each are siphoning a portion causing a drastic loss'... Tatum said that Barr then dialed another number immediately reaching then governor Bill Clinton. Barr explained the missing money problem to Clinton explaining that over $100 million of the Enterprise monies had disappeared... warning that the matter must be resolved or 'it could lead to big problems.'"

The problems were evidently ironed out. Bill Clinton became president, one of the CIA's "few groomed men," who was promised his position on the "short list" for the job, according to *Compromised* authors Terry Reed and John Cummings.

Oliver North – "Patriotic" Drug Smuggler

In another instance, Tatum described "flying the group to Santa Ana, Honduras meeting with Enrique Bermudez and other Contra leaders and visiting a cocaine processing facility. Tatum described the strong smell of jet fuel and acetone and the large fuel pods that had the tops stripped off them and in which were fuel and leaves," writes Stich. "Tatum repeated what Oliver North said, 'One more year of this and we'll all retire.'"

(Or, if not retirement, how about an Ollie North syndicated radio talk show? Or what about a run for senator, maybe even president — on the Anti-Drug, Law and Order platform? The hubris of criminals like Oliver North is unbelievable.)

"North added, 'If we can keep those Arkansas hicks in line, that is,' referring to Barry Seal and Governor Clinton... As Tatum listened to these conversations he remembered the army officer's remarks, 'Tell no one. There's no one big enough in your chain of command.'"

No kidding. Hearing Oliver North discuss the involvement of George Bush and Bill Clinton in drug smuggling, Tatum wisely followed this advice.

And Who Is Rodney Stich?

Former US government investigator Rodney Stich is one of today's unsung heroes. His single-minded dedication in exposing government crimes and coverups has resulted in his own harassment, imprisonment and bankruptcy.

Hounded and nearly destroyed by government agents, his story will remind you of the persecution of dissidents in the former Soviet Union.

In today's National Security State of America, he has however persevered.

His encyclopedia-sized 753-page book, *Defrauding America*, in its third expanded and revised edition, is clearly a labor of love. It also happens to be the definitive history of crime, corruption and coverups by the US Federal Government in the 20th century. This book is not merely important. It is indispensable for every person who wants to know the behind-the-scenes maneuvers of Big Government, Big Business and Organized Crime — in many instances, different branches of the same beast.

Future generations will regard this book as an historical milestone like Edward Gibbon's *Decline of the Roman Empire*. Why? Because *Defrauding America* contains *prima facie* evidence of legal and judicial corruption, so horrendous and so monstrous as to defy imagination.

And how did it happen? Rodney Stich used to be a Federal Aviation Agency investigator. After many years and continuous reports of airline maintenance abuse and negligence, he became a whistleblower. But because of the powerful forces he had challenged, he was set up, falsely charged and imprisoned.

During his "diesel therapy" — being constantly moved from one prison to another so there would be no time for him to file court appeals — he met and interviewed other whistleblowers from other US government agencies. He accumulated more and more information and was able to write and publish *Defrauding America.*

Why Stich Was Falsely Charged and Imprisoned

In a recent interview, Stich says, "My initial imprisonment was due to so-called 'contempt of court.' As you may know, I had discovered extremely serious government misconduct related to a series of air disasters. That started me into becoming a kind of an activist in government corruption."

"As I was aggressively pursuing this and acquiring more information from other government agents over a period of years, I started discovering other forms of government corruption. Involved with all of this was the United States Justice Department cover-up, which I encountered for the last thirty years. So if the Justice Department is obstructing justice, there isn't much one can do. But I discovered a particular statute — I may be the only one that ever used this — and the wording is very clear."

"This is Title 18 Section 4," continues Stich. "It states that 'anyone who knows of a federal crime who does not promptly report it to a federal judge or other federal officer becomes guilty of the crime of subornation of a crime.'"

"So I thought this is an excellent way to circumvent the obstruction of justice by the US Justice Department. I filed action demanding that the judge receive my evidence and the evidence of some of the other agents I had become acquainted with. By law they're required to do so. Instead they refused to receive it."

So then what happened? "Sometimes they dismissed it without a hearing," says Stich, "and never even allowed me to get to that point. Then they also rendered an order, and this was repeated several times — forever barring me access to the federal courts. This is, of course, unlawful and unconstitutional. And also it's obstructing justice."

"As my knowledge of criminal activities in government increased — when I started getting heavy evidence of CIA drug trafficking — I filed actions again, even though federal judges barred me access to the federal court, which they legally can't do, but they do it. Then they held me in contempt of court for even trying to report the criminal activity that I must report."

Because he had been betrayed by attorneys many times before, Stich represented himself *pro se* having learned the details of navigating in the corrupt waters of the US judicial system. There were lots of shoals and his own shipwreck was his eventual imprisonment.

"As attorneys would tell me over the years," Stich says laughing, "'If I represent you, that would be the end of my career because the government is very powerful and government can very easily affect an attorney's career.'"

"The initial imprisonment was six months in federal prison for contempt of court," continues Stich. "In other words, here I am trying to report crime that the Justice Department and federal judges were actually involved in the cover-up. Incidentally, to do this the federal judges had to have the cooperation of the Justice Department because the Justice Department would then file the charges and prosecute."

Is it really possible that they worked hand in glove to cover up the exposure of these criminal activities?

"Yes," says Stich, "and it's interesting to note that in the early stages in one of my earlier books in the second edition of *Unfriendly Skies*, I was naming federal judges and Justice Department personnel who were blocking the reports I had of the criminal activities related to a series of air disasters. Of course, later on when I'm going to federal court with other offenses, these same groups are now charging me with contempt of court for trying to expose criminal activities in which they were implicated."

"And justice for all" from the American Pledge of Allegiance turns out to be nothing but a sick joke.

Exposing the Power Elite Criminals

"This book reveals criminal and subversive activities implicating high level personnel in the three branches of the federal government," writes Stich in his introduction to *Defrauding America*. "It reveals why most of the public is dangerously uninformed about the criminal acts perpetrated against the United States and its people by the very people entrusted to prevent such happenings."

"Many criminal activities such as CIA drugging of America will be difficult to believe by most Americans who have been shielded from the truth by a duplicitous Congress and much of the media," he continues.

"For those of us who have seen these events as insiders, including those who actually participated in them, questioning whether the CIA would engage in drug trafficking is like asking pilots, 'Will planes really fly?'"

"Yes, planes actually fly, and yes, the CIA has been smuggling drugs into the United States for the past 50 years."

Evidence of CIA Drug Trafficking

One of the most explosive chapters in the book is entitled, "CIA and DEA Drug Trafficking." This includes first-hand accounts of former CIA operatives and DEA agents who were part of these operations.

Stich writes, "My phone was used for hundreds of hours of three-way conference calls between CIA and DEA personnel, their wives, a Mossad agent and even Ross Perot. Often the conversations were of the nature of one pilot describing to another events that they experienced each one knowing that any fabrication would be recognized by the other. My position was like a secret mole inside covert CIA activities, adding to the discoveries I made while a federal investigator and while being victimized in one of the many criminal enterprises."

Cross corroboration between testimony by CIA operatives Gunther Russbacher and Trenton Parker, for instance, indicates that the Colombia drug cartels were actually organized by the CIA.

"Parker told how the CIA set up the meetings in which various Colombian drug dealers organized into a drug trafficking cartel," writes Stich. "... He stated that the first meeting occurred with twenty of the biggest cocaine dealers in Colombia present, that the second and final meeting was held at the Hotel International in Medellin attended by about two hundred drug dealers. The Medellin Cartel was established in December 1981, and each of their members paid an initial $35,000 fee to fund a security force for the cartel members to protect their drug operations."

In another part of the book, Stich writes that "CIA operative Gunther Russbacher, confirmed the meetings that Parker mentioned and that there had been a preliminary meeting in September 1981 in Buenaventura, Colombia which established the format for subsequent meetings. Russbacher attended the September 1981 meeting which was initiated by the CIA to facilitate drug trafficking into the United States, permitting the CIA to deal with a group rather than many independent drug dealers."

What does that mean? The phony so-called "war on drugs" is simply an operation to eliminate any competition to state-sanctioned drug trafficking.

"The average American is unaware of the gravity of the CIA's criminal activities thanks to the orchestrated cover-up and disinformation by the establishment media," writes Stich. "The corrupt mindset has existed for years. Initiating wars as in Vietnam and assassination activities as in Vietnam and Central America are routine."

"Although the CIA is not permitted by law to operate within the United States, it has done so. It has engaged and is engaging in many forms of criminal activities against the American people. Through fronts, cutouts and proprietaries, the CIA has defrauded all types of US financial institutions including savings and loans, banks and insurance companies. The CIA is a major player in the looting of Chapter 11 assets, making the exercise of Chapter 11 statutory protections a trap for unwary Americans."

DEA Drug Trafficking

According to Stich's informants, who are former Drug Enforcement Agency (DEA) whistleblowers, this US federal agency supposedly created to stem the influx of drugs into the United States has become so corrupt that it makes you wonder if the purpose of the DEA was simply to act as a liability control asset of the drug cartel. These serious criminal activities have never been investigated by the US Justice Department, which itself is compromised by its participation in illicit and criminal activities.

"On April 4, 1993, I received the first of a series of phone calls from a former DEA pilot, Basil Abbott, who had flown drugs from Central and South America for the DEA in DEA aircraft since 1973," writes Stich in his book.

"Abbott was in federal prison, being charged with a parole violation while on a trip from Austin Texas to Missouri. The parole violation consisted of failure to convince the DEA agents that he was not doing anything to violate his parole. The actual reason for his arrest was that Abbott tried to interest the media and the networks in his charges that the DEA routinely engages in drug trafficking into the United States."

"... Abbott named other DEA pilots who, acting under DEA orders, flew drug-laden aircraft from Central America to the United States. These included Floyd Carlton, Cesar Rodriguez, Daniel Miranda and George Phillips among others..."

"The intensity of the drug trafficking flights was revealed by Abbott as he described the large number of aircraft arriving and departing, 'It was like Grand Central Station at some airstrips in Belize and Nicaragua.'"

"These flights were profitable for everyone involved, including the pilots. In addition to their government salary, DEA pilots received additional money or perks. Abbott received $60,000 and fifty pounds of pot for this one week of flying to the Miskito Indians..."

"Abbott described a flight to Panama with DEA agent George Phillips (Phillips was a CIA contract agent assigned to the DEA). While stopped for fuel at Belize, Phillips opened an aluminum suitcase in which there were rolls of tapes and disks marked Inslaw. Phillips stated to Abbott that the tapes were money records of a fake company used by drug dealers. This software, called PROMIS, was initially stolen from the Inslaw people by Justice Department officials and business associates, and then sold to foreign governments and drug cartels."

"Abbott described his frequent contacts with DEA Central America Bureau Chief, Sante Bario, and how the DEA silenced Bario when it suited the agency. DEA and Justice Department personnel charged Bario with federal offenses, seeking to cause his imprisonment, and to discredit anything he might say about the DEA drug trafficking. When brought before US District Judge Shannon in San Antonio, Bario tried to describe his DEA duties and the DEA drug trafficking, but Justice Department attorneys and the judge blocked him from proceeding. While in jail awaiting trial, a prison guard gave Bario a peanut butter sandwich laced with arsenic and within minutes Bario collapsed experiencing great pains. He later died."

Celebrity Criminals

Stich names lots of names in his book, public officials and well-known politicians, as participants in serious criminal offenses. These of course include celebrity status politicians like the unindicted Bill Clinton, George Bush, William Barr and Oliver North.

It makes you wonder if Stich was ever sued or threatened by anyone for libelous content or anything that was untrue in his books?

"No, I never have," says Stich. "Something interesting did happen a few months ago. There was one drug enforcement agent, Michael Hurley, who was agent in charge at Mena, Arkansas."

Mena, by the way, was the site of a small rural airport in Arkansas, the staging area for drug shipments into the United States during the late 1980s.

"His name originally came up in the Inslaw matter," continues Stich. "Michael Riconoscuito was involved in altering the Inslaw software which was stolen by the Justice Department people from the Inslaw company. So when Congress wanted Riconoscuito to testify to these matters, he was called by a Justice Department official and told that 'if you testify, we'll get you.' He goes and testifies and a week later Michael Hurley, who was a DEA agent in Nicosia, was transferred to the state of Washington and was then involved in filing what I feel are false drug charges against him."

So Hurley was the one who initially set up Riconosciuto?

"Hurley was chief agent for the DEA in Mena and was well aware of the smuggling in early 1980s."

And this is the crossroads where different crimes and coverups intersect — what the late journalist Danny Casolaro called "The Octopus," a global cabal of dirty tricksters involved in deals around the world.

According to Casolaro, "The Octopus" was a loosely knit international network of former CIA operatives, military men, organized crime figures, and other "beltway bandits" (former government officials) who worked together on various projects. What kind of projects? Arms manufacturing and weapons sales, money laundering, procurement fraud, and kickbacks.

"Meanwhile," Stich continues, "Lester Coleman, author of *The Trail of the Octopus*, was working out of Beirut and Nicosia as an agent for the Defense Intelligence Agency. He was instructed to spy on the DEA while he was working under the cover of the Christian Broadcast Network."

And why didn't the DIA trust the DEA?

"My understanding is that DIA felt that the DEA was heavily involved in drug trafficking," says Stich. "They just wanted to know what was going on. Coleman was an operative in Nicosia. The DIA was using [Pat Robertson's] Christian Broadcast Network as a cover. While Coleman is working in Nicosia, he finds out that Michael Hurley and the DEA is involved in a drug pipeline that involves the CIA, the DEA, the Syrian drug traffickers, and Lebanese drug traffickers and that they were using Pan Am aircraft for smuggling the drugs."

"It was this drug pipeline — the way it was being operated — that permitted the terrorists to put the bomb on board PanAm 103. This is where Michael Hurley comes in. Coleman says that the DEA and Hurley were aware of and were involved in this drug pipeline."

"Michael Hurley sent me a fax four months ago," says Stich. "He said that he heard me referring to him on the internet and he would sue me if it were untrue. So I faxed him back and said 'frankly I haven't mentioned you at all on the internet; however since we're in contact, I want you to confirm to me that you were the DEA agent in Arkansas in the early '80s.' He never answered. But I talked with Lester Coleman, and he confirmed that, 'yes, it was true.'"

Just another unindicted criminal?

"As far as unindicted criminals are concerned," notes Stich, "you'd have a good part of the US Justice Department. But who's going to prosecute?"

Corruption in the US Department of Justice

So what's Stich's sense of this institutional corruption which has gone on through several administrations for at least thirty years?

"As far as Justice Department corruption is concerned, I was able to document it for the last thirty years, while I was a federal investigator," replies Stich. "In fact, while I was a federal investigator, I even accused, in writing, J. Edgar Hoover of criminal cover-up and obstruction of justice, while I was with the FAA in the 1960s."

"You know a federal employee can not get away with that. And there's some particular federal directives that makes that a very serious offense if you do that [accuse a public official] without having evidence. Now I had plenty of evidence. It was about 1965. I had been in contact with him for some time, bringing to his attention the criminal activities that I discovered in the FAA — also while I was acting as an independent prosecutor. I was able to document other criminal activities, not only in the FAA related series of air disasters. I was so incensed by about what was going on and the constant accidents. Every six months there would be another fatal crash. So what I did — I forced a four-month hearing upon the FAA during which time I acted as an independent prosecutor. During this time I conducted the hearing, brought testimony and hard evidence into a 4000 page transcript. During this hearing, I had FAA management engaging in perjury, subornation of perjury, and fraud that I was able to document."

"People don't realize the significance of this, which I describe in *Unfriendly Skies*. This has never happened in the FAA and probably never will — where a key FAA investigator is forcing a hearing on the FAA and during which it is turned into an adversary hearing. I'm getting witnesses to testify and I'm introducing documents and where there are some really unusual events are going on. Plus, during the hearing two more air disasters occur, in one of them over a hundred people were killed. This is due to problems that I was identifying and the crashes occurred in my area of responsibility. They were due to the same problems I would bring out and that FAA management was fraudulently denying that existed. It makes for a helluva story."

And what are the reasons for the corruption? Were airline officials just paying off the FAA top officials? What was the motivation for these continuing crimes and coverups and air safety violations?

"There are several reasons," Stich explains. "One, the revolving door syndrome which is in many government agencies. A government employee, usually management, is placating industry doing anything they can to get brownie points with them so that when they leave government service, they got high paying jobs in industry."

"Then of course, there's pressure on the FAA from members in Congress who are of course getting healthy contributions from industry. And when that pressure is put on the top of the FAA, it goes all the way down the line. And all of these FAA people who cooperate, there's different ways they can be rewarded. So the fellow who s trying to do his job and insists upon doing it, he suffers retaliation. But for all those who play the game — there are various rewards that they get."

"Then of course you have the incompetents in the FAA. You get someone at management level. He doesn't want to fight with industry. First of all, he's not competent to take them on. The point of an inspector is to bring out unlawful or unsafe practices. The management people don't want to hear this. Reports are made and destroyed. If an inspector persists, there are many ways that he can be retaliated against — if he doesn't get the message."

"The FAA came into being in 1958 from the Civil Aeronautic Association, after a United Airlines rammed into a TWA airliner over the Grand Canyon. That received so much publicity that Congress legislated the Federal Aviation Act of 1958. I went with the FAA shortly thereafter. The function of the FAA was to promote safety and issue rules and regulations and have inspectors to see that they're carried out. But there are many problems in the system."

No kidding. The biggest problem seems to be to figure out who will watch the "watchers"? How can government agencies remain accountable to the citizens rather than so-called special interests and industry groups?

Another obvious parallel in the United States is the relationship between the Food and Drug Administration (FDA), which is supposed to be a public guardian of health and the pharmaceutical industry which is involved with the same kind of corrupt practices, bribery and "revolving door" of agency employees and industry executives. Also the Securities Exchange Commission (SEC) and the so-called securities industry is another case in point.

So what can be done to break the chains of corruption?

"If we could clean out the Justice Department for one thing and provide some type of workable solution where inspectors or government agents could get protection if they are being retaliated against," says Stich.

Isn't that what the Whistleblower Act is all about?

"It doesn't work for those who are reporting high level government corruption," says Stich. "That's okay if you report misconduct of industry and that industry is not being protected by high level government management. Let me quickly mention that over a period of years as I'm getting more publicity, I'm getting more and more government agents coming to me all the time. I can think of a dozen of these people who attempted to report serious high government corruption and they suffered retaliation."

The Dark Night of the Soul

Defrauding America is essential reading for everyone who cares about freedom. It's exhilarating — and disheartening — because it contains hard evidence of state-sponsored terrorism by the US government against its own citizens.

When Rodney Stich found himself in prison because of his whistleblower activities, his own personal nightmare was in full swing.

"Many times I thought to myself, 'My God, how can this be happening to me?

This can't be,'" he writes. "I couldn't believe that what started out with discovering deadly air safety and criminal violations at United Airlines could have such devastating consequences for me… How could I be in prison for refusing to commit the crime of cover-up? Where was the media, the so-called protectors against government tyranny?"

"It was all so incomprehensible. I had been financially well off. I had a good life. I had a reputation throughout the United States as an air safety activist and suddenly I found myself in prison and stripped of the assets I worked for the past twenty years to acquire all because I felt a sense of responsibility…"

"Sometimes I just wanted to die. The strain of all this was getting to me. Flung into prison, things looked bleak. Everything was accumulating. The six years of judicial persecution, the loss of my home, my business, my assets, the humiliation, the character assassinations, the loss of privacy and the hopelessness. There is only so much a person can stand."

"It caused me to think more than once of ending it all," he continues. "I had been through World War II as a Navy pilot in the Pacific. I had flown for almost fifty years, experiencing all kinds of aircraft emergencies. All these stressful conditions put together did not equal the fear I now experienced. I looked at the plastic bags used for laundry and thought how peaceful things could suddenly become if one was slipped over one's head and the misery ended. The primary thing preventing me from doing such a thing was the hope that I could expose the corruption in government and somehow motivate the American people to exercise their responsibilities under our form of government. What a dreamer I must have been."

Not only a dreamer, Rodney Stich is a courageous individual who has put his sense of justice above everything else.

Whistleblowers' Clearinghouse

Former US Federal Aviation Agency investigator Rodney Stich is the author of several book-length exposés — Defrauding America, Unfriendly Skies, Drugging America and Disavow. By virtue of his life work, he has become a one-man whistleblowers' clearinghouse.

"You could put it that way. I've been saying that I've become a focal point for whistleblowers," says Stich. "One of them was an FBI agent for ten years, Richard Taus. He worked with Louis Freeh, the FBI director, on the Pizza Connection drug cases and during this investigation he found evidence of CIA involvement with organized crime in the New York City area."

"Another is Jimmy Rothstein, who was on the New York Police Department vice squad and discovered the same thing — CIA drug trafficking with organized crime. Both of those people suffered retaliation."

FBI Whistleblower Richard M. Taus

"They either had adverse job performance reports or they filed false charges against him, as in Richard Taus's case," says Stich. "He's in prison now, and he'll be there for the next 80 years, if we don't do something about it."

"Richard Taus was a highly decorated Vietnam helicopter pilot," continues Stich. "He's had many high commendations. He was a Lieutenant Colonel in the National Guard in the New York City area as a helicopter pilot. He was also an FBI agent."

"Incidentally while he was in Vietnam, he reported drug trafficking by the CIA in Air America. Somehow Congress heard about it, and a Congressman came over there. He discovered about two thousand pounds of drugs in a Air America plane that was forced down. Taus was in a helicopter so he quickly went there to help the crew and while he's there his crew chief sees all of the drugs on board the plane. So Taus reports it when he gets back to his base. The Congressman came over and he was told that this was for the crew's own use, that it was not for distribution."

"But two thousand pounds?" Stich asks. "They're still probably using it."

And how did Taus become a CIA fall guy? "They set him up the same way they set up two other sources I have — Jimmy Rothstein and someone who was a member of the Mafia in New York, who was also a CIA paymaster working with both Mafia and the CIA. I've talked to his daughter about it."

Stich is referring to Dee Ferdinand, daughter of mafia figure Albert Carone. He says that "having grown up in a Mafia family and being friends with top Mafia bosses, Dee was very helpful in explaining the complex relationship between the Mafia and the CIA. She explained details of her father's activities as a CIA pay-master moving money to and from the Mafia families in New York, New Jersey and Pennsylvania, the CIA, the Mossad and payoffs to the New York City police department."

Not to forget — mob boss Sam "Momo" Giancana used to say, "The Outfit and the Agency — it's like two sides of the same coin."

The Outfit is of course the Mob, and the Agency is the CIA.

Regarding the set-up, Stich continues. "They suddenly charged Taus with 'playing with little boys.' It doesn't seem to be too hard to get little boys to tes-tify against him — especially if their families are under threat of prosecution."

So now Taus is in prison on phony pedophilia or child molestation charges?

"Yes," says Stich. "First the feds filed charges against him and as Ted Gunderson, former chief special FBI agent in the Los Angeles area, has said there's no federal offense for that. The feds filed it just long enough to get Taus out of circulation because Bush was coming up for reelection and some of the corruption had to do with Bush."

"Then after Taus is removed from active duty with the FBI, the state of New York took over. With Taus, it will be more difficult because it's a state offense. If it was federal, it's easier to show retaliation. When you have to go to the state level, it's more difficult to show that it's retaliation for reporting corruption by high level federal officials."

CIA Whistleblower Stephen Crittenden

To his credit, Rodney Stich's publication of *Defrauding America* has helped release former federal agent-whistleblowers from prison, especially Stephen Crittenden, head of Crittenden Airlines, a highly secret CIA front corporation.

"Crittenden was the fellow who was head of a CIA airline for 16 years," says Stich. "He was hauling drugs for the CIA and he's given me detailed affidavits about it. He got tired of it after a while and shut down the airline. He had C-130s all over the world and especially in the Far East. So naturally the CIA wasn't happy with him."

"Eventually they filed false charges against him," Stich continues. "He went to prison. He was complaining to his CIA handler, and the handler said 'just keep quiet and we'll get you out before long.' Well, they didn't get him out. About the time he was to be released five years later, they filed new charges against him that would get him twenty years. And that's what the Justice Department was requesting. About this time he contacts me. What I did was file a friend of the court brief in the US District Court in Phoenix, Arizona and attached to it an affidavit that Crittenden gave me describing in detail the drug trafficking he was doing and also a draft of the chapter on Crittenden that would be in the next book (the next edition of Defrauding America)."

"At the hearing the judge cleared out the courtroom and gave Crittenden a choice, 'You recant this affidavit, or you're going to get twenty years.' So Crittenden recants and gets out, and then I get a new affidavit from him reaffirming what he told me in the first place. He's one of the fellows who got out."

Dos and Don'ts for Whistleblowers

Since Rodney Stich has the experience, what kind of suggestions would he give to a potential whistleblower?

"No one had better do what I did," Stich states unequivocally. "The system is too corrupt. And the checks and balances don't work. There's enough corrupt people in the Justice Department and the federal courts, and they have access to government officials on the state level. So almost anybody can be pretty much destroyed. And with the media so implicated in the cover-up, it's very difficult for any individual. And then the public doesn't really care."

"For instance, in my naive thinking twenty years ago, when I came out with the first edition of *Unfriendly Skies*, I thought that the public wanted to know and that sufficient percentage of the public had enough courage to help," continues Stich. "That unfortunately does not work because the public is more interested in trivia like sports, and those few who do know don't do anything. And things have just gotten worse. The corruption has gotten worse in government. And it's so spread out now that there's virtually no one there to do anything with this corruption. It's up to the public and you might as well forget it because the public haven't gotten it."

So do we deserve this because there have been no outcries of outrage?

"I definitely feel that most of this corruption could not exist if it wasn't for the illiteracy of the public and their indifference to it all," says Stich. "And as other people have said to me, maybe they deserve what's being done to them. I'm not sure I would disagree with that."

"One thing I've always tried to do is stay very factual. I don't get into any conspiracy theories or any far out matters. What I'm trying to do is get the person on the street from the state of ignorance — which incidentally I was in when I was an airline pilot like most pilots — and convey to them some of the hardcore corruption that's going on in government that's affecting very tragically many innocent Americans who don't even know they are suffering because the media again does a good job of keeping the lid on it."

TWA Flight 800 Disaster and Cover-up

There has been plenty of speculation regarding the reasons for the downing of TWA Flight 800. Rodney Stich, an aviation safety activist and investigator, has gathered his own evidence regarding the whys and wherefores of the crash and the subsequent poorly staged cover-up. He shared this research and conclusions in a recent interview.

"It's unprecedented in the history of aviation for so much disinformation and cover-up to occur by the NTSB (National Traffic Safety Board) and the Justice Department," says Stich.

"In my book *Unfriendly Skies*, I document repeated instances of NTSB cover-up when serious misconduct was involved. In TWA Flight 800, there were almost 200 witnesses who report seeing a missile trail, including one person whom I call a missile trail expert."

"This is a helicopter pilot who had taken off from Long Island [New York]," continues Stich. "He was facing the ocean just as the missile was going up. He had seen dozens of missiles fired in Vietnam including missiles fired at him, so he knows what a missile trail looks like. This is how he describes it — 'it was a thin missile trail going up, and the first explosion is a missile type of an explosion, different from a fuel tank explosion.' That was followed by explosions of fuel tanks, a totally different color."

And this is where it gets interesting as the "legend"— a false story concocted by spooks to distract the public from the facts, is created.

"Here's what the FBI says about all these people that saw the missile trail," continues Stich. "They're saying it's fuel that was coming out of the ruptured fuel tanks and ignited. But it's really not a thin pencil trail, it's a massive fireball. And the FBI expects you to believe that. And then they got the CIA involved. It's unheard of for the CIA to be involved in an accident investigation. The CIA has an animated video they showed on TV where the plane is going along and they claim the center fuel tank blew up and this is what did it."

It sounds like the "magic bullet" that supposedly killed JFK. This was the famous bullet that did a U-turn inside of Kennedy's body — the wacky "conspiracy theory" invented by Arlen Specter, currently US Senator from Pennsylvania.

"This is even better," says Stich. "The CIA says that the plane then climbed a few thousand feet — after the explosion. The NTSB by law has the responsibility to conduct a meaningful investigation. At the NTSB hearing December 8, the FBI had notified the NTSB that they are not to allow anybody to testify or make any reference to a missile, according to *Aviation Week and Space Technology* magazine."

Covert operations and criminal politics again take precedent over air safety and passenger security.

"Here we have the CIA and FBI involved and blocking the NTSB," continues Stich. "And one of the possible reasons for the cover-up? The FBI and CIA were involved in negotiating with Afghan rebels. The rebels wanted to give thirty to forty surface-to-air missiles back to the United States at no charge. In exchange they wanted the release from federal prison of the son of one of the rebel leaders. He was there on relatively minor drug-related charges. They had evidently over a hundred Stinger missiles left over from the Afghan war. They provided serial numbers of the Stingers that they had and the serial numbers were confirmed."

"The CIA, FBI and Justice Department were negotiating and one of the key negotiators was a friend of mine, a former CIA asset, Ron Rewald. Rewald turned over documents to me. While he was in prison, he met the man whom he had previously met in Honolulu in 1995. And now the CIA was dragging its feet about the negotiation."

Stich suddenly makes a chilling comment. "Maybe they were more interested in the missiles getting in the hands of the terrorists for all we know. It was known that terrorists were bidding on the missiles."

Now there's a thought to quicken your pulse — what if...?

"If a plane was shot down, that would help justify the CIA's existence," says Stich. "It's almost like the Persian Gulf War. When you don't have a credible enemy, you build up Saddam Hussein to make the Pentagon seem worthwhile."

A parenthetical note: according to John Loftus, author of *The Secret War Against the Jews*, the San Francisco-based Bechtel Corporation was responsible for building Saddam Hussein's poison gas factory.

It's not ironic then that the United States continues building the "best enemy money can buy," as historian scholar Antony C. Sutton has shown. First it was Hitler's Germany, then the Soviet Union, and more recently there has been a massive technology transfer to Red China. This strategic build-up of future "enemies" in fact is part of a long historical tradition.

"Here we have hard evidence that missiles were offered to the United States, were rejected, knowing that terrorists would get them. The missiles are out there and they're going to be used eventually," concludes Stich.

"This is far more evidence than the NTSB has used in many air disasters to come up with the most probable cause. And the cover-up by the FBI, the pressure on people is enough to reflect on the mindset in the FBI."

The Rise and Fall of a CIA Front Man

So who is this former CIA asset Ronald Rewald?

He's an international wheeler-dealer and the subject of another book by Stich called *Disavow*. "Disavowed" means — once your cover is blown, you're on your own, pal.

Rewald hobnobbed with the world's movers and shakers, living the lifestyle of the rich and famous. He had a $2 million estate in Hawaii. A chauffeured limo took him to work everyday, and he even played polo with the Sultan of Brunei, reportedly the richest man in the world.

Nevertheless Rewald had a dark secret. He was a front man for the CIA, an informant since college when he began spying on "subversive" organizations like the SDS (Students for a Democratic Society) during the late 1960s and '70s.

Later as chairman of BBRDW — Bishop, Baldwin, Rewald Dillingham and Wong — a CIA front masquerading as a worldwide investment company, Rewald thought he had nothing to fear. But then came the setup and betrayal. Today after spending ten years in prison as the fall guy for the CIA, Rewald is reportedly still in denial.

According to Stich, BBRDW was a CIA proprietary (a company wholly owned by CIA operatives) started, operated and funded by the CIA in 1979 using many of the same high level people that had staffed Nugan Hand Bank.

Nugan Hand Bank, of course, was the infamous Australia-based money laundry used by CIA to disburse Southeast Asian drug revenues.

In a chapter of *Defrauding America*, Stich writes that "the CIA used BBRDW as an international investment company cover with 120 employees staffing offices in 16 countries including Hong Kong, India, Indonesia, Taiwan, New Zealand, Singapore, London, Paris, Stockholm, Brazil and Chile. CIA personnel opened and operated these far flung offices."

When his cover was blown by a Honolulu reporter, Rewald never saw it coming. Since he'd been working for the CIA since his college days, he just assumed that the CIA takes care of its own. Rewald was wrong.

Disavow by Rodney Stich and T. Conan Russell should be required reading for every person who's even thinking about working for any of the so-called "intelligence" agencies (CIA, DIA, NSA, FBI, ONI, etc.). Just as there is no honor among thieves, there is even less honor among "spooks" — the spies of the world.

Disavow deals with global realpolitik, the important business of state — making drug deals, laundering money, and buying elections — all the professional expertise for which the CIA is absolutely unparalleled anywhere on earth.

Ronald Rewald found out the hard way. If he ever writes his autobiography, he should call it, "I Was a Chump for the CIA."

October Surprise and Cover-up

Yes, Virginia there really was an "October Surprise" and the cover-up continues even now, typically dismissed — or ignored — by the global mega-media cartel.

An entire chapter in *Defrauding America* covers this crime, scandal and cover-up. The evidence is clear. A gross and unpunished violation of the US Constitution occurred when George Bush tried to manipulate the Iran Hostage Crisis, so that Ronald Reagan would win the presidential election over President Jimmy Carter.

Simply put, the intent of the scheme was to bring about the defeat of President Carter and elect Reagan. The Reagan-Bush team promised the Iranians billions of dollars of US military equipment and $40 million in bribes in exchange for freeing the hostages after the election of 1980.

Stich writes that "the establishment media sought to discredit the CIA whistle blowers who could prove the existence of the October Surprise operation... The evidence required impeaching President George Bush and filing criminal charges against key officials in the executive, legislative and judicial branches. Never in the history of the United States was there such a serious criminal conspiracy inflicted upon the US by people in control of the White House..."

"Iran-Contra"

Was CIA asset and drug kingpin Oliver North of the US National Security Council rewarded for his silence with a national radio show in America? The facts speak for themselves.

Former pilot trainer and whistleblower Terry Reed, author of *Compromised*, states unequivocally that his CIA handler was Oliver North, who used the pseudonym "John Cathey."

Stich writes that "the ugly side of the Contra connection was carefully kept from the American public by the establishment media and Congress. Oliver North and others involved sought to place a humanitarian cloak over their activities. They claimed they were helping an oppressed people fight communism. But the CIA representing the American people traded arms for drugs... Aircraft carrying arms to Central America returned with the drugs that were used to pay for the arms."

North's reprehensible cover story of "fighting communism" and "protecting national security" are just the feeble excuses of a treasonous self-serving liar, or as Samuel Johnson said, "Patriotism is the last refuge of the scoundrel."

"It wasn't only the Contras to whom the CIA furnished arms," writes Stich. "The CIA were selling and delivering arms to the opposition Sandinistas. One CIA operative said to me, 'How else could we keep the fighting going?'"

Review in the CIA

According to Stich, "the CIA has hundreds of dummy corporations in the United States in the form of proprietaries, fronts and cooperating assets. These include law firms, financial companies such as banks and bond brokerage houses, insurance companies and airlines..."

"It becomes very easy for the CIA to deny blame for their acts. They simply deny any knowledge of what the front-company or contract agent is doing in addition to their standard practice of lying. There is no danger to this practice, since Justice Department officials protect their lying and their corrupt operations and most of the mainstream media also covers for them as well as members of Congress."

Case in point? Here's a classic — an Associated Propaganda, er, I mean, Press, article from December 19, 1997. The headline actually reads, "CIA clears itself over sales of crack cocaine in US Washington (AP) The CIA found no evidence that its employees or agents colluded with allies of the Nicaraguan Contra rebels involved in crack cocaine sales in the United States, a senior official said Thursday."

Just imagine if you could "clear" yourself of high crimes and treason, just by saying so. And having Associated Propaganda publish it.

To reiterate Stich, "They simply deny any knowledge of what the front company or contract agent is doing in addition to their standard practice of lying."

Then they proclaim "Case Closed," as CIA asset and strategic writer Gerald Posner would say. "Strategic writer" is evidently an actual job title in the Agency, but it's really just a euphemism for "highly-paid liar."

Bank of Lavoro and Iraqgate

Stich has an entire chapter on the background of the Persian Gulf War. Not only were Americans brainwashed by the government, CNN and other media to accept a totally bogus war in support of George Bush's so-called "New World Order," but the Gulf War was also used to test experimental vaccines on unknowing subjects aka human guinea pigs — US and British armed forces personnel.

Stich includes the behind-the-scenes story of how the Bush Administration built up Saddam Hussein's regime with US loans, guaranteed by US taxpayers, to buy chemical and biological weapons.

Result? The Persian Gulf War was a planned and programmed event guaranteed to make money for criminal corporate-government insiders.

More Hard Evidence of CIA and DEA Drug Trafficking

Stich writes that "many pilots have admitted to me during the past 40 years that they hauled drugs under the direction of the CIA, DEA and the military..."

"The CIA-engineered Vietnam War provided the logistics making possible massive transportation of drugs from the Golden Triangle area of Asia into the United States. The CIA-engineered conflict in Nicaragua resulted in and made possible massive transportation of drugs from Central and South America into the US These developed into multi-billion dollar a year profits for the CIA..."

"It is no longer far-fetched to consider that the CIA may have deliberately generated these conflicts to develop its drug trafficking operations into the United States. Nor is it far-fetched to consider that these acts and consequences may be a part of a scheme to financially and morally destroy the United States."

Is the US Federal Government a Criminal Enterprise?

Stich writes that "as stated in the 1978, 1980 and 1990 editions of *Unfriendly Skies* [Stich's classic expose of air traffic safety] and in *Defrauding America* at the epicenter of the corruption described within these pages are attorneys and officials in the US Department of Justice and federal judges. Without their criminal conduct, none of these criminal activities could have been perpetrated or continued. The same applies to the mainstream media and to members of Congress, all of whom played key roles in the obstruction of justice."

U.S. Secret Killer Squads

One of the most astounding — and sickening — revelations in the book is the exposure of the Secret Death Squad (SDS) or Experimental Assassination Team, officially listed by the CIA as MACSOGSDODV, or Military Assistance Command Strategic Operational Group Special Detachment, Department of Defense, Vietnam.

According to Stich, his informant Robert L. Freeman described to him an all black assassination team, trained by the US military for an ultra secret operation intended to destabilize Vietnam, Laos and Cambodia.

"Freeman was one of 45 blacks trained by the US Army, US Navy and CIA for the sole purpose of killing anyone, including US service men and advisors," writes Stich. "He described in great detail how his group was mentally brainwashed, trained and armed, engaged in random and indiscriminate killings to destabilize the region and justify US intervention…"

"Freeman was the head of a five man assassination team ordered by the team's CIA handlers to kill anyone they encountered and leave evidence that another faction had done the killings. Freeman said that for several years his team went on a killing spree, sometimes wiping out an entire small village."

In the book, Stich includes Top Secret US documents from 1963 and 1964 confirming the assassination of South Vietnam's President Ngo Dinh Diem by Freeman's team.

In other words, the CIA sets up their puppet rulers, then murders them when it becomes expedient.

But there's more. Freeman also has hard evidence proving that his team was ordered by his CIA handlers to assassinate American POWs and how his team carried out the orders.

Stich writes that "those documents provided sufficient corroboration to make Freeman's descriptions believable. Not that the assassination of American GIs ordered by Washington were the biggest crimes ever inflicted upon Americans, but these were crimes that the average person could understand."

Repealing the National Security Act

As far as the US is concerned, the National Security Act of 1947 can be considered the root of evil described in Stich's books. It continues to provide an impenetrable shield for the arrogant abuse of power by government officials — namely the National Security Council, which operates under questionable constitutionality — as well as the so-called intelligence agencies like CIA, NSA, and NRO.

These agencies' Cold War *raison d'etre* has disappeared into the black hole of the phony ideological battle known as the "capitalism vs. communism" scam. Now they remain as the last refuge of criminals and corrupt officials whose illegal practices continue under the guise of so-called "national security."

Like the old guard Soviet nomenklatura and its attendant apparatchiks, these agencies and the faceless bureaucrats who run them have garnered enormous power — most likely due to the cash flow from the massive drug trafficking over the last fifty years.

And so it goes. Rodney Stich's life work — his books, especially *Defrauding America*, which he subtitles "An Encyclopedia of Secret Operations by the CIA, DEA and Other Covert Agencies" — is clear evidence that the National Security Act of 1947 must be repealed. Why? Because the secrecy, amorality and degeneracy it has spawned has changed the character of not only the United States but the world at large. Worst of all it has brought about an institutionalized corruption and depravity in America that parallels nothing but the final days of the Roman Empire.

From Grassroots Awareness to Informed Action

Today every individual must know and understand the secret history of the world as well as knowledge of the alternatives. What Rodney Stich has documented — criminal behavior by public officials entrusted with government — can no longer be tolerated.

Like Amnesty International, which works to release political prisoners in repressive regimes, there ought to be locally-based grassroots groups for expanding public awareness of government crimes, coverups and corruption.

How about "Whistleblowers International"?

Rodney Stich has established a precedent. The brave individuals who have spoken out against this evil have continued to expose the treacherous conduct of those who have betrayed public trust.

By now there's no other choice. It's up to us.

As it's been said before — you know you got to run the hoodoo out of town.

Bibliography

Castillo, Celerino and Harmon, Dave *Powderburns: Cocaine, Contras and the Drug War* (Mosaic Press, 85 River Rock Dr. Suite 202, Buffalo, NY 14207, USA)

Eddy, Paul with Hugo Sabodal and Sara Walden *The Cocaine Wars*, (Bantam Books, New York)

Goddard, Donald & Coleman, Lester K. *Trail of the Octopus: From Beirut to Lockerbie — Inside the DIA* (Penguin 1994 (Unavailable in USA)

Gritz, James "Bo" *Called To Serve* (CPA, c/o HC 11, Box 307, Kamiah, Idaho 83536)

Hougan, Jim. *Spooks: The Haunting of America — The Private Use of Secret Agents* (William Morrow & Co., New York)

Kruger, Henrik *The Great Heroin Coup: Drugs Intelligence and International Fascism* (South End Press Box 68 Astor Station Boston MA 02123)

Kwitny, Jonathan *The Crimes of Patriots: A True Tale of Dope, Dirty Money and the CIA* (Simon & Schuster Inc, New York)

Levine, Michael. *The Big White Lie: The CIA and the Cocaine Crack Epidemic,* (Thunder's Mouth Press, 632 Broadway, 7th Floor, New York 10012 USA)

Lyne, William, *Space Aliens from the Pentagon* (Creatopia Productions, Lamy New Mexico 87540 USA, 505-466-3022)

McCoy, Alfred W. *The Politics of Heroin: CIA Complicity in the Global Drug Trade* (Lawrence Hill Books, An Imprint of Chicago Review Press, Inc. 814 N. Franklin St., Chicago, Il 60610 USA)

Reed, Terry & Cummings, John. *Compromised: Clinton Bush and the CIA — How the Presidency Was Co-Opted by the CIA* (SPI Books, 136 West 22nd St., New York, NY 10011, 212-633-2022)

Stich, Rodney (and T. Conan Russell) *Disavow*

Stich, Rodney *Unfriendly Skies*
  Defrauding America: Encyclopedia of Secret Operations by the CIA, DEA and Other Covert Agencies (Diablo Western Press, PO Box 5, Alamo, CA 94507,USA, 800-247-7389) URL: http://www.defraudingamerica.com

Sutton, Antony C. *America's Secret Establishment: An Introduction to the Order of Skull and Bones* (Liberty House Press, 1517 14th St. #216C, Billings, Montana 59102 USA)

Tatum, Gene "Chip," *The Tatum Chronicles*, URL: http://www.aci.net/kalliste/black ops

Thomas, Kenn and Keith, Jim. *The Octopus: Secret Government and the Death of Danny Casolaro*, (Feral House)

Webb, Gary. *Dark Alliance: The CIA, the Contras, and the Crack Cocaine Explosion* (Seven Stories Press, 140 Watts St., New York, NY 10013)

Chapter 27

Gun Control: The Genocide Agenda

ARON ZELMAN, EXECUTIVE DIRECTOR of the Jews for the Preservation of Firearms Ownership (JPFO), sells politically incorrect posters and T-shirts. There's a picture of Hitler with a Cheshire cat grin. His right hand is extended in the sieg heil salute.

The caption says, "All those in favor of gun control, raise your right hand."

Genocidal Roots of Gun Control

According to Zelman, the case against gun control is self-evident. The downside of the issue, of course, is genocide. In other words, without a weapon, you can't prevent your own murder.

In the 20th Century, there have been at least seven major genocides, says Zelman. At least 56 million persons, including millions of children, have been murdered by officials of governments "gone bad." Here's a reminder.

1. Ottoman Turkey (1915-1917) — 1.5 million Armenians murdered
2. Soviet Union (1929-1953) — 20 million people who opposed Stalin murdered
3. Nazi-Occupied Europe (1933-1945) — 13 million people, including Jews, Gypsies and others who opposed Hitler, murdered
4. China (1948-1952) — 20 million anti-communists not including Tibetans murdered

5. Guatemala (1960-1981) — 100,000 Mayan Indians murdered
6. Uganda (1971-1979) — 300,000 Christians and rivals of Idi Amin murdered
7. Cambodia (1975-1979) — 1 million persons murdered

In every case, before the wholesale murders began, at least one so-called "gun control" law was on the books. In recent cases of US armed intervention, in which citizens were murdered in their own countries, Haiti had a "gun control" law (Dec 22, 1922, amended Oct 1, 1980) and so did Bosnia, as part of the former Yugoslavia (Sept. 17, 1964).

The cynical arms embargo against the Bosnian Muslims, by the way, prevented them from defending themselves against Bosnian Serb ethnic cleansing.

Nazi Parallels with American Gun Control Laws

In a fascinating book called *Gun Control: Gateway to Tyranny*, authors Jay Simkin and Aaron Zelman show that the Nazi Weapons Law (March 18, 1938) is the actual source document used as a model the US Gun Control Act of 1968.

The official German text of the Nazi law is presented side-by-side with its American counterpart. A section-by-section comparison with the American Gun Control Act of 1968 shows the undeniable lineage. Thus America's draconian gun control laws remain one of Hitler's lasting legacies, a sordid reminder to all Americans that contrary to historians' lies, the Nazis really did win World War II.

According to the authors, the Nazi Weapons Law of 1938 replaced a Law on Firearms and Ammunition (April 13, 1928). The 1928 law was enacted by the German government to curb "gang activity," actually violent street battles between Nazi and Communist thugs.

Sound familiar? In America, so-called "gang activity" has also been used as a pretext by strident anti-gunners.

"Gun control did not save democracy in Germany," says Zelman. "It helped to make sure that the toughest criminals, the Nazis, prevailed. Then when the Nazis inherited the lists of firearms owners and their firearms when they took over in March 1933, the Nazis used these registration lists to seize privately-held firearms from persons who were 'unreliable.'"

"In 1938, five years after taking power, the Nazis enhanced the 1928 law with the Nazi Weapons Law which introduced handgun control. Firearms ownership was restricted to Nazi party members and other 'reliables,' while Jews were barred altogether." (http://www.jpfo.org.htm)

Conclusion? A disarmed population can be slaughtered much more efficiently.

NRA Maintains Status Quo, Does Nothing

Controlled opposition groups like the National Rifle Association (NRA) have done precious little to stop the march of totalitarian-style gun control.

Current NRA president Charleton Heston, for example, continues the tradition of compromise and ineffectual efforts to protect the right to bear arms.

In fact, it could be argued that the one-step-forward, two-steps-backward mentality of the NRA has itself been responsible for creeping gun control in America.

"We [JPFO] are very different from the NRA. We believe that gun control should be destroyed," says Zelman in a recent interview. "We view gun control as a cancer, a cancer that will destroy the guardian of the Second Amendment of the Bill of Rights."

"The National Rifle Association pooh-poohs the idea of destroying gun control," continues Zelman, "They look for ways to compromise and work within the system. In doing so, they keep gun control alive."

"The Gun Owners of America differs from JPFO in that they do a wonderful job of aggressively lobbying politicians, and they use a lot of our material," says Zelman. "So we heartily endorse the GOA."

NRA, on the other hand, liberally spends its members' dues by publishing full-page vanity ads in the Wall Street Journal. An ad headlined "America needs to hear what its president won't" continues the dance with the gun grabbers, instead of challenging them on their own turf.

The NRA, the self-styled so-called gun lobby, acts as a Trojan horse, playfully sparring with the radical agenda of the Gun Control Nazis. It has called for a "National Instant Check System," claiming that "when a felon tries to buy a gun... none has been prosecuted in the past 3 years."

Forever tooting their own horn, the ad brags that "the NRA has invested tens of millions of dollars teaching childhood accident prevention, promoting firearm safety, educating hunters, training police instructors."

There's no mention, however, of their sorry record in opposing gun control laws, which are periodically introduced — right after a high profile, highly suspect schoolyard shooting. Stockton, California, Jonesboro, Arkansas and Littleton, Colorado come to mind. Oh, no, not another "coincidence."

(When was the last time you saw a Big Media headline that read "Frequent Shootings Raise Questions About Mind Control"? Unless you read independent alternative media like Conspiracy Digest (http://www.conspiracydigest.com) Steamshovel Press (http://www.steamshovelpress.com), or Conspiracy Planet (http://www.conspiracyplanet.com), you never will.)

Those Rebellious Canadians

Even the traditionally milquetoast Canadians have recently looked back in anger at gun control laws.

Since December 1, 1998, a law went into effect requiring 3 million gun owners to register as well as their estimated 7 million rifles and handguns. Gun owners, exempt from previous registration, are refusing and have even taken to the streets in protest.

"Canadians should get upset," contends Zelman, "because of 'home invasions' where brazen armed criminals barge right in during daylight. The suspected victims are unarmed, so they [armed robbers] can just march right in there. I don't know how far the Canadian people are going to go with their disgust, but fortunately there is a growing number of people who are voicing their opposition."

Gun control laws did nothing to prevent a 14-year-old student from opening fire and killing a 17-year-old classmate in an Alberta High School, or a former Ottawa transit worker who went "postal" killing four, then shooting himself to death.

The Canadian constitution, by the way, does not include the right to bear arms.

Handgun Control's Spooky History

Rumors have persisted for many years that the well-funded and well-publicized anti-gun lobby, Handgun Control Inc., headed by Sarah Brady, is a CIA front.

"I don't think it's a CIA front," says Zelman. "The facts are that Edwin Wells, who worked with CIA until he retired, actually helped fund Gun Control Inc. He helped Pete Shields get Handgun Control Inc. off the ground and running. It's interesting that Pete Shields started Handgun Control Inc., when one of his sons was murdered in what was known as the 'Zebra Slayings' in San Francisco. Conveniently enough, when Mr. Wells held dinners in his Georgetown home and invited people in to raise money, he learned about Pete Shields' pet project."

"Bill Casey, former director of CIA, was also a promoter of Handgun Control," continues Zelman. "These people always talked about how they found out how dangerous handguns were in the hands of civilians. Civilians could kill those who were coming to kill them. And they didn't like that."

"The whole anti-gun movement, the whole anti-freedom movement has very murky beginnings," concludes Zelman. "But it shouldn't surprise anybody. During World War II, before the CIA was organized, the OSS [CIA's predecessor] brought in all of the Nazis. This has been documented in a number of books, for example [Christopher Simpson's] *Blowback*."

Other books which deal extensively with the subject, from a scholarly perspective, include *The Belarus Secret* by John Loftus (1989) and *The Paperclip Conspiracy: The Hunt for Nazi Scientists* by Tom Bower (1987).

"A lot of these people moved into the CIA, so why shouldn't we have Nazi gun control laws in America?" Zelman asks rhetorically. Why not indeed?

The Tyrants' Agenda

So was the Columbine School Massacre a gun-control-agenda-forwarding-event?

"The timing of this was most curious," says Zelman. "If you look at Charlie Schumer and what he's doing, it's as if they were waiting. They were totally prepared. I think they had the legislation waiting for an incident, and they were prepared to bring it out as soon as the incident happened. And that's what they did. The timing was perfect. And they furthered their agenda. I think what's curious [is] how we see so frequently that these individuals who commit these heinous crimes so conveniently commit suicide. Or they're conveniently killed by somebody to make it look like it's suicide."

It's almost like watching a non-stop replay of the Lone Nut Theory — year after year, decade after decade. They must figure if Americans are too stupid to connect the dots, why bother changing the cover story?

Instead of examining the role of illicit mind control experiments used in conjunction with powerful psychoactive drugs like Ritalin and Prozac prescribed to schoolkids, the Big Media Cartel promotes the disarmament of the American people.

Never Again? Don't Hold Your Breath

Aaron Zelman certainly has a lot of work ahead — especially in the current media environment. He understands that individual self-defense is the greatest virtue in any culture or religion. And without the right to bear arms, future holocausts are not only probable. They're a sure bet.

"We published a booklet called *Gun Control is Racist*," says Zelman, "It explains to people the history of why we even have gun control in America. It all started two hundred years ago with racism."

"The racist gun control laws were designed to make sure that a black person would have to have a permit to have a firearm, would have to pay a tax, would have to be registered and licensed," says Zelman. "And that's the same kind of gun control laws they want to implement for everyone."

"JPFO is unique among pro-firearm ownership organizations," concludes Zelman. "After all no one can label JPFO as 'anti-Semitic.' As a result, JPFO confronts Jewish politicians and organizations, which urge disarmament of law-abiding Americans. And JPFO also exposes non-Jewish gun prohibitionists like Sarah Brady whose falsehoods erode the Constitution's protections that are most vital to Jews and other minorities.

(JPFO can be contacted at P. O. Box 270143, Hartford, WI 53027, 414-673-9745)

Chapter 28

Global Conspiracy 101:
An Interview with John Coleman

J OHN COLEMAN IS THE AUTHOR of *Conspirators Hierarchy: The Story of the Committee of 300*, *Diplomacy by Deception*, and *Socialism, the Road to Slavery*, as well as more than 400 white papers / monographs on a variety of economic and political topics.

As a former British intelligence officer, he was stationed in fourteen different countries for twenty years. Since 1970, he has published *World in Review*, a monthly intelligence and economics newsletter.

John Coleman holds a doctorate in political science and economics, having studied for five years at the British Library and British Museum in London. He is a highly regarded historian, as well as a political analyst of current events.

And how did he first find out about the Committee of 300 and what happened that he became determined to expose them?

"During the course of my professional career, I was given documents that were marked 'Code: Word,'" Coleman replies. "'Code: Word' is the highest type of classification you can get. It's far above 'Top Secret' or anything of that nature. And in these documents was a plan laid out between the British government and the United States government as to how they would handle future conditions in Africa. We were there ostensibly fighting communist penetration, trying to keep the communists out of Angola and Rhodesia and later South Africa, when in fact, we were laying the ground work for a total communist take-over. So we were there supposedly for one purpose, but in fact, we were carrying out the future plans of the New World Order."

And what happened to him when he objected to what he called the "inimical goals of the Olympians?"

"The inimical goals of the Olympians, of course — it's the same thing as the Committee of 300. In intelligence circles, that is what their name is, the Olympians. But they didn't refer to them as the Olympians. They referred to the 'Higher Committee' and they referred to the 'Controlling Body.' It was only later that I found out who this controlling body actually is. By backtracking on the name 'Olympians,' I was then able to come up with the classification, that this was the Committee of 300."

And what is the origin of the term "Committee of 300?"

"It goes back to the days of the major drug trading empire," Coleman replies. "The British Empire is based upon drug trading. The British East India Company was a very powerful company dealing primarily in opium, which they grew in India, in Benares and the Ganges Valley, and then shipped to China and sold to Chinese buyers. It was directly controlled by the British government — for enormous profits. If you take a year like 1973, for instance, where car profits were very good, and you combined General Motors and Ford, their sales for those two years, it would approximate about one-tenth of the sales of the general revenue earned by the British East India Company from opium sales in China. It was a huge and lucrative business, actually backed by the British government.

"'The 300' refers to the actual structuring of this company. They knew from past experience that if you have people with unequal powers, there's going to be trouble. So they structured it in such a way that there were 300 members of the board of this company, each with equal voting rights, each with an equal share approximating an equal sum of money, and with the proviso that nobody could gang up on anybody else, to outvote any member, or to oust any member."

The 300 was basically an outgrowth of the British East India Company, then?

"Yes, it was named after the controlling body that ran the British East India Company, the 300 members of the board of directors of this company that ran everything. That organization continues to this day. But, of course, it's now very much broader. It's not only introducing and expanding the drug trade in the United States. That's only one aspect. They're now into political control, not only of the United States, but Germany, France, Italy, in fact, virtually every country of the world. Even Russia, but they've bumped their heads in Russia, first of all, against Stalin, who refused to bow to their dictates, which is why the Korean War was fought. And secondly, by the fact that we have a new leadership, that refuses again to bow to the British colonial form of government through this Committee of 300. And they were successful, as Stalin was successful, in keeping them out of Russia. And the new breed in Russia and Lebed, by the way, 'World in Review' [Dr. Coleman's newsletter] first mentioned in the West, probably one of the first publications to do so, back in 1986. We talked about him.

"Lebed was a general in the army. And he has come out very strongly against this Committee of 300, which he is fully aware of, because he's got a copy of my book."

And he is characterized typically as a "rabid nationalist?"

"He is characterized as a rabid nationalist, who is on the bus with the communists. The idea of being on the bus with the communists — you at times get on a bus to go downtown and happen to be sitting next to a gang of thugs dealing in opium. That doesn't mean to say that I'm part of them."

So it's a temporary alliance with them?

"No, I don't think it's a temporary alliance because I don't think that the Russian Communist Party is a communist party. It's definitely socialist, but they're not of the caliber of Stalin and Lenin. And they will form an alliance with Lebed and the army, and the other, Pamyat and the Russian National Monuments. These are all patriotic Russians. They hate Wall Street and they hate Clinton, and they hate the United States for trying, for the second time, to bring their country down to ruin. Because, let's face it, we did that. We bolshevized Russia, we being the British government and the United States government in 1917."

In his book, *Conspirators Hierarchy*, Dr. Coleman writes that the Committee of 300 is "the ultimate secret society made up of an untouchable ruling class, which includes the Queen of England, the Queen of the Netherlands, the Queen of Denmark and the royal families of Europe. These aristocrats decided at the death of Queen Victoria, the matriarch of the Venetian Black Guelphs, that in order to gain worldwide control, it would be necessary for its aristocratic members to go into business with the nonaristocratic, but extremely powerful leaders of corporate business on a global scale, so the doors to ultimate power would open to what the Queen of England likes to refer to as the commoners."

Historically speaking, was there a meeting that took place, or how was it decided?

"No, they all got together. All the royalty got together, and then they acted through their ministers. They kept themselves at a distance. The Queen never dirties her hands with anything direct. She has her ministers. She has the Duke of Kent, who is, let's say, her executive, who takes her place as the ruler of England when she is out the country. Then the instructions are handed down right until you get to the gutter level, which is the mafia. The mafia is part of this crowd, but they keep their distance from them. They would never associate with them or report any connection whatsoever. Nobody knows where it was held, but there is some thought that it was held in one of their castles up in Scotland."

An obvious out of the way place?

"That's right, because nobody can gain access there."

What evidence did he see or did he come across that this meeting actually took place?

Coleman says, "The evidence that this meeting took place was contained in the records by the German who was responsible for managing the finances of the Kaiser of Germany and managing the finances of the Rothschilds and one would imagine that he would know exactly what was going on. And he not only made reference to the meetings, but he said quite distinctly that — his name was Walter Rathenau — that here is a Committee of 300 known only to each other and they rule the world. It was 1923. And a year later, of course, he got a bullet in the back of his head for his trouble."

In *Conspirators' Hierarchy*, Coleman also writes that "the Committee of 300 consists of specialists in intelligence, banking, and every facet of commercial activity... Included in the membership are the old families of the European Black Nobility, the American Eastern Liberal Establishment (in Freemason hierarchy and the Order of Skull and Bones), the Illuminati, or as it is known by the Committee, 'Moriah Conquering Wind,' the Mumma group, the National and World Council of Churches, the Circle of Initiates, the Nine Unknown Men, Lucis Trust, Jesuit Liberation Theologists, the Order of the Elders of Zion, The Nasi Princes, International Monetary Fund, the Bank of International Settlements, the United Nations, the Central British Quator Coronati, Italian P2 Masonry, especially those in the Vartican hierarchy, the Central Intelligence Agency, Tavistock Institute, selected personnel, various members of leading foundations and insurance companies, the Hong Kong Shanghai Bank, the Milner Group-Round Table, German Marshall Fund, NATO, Ditchley Foundation, Club of Rome... literally, hundreds of other organizations."

It seems to be a lot of disparate groups. How do they keep order and coordinate strategy?

"They do it in exactly the same way as a giant corporation keeps order," says Coleman. "You take a company like General Motors, for instance. How do they keep order? They've got banking, sales, advertising, management, government, and public relations. There are thousands of different departments, but each department head is designated with a specific task and he is answerable to one of the specific directors on the board. That's his field of expertise."

So it's just a straightforward corporate hierarchical organization. But on a global level, who is at the top of this power structure?

"Well, they say in papers of this Committee of 300 that there is no end. But we all believe — and when I say we, all intelligence people I have ever spoken to, and I've spoken to a lot of them about it — that it's the Queen of England."

So she's the chairperson of the world, so to speak?

"She's also the richest and most powerful lady in the world. She gets daily briefing from MI6 [British Intelligence] of what's going on in the world. Once a week, she meets with the head of MI6, and he gives her a very in-depth briefing of every event that has taken place. She is far better informed than anybody else, even the British Prime Minister. These people are answerable only to her. They are not answerable to the British public or the British Parliament."

When he first wrote his exposé, were there threats on his life?

"Well, there were a lot of problems we went through in the beginning," he answers cautiously, "but we reached an understanding that if I don't cross a certain line, I'm not going to be bothered by them. What that line is, of course, I can't tell you."

Probably one of the most controversial points in his book is that the Beatles and rock music in general were the creation of the Tavistock Institute of Human Relations in England. What kind of documents did he see that brought him to this conclusion?

"Well, I got hold of all of the documents concerning Theodor Adorno, who was kicked out of Germany by Hitler because Hitler came across the fact that he was working with music which was designed to so confuse the mind of the listeners, directed primarily to the youth, that they would be susceptible. Adorno was a musician, a professor of music.

"What he was doing — he was taking the music of the priests of Baal and he was using this, which is really a repetitive beat, incessantly played over and over with some variations, the variations being on a discordant note, atonal, which repetitively played, would make people become virtually disoriented. He was commissioned by the Committee of 300 to prepare the way for their huge drug invasion in America. Don't forget, they had this enormous, profitable drug empire in China, worth billions of dollars. They were now bent upon doing exactly the same thing in the United States, with the youth of America. And they needed a vehicle by which this effort could be launched, and the obvious conclusion they drew was that certainly pop music was a great opportunity, because it ostensibly was a self-generating impulse amongst the youth, to kick over the traces and defy authority.

"Adorno studied the music of the ancient priests of Baal," Coleman continues. "All that stuff is available in the British Museum, by the way. Every bit of it is available there. And he also studied the music of the cult of Dionysus, which is a type of satanic cult. And the Dionysus people had taken the music of the priests of Baal a step further. What Adorno did was combine the two of them and then add even more jarring notes to it, so that people after hearing it at a given time, especially if played loudly, would become totally disoriented. That's exactly the basis of it all."

And how successful was the creation of rock music as a marketing strategy for promoting the sale of drugs to young people?

"Look around and you'll see," he answers. "There are more drugs in America now. The increase in the usage of drugs by the youth is astronomical. The drug war is a failure. Clinton is hiding a memo from one of his own agencies that said his policy on drugs is a total failure. He has refused to turn this document over to the House committee investigating drugs. All the money that he is wasting on the war on drugs, you might as well take it, tear it up and throw it down the toilet."

Brian Desborough, in his book *They Cast No Shadows* (2002; IUniverse.com), writes "John Lennon publicly claimed that the Beatles singlehandedly introduced narcotics to the world's teen population. This suggests that the Beatles unwittingly may have been under covert Tavistock control, something Lennon alluded to in a magazine interview not long before his assassination; the lyrics to Lennon's song 'Imagine' are typical New World Order propaganda. Prior to his untimely death, Lennon was clearly his own person and therefore considered a political loose cannon by the Illuminati. This could be the motive for his assassination by CIA asset Mark David Chapman, who displayed obvious signs of mind control at the time of his arrest."

One of the front men in the creation of the so-called counter-culture or Aquarian Age phenomenon in America was a man by the name of Willis Harmon. "He was specially chosen, a professor at Stanford University in the Stanford Research Institute, a division of Stanford University," explains Dr. Coleman. "He was picked by the Committee of 300 as a person who was able to devise the strategy to usher in the so-called new age among the youth. They said this is no longer the Age of Pisces, but the Age of Aquarius. In other words, the age when 'anything goes.' If it feels good, do it — without any regard to the consequences for your actions. And they called this the Age of Aquarius, which was really the entry vehicle for the youth into the New World Order — outside of politics."

So typically, a modus operandi, if you will, would be to take a kernel of truth and subvert it to the purposed of the Committee of 300?

"Don't forget, the Committee of 300 is strictly a communist organization," Coleman continues. "They believe in communist principles. They are against the family. They are against any form of religion that would become a religion accepted by all the people. They are against private property. They are against capitalism. They want to rule the world and they say they are the gods of Olympus, that God has given them the title and the right to rule everybody else. Therefore, everybody else is to have nothing, except what they in their magnanimity will grant them."

And how did they rationalize the failure of their system in the former Soviet Union?

"That was a trial run," he says. "Communism is not dead. The new communism is in America. We have a communist leader in the White House, ten times worse than Roosevelt and probably approximating the zeal of Stalin."

So it's basically a control system, nothing more, nothing less.

"That's all it is. Don't think communism is dead. They weren't able to penetrate Stalin too much, and the new nationalists are keeping them at bay. They've played down that operation."

You're certainly not defending Stalin's tactics in genocide, I said.

"I'm not defending his genocide at all. In fact, he is probably one of the most evil men who have ever lived. We know for a fact that he murdered 60 million Christians. These are documented figures. This is not a figment of the imagination. But, what we do owe him is that he showed by tenacity of purpose, that it is possible to defeat this organization."

I'm not following, I said. What exactly shows the defeat of the organization?

"Well, Stalin was most tenacious. He said, I know what you guys are up to. I know exactly what you want to do — you want to come in and take over Russia as part of your New World Order. I'm not going to allow that to happen. And he fought them tooth and nail, even to the point where they had the Korean War to show him that he could not operate without their say-so."

Coleman has stated that people are sent to the Tavistock Institute, which he calls the "premier brainwashing institution in the world," for what has been called "training." What exactly does this so-called training entail?

"Well, I use the word brainwashing, because that's a term that everybody knows and understands. It was founded by Brigadier General John Rawlings Reese. He hit upon a great idea and a very simple one. He said, in psychiatry, people come to me to be healed. I can make people who are not sick — I can make them sick by the same techniques."

Reverse the process?

"Exactly, and that simple thing he thought of, 80,000 British troops were given to him as guinea pigs. And he found out it works in the most fantastic way.

And he evolved theories, which he then put into practice. Basically, he expressed the view that everybody can be controlled. It's just a matter of applying the correct techniques. Of course, those techniques are worked out by people under his control."

So psychiatry was subverted then, or was it initially a discipline strictly created for this purpose?

"It was strictly created for this purpose. People talk about Freud and so on, but these people had another ulterior motive altogether and that was to obtain full control of individuals, groups, major and minor, and eventually whole nations. The Tavistock group has been at war with this country since 1946.

"Just to give you an example they worked out during the war — the war criminal Churchill came to Tavistock and said, 'We need a method of how we can defeat the Germans. They're too good for us in the military field. We can't beat them. They've bested the best of us. What can we do?' So they got their people to work and they worked out a plan, which they called the Prudential Bombing Survey, which was this. They knew how much stress that people could take in their lives before cracking, before breaking. And what they worked out was that, if the American and British bombers could bomb 60% of German worker housing into extinction, the stress and the shock would be so great that the German public would no longer support the war effort and the war would come to a halt.

"And that is exactly what they did. All of those great movies we used to see in the British theaters. The RAF went over Dusseldorf and destroyed all the steel mills. Don't believe it. It's a pack of lies, because the steel mills and those making shells and artillery pieces are owned by both sides and financed by both parties. The Warburgs and the Rothschilds financed both sides of the war. They weren't going to go in and destroy their assets. What they were doing is destroying German worker housing. It didn't cost them anything. When they got up to a saturation of 60%, that's exactly when Germany collapsed."

So they predicted it at 60% and it came out to be true?

"Exactly right. Now you have the same thing happening in America. The technique is for 'long-range penetration' and 'interdirectional conditioning.' What it means is that over a long period of time the American people are being subjected to a barrage of new ideas, strange ideas, ideas they can't cope with, so that their minds become so penetrated, they are presented with so many alternatives, that they can't handle it. They don't know what to do."

So after this numbing takes place, then what happens?

"Then, like a soldier in battle, you'll sit down in the thick of shells crashing and bullets whistling and just sit there and begin to sing a song or take out a book and read it. This used to be called 'shell shock.'"

Are you talking about a disassociation from reality?

"Exactly right. So that the American people become shell shocked. They don't know which direction to go. Then the Tavistock Institute will show them the way to go. And they will think that what they are working with are their own ideas, but they are not. They are ideas presented by the Tavistock Institute and sublimated into their brains. Then they follow this ritual. And that's how we have all of these strange things happening in America today."

John Malone, the CEO of TeleCommunications, Inc. (TCI) has a doctorate in "Operations Research." What exactly is it, and how could it be used by mass media conglomerates to mold public opinion?

"They use the Tavistock method. They present a set of alternatives. They create a problem, and a set of alternatives to solve the problem. There are so many choices that people don't know how to make choices and in the end they give up making choices."

And what is Dr. Coleman's perception of the Kennedy assassination?

"Kennedy was one of the few men who stood up against this group. When he unraveled their plans for Cuba — that's a very long story. When he disobeyed them regarding the printing of treasury notes. He said, 'we're not going to use the Federal Reserve; we don't need them; we're going to print our own US Treasury notes issued upon prayers of the people.' They told him, 'Mr. Kennedy, Look, you're overstepping the bounds. We are giving you orders and you are going to obey them.' And he said, 'I'm not obeying orders. I'm the President of the United States.' In order to show his associates, those immediately around him, would-be successors, would-be people in line for the presidency, that they are the boss, they publicly executed him in the most brutal fashion. In full view of millions and millions of Americans."

Was he warned first?

"He was warned several times to stop and to take orders. They told him bluntly, 'You are here to take orders,' and he refused to take the orders."

Who were primarily the messengers of these orders?

"Arthur Schlesinger and people of that nature, in exactly the same way as Colonel House used to give his British intelligence orders to Woodrow Wilson, for example. It will be in the new edition of the *Committee of 300*. We're expanding the book to take in the full story of the Kennedy assassination, the bandits who executed it and why."

And why is population control so important to the Committee of 300? In other words, how does the promotion of abortion, euthanasia, and suicide fit into the plans of achieving the goals of "Global 2000"?

"Global 2000, as you know, was a paper prepared by the Club of Rome under the auspices of Cyrus Vance, who then presented it to President Carter three days before his term ended and told him, henceforth this is official US policy. And Carter, being a good servant, said, 'OK, this is our policy.' And it was adopted as US policy and still is today. What it basically called for was the diminution of the world's population by half by the year 2000.

"In terms of the blueprint, they said that there are just too many useless eaters in the world and that the world does not have unlimited resources and these people, the useless eaters, are consuming these natural resources at an alarming rate. Also, they are polluting the earth, the rivers and the streams, and the land itself is being polluted by people. In fact, the president of the Club of Rome said, there is a cancer in the earth and the cancer is man. [*Mankind at the Turning Point* by Mesarovic and Pestel]. We've got to get rid of him. And so they devised plans to get rid of 2.5 billion people by the year 2000. And they went about it. AIDS is one of their means of achieving that. Bertrand Russell said that wars seem to have been disappointing. They haven't killed enough people. In fact, he said, we need the return of the Black Plague. AIDS, you can say, is the return of the Black Plaque, greatly upgraded."

What are the latest programs introduced by the Tavistock Institute in order to continue changing American society?

"They are still working on exactly the same formulas. They have expanded their communication system, but the formulas have not changed. Barrage people with ideas, confuse them, give them alternatives — this is the newest thing that is coming down and you have to accept it. You can't fight against it, and people get tired of fighting and they just give up."

During the 1980s, tens of billions of dollars were spent on SDI (Strategic Defense Initiative) and there's nothing to show for it. Recent evidence shows that this money has gone into mind control research and implementation, programs by the Department of Defense, NSA, DIA, and the CIA. What do his sources tell him?

"They tell me that the worst of them is the NSA. The NSA turned into a huge surveillance machine. They have 50,000 operatives who have the authority, not from the Constitution, but from the NSA. They can surveill anybody that they want. If they take an interest in you, they can bring tremendous forms of surveillance to bear upon you. They can even plant images in your mind. They can do it from computer to your mind, or they can do it by sound, by bypassing the auditory nerves in the cortex of the brain, and bypassing the optic nerves in the cortex of your brain. They can create images that make you think that you are doing things because you want to do them, when, in fact, you are listening to the commands that are outside of your body. And this has been proven over and over again. That's why I'm probably going to earn the wrath of a lot of these people who say they've been kidnapped and taken aboard the space ships, but what those people experienced was just computer-to-mind transferals or signals, bypassing the optic nerves in the cortex of the brain, which showed them a picture of them being taken aboard these ships with these little aliens."

Regarding SDI — was all the money allocated by Congress for national defense of the United States squandered on mind control research?

"I would say that as much as 90% of it went down that rat hole. Because of the sudden burgeoning of all these systems. I haven't dealt with any of them in this interview, but there are so many systems working today in electronic surveillance and mind control systems that took huge amounts of money to develop the proprietary systems — let's put it, for want of a better term — machinery belonging to the NSA that no one else can handle. I mean, they are 18 years ahead of any computers today in the world."

Aside from the black budgets that they have, was this funding subverted into this program?

"I absolutely believe it. Because they could not have done it without this money. Because these systems cost such a huge amount of money."

In his book *Socialism, the Road to Slavery*, he writes that the real reason behind the planned global mass genocide for population control is to create a climate of instability, destabilize the nations, set people's hearts fluttering with fear. Where is a part of that plan?

"If you look around, let's take an analysis of the news over the last two years. It's nothing but alarmist. There's nothing about the possibilities of peace. It's all about the possibilities of disasters. People's minds are fainting for fear. And as far as the next conflict, the Middle East, of course, is guaranteed."

The NSA, FBI and CIA, Coleman writes, are illegal and unconstitutional federal agencies. What is the basis for his contention, and what can be done about it?

"I will answer your last question first. If the Congress would do its duty, it could put these agencies out of business by the stroke of a pen. Because they are not authorized by the Constitution. For something to be lawful, or for a bill to passed by the legislatures, it has to be related to something already in the Constitution. You can't just, out of fresh air say, I'm going to pass this bill. If it's not already related closely to something in the Constitution; if it's not mentioned in the Constitution, if it's not by implication, of anything that's contained there, then it's a prohibition of those powers. Neither the name of the National Security Agency, the FBI, the CIA or ATF, none of these agencies are mentioned in the Constitution. Therefore, they are without a mandate. Therefore, they are unconstitutional, and anything unconstitutional is unlawful."

The National Security Act of 1947 is also regarded as an unconstitutional breach in the nation's affairs. What can be done to rescind it?

"As I said, if the Congress would do its duty, they could rescind it overnight, or refuse to fund it. They could take two steps immediately, saying, we are not going to allocate any more money — and that's what they were afraid of, so they took that money. The Congress might very well do that. Congress can say, we are passing a resolution today that we refuse to fund the activities of the FBI, the NSA, and that would put them out of business. Where would they get their money from to pay for their agencies? Or they could point to the unconstitutionality — that these agencies are operating without a constitutional mandate, and say that we declare them null and void. They have no standing. The Congress could do that overnight."

So, how can people defend themselves from the onslaughts of the change agents?

"They've got to, first of all, know the Constitution. That's number one. And they've got to use that Constitution to get rid of legislators who won't do the will of the people, and even to impeach the President. He is impeachable. I have about 30 articles of impeachment. If I can get somebody to take them up, he would be impeached."

In the face of all the overwhelming information you have published, what can people do to take control of their lives?

"The main thing to do is have faith in their country, have faith in the institutions of the Republic upon which it is founded. We are not a democracy. We are a confederated republic. Know the Constitution. Don't forget our laws are based on the laws of God. We all need to turn back to God and ask Him to help us. We need to be able to invoke the Constitution when people come with bills that are 100% unconstitutional and that have the stamp and the mark of the Communist Manifesto of 1848. We need to know history. We need to know the Constitution. When we've done that, we can be well on the road to taking charge of our own destiny."

(Dr. John Coleman's books are available from Joseph Publishing, 2533 North Carson St., Carson City, Nevada 89706, 800-942-0821)

Chapter 29

AP — *Associated Propaganda, Er, I Mean, Press*

S AME AS IT EVER WAS — the history of Associated Press (AP) reveals a pro-establishment and anti-populist bias that stretches to its beginning as the seed of the Big Media Cartel / Monopoly Press.

Rejected by Americans at its inception, the media behemoth called Associated Press has become the universal mouthpiece of propaganda, unrivalled in its reach and influence.

Historian J. Anthony Lukas, in his remarkable book *Big Trouble*, describes the origin of the ubiquitous AP. He writes that "Americans were aghast that a great octopus like the AP could embrace eight hundred member papers, putting its product before as many as twenty-five million readers every day. 'Here,' wrote one stupefied editor, 'is the most tremendous engine for power that ever existed in this world... If you can conceive all that Power ever wielded by the great auto-crats of history... to be massed together into one vast unit of Power, even this would be less than the power now wielded by the Associated Press.'"

That was more than a hundred years ago. Even then, before the consolidation of press, radio and television in what CIA's propaganda-meister Frank Wisner dubbed the "Mighty Wurlitzer" of media orchestration, Lukas writes that "the AP's puissance was measured as much by organizational rigor as by sheer size, for in an era of trusts, it was one of the nation's most effective monopolies. A news-paper with a precious AP franchise was protected against any competitor in its territory seeking one, while the AP itself had dread powers to discipline a paper that dealt with a rival news service."

A parallel in history is, of course, the Rockefeller dominated and controlled Standard Oil Trust, which through organized-crime strong-arm tactics and unscrupulous treachery, succeeded in monopolizing the entire oil industry in the United States.

And how did AP get that way, becoming a media octopus with tentacles stretching into every town in the country? This history should be known by everyone. "In 1898, facing charges of trafficking with the enemy, the Chicago 'InterOcean' challenged the AP's structure in court," writes Lukas.

"When the Illinois Supreme Court upheld the suit, finding that the AP was 'so affected with a public duty' that it must provide its news to any applicant, the AP abruptly dissolved as an Illinois corporation and reorganized in New York, this time not as a business corporation, but as a mutual association — like a literary society or fishing club — permitting it arbitrarily to expel any member who protested publicly against the way the organization was run. Henceforth all insurgency was doomed."

In an astute analysis of the precursor of today's "monopoly media," Lukas writes that "to its critics, the AP was fond of stressing this 'mutuality' arguing that it was merely a 'clearing house' drawing news primarily from its members and distributing it to other members."

"In fact, the AP stood for the notion that news was private property, fiercely retaliating against anyone who poached on its preserve," continues Lukas. "It was dominated by an inner circle of large metropolitan newspapers that at the time of the service's reincarnation in 1900 had each purchased a thousand dollars in bonds worth forty votes, compared to the single vote held by ordinary members."

"Buttressed by this margin, old-guard papers like the *Chicago Tribune* and the *Washington Star* were firmly in the saddle," concludes Lukas. "Where it drew news from a member paper, which generally supported the community's most substantial interests, the AP reflected the outlook of that city's power structure."

Currently AP's offices in New York's Rockefeller Center reflect the globalized nature of the Establishment's concern for tight and rigid news control and subsequently the very important molding of public opinion. Obviously the Internet and its vast menu of choices in lieu of the Mega Media Cartel's control of what constitutes news and what's "fit to print" is a major stumbling block in their Command and Control mentality.

For Upton Sinclair, writes Lukas, "the AP's vast reach ensured that American public opinion was 'poisoned at the source.'"

(By the way, where does your hometown paper get its so-called "news"? If you see that "AP" in front of every story, you should realize that you're reading calculated and biased disinformation.)

"In large cities and some state capitals, the AP maintained bureaus staffed by its own men and to cover major events like the Haywood trial it dispatched its own reporters," writes Lukas. "But that did little to diversify the AP's menu... To Oswald Garrison Villard of *New York's Evening Post*, the AP had 'always bowed down before authority and rarely ever stood up to the government in any controversy.'"

In other words, AP remains the same yesterday, today, and most likely tomorrow — a propaganda organ for the Power Elite. Political dissent is not to be tolerated (or reported without bias), a standard AP *modus operandi*.

"The Hayward case [the subject of *Big Trouble*] may have been the first trial in American history in which the real target wasn't so much the jurors in the box as the larger jury of public opinion," writes Lukas. "It bore the signs of a spectacular show trial, a great national drama in which the stakes were nothing less than the soul of the American people."

Today, few Americans believe the truthfulness of news reported by the networks and Media Cartel. Recent Pew Research Center surveys show that a majority of the public — 56% — now believes news stories are often inaccurate.

People instinctively and subconsciously know that the Government-Media Cartel lies, manipulates and distorts the truth. Their intuition is absolutely correct, when you consider the words of John Swinton, former Chief of Staff for the *New York Times*, called "The Dean of His Profession." Swinton himself said as much to his colleagues at a dinner before the New York Press Club:

"There is no such thing as an independent press in America. You know it and I know it. There is not one of you who dares to write his honest opinion, and if you did, you know beforehand that it would never appear in print..."

"The business of journalists is to destroy the truth; to lie outright; to pervert; to vilify; to fawn at the feet of mammon and to sell his country and his race for his daily bread. You know it and I know it, and what folly is this — toasting an independent press? We are the tools and vassals of rich men behind the scenes. We are the marionettes. They pull the strings, and we dance. Our time, our talents, our capacities and our lives are all property of these men. We are intellectual prostitutes."

You can imagine the lack of applause, or silence, he got after that little confession.

So remember this quote by Swinton the next time you watch CNN, CBS, ABC, NBC, Fox, etc.

And when you see that symbol "AP" at the beginning of a so-called "news" story — think "Associated Propaganda."

BUSHWHACKED

Chapter 30

One Good Hoax Deserves Another

J UST AS GEORGE ORWELL'S 1984 (originally entitled 1948) accurately predicted the surveillance society of today's National Security State of America, the reprinting of *Report from Iron Mountain on the Possibility and Desirability of Peace* likewise holds awesome prescient powers, especially in retrospect.

According to the *New Yorker* Magazine legend / cover story of May 13, 1996, the authors of *Report from Iron Mountain* were just a bunch of happy-go-lucky lefties who thought it would be a kick to publish a "satire" disguised as a think-tank study and pass it off as the real thing.

These three were novelist E.L Doctorow, freelance writer Leonard C. Lewin and *Nation* publisher Victor Navasky. They later enlisted fellow prankster Harvard professor John Kenneth Galbraith who vouched for its authenticity in a *Washington Post* book review. Gotta love those "pranks."

Curiously, however, the book holds up remarkably well as a prophetic document. So is it really a satire? Or has it become a blueprint for the future — the "future" as in "right now"?

Whatever its origin or intent, the book seems to accurately predict the current amoral, cynical and dissembling state of affairs in US government policies.

When it was first published in 1967, the supposedly controversial hoax document *Report from Iron Mountain*... concluded that economic surrogates for war must meet two principal criteria. They must be 'wasteful,' in the common sense of the word, and they must operate outside the normal supply-demand system."

What does that mean? It certainly sounds like government-sponsored social programs since "the book cites, 'Health. Drastic expansion of medical research, education and training facilities.'" (p. 59)

Could that be a prediction of the on-going, never-ending, always-increasing "War on Cancer"? Or the "War on AIDS"? Or the "War on Drugs"? Or maybe the "War on Violence" sponsored by the Center for Disease Control itself?

How about "the general objective of complete government-guaranteed health care for all at a level consistent with current developments in medical technology..." (p. 59)?

Then, believe it or not, *Report from Iron Mountain...* predicts the massive corporate welfare programs for space and "defense" research.

"Another economic surrogate that has been proposed is a series of giant 'space research' programs. These have already been demonstrated in their utility in more modest scale within the military economy. What has been implied, although not yet expressly put forth, is the development of a long-range sequence of space-research projects with largely unattainable goals." (p.61)

Remember "Star Wars?" Where did the billions upon billions of dollars spent for Research and Development disappear? The US certainly has nothing to show for it.

Continuing in this vein, those clever Iron Mountain hoaxers write that "space research can be viewed as the nearest modern equivalent yet devised to the pyramid building and similar ritualistic enterprises of ancient societies." (p. 62)

NASA still gets funding despite its lack of success in any measurable regard.

What's really striking, though, is the "prediction" of using the US Military as a U.N.-based Rent-a-Cop Agency for trouble spots throughout the world. Here's what the hoaxers wrote about that scenario:

"A more sophisticated variant is the proposal to establish the Unarmed Forces of the United States. This would conveniently maintain the entire institutional military structure, redirecting it essentially toward social welfare activities on a global scale. It would be in effect a giant military Peace Corps. There is nothing inherently unworkable about this plan, and using the existing military system to effectuate its own demise is both ingenious and convenient." (p. 64)

Is that why there are still US Armed Forces in Bosnia — in UN uniforms no less? And Macedonia? And Somalia? And Haiti? Is Columbia next?

Report From Iron Mountain looks more and more prophetic by the moment.

Was *Report* author Victor Navasky, founder and editor of the *Nation Magazine*, just another "strategic writer" for the CIA? Evidence of CIA/Secret Government funding of so-called "Left-Wing" publications can be traced back as far as the seminal work of historian Carroll Quigley's *Tragedy and Hope*, which exposed this ongoing strategy.

And then there's the UFO bugaboo. Was its popularization another strategy of the Power Elite? Here's what the *Iron Mountain* "hoaxers" write:

"Credibility, in fact, lies at the heart of the problem of developing a political substitute for war. This is where the space-race proposals, in many ways so well suited as economic substitutes for war, fall short. The most ambitious and unrealistic space project cannot of itself generate a believable external menace. It has been hotly argued that such a menace would offer the last best hope of peace etc. by uniting mankind against the danger of destruction by 'creatures from other planets' or outer space. Experiments have been proposed to test the credibility of an out-of-our-world invasion threat; it is possible that a few of the more difficult to explain 'flying saucer' incidents of recent years were in fact early experiments of this kind." (p. 66)

More recently motion pictures like *E.T.*, *Close Encounters*, *Communion*, *Fire in the Sky*, *Roswell Incident*, and *Independence Day*, as well as TV shows like *X-Files* continue to promote the on-going fascination and "academic" debate regarding the "reality" of UFOs.

The *Report from Iron Mountain* authors might be unsung prophets after all. Imagine — in 1966, they predicted the "Environmentalist Movement." Here's what they wrote:

"Nevertheless, an effective political substitute for war would require 'alternate enemies,' some of which might seem equally farfetched in the context of the current war system. It may be, for instance, that gross pollution of the environment can eventually replace the possibility of mass destruction by nuclear weapons as the principal apparent threat to the survival of the species. Poisoning of the air and of the principal sources of food and water supply is already well advanced and at first glance would seem promising in this respect; it constitutes a threat that can be dealt with only through social organization and political power."

"But from present indications it will be a generation to a generation and a half before environmental pollution, however severe, will be sufficiently menacing, on a global scale to offer a possible basis for a solution." (p.67)

Could this really have been the blueprint for the popularization of the so-called Environmentalist Movement of today? The Power Elite plan ahead for generations.

"It is true that the rate of pollution could be increased selectively for this purpose; in fact the mere modifying of existing programs for the deterrence of pollution could speed up the process enough to make the threat credible much sooner. But the pollution problem has been so widely publicized in recent years that it seems improbable that a program of deliberate environmental poisoning could be implemented in a politically acceptable manner." (p. 67)

"Deliberate environmental poisoning?"

Is that satire or what? I mean, talk about droll humor. Lewin and Navasky must be just plain giddy in their merriment.

And then there's the sociological aspect of "substitutes for the functions of war."

What activities can provide a good excuse for compulsory government service, a form of sophisticated slavery, if you will?

Lewin and the Boys got it all figured out, and it actually sounds like — surprise! — well, it sounds just like current US policy.

What do you do with the riff-raff? Put them in a mandatory "Volunteer Service." Here's what the Iron Mountain Prankster Boys write:

"Most proposals that address themselves, explicitly or otherwise, to the postwar problem of controlling the socially alienated turn to some variant of the Peace Corps or the so-called Job Corps for a solution. The socially disaffected, the economically unprepared, the psychologically unconformable, the hard-core 'delinquents.' the incorrigible 'subversives' and the rest of the unemployable are seen as somehow transformed by the disciplines of a service modeled on military precedent into more or less dedicated social service workers..." (p.68)

President Clinton must have taken the Report to heart. He's created a program called Americorps National Service for "thousands of Americans will soon be getting things done through service in exchange for help in financing their higher education or repaying their student loans."

President Bush continues the drumbeat with his new program for Homeland Security and the Neighborhood Watch.

Indentured servants. There's a place for everyone in the New World Order of Global Fascism.

The Report continues: "Another possible surrogate for the control of potential enemies of society is the reintroduction, in some form consistent with modern technology and political processes, of slavery... It may be an absolute prerequisite for social control in a world at peace. As a practical matter, conversion of the code of military discipline to a euphemized form of enslavement would entail surprisingly little revision; the logical first step would be the adoption of some form of 'universal' military service." (p.70)

Even slaves have a place in this system. Property of the US Government. Get in line for your I.D. microchip.

Currently, federal mandates for high school graduation include mandatory "volunteer service to the community." You have to admit it. It's kind of clever to have a "mandatory" "volunteer" service, right?

The author(s) of Report from Iron Mountain fret, however, that the "alternate enemy" must imply a more immediate, tangible and directly felt threat of destruction. It must justify the need for taking and paying a "blood price" in wide areas of human concern.

And this is where the world of mind control programming, TV news and entertainment intersect. When Government Propaganda and Monopoly Media work together like an iron hand in a velvet glove, you can call it "Government-Media." Here's what you get from the Iron Mountain Boys:

"Game theorists have suggested, in other contexts, the development of 'blood games' for effective control of individual aggressive impulses... More realistically, such a ritual might be socialized, in the manner of the Spanish Inquisition and the less formal witch trials of other periods, for purposes of 'social purification,' 'state security' or other rationale both acceptable and credible to postwar societies."

So here's the program. Social purification? You betcha. American Dissidents Killed. Live on TV. (A big boost to the ratings too.)

Randy Weaver's wife and son shot dead in Ruby Ridge, Idaho.

David Koresh and his followers burned alive in Waco, Texas.

The World Trade Center destroyed live on TV.

The killers walk away untouched. Why? It's just a program of "social purification." Plus it's a really good commercial for the State philosophy — "step out of line? The Man come and take you away."

And how about State security?

You saw the Oklahoma City Bombing. Live on TV. Added benefit for the State? The National Security States of America passed a so-called "anti-terrorism" bill making America more of a Police State than ever before.

Then there's the pesky US Constitution's Bill of Rights. So how do you get around that? More Globalist organizations:

"A number of proposals have been made governing the relations between nations after total disarmament; all are basically juridical in nature. They contemplate institutions more or less like a World Court or a United Nations, but vested with real authority." (p. 65)

There's NAFTA, GATT and the World Trade Organization. How about a World Parliament next?

And then there's the population control problem, but they've got a handy eugenics solution.

"The real question here, therefore, does not concern the viability of this war substitute, but the political problems involved in bringing it about. It can not be established while the war system is still in effect. The reason for this is simple: excess population is war material." (p.74)

That's right. Read it again: "excess population is war material."

Too many damn people. These are exactly the sentiments of UN shill and

Canadian industrialist-environmentalist Maurice Strong. War, you see, is not only useful because of its 'wasteful expenditures' but it also gets rid of the 'cannon fodder'" (Strong's exact words).

There are some interesting parallels between one controversial hoax document called *Report from Iron Mountain*, allegedly from the Left, and another controversial hoax-document, *The Protocols of the Elders of Zion*, allegedly from the Right. Whether it's a "satire" or a "hoax," it's the same state of mind. And it's the same game.

Compare them and decide for yourself.

For example, here's the *Protocol No. 10* on "Government":

"When we have accomplished our *coup d'etat* we shall say then to the various peoples: Everything has gone terribly badly, all have been worn out with sufferings. We are destroying the causes of your torment - nationalities, frontiers, differences of coinage."

Compare that with this excerpt from *Report From Iron Mountain*.

"We have already pointed out that the end of war means the end of national sovereignty, and thus the end of nationhood as we know it today. But this does not necessarily mean the end of nations in the administrative sense, and internal political power will remain essential to a stable society." (p .65)

And here are some words on "Social Programs and Entertainment":

From *Protocol No. 13*: "... In order that the masses themselves may not guess what they are about we further distract them with amusements, games, pastimes, passions, people's palaces... Soon we shall begin through the press to propose competitions in art, in sport of all kinds: these interests will finally distract their minds from questions in which we should find ourselves compelled to oppose them. Growing more and more disaccustomed to reflect and form any opinions of their own, people will begin to talk in the same tone as we, because we alone shall be offering them new directions for thought."

And from *Report From Iron Mountain*: "Substitutes for the Functions of War: Models... 3. Sociological: Control functions. a) Programs generally derived from the Peace Corps model. b) A modern sophisticated form of slavery. Motivational function. a) Intensified environmental pollution. b) New religions or other mythologies. c) Socially oriented blood games. d) Combination forms." (p. 84)

And here are some words on "Disarmament":

From *Protocol No 5*.: "Nowadays it is more important to disarm the peoples than to lead them into war; more important to use for our advantage the passions which have burst into flames than to quench their fire: more important to catch up and interpret the ideas of others to suit ourselves than to eradicate them. The principal object of our directorate consists in this: to debilitate the public mind by criticism; to lead it away from serious reflections calculated to arouse resistance; to distract the forces of the mind towards a sham fight of empty eloquence."

From *Report From Iron Mountain*: "The economic impact of general disarmament, to name only the most obvious consequence of peace, would revise the production and distribution patterns of the globe to a degree that would make the changes of the past fifty years seem insignificant. Political, sociological, cultural and ecological changes would be equally far-reaching. What has motivated our study of these contingencies has been the growing sense of thoughtful men in and out of government that the world is totally unprepared to meet the demands of such a situation." (p.8)

"The important point is that the *Report*, whether written as a think-tank study or a political satire, explains the reality that surrounds us," writes G. Edward Griffin, author of *Creature From Jekyll Island*.

"Regardless of its origin, the concepts presented in it are now being implemented in almost every detail. All one has to do is hold the *Report* in one hand and the daily newspaper in the other to realize that every major trend in American life is conforming to the blueprint."

"So many things that otherwise are incomprehensible suddenly become clear: foreign aid, wasteful spending, destruction of American industry, a job corps, gun control, a national police force, UN army, disarmament, a world bank, world money, the surrender of national independence through treaties, and the ecology hysteria."

"*Report From Iron Mountain* is an accurate summary of the plan that has already created our present. It is now shaping our future."

Is it satire, hoax, or disinformation?

It doesn't matter. Like H.G. Wells, another dead propagandist for the New World Order, whose book *The Open Conspiracy* is another blueprint for world domination, the "policy makers" behind both *Report from Iron Mountain* and the *Protocols* have the same agenda — tyranny, enslavement, and the subjugation of the human race.

BUSHWHACKED

Chapter 31

Allan Dulles: Father of Lies

W HAT CAN YOU SAY ABOUT a dead white guy whose own wife called him "The Shark?" Yes, Allen Dulles was a lawyer. He worked for the powerful illuminati law firm Sullivan & Cromwell, where conflicts-of-interest were a way of life, whose clients included multinational corporations and foreign governments, and whose big money deals shaped the destiny of the planet.

In his high profile career which spanned two World Wars as well as the Cold War, Dulles was also a director of the Central Intelligence Agency and a director of the Council on Foreign Relations.

Dulles was a moral, intellectual and physical cripple. His philandering was notorious. His acquiescence to the wishes of his masters — the Anglo-American Establishment — is a matter of historical record. And ironically, he also had a club foot, like Dr. Sidney Gottlieb, the amoral director of the CIA's Technical Services Division, responsible for the Agency's devilish mind control programs.

James Srodes, author of *Allen Dulles: Master of Spies* (Regnery)has produced a sanitized whitewash of a biography, completely avoiding Dulles's culpability in many heinous crimes against humanity.

During Dulles's tenure, after all, the CIA continuously used people as involuntary human guinea pigs. In their hubris, the arrogant spymasters believed they were accountable to no one, the lives of their victims mere Olympian playthings.

This dysfunctional mindset of the power elite is the psychopathology of Dulles himself and many others who consider themselves the movers and shakers of the twentieth century.

Nazis Bankrolled by Wall Street

With blithe disregard, Srodes downplays the importance of the collusion between Big Business and Big Government, writing "there is little doubt that a close relationship between the State Department and the senior partners of Sullivan & Cromwell suited all the parties well... Questions of conflicts of interest rarely arose in a time when the interests of commerce and government were so closely allied."

Closely allied? That's Srodes quaint way of saying that the Old Boys Club parasites infested government as well as business.

Most bothersome, however, is Srodes's dedicated ignorance of the build-up of the Nazi War Machine by Wall Street investment bankers. For instance, in dealing with the Schroeder bank's involvement with financing Hitler, Srodes is disingenous at best. He claims that it was a "different" Schroeder bank because of the different spelling of the surname, even though the name was anglicized in its British incarnation.

"There never was any proof that Sullivan or Cromwell or the Dulles Brothers of the London Schroeder Bank ever had ties to or dealings with von Schroeder," huffs Srodes.

The facts remain that Srodes's disinformational biography disregards well known facts recounted in former Hoover Institution scholar Antony C. Sutton's landmark history, *Wall Street and the Rise of Hitler* (1976), available at http://www.buccaneerbooks.com.

"Who was Schroeder?" asks Sutton in his book. "Baron Kurt von Schroeder was born in Hamburg in 1889 into an old established German banking family. An earlier member of the Schroeder family moved to London, changed his name to Schroder (without the dieresis) and organized the banking firm of J. Henry Schroder in London and J. Henry Schroder Banking Corporation in New York."

In his well-documented story of the American financiers who provided the money and materiel Hitler used to launch World War II, Dr. Sutton recounts how Nazi Baron Kurt von Schroeder "acted as a conduit for I.T.T. money funneled to Heinrich Himmler's S.S. organization in 1944, while World War II was in progress and the United States was at war with Germany."

Furthermore, in recent correspondence with this author, Dr. Sutton writes that "New York was so determined to conceal the WWII links that a vice president of New York Schroeder Bank (Bogdan) was put in uniform and sent to Germany to grab the [incriminating] paperwork before US troops even reached Cologne."

The American subsidiary of the notorious Nazi firm I. G. Farben, called American I.G., was under the control of an American citizen named Halbach, nominally a consultant to the firm.

When his bank accounts were blocked after Pearl Harbor, Sutton writes, "Halbach filed suit against the Alien Property Custodian through the Establishment law firm of Sullivan and Cromwell to oust the US Government from its control of I. G. Farben companies. These suits were unsuccessful, but Halbach was successful in keeping the Farben cartel agreements intact through World War II."

"This tells me someone even today wants to keep history concealed," says Sutton. "The work of the Control Commission for Germany would be a very productive research project," he concludes.

Dulles and the Wilson Puppet

In spite of himself, Srodes lest the truth out during unguarded moments.

For instance, describing the way that President Wilson was controlled by his notorious handler "Colonel" House, Srodes writes that "Wilson created a special advisory group, The Commission of Inquiry. It quickly became known as the Inquiry and the press called it Wilson's brain trust. Under Colonel House's direction, the group was made up of historians, geographers, economists and other experts on world affairs… With typical Wilsonian confidence, the president told his advisors not to bother him with the details of the issues he would confront, 'Just tell me what is right, and I will fight for it,' he said." In other words, Wilson handled himself like an obedient puppet.

Srodes also does nothing to illuminate Wilson's obsession with the League of Nations, a failed precursor of the UN. "His fixation, which used the young Allen Dulles and his brother Foster Dulles, resulted in the Treaty of Versailles, which by carving up ethnic groups and nations was in due course responsible for setting the stage for World War II."

"Major participants began to flee Paris at once," writes Srodes,"though there remained an enormously detailed set of agreements on borders, arms trade and nationalities — thirty five separate committees in all —that would have to be worked out for the final act of the drama, the Treaty of Sevres signed in August 1920."

Allen Dulles, meanwhile, failed upward — getting more responsibility from the Power Elite to fulfill their mandates.

Mind Control — The Solution to Dulles's Problem Wife

The illuminati double standard in sexual ethics — "do as I say not as I do" —

329

is underscored by Dulles's "private" behavior.

"Allen Dulles was a womanizer by any standards," writes Srodes. "It is inconceivable that he would have been hired by the CIA at all, let alone serve as its director for as long as he did, if today's intense scrutiny and censorious attitudes had existed in the 1950s.

"His penchant for flirtations and flings [Srodes can't bear to call them affairs] drew frequent rages and warnings from Clover [Dulles's wife]," pontificates the author.

"Clover had come to terms with her husband's philandering," writes Gordon Thomas in *Journey into Madness: The True Story of CIA Mind Control and Medical Abuse* (1989).

"It had been strong enough to have driven her to contemplate suicide," continued Gordon. "Each time she had discovered a new adultery she had gone to Cartier. She had filled a jewel box with expensive baubles marking his infidelities."

"Over the years Clover had also consulted several psychiatrists who had prescribed drugs that only momentarily masked her pain. It had been an Agency doctor, a kindly man, who had finally taken her aside during a reception at the French Embassy for Bastile day and said she could benefit from seeing a Dr. Cameron."

This was the notorious criminal Doctor Ewen Cameron whose hospital in Montreal became a living hell, the horror show setting for mind control experiments directed by CIA director Allen Dulles.

Sanitizing the CFR

Srodes is just another spinmeister, sanitizing history in the tradition of other Establishment hacks.

"His [Dulles's] early membership in the Council on Foreign Relations would prove much more important to his development," writes Srodes. In other words, if joining the Old Boys Club doesn't help your career, nothing will.

Srodes doesn't explain the significance of the CFR, a defacto U.S. Politburo, sister organization of the Royal Institute of International Affairs, whose mutual origin in Cecil RhodesUs Roundtable Group remains ground zero for contemporary globalists who dominate US government policies and agendas.

The Council on Foreign Relations, the preeminent cabal of control freaks, is even quoted in the book from the 1944-45 Report as pronouncing, "Peace will need to be worked out as diligently as war has been."

The CFR's penchant for globalist micro-management has been a bane for America ever since.

"From 1939 onward, Dulles had become one of the leading public proponents of the view that America's own defense security was inextricably entwined with that of Western Europe and particularly with that of Britain," writes Srodes.

"That year, he and Hamilton Fish Armstrong published a sequel to their 1936 argument against isolationism," he continues.

Undoubtedly Dulles's dull propaganda tract called "Can We Stay Neutral?" set the agenda for public acquiescence to the burgeoning war industry and further profiteering by Wall Street allied industries.

After all, how could you make money without a designated enemy?

The Washington "Kremlin"

Ironically, home to the OSS and the CIA — a compound of buildings at 2430 E. Street N.W. — was called "the Kremlin."

This bizarre moniker betrays the police state mentality of the OSS-CIA veterans who became the ardent fighters of communism.

As far back as 1945, the CIA has been called an "American Gestapo," most notably in a series of articles written by Walter Trohan in the Chicago Tribune.

During that time, General George Strong argued that the OSS was "possibly dangerous" and that "it ought to be liquidated in a perfectly natural logical manner."

The specious argument that America "needed" an intelligence agency is betrayed by the fact that there were no less than eight different spy agencies in the US at the time.

CIA-Media Propaganda

"With a combination of hard dollar contributions and soft dollar services, major American corporations were enthusiastic supporters of both government and private cloak and dagger campaigns," writes Srodes.

"Correspondents for major newspapers, magazines and broadcast networks (notably Time-Life, NBC and CBS) doubled as collectors while the media outlets themselves shaped programming to propaganda needs," continues Srodes.

According to Deborah Davis, author of the definitive *Katharine the Great: Katherine Graham and Her Washington Post Empire* (1991), it was much worse.

Interviewed in Kenn Thomas's edition of *Popular Alienation* (1995), Davis says that "Philip Graham was Katherine Graham's husband who ran the Post in the 50s. He committed suicide in 1963. That's when Katherine Graham took over. [Benjamin] Bradlee was close friends with Allen Dulles and Phil Graham. The paper wasn't doing very well for a while and he was looking for a way to pay foreign correspondents and Allen Dulles was looking for a cover."

"So the two of them hit on a plan," says Davis. "Allen Dulles would pay for the reporters and they would give the CIA the information that they found as well as give it to the Post. So he helped to develop this operation and it subsequently spread to other newspapers and magazines. It was called Operation Mockingbird."

The Washington Post is a CIA front. You can deal with it best by ignoring its pretentious pronouncements disguised as "news."

CIA infiltration of the mass media is an historical fact. Is it taught in the prestigious Schools of Journalism around the country? Very unlikely..

The Dulles-Mafia Connection

In mobster Sam Giancana's revealing biography, *Double Cross* (1992), "Mooney [Giancana] went on to say that CIA director Allen Dulles was the one who originally come up with the idea of taking out Castro."

"Two officials, Richard Bissell and Sheffield Edwards, were selected to put the scheme into action," write co-authors Sam and Chuck Giancana, godson and brother of mob boss Sam Giancana. "For the liaison to the Outfit [the Chicago-based Mob], Mooney said they called on Bob Maheu [a Howard Hughes operative]."

"The guy from the FBI? The guy who used to be with the FBI. He has a cover, a detective agency," answered the elder Giancana. "He's working for our Teamsters attorney friiend, Williams. That's how a lot of the guys work. Like Bannister… Maheu and Banister work for the CIA all the time… They're good, damned good. And they've made me a lot of money."

The CIA's use of "cutouts," or go-betweens, put distance between the CIA's murderous deeds and the killers they hired. Most recently this practice has been called "privatization."

"After Mooney's initial meeting with Maheu, one arranged by his lieutenant Johnny Roselli, Mooney told Chuck he instructed Roselli to tell Santo Trafficante amd Carlos Marcello he wanted them to provide the assistance necessary — their Cuban connections — to pull off the CIA assassination plot," the book continues.

"Mooney made Roselli the go-between with Maheu and the CIA. Meanwhile Mooney said he put Jack Ruby back in action supplying arms, aircraft and munitions to exiles in Florida and Louisiana, while the former Castro Minister of Games, Frank Fiorini, joined Ruby in the smuggling venture along with a Banister CIA associate, David Ferrie."

These intimate connections between a notorious cast of characters from CIA, the Outfit and the JFK assassination players put credence to Giancana's contention, "That's what we are, the Outfit and the CIA, two sides of the same coin."

Dulles and the JFK Murder

Then President John F. Kennedy had the audacity to fire Allen Dulles as director of the CIA. Why? He blamed himself and the CIA chief for the Bay of Pigs failed invasion of Cuba.

Enraged at the fiasco, Kennedy vowed to "splinter the CIA into a thousand pieces." Shortly thereafter the men who caused him public humiliation were fired — CIA veterans Allen Dulles, Richard Bissell and General Charles Cabell.

It has been duly noted that CIA agents loyal to Dulles had been placed throughout the United States. Also the Nazi spymaster Reinhard Gehlen's German and Eastern European agents, exfiltrated after WWII, were positioned in Houston, Dallas, Fort Worth and New Orleans, where they would be later useful in providing a smokescreen for the Warren Commission's coverup of JFK's murder.

When President Johnson appointed Dulles to be a member of the Warren Commission to probe the JFK assassination, there was more than a little irony that the former CIA spymaster got the job.

When you need a first-class coverup, call a professional.

The blatant conflict of interest was once again covered up by the media watchdogs turned lapdogs. The fix was in.

Interestingly enough, Srodes writes that "the correspondence in Dulles's personal papers shows that a major preoccupation of all the commission members was to satisfy the American public that Lee Harvey Oswald had acted alone and above all, had not had any ties to the CIA, the FBI or any other arm of the government."

The Lone Nut Conspiracy Theory was born, and the Dulles-directed Warren Commission Report was produced — a better historical fraud than even the Piltdown Man hoax.

Dulles — Illuminati Gofer

Even though "gofer of the illuminati" might be too harsh a sobriquet for Dulles, it is certainly not inaccurate.

As the ultimate insider and member of the ultra-secret Pilgrim Society, Dulles consistently followed his masters' agenda of internationalism. He steadfastly promoted globalism and the oligopoly's control of resources and nations, which the "useful idiots" — as the Soviets used to call them — believe will lead to the inevitable One World Government.

Allen Dulles: Master of Spies is a prime example of revisionist biography at best, — or blatant hagiography at worst. It's another sanitized whitewash of a man who could be liberally characterized as a world-class criminal.

In his conclusion to the 570-page doorstop of a book, Srodes flirts with the truth and even briefly touches it. He writes that "Dulles was indebted to both his grandfather and uncle for his conviction that the safety of a free society must be protected by that institutional paradox, a publicly accountable secret service."

It is certainly secret, but most certainly not accountable.

"If that ideal was wrong, then Dulles was wrong and the concept on which the CIA was founded was also wrong," concedes Srodes. "If the past fifty years were wrongly cast, then the Truman Doctrine, the Marshall Plan and the Cold War were all ghastly mistakes."

And that ghastliness remains Dulles's lasting legacy.

"His monument is around us," concludes Srodes, referring to the bas-relief medallion with Dulles's portrait, hanging in the central lobby of the CIA head-quarters building.

But Srodes is wrong there too. The real "monument" to Dulles is today's sur-veillance society.

Allen Dulles — Godfather of the National Security States of America.

Chapter 32

Friedman Sez, "Shut Up & Eat Yer Globaloney"

A LLEGEDLY A BEST-SELLER, *The Lexus and the Olive Tree* is the latest salvo by the Power Elite to promote their agenda. Their frontman is Thomas L. Friedman, the globe-trotting, name-dropping Foreign Affairs columnist for the *New York Times*.

The dubious honor of popularizing globalism, or globalization, and making it appear inevitable has fallen to Mr. Friedman. As an American internationalist, Friedman promotes the idea that if the United States gets even more entangled with other nations and mega-corporations in financial-economic alliances like WTO, GATT, NAFTA, MAI, and IMF, global peace and prosperity are a sure thing.

As a promoter of Pax Americana, Friedman writes that America truly is the "ultimate benign hegemon and reluctant enforcer" — as if globalist noblesse oblige will convince everybody to hand over their liberty.

"The very reason we need to support the United Nations and the IMF, the World Bank and the various world development banks," writes Friedman, "is that they make it possible for the United States to advance its interests without putting American lives or treasure on the line everywhere, all the time."

In fact, making the world safe for Coke, Windows, McDonald's and other multinationals seems to be the driving force behind the globalist agenda.

Opponents, on the other hand, are branded "isolationists," a term so uncool that the Big Media Cartel likens it to political neanderthals.

"Americans were ready to pay any price or bear any burden in the Cold War because there was a compelling and immediate sense that their own homes and way of life were at stake," continues Friedman. "But a large majority don't feel that way about North Korea, Iraq or Kosovo... That's why Americans are in the odd position of being held responsible for everything, while being reluctant to die for anything."

You got that right, pal. Dying for NATO or the United Nations just doesn't sound that exciting. But, who knows? With a little more brainwashing by Friedman and his ilk, the possibilities are endless.

No Realpolitik in Friedman's World

Interestingly enough, Friedman counts Lawrence Summers, former US Treasury Secretary and current Harvard University president, his friend. Summers himself is a Bilderberger, an attendee of the super-secret Global Politburo, which meets on a yearly basis to plan the direction of the world's economy and God knows what else. Meetings are strictly off the record, closed to journalists, and on the QT.

Friedman likewise makes no mention of the Global Power Elites and their highly questionable agenda of global command & control economics. As far as he's concerned, the Bilderbergers, Council on Foreign Relations, Royal Institute of International Affairs, and the literal swarm of tax-free fronts like the Ford Foundation, Rockefeller Foundation, and so on, are not even relevant to the global economy. He pointedly ignores them, although he does mention in passing the World Economic Forum at Davos.

Instead Friedman tries to amuse — and impress — his readers with anecdotes about his exotic adventures in far-off places. Since he is a good storyteller, you can assume that the behind the scenes manipulations of realpolitik are just not that interesting.

Shiny Happy Globalists

His goofy book title *The Lexus and the Olive Tree* is supposed to refer to an epiphany he received in Japan in 1992 when he visited the Lexus luxury-car factory.

(No, he didn't get run over by a Lexus.)

"It struck me then that the Lexus and the olive tree were actually pretty good symbols of the post cold war era," he writes. "Half the world seemed to be emerging from the cold war intent on building a better Lexus... And half the world — sometimes half the same country, sometimes half the same person — was still caught up in the fight over who owns which olive tree."

In other words, the smart worker bees were plugging into the global economy selling luxury cars to those who could afford them, while the stupid worker bees were still trying to carve up the land according to their antiquated notions of nations and ownership.

Silly peasants — when will they learn?

Friedman is also very creative. He invents cutesy terms like "Golden Straitjacket" which means conforming to draconian IMF policies without a whimper.

Friedman's other term, "Electronic Herd," refers to global speculators who invest in whatever at the speed of a keyboard click. The schmuck probably meant "digital goyim" but that was probably too politically incorrect even for his publishers. According to Friedman, then, an investor is just another head of cattle looking for greener pasture.

Friedman doesn't disclose whether the very title of his book, *The Lexus and the Olive Tree* is the result of some very shrewd product placement.

After all, he could have called it "The Infiniti and the Olive Tree" and who would have known the difference?

Or even "The Mercedes and the Olive Tree."

The Brady Bond Scam

Friedman's book is a fascinating stewpot of misinterpreting problems, solutions and results. For instance, in describing the so-called "Brady Bond" scam in which individual investors paid for the bad judgments of major investment bankers, Friedman calls it "democratizing investment."

He positively glows as he writes that "suddenly you and I and my Aunt Bev could buy a piece of Mexico's debt, Brazil's debt or Argentina's debt — either directly or through our pension and mutual funds."

Talk about spin. Instead of just banks holding bad paper, it was "diversified" so that the "little people" could throw their own good money after bad — just like the Big Boys. Except nobody bails the "little people" out when they default.

Does Friedman not understand that it's just a matter of spreading the risk and the potential for default? Or is he playing dumb?

After all the US Government sponsored bankers won't bail you out like they did with Long Term Capital Management.

Global Casino? What Global Casino?

With nary a peep about speculation in the global casino, Friedman ignores the dangers of globalism, like overleveraging non-existent assets (derivatives).

In fact the likelihood of a financial contagion of bad bets cascading domino-like in a global market freefall is barely mentioned. He even pooh-poohs these dangers by writing that "the paranoid illusionist believes more than nothing — he believes that there are hidden debts and off the books liabilities all over the place."

(Hey pal, ever heard of the trillion dollar per day off balance sheet derivatives market?)

Friedman also ignores other dangers of monoply capitalism, i.e. globalism, including the cartelization of commodities and global price-fixing, but does admit that the "scary truth is we don't fully understand what it means to be inter-linked."

"If you talk to Wall Street investment banks today they will tell you that the thing that absolutely took them by surprise in the market melt-down of August-September 1998 was how much more interconnected the system was than they realized," writes Friedman.

"None of their risk models which were based on past correlations between investments and certain events had anticipated the sort of chain reactions that in 1998 made a mockery of the whole concept of diversification," he continues.

"Companies that thought they were diversified by investing in different financial instruments with different maturities, in different currencies, in different markets, in different countries found out quickly that all their investments were part of one big interlinked chain from which they could not escape when markets started to nosedive."

Yikes.

Global Elite Rules

Friedman is an anti-populist and a false prophet of a false religion. But is he really the Karl Marx of Globalism? Only time will tell. He does, however, seem to be in love with another term he invented — DOSCapital 6.0

He also conspicuously quotes Rockefeller asset Fareed Zakaria, editor of the CFR organ *Foreign Affairs*. Zakaria is also a command and control globalist who told Friedman, "That's why it's not enough to just harness the market; you have to regulate it. But to regulate it, you need elites who are ready to protect things from the market..."

OK, you proles, repeat after me: "We need elites. We need elites. We need elites."

"It is usually only elites, secure in their own wealth, who are ready to worry about these things," continues Zakaria. "The Rockefellers helped set up the national park system in America. The Metropolitan Museum was founded by great capitalists who said we need a museum that has nothing to do with the market."

Who knows? Maybe Friedman — or Zakaria — never heard of tax write-offs.

Just remember — Friedman's book *The Lexus and the Olive Tree* is like a commercial for the American Empire.

"American Hubris. Don't Leave Home Without It."

Chapter 33

New (Reptilian) World Order

W HAT IF PLANET EARTH WERE OSTENSIBLY run by a race of shape-shifting reptilians? Believe it or not, this outré political-science-fiction scenario has become a focus of historical researchers as well as spiritual visionaries. In fact, the resonance of corroborating evidence from science and metaphysics has a synchronicity that is nothing but astonishing.

Serpents and flying dragons, of course, have been a staple of ancient myth and legends of indigenous people around the world. The assumption has always been, however, that they are metaphor or allegory — and not a literal description of actual beings.

But what about the admonition of Jesus and John the Baptist when they chided the "generation of vipers" and "serpents"? What if they saw these creatures with their spiritual vision — the overshadowing of humans by astral beings from another dimension? How would they communicate this vision to others?

And what about the stories from the *Book of Enoch* and the *Forbidden Books of the Bible* which refer to the Nephilim — literally "Those Who Were Cast Down" — and the Watchers, the Fallen Angels?

Sumeria: The Cradle (Or Test Tube) of Civilization

Scholars and historians have been totally confounded by the abrupt rise of the Sumerian culture nearly 6,000 years ago in the Fertile Crescent of the Tigris and

Euphrates Rivers. This "sudden civilization" seemed to appear out of thin air and refused to conform to the popular historical theory of linear development.

Historian Professor Charles Hapgood squarely faces the issue when he writes "today we find primitive cultures co-existing with advanced modern society on all continents... We shall now assume that 20,000 years ago while Paleolithic peoples held out in Europe, more advanced cultures existed elsewhere on earth."

Likewise the rise of Sumeria has been a major puzzle. Joseph Campbell in *The Masks of God* writes, "With stunning abruptness... there appears in this little Sumerian mud garden... the whole cultural syndrome that has since constituted the germinal unit of all high civilizations of the world."

William Irwin Thompson puts it even more succinctly. "Sumer is a poor stoneless place for a Neolithic culture to evolve from a peasant community into a full-blown civilization," he writes, "but it is a very good place to turn the plains and marshes into irrigated farmlands... In short, Sumer is an ideal place to locate a culture already having the technology necessary for urban life and irrigation agriculture."

A more stunning conclusion was reached by Professor Samuel N. Kramer, one of the greatest Sumerologists of our time. He reviewed the table of contents from the Tablets of Sumer and found that each one of the 25 chapters described a Sumerian, and in fact a world-first, type of achievement.

The Sumerians had the world's first medicine and pharmacopoeia. The world's first brain surgery. The world's first agriculture and farmer's almanac. The world's first cosmology and astronomy. The world's first law codes. And they utilized a highly advanced technology capable of sophisticated metallurgy, smelting, refining and alloying as well as petroleum fuel refining. Most importantly, the Sumerians were responsible for the world's first genetic engineering.

Like a mystery without a suspect, the Sumerian story remained a riddle until historian-archaeologist Zechariah Sitchin published a remarkable book called *The 12th Planet* (1979). In his subsequent series entitled *The Earth Chronicles*, Sitchin describes in great detail the crossbreeding program of the Sumerian "gods" through genetic manipulation.

Having spent thirty years studying Sumerian, Assyrian, Babylonian and Hittite texts and the Old Testament in the original Hebrew, Sitchin deciphered the ancient scripts, transcribed them, transliterated them and finally translated them.

His conclusion? Sitchin writes that the Sumerian civilization did indeed appear out of thin air. The forerunner of Greek and Roman civilization was initiated by a highly advanced race of extraplanetary colonists who came to earth, established their settlements, and began the single-minded pursuit of wealth and power by mining gold and other minerals necessary to sustain their high-tech high-maintenance lifestyle.

And who were these "colonists"? The Sumerians themselves described them as the "gods of heaven and earth." They were also called "the ancient gods," or the "olden gods," and according to Sumerian lore, they had come down to earth from heaven. In the Hebrew text of the Old Testament, the Sumerian gods of heaven and earth are referred to as the Nephilim. The Sumerians themselves called the colonists the Anunnaki.

The *Bible* and *Strong's Concordance* does not mention the Nephilim specifically by name, but *Nelson's Concordance* has several listings. Sitchin translates the biblical verses from Genesis 6:4 as, "The Nephilim were upon the Earth, in those days and thereafter too, when the sons of the gods cohabited with the daughters of Adam and they bore children unto them. They were the Mighty Ones of Eternity."

And what does "Nephilim" actually mean? Normally translated into English as "giants," the word stems from the Semitic root NFL ("to be cast down"). It means exactly what it says — "Those who were cast down upon Earth."

"Contemporary theologians and biblical scholars have tended to avoid the troublesome verses," writes Sitchin, "but Jewish writings of the time of the Second Temple did recognize in these verses the echoes of ancient traditions of 'fallen angels.'"

Tracks of the Nephilim and the Watchers

Apocryphal texts like the *Book of Enoch*, the *Pseudepigrapha*, and other politically incorrect "Lost" Books of the Bible reflect a precise knowledge of fallen angels on Earth. In fact, scholars maintain that there were two accounts of separate "falls" of the angels. First, there was the archangel's rebellion against God and his fall through pride, in which he was followed by other angels — the Nephilim. And second, there was the story of angels who fell through lusting after the daughters of men —the Watchers.

According to the *Book of Enoch*, a band of angels led by Samyaza "became enamored of the daughters of men" and decided to go after them, saying "come let us select for ourselves wives from the progeny of men, and let us beget children." So they all took an oath, all two hundred of them, and descended to earth. "Then they took wives, each choosing for himself; who they began to approach, and with whom they cohabited; teaching them sorcery, incantations... Moreover Azazyel taught men to make swords, knives, shields... Then Michael and Gabriel, Raphael, Suryal and Uriel, looked down from heaven, and saw the quantity of blood which was shed on earth, and all the iniquity which was done upon it..."

Indeed, bloodshed, including ritual abuse and human sacrifice, are hallmarks of these creatures.

Invasion of the Serpent People

In a book called *Flying Serpents and Dragons: The Story of Mankin's Reptilian Past*, R.A. Boulay, a former NSA cryptographer, writes that "from a combination of ancient secular and religious sources, it is possible to piece together the story of our ancestry which lies in the coming of the alien serpent-gods or astronauts who colonized earth many eons ago."

In fact, the evidence lies in a complete reappraisal of the legends, myths and "history" of the world. The Sumerian legend of Gilgamesh and Agga points to this interaction of "humans" and "serpents." And of course, there are the well-known "serpent gods" of the Indus Valley, the Nagas or Serpent race of Ancient India, and the Hindu epics, *Ramayana* and *Mahabharata*, which also deal with the serpent-gods. In Chinese history, *Vih King* describes how man and dragon lived peacefully together and even intermarried. And the serpent gods in American mythology are described in the Mayan book *Chilam Balam* where Itzamna, the serpent god is revered by the "people of the serpent."

The story of St. George overcoming the "dragon" in England and St. Patrick driving the "serpents" out of Ireland are also part of Christian iconography.

The predominance of these "serpent" references points to a pattern of willful ignorance on the part of the ivory tower mainstream and its so-called scholars.

Before the Flood

According to Boulay, the Anunnaki genetic engineering was done by "combining the characteristics of the native ape man or Neanderthal with their own saurian nature" producing the so-called "Adam" of the Old Testament. "This Adam was half-human and half-reptile, however, and being a clone could not reproduce himself."

Berossus, the Babylonian priest writing in 3rd Century B.C Athens, claimed that man's ancestry and origin can be traced to "Oannes," an amphibious creature that came out of the Persian Gulf to teach the arts of civilization to man. "Berossus called them 'annedoti' which translate as the 'repulsive ones' in Greek. He also refers to them as 'musarus,' an abomination," writes Boulay. "If the tradition had been invented, a more normal attitude would have been to glorify these creatures as splendid gods or heroes, yet the fact that they chose to describe their ancestors this way argues for the authenticity of the account."

"The Sumerian gods regarded Man as a convenience and nothing more," writes Boulay. "He supplied their wants, kept their cities, and provided cannon fodder for their various military ventures." (Sound familiar?) "The gods could be cruel and unsympathetic masters. They considered humans merely as unruly children, not more important than pets, to be governed ruthlessly and without sentiment."

The ruthless "policy" of the New World Orderlies reflects this ancient bias in the incessant propaganda that a population "crisis" exists on the planet and that the best way to remedy the situation is through wars to kill off the "cannon fodder" or through abortion to kill off future "useless eaters."

Boulay contends that the Old Testament begins at Sumer and there is a large body of religious literature besides the Book of Genesis, which deals with the period before the Deluge. He cites sources such as the three Books of Enoch, the Book of Jubilees, Gnostic teachings, the Dead Sea scrolls, the Haggadah of the oral tradition of the Jews, the Rabbinical writings, the works of Josephus, and the Books of the Pseudepigrapha, especially the Book of Jubilees.

What Was the "Serpent" of Eden?

Carl Sagan cryptically titled one of his books *The Dragons of Eden*, but ancient Jewish legends describe the Serpent of Eden as man-like. In other words, he looked like a man and talked like a man. What does this mean?

"The section of the Haggadah that deals with the creation describes the Serpent who inhabited the Garden before the creation of Adam as an upright creature that stood on two feet and was equal in height to the camel," writes Boulay. "The serpent was man-like in many ways. He was tall and stood upright on two legs. He did all the work of the gods particularly the mining and agricultural work. And above all the Serpent had an intellect superior to Man. These are all the attributes of the Anunnaki."

Boulay says that "according to the Haggadah, the bodies of Adam and Eve 'had been overlaid with a horny skin' and moreover of Adam's skin, it was said that 'it was as bright as daylight and covered his body like a luminous garment. Adam thus had the outward appearance of a reptile with its scaly and shiny skin. It was for this reason that Adam and Eve did not wear nor did they need clothing for protection or comfort.'"

"The reptilian appearance of the Biblical gods was a well-kept secret and only occasionally is it perceptible in the Old Testament," writes Boulay. "In a radical reinterpretation of scripture, he says that in the Haggadah, the source of Jewish legend and oral tradition, it is revealed that Adam and Eve lost their 'lustrous and horny hide' as a result of eating the forbidden fruit. The Gnostics, rivals to the early Christians, relate that as a result of eating the fruit, Adam and Eve achieved knowledge, part of which was to realize that their creators were beastly forms."

The Haggadah also explains what happened in the Garden after Adam and Eve ate the forbidden fruit. "The first result was that Adam and Eve became naked. Before their bodies had been overlaid with a horny skin and enveloped with a cloud of glory. No sooner had they violated the command given them that the cloud of glory and the horny skin dropped from them and they stood there in their nakedness."

Even the bizarre ritual of circumcision may have a reptilian connection. "Just as the serpent achieves long life through sacrificing and leaving off part of himself, so man may also be saved by ritually sacrificing part of himself," continues Boulay. "The rite of circumcision also served as a perpetual reminder to man that his true origins lay in the serpent-god creator and that he existed at the forbearance of these gods."

Why Cain Killed Abel

In a fascinating reassessment of the well-known Bible story of Cain and Abel, Boulay proposes an alternative rationale. For instance, in the *Apocalypse of Adam*, a Gnostic document of the First Century AD, Adam reveals to his son Seth "that the Lord who created us created a son from himself and Eve your mother."

"If the deity was the father of Cain, while Adam sired Abel," writes Boulay, "it would explain further events — Cain would be semi-divine, part-reptilian and more 'god'-like. About the birth of Cain, this document observes that Eve 'bore a son and he was lustrous' — a description of shiny luminous hide of the reptile gods. The Apocalyptic version of this text also describes Eve's dream. She tells Adam, 'My Lord, I saw a dream last night, the blood of my son Amilabes, called Abel, being thrust into the mouth of Cain his brother and he drank it mercilessly... And it did not stay in his stomach but came out of his mouth.' They got up to see what happened and found Abel killed Cain.'"

The crime of Cain was apparently not only to commit fratricide, but to eat the flesh and blood of his brother. "This behavior seems more reptilian than human since Cain was sired by the deity unlike his brother who had Adam as his father," concludes Boulay.

The "Serpent" Gods

What did the ancient "gods look like? "The coming of the Anunnaki coincided with the end of this period as the Earth began to dry out and the meat-eating dinosaurs and small mammals appeared," says Boulay. "The reptile gods needed moisture and warmth and probably the reason why civilizations were founded at the mouth of great river systems — the Nile delta, the Indus River valley and the Tigris Euphrates system."

"In appearance the serpent gods were tall, at least 8 to 10 feet, and walked on two feet. They had a tail like a reptile and a tough hide somewhat like a lizard but with a large amount of horny or scaly skin. Their hide was generally lustrous and smooth, somewhat like a chameleon and probably varied in different hues of green and gray... They had short horns on their head which they considered to be a sign of divinity. Humans were repulsive to them because they were hairy, had soft skins and bony limbs."

"The sons of the Serpent gods, the Nephilim of the Bible, which descended before the Deluge and mated with human women also dabbled in genetic engineering," concludes Boulay. "Eventually mankind will have to learn the truth about his origins and face the fact that his gods and ancestors were reptiles, truly monsters by any of our current definitions. There will be a great cultural shock as we have never seen before," Boulay predicts.

Reptilians Among Us

"Researchers into the reptilian phenomenon conclude that at least some originate in the Draco star constellation," writes David Icke in his book *The Biggest Secret.*

"There are three suggested origins for the Anunnaki reptilian intervention in human affairs," writes Icke. "1 They are extraterrestrials; 2 They are 'inner' terrestrials who live within the earth; 3 They manipulate humanity from another dimension by 'possessing' human bodies. I think they are all true."

Icke's book is a repository of mind-bending, paradigm-shifting information, which sounds like a grade-Z sci-fi movie — until you read the evidence. His premise is simple — what if the Global Power Elite are part of these reptilian bloodlines still controlling and ruling Planet Earth as their own private galactic fiefdom?

"These bloodlines," writes Icke, "became the British and European aristocracy and royal families and thanks to the 'Great' British Empire, they were exported across the world to rule the Americas, Africa, Asia, Australia, New Zealand and so on. These genetic lines are manipulated into the positions of political, military, media, banking and business power and thus these positions are held by lower fourth dimensional reptilians hiding behind a human form or by mind-puppets of these same creatures."

"These same reptilians have been occupying the bodies of all the main players in the conspiracy going back to ancient times," continues Icke. "The obsession with interbreeding within the [Babylonian] Brotherhood bloodstreams comes from the need to hold the reptilian genetic inheritance and therefore maintain the vibrational connection between the human body on the third dimension and its controlling force on the lower fourth. It was to hide this truth that they arranged the destruction of ancient historical records, texts, and accounts over the centuries as they ravaged and raped the native societies of the world. The reptilians wanted to destroy all memory and records of their earlier open existence and control in the past. If they could do that, humanity would have no idea that they were being controlled through physical bodies that look human by a fourth dimensional force."

Out of Africa: More Corroboration

In a remarkable three hour video called *The Reptilian Agenda*, David Icke interviews Zulu *sanusi* (shaman) Credo Mutwa, who describes African traditions and histories of indigenous "interactions" with the Chitauri, his name for these alien creatures, who are known as "Children of the Serpent."

"You white people say that there are alien beings on this earth," he says. "No, you are wrong. The earth on which we live has produced twenty-four different races during its long existence…"

"Some of the Chitauris have horns on their heads… *Star Wars* shows creatures, which certainly exist, which even the most uneducated Africans can identify. In there is a creature called Darth Maul. Darth Maul is a red and black being with a ring of horns around his head. That is exactly what the Chitauri look like. The Royal Chitauri have a ring of sharp horns around their heads."

In an astonishing parallel with the Book of Revelation of John the Divine, Credo Mutwa says that "African tradition says that the Chitauri engaged God himself in a terrible war. God, the real God, the Creator, defeated them and he closed their mouths so they are unable to talk or eat food anymore."

"We are told that the Chitauri fatten on the energy that we human beings give them," he continues. "They eat what we call the 'dark power' when they destroyed the planet on which they live. They live on negative emotions like fear and hatred, very intense human emotions. We are told that the Chitauri eat energy when humans start thinking at certain levels."

Incarnation of the Lizard-People

With a background in Jungian psychology, author Barbara Hand Clow excels in shamanic cosmology, an intuitive storytelling technique that integrates history, legend and myth using her own internal guidance. In the third volume of her *Mind Chronicles Trilogy* called *Signet of Atlantis*, she also tackles the problem of the "lizard race" from her own perspective.

Clow refers to the physical incarnation of this race on Earth. "They [the Anunnaki] nevertheless have received a measure of control over the planet's surface," she writes. "Most notably they have achieved the ability to incarnate. No longer will they have to persuade the people to build temples in order to link up to their own control centers; no longer will they require a channel to enter Earth; now they can become humans themselves."

"The various non-physical lizards creeping around the canals of Baalbek are considerably attracted to the idea of taking human form through incarnation," she continues. "They look forward to creating fear more directly. These monsters are not content to lumber around as fourth dimensional reptiles, occasionally eating someone up. Much more appealing to them is the idea of actually entering the third dimension — in the twentieth century, for example, actually becoming an Adolf Hitler, a Charles Manson, a Stephen King, or making the twentieth century film that creates fear of the act of eating, the *Night of the Living Dead*. They will even baldly show themselves for who they really are by creating a movie called *V*."

Other sci-fi movies with this theme of alien-reptilians on Earth include *The Arrival*, *They Live*, and *Alien Resurrection*.

"You must realize that the Holy Land is a laboratory of stellar control patterns," writes Clow. "In temple secrecy, we were taught everything about the visitors, but this information was taken out of the Bible. For 300,000 years, the central agenda by the Nibiruans [colonists from Nibiru, also called Marduk] has been to control the Earth and the use of its resources."

It is also a special time, the return of humanity's spiritual powers and the choice of self-transcendence. "The return of these archetypal powers is also a result of your ability to perceive wider spans of the light spectrum," she continues. "This expanding vision is your key to integrating all the dimensions into your awareness. This broader awareness is natural, but it was once taken from you by the 'gods.' The Nibiruans and other visitors — those demigods who felt disconnected from their Source — narrowed your perceptive abilities in order to help themselves materialize on Earth."

"The Nibiruan mind-set that has poisoned planet Earth has most recently manifested as the reptilian attitude that American political leaders call the 'New

World Order.' This is a mind-set that believes in scarcity and limitation when the Earth is actually abundant and unlimited. This is the mind-set that would throw all the people into crocodile pits. The world's power brokers are gluttons who control more resources than they need in order to protect themselves against the scarcity they fear."

Clow calls them the World Management Team, which she defines as "individuals in the third dimension who are controlled by the Anunnaki who impulse them to carry out plans that benefit Nibiru and not Earth. All individuals working in Team agencies — such as in the Vatican, secret societies, banks, governments, school systems, the medical system and many businesses — are agents of the Anunnaki, unless they are conscious of the Annunaki vibrations and do not carry out their plans. In recent days, the World Management Team has been calling itself the New World Order."

The Coming of Christ

"Since the coming of Christos, the time has come to choose life over death," writes Barbara Hand Clow in *Heart of the Christos*. "The death wish comes from the paralyzing fear of the black place — Orion. In the wars with Orion, pain and separation were first experienced, and after that point many souls chose to cease to be. But all changed with Christos. A being of such love and compassion came to Earth that now all souls have access to the desire to be alive, to be alive just to experience the love of Christos."

"The fallen angels have sidetracked themselves by playing around with various experiments which have been creative but without wisdom. As the third dimension has become increasingly complex, especially during the last five thousand years, the angels have amused themselves by being voyeurs of the results of materializations. Technology with no divine inspiration or wisdom has been the latest project of the [fallen] angels."

After all, Christ himself said, "Be ye wise as serpents." What did he really mean?

The Rape of the Anunnaki

According to many leading experts, sex has gotten a bad name ever since the trauma of the Anunnaki who came to this planet and raped the women of Earth.

In *The Pleiadian Agenda*, Barbara Hand Clow writes that "the Anunnaki selected women to have sex with them so they could actually birth themselves into the incarnational cycles of Earth, and that was something that had never occurred before."

Prior to this time, she contends that "all sex was very natural. You easily merged electromagnetic fields and your physical bodies, and the vibrations of the Moon, Sun and planets flowed through your kundalini channels. You were drawn to each other by planetary affinities in your birth charts and merging was always easy and pleasurable. Sex with the Anunnaki was forced and unnatural in so many ways because there were few energy affinities. You became confused while the gods felt kundalini energy for the first time. They loved it. Male gods even had a lot of sex with each other and with the few female goddesses once they found out what sex felt like on Earth…"

"All imbalances between men and women today come from energetic imprints of incompatible energy fusion from these ancient times," writes Clow. "Your loathing for reptiles also comes from this phase of your evolution because the most embodied Anunnaki were very reptilian, and those Anunnaki were the ones who could mate with human females."

The Satanic Ritual Abuse - Mind Control Connection

One of the most disturbing recent revelations is that so-called ritual abuse, ceremonial murder and diabolical mind control technology is so widespread on Planet Earth. Survivors of these horrendous atrocities have corroborated evidence of celebrity perpetrators, a global criminal power elite, who continue to act in callous disregard of human rights. They perform these Satanic rituals which, according to their beliefs, conjure up powerful forces — demons and entities from other dimensions.

"The reptilians and their crossbreed drink blood because they are drinking the person's life force and because they need it to exist in this dimension," explains Icke. "They will often shapeshift into reptilians when drinking human blood and eating human flesh, I am told, by those who have seen this happen. Blood drinking is in their genes and an elite high priestess or 'mother goddess' in their hierarchy who performed rituals for the Brotherhood at the highest levels told me that without human blood the reptilians cannot survive in this dimension."

"The closer the earth's field is vibrationally to the lower fourth dimension, the more power the reptilians have over this world and its inhabitants. Satanism is not just a sickness and a perversion, although it is that also, its main reason is to control the Earth's magnetic field; to worship and connect with their reptile masters; to drink the life-force of their sacrificial victims; and to provide energy for the reptilians who appear to feed off of human emotion, especially fear."

The fact that the Earth's electro-magnetic field has been steadily decreasing over the last two thousand years has been described in the work of Gregg Braden and his books *Awakening to Zero Point* and *Walking Between the Worlds*.

"We are clearly being prepared for revelations about the reptilians, because the highly charged, higher frequency energies will increase dramatically the number of people who see the reptilians of the lower fourth dimension," Icke claims. "Arizona Wilder told me that the number of sacrificial rituals has increased massively since the 1980s because the reptilians need more and more human blood and energy to hold their human form."

Revelations of a Mother Goddess

A mind control survivor by the name of Arizona Wilder, whose title was "Mother Goddess Starfire" in the Satanic hierarchy, participated in many black magic, human sacrifice ceremonies attended by the world's power elite and members of the so-called Royal Family. Her title, role and performances have been confirmed and cross corroborated by other mind control survivors including Cisco Wheeler.

(It makes you wonder — what did the punk rock group Sex Pistols really mean when they sang, "God save the Queen/She ain't no human bein.'"?)

"At outdoor rituals, Arizona says she wore a red robe and stands in the centre of a pentagram which is surrounded by a hexagram," writes Icke in *The Biggest Secret*. "She was triggered into her 'Isis' program and conducted the Drawing Down of the Moon ceremony which she says made four snarling hideous creatures materialize in the Satanists' circle."

These entities could be the so-called "Ancient Ones," demons or fallen angels imprisoned in the lower astral plane, an extra-physical dimension. Arizona says that they were conjured up through a series of incantations from her grimoire, a black magic spellbook.

"The sacrificial victims, who have been bred from birth for the role, are ritually killed by slashing the throat from left to right. The blood of the victims is collected and mixed with arsenic, which appears to be a necessary element for those of the human-reptilian bloodlines," continues Icke. "This is poured into goblets and consumed by the Satanists, together with the liver and the eyes. This is supposed to provide strength and greater psychic vision..."

"The Mother Goddess says that by this time the participants are in such a high state of excitement that they often shape-shift into reptilians and mostly manifest, she says, in a sort of off-white color. They are also terrified, because at this point, the Mother Goddess points out four of them and they are then ritually murdered."

"Clare Reeves, President of Mothers Against Sexual Abuse in the US told me that at least 12 ritually abused clients reported that the participants shape-shifted into reptilians," Icke concludes.

The Metaphysics of Fallen Angels

Regarding the existence of this fallen race, Elizabeth Clare Prophet, author of over 30 books on spiritual topics, writes that "the Canaanite evolutions were worshippers of the Serpent both as the person of the fallen one and as the life-force sealed in the white fire core of the base-of-the-spine chakra."

"From this religion of the fallen ones comes all the phallic and fertility rites of primitive cultures. Their archetypes can be seen in the Ugarithic pantheon whose chief deity is Il or El. This syllable comes form the El, the power of Elohim usurped by the fallen ones. This Il, L, is the abbreviation for the name Lucifer, called the sky god."

"He is known in numerous cultures as the father of the gods, their supreme lord and ruler in their assemblies. The councils of the false hierarchy gathered on certain mountains of what is now North America as well as in the Middle East."

"Baal and his wife Asherah along with Tammuz and Ishtar are among the many fallen angels who fell, they and their twin flames. They were a race of giants feared by the descendants of Seth."

"These fallen angels were now embodied in the physical earth because they were cast out of the higher octaves for their rebellion against the Son of God and the heavenly orders of hierarchy. Their unions with the daughters of Cain were not in the spiritual order of God's progeny who are born solely out of the Christi seed. "

"This cursed lifewave, the 'mighty men which were of old, men of renown,' became the mere natural man, without soul or conscience or spark of the divine potential. The natural man, now called Homo sapiens, was a 'kind of man' but not a God-free being after the descent of Adam from Seth to Noah. Hence the crossbreeding of the Watchers and their godless creation with the children of Cain opened the door for laggard evolutions to embody on earth and the interchange of these several fallen evolutions became known in general as 'mankind.'" (Pearls of Wisdom, Vol. 42, No.2)

In another remarkable cross-corroboration of this alien fourth-dimensional race, she writes, "Once upon a time, the astral plane, hitherto sealed, was forced open by an intergalactic evil. And whosoever descended the thirty-three steps leading to oblivion fell into the darkness of Old Night. It was pitch black and the creatures of the deep, reptilian in nature, writhed in the bottomless pit. These creatures piled their bodies one upon the other and even the trenches of hell could not contain them. Those who descended into hell are playing out their unreality to the end." (Pearls of Wisdom, Vol. 40, No. 25)

351

The Evolutions of Earth

Prophet believes that there are many lifewaves and evolutions on Earth. Despite the commingling of races through complex genetic engineering over the last half-million years or so, she makes a distinction between those who aspire Godward and those who do not.

"The sons and daughters of God and their children are a distinct race of the I AM consciousness," she writes. "And they are called the I AM Race. It was to them that Moses spoke when he hurled to them his fiery fiat to break the hypnotic spell of the Watchers and their slave race: 'I have said, ye are gods, and all of you are children of the Most High.'"

"I AM" refers to the name of God revealed to Moses through the burning bush — I AM THAT I AM.

In *Planet Earth: The Future is to the Gods*, Prophet says that "in the records of the retreats of the Great White Brotherhood are the missing links which archeologists have not found. How the scientific analysis of artifacts confirms the hidden mysteries of God can only be revealed by the spirit of prophecy. When there is a gap in scientific or historical awareness, God does not leave us comfortless."

"In the Bible these soulless beings are referred to as 'the wicked,' for they have seen to it that all more specific descriptions of their race have been removed — lest mankind discover them and rise in righteous indignation against their overlords."

The reptilians or serpent gods have their origin in the so-called "fall" from higher dimensions or octaves, she believes.

"Who were these Nephilim? These fallen ones were a part of the original angelic and archangelic bands created even before the Sons of God were created," says Prophet.

"The angels occupy a position in the panoply of the kingdom of God as servants of the Sons of God. Like teachers or protectors, they came first to prepare for the Incarnation of the Word, the incarnation of Christ — not in one son of God, but in many many sons and daughters of God throughout the universes."

These Nephilim, in other words, may be the same fallen ones referred to collectively as "the dragon" in Saint John's vision of the Apocalypse, the Book of Revelations — "And there was war in heaven: Michael and his angels fought against the dragon; and the dragon fought and his angels, and prevailed not; neither was their place found any more in heaven. And the great dragon was cast out, that old serpent, called the Devil, and Satan, which deceiveth the whole world: he was cast out into the earth, and his angels were cast out with him."

Serpents. Dragons. Reptilians. Coincidence, or not, the parallels are simply astonishing. Satan and the fallen angels are often pictured as serpent-reptilians, especially in Gustave Dore's world-famous illustrations.

It's also recorded that Jesus rebuked them often, saying, "Ye serpents! Ye generation of vipers, how can ye escape the damnation of hell? Wherefore behold, I send unto you prophets and wise men and scribes, and some of them ye shall kill and crucify, and some of them ye shall scourge in your synagogues and persecute them from city to city, that upon you may come all the righteous blood shed upon the earth, from the blood of righteous Zacharias, son of Barchias, whom ye slew between the temple and the altar." (Matt. 23)

The bloodlust and the modus operandi of the embodied Watchers has changed little in two thousand years since.

More references to the "generation of vipers" are in Matt. 3:7, Matt 12:34-35 and Luke 3:7. They are also called "princes of this world." Despite censoring, tampering and editing the Bible, codewords for this race in the Old Testament include terms like "the wicked," "mighty men," "the giants," and "evildoers."

Gods, Gods and More Gods

"Archeology reveals the history of the fallen ones and their mechanization man," Prophet continues. "We have to go to the retreats of the Great White Brotherhood to realize that we are not this creation, but that we have beating within our hearts an eternal flame that makes up an eternal part of God. There are two types of evolution on this planet, and it's becoming evident every day as you look around and try to understand what kind of people would do the things that are being perpetrated against innocent people by governments, nations and all sorts of multinational corporations."

"The Nephilim did not create life on earth," she says. "They did not create the sons of God or the children of God. Nor did they create mammals or primates. What they did was take an ape-like man Homo erectus and drastically alter his capabilities by implanting in him their own image and likeness. A new species, Homo sapiens, was mass produced. It's safe to assume that the Nephilim being capable of space travel 450,000 years ago were equally advanced in the life sciences. Whether they use cloning, cell fusion, genetic transplant or methods yet unknown to us, they were able to set up a production line and mass produce or manufacture man."

Prophet's conclusion concurs with other contemporary spiritual teachers. "People today are simply not willing to face the facts," she says. "The Nephilim and their godless creation are alive and well on planet Earth. They are the spiritually wicked in high places — of church and state, government, education, the arts, the media and in the science."

"The Nephilim say, 'we are the gods and the future belongs to us.' Now it is up to us to say, 'Nay.' The future is to the Word Incarnate and I elect to be that Word. God has given that option to us. We can elect to be joint heirs of the universal Christ consciousness that Jesus embodied, that Gautama Buddha embodied, that the Saints of East and West have had. The words and works of the Sons of God set them apart from the Nephilim."

"Lizzies" and the Human Dilemma

Barbara Marciniak, author of *Bringers of the Dawn*, *Earth* and *Family of Light* comes to a similar conclusion about Earth and the reptilian agenda.

"The creator gods who have been ruling this planet have the ability to become physical, though mostly they exist in other dimensions," she writes. "They keep energy at a certain vibrational frequency while they create emotional trauma to nourish themselves."

"You have only dealt with gods who have wanted to be admired and to confuse you and who have thought of Earth as a principality, a place that they own out in the galactic fringes of this free-will universe."

Marciniak semi-facetiously calls these part-human part-reptilian beings, "Lizzies." "These beings, who are neither spiritually informed nor learned in spiritual ways, deny the existence of a spiritual force," she writes. "They have developed scientific principles and technologies that scatter the laws of spirituality... It is possible to become a brilliant master of manipulating matter and reality without understanding spiritual connections."

What if a race of godless materialistic "Lizzies" really are diddling with Planet Earth? It would go a long way to explain the madness of scientists and their bizarre obsessions with genetic engineering, cloning, trans-genic chimeras, and patented life-forms — and, of course, those who would create mind-controlled slaves as their own high-tech playthings.

Playing "god" seems to be a deadly serious game of one-upmanship for these fallen creatures, descendants of the sibling rivalries of Enki and Enlil, the original Nephilim gods.

Breaking the Spell

And why does the spell continue? Obviously the shedding of blood through satanic ritual murders and wars replenishes the energies they feed on. Negative emotions are another source of their power.

"The reptilians manipulate from the lower fourth dimension, the so-called lower astral frequency range," writes Icke. "To control this planet they have to keep the mass of humanity at or below that level and disconnect them from anything higher. Crucial to maintaining the human psyche in disconnected igno-rance is the manipulation of low vibrational emotion, fear, guilt, resentment, dis-like of self and condemnation of others, which in the end are all expressions of fear. These are the very emotions which resonate to the frequency range of the lower fourth dimension and once we succumb to domination by these emotions, we succumb to the control of the reptilian consciousness."

Icke says that "the more you open your heart, the more powerful this flow and the quicker you will synchronize with the rising vibrations and transform into a higher state of consciousness. If you close your heart and you close your mind, you will be resisting these changes and more and more of your energy will be spent fighting the very energies that will transform your life and set you free."

Marciniak writes that the "3-D world is headed for a collision of dimensions — not a collision of worlds, a collision of dimensions. Many dimensions are going to come crashing into each other. The test, the initiation [will come] — and initiation always means to move through another reality, to conquer it and transmute it."

"The battle of light and dark and good and evil is only between portions of yourself," Marciniak continues. "These portions are multidimensional extensions or reincarnations of the same collective of energies that you are a part of as an individual…"

"The avatars and masters have now permeated the gridwork of the world bringing with them their own tools for teaching… This hierarchy works with love, cherishes who you are and has been able to see through the time mecha-nisms that are keyed into the planet to know that consciousness is ready for the evolutionary leap."

Credo Mutwa ends his interview with David Icke by quoting an African proverb, "God is greater than all the wizards and sorcerers of the earth."

"Already there are signs that the Chitauri are getting desperate," he says. "Why? There are signs that the human being is trying to bring out the God with-in himself. We are trying to become gods and we are succeeding."

Credo Mutwa is right when he says that the future will be won by using the power of the Spirit. "Let the power of Light shine in the dark corners of con-spiracy and as it shines, let humankind be saved."

Prophet contends that praying for divine intercession is a vital component of spiritual warfare. In fact, one of the most important components of her spiritual teachings concerns calling the angels to deal with these beings.

"There's a very important law," she says. "The legions of light can not come into this earth plane unless we invoke them because God gave us dominion in the Earth and free will. It's our Earth. It doesn't belong to the Nephilim. It doesn't belong to their godless creation. It belongs to the children of light and the sons of God."

"If we want divine intercession, we have to ask for it," continues Prophet. "And that's through prayer, dynamic decrees, and meditation. [We can] invoke God's Presence, 'God, come down to Earth. Take over. Judge the fallen ones and bring Earth to this victory.'"

Through the publications of the Summit Lighthouse, she has even offered powerful decrees and invocations, which can be used to exorcise the earth of these demonic forces in other dimensions in the exercise of spiritual warfare.

What comes to mind is Paul's admonition to the Corinthians, "Know ye not that we shall judge angels?" (1 Cor 6:3) The "fallen angels" whose time is up are also well aware of this cycle. They know that it's time for the judgment, especially when it's invoked and qualified by God's Will.

"The future is to the children of God who know that the only God that is real on earth is the God who lives within his holy temple — the temple of his people," says Prophet. "The future is to his people who have heard the Word and know that they are God Incarnate. The future is to those who exercise free will to elect to become the Sons of God."

It is an awesome choice for the residents of Planet Earth — to be or not to be the Christ. Especially in the face of at least two thousand years of indoctrination that nobody but Jesus is worthy. Hard-core, deep-seated programming that so-called "sin" is our original legacy. Continuous mind control that guilt and fear are mankind's "natural" estate.

It's time for these matrices of fear, death and mortality to be shattered forever. It's time for their plans for a New World Order to be cast asunder. And it's time for the false gods and their illuminati gofers to be overthrown.

Sifting out the so-called "tares among the wheat" is an ongoing process — within oneself and the planet as a whole. On a personal level, each decision to act ethically and morally is crucial. If fear is the lock on the virtual prison of Planet Earth, then Love is the key to soul liberation. The victory over the Nephilim enslavement of humanity however is ineluctable.

After all, we're playing for keeps.

Bibliography

Author interviews with David Icke, Arizona Wilder, Brian Desborough, Barbara Hand Clow, and Barbara Marciniak

Boulay, R.A. *Flying Serpents and Dragons: The Story of Mankind's Reptilian Past* (1990) The Book Tree, PO Box 724, Escondido, CA 92033, www.thebooktree.com

Braden, Gregg. *Awakening to Zero Point* (1994)
  Walking Between the Worlds (1998),
  (Laura Lee Productions, P. O. Box 3010, Bellevue, Washington 98009, 800-243-1438, www.lauralee.com)
Clow, Barbara Hand. *Eye of the Centaur* (1986)
  Heart of the Christos (1989)
  Signet of Atlantis (1992)
  The Pleiadian Agenda (1995)
deMause, Lloyd. *Foundations of Psychohistory* (1982) Institute of Psychohistory, 140 Riverside Dr., New York, New York 10024, www.psychohistory.com
Kramer, Samuel Noah. *History Begins at Sumer* (1959) Doubleday Anchor
Marciniak, Barbara. *Bringers of the Dawn* (1992)
  Earth (1995)
  Family of Light (1998) Bear & Company, P. O. Box 2860, Santa Fe, New Mexico 87504
Pagels, Elaine. *The Gnostic Gospels* (1979) Vintage Books, New York
The Origin of Satan (1995) Vintage Books, New York
Prophet, Elizabeth Clare. *Fallen Angels and the Origin of Evil* (2000)
  Planet Earth: The Future Is to the Gods (1980)
  How to Work With Angels (1998)
  The Creative Power of Sound (1998)
  Access the Power of Your Higher Self (1997), Summit University Press, P. O. Box 5000, Corwin Springs, Montana 59030, www.tsl.org
Rhodes, John. www.reptoids.com
Russell, Jeffrey Burton. *The Prince of Darkness: Radical Evil and the Power of Good in History* (1988) Cornell University Press, Ithaca, New York 14850
Sitchin, Zechariah. *The Twelfth Planet* (1976)
  The Stairway to Heaven (1980)
  The Wars of Gods and Men (1985)
  When Time Began (1993)
  Genesis Revisited (1990)
  Divine Encounters (1995)
  The Cosmic Code (1998) Avon Books, 1350 Avenue of the America, New York, NY 10019, www.avonbooks.com (Bear & Co.)
Thompson, William Irwin. *At the Edge of History* (1971) Harper Colophon
  Islands in Time (1990), Bear & Co., Santa Fe, New Mexico